BRITISH–IRISH RELATIONS
AND
NORTHERN IRELAND

To Áine, Camille
and, above all,
Caroline
– for everything

BRITISH–IRISH RELATIONS AND NORTHERN IRELAND

From Violent Politics to Conflict Regulation

Brendan O'Duffy
Queen Mary, University of London

IRISH ACADEMIC PRESS
DUBLIN • PORTLAND, OR

First published in 2007 by Irish Academic Press

44, Northumberland Road,	920 NE 58th Avenue, Suite 300
Ballsbridge	Portland, Oregon
Dublin 4, Ireland	97213-3786

www.iap.ie

British Library Cataloguing in Publication Data
An entry can be found on request

ISBN 978 0 7165 2953 8 (cloth)
ISBN 978 0 7165 2954 5 (paper)

Library of Congress Cataloging-in-Publication Data
An entry can be found on request

Typeset in 10.5/12pt Times NR by FiSH Books, Enfield, Middx.
Printed by Biddles Ltd., King's Lynn, Norfolk

Contents

List of Figures and Map

MAP

Abbreviations

AIA	Anglo-Irish Agreement (1985)
AIIC	Anglo-Irish Intergovernmental Conference
APNI	Alliance Party of Northern Ireland
BBC	British Broadcasting Corporation
BIA	British-Irish Agreement (1998)
CAB	Records of the Cabinet
CLMC	Combined Loyalist Military Command
CO	Records of the Colonial Office
DO	Records of the Dominions Office
DSD	Downing Street Declaration (1993)
DUP	Democratic Unionist Party
EEC	European Economic Community
EU	European Union
GFA	Good Friday Agreement
HC	House of Commons (Westminster)
HL	House of Lords (Westminster)
HMSO	Her Majesty's Stationery Office
IICD	Independent International Commission on Decommissioning
INLA	Irish National Liberation Army
IMC	Independent Monitoring Commission
IRA	Irish Republican Army
IRB	Irish Republican/Revolutionary Brotherhood
MLA	Member of the Legislative Assembly (Northern Ireland)
MP	Member of Parliament (UK)
NI	Northern Ireland
NICRA	Northern Ireland Civil Rights Association
NILP	Northern Ireland Labour Party
NIO	Northern Ireland Office
OIRA	Official Irish Republican Army
PD	People's Democracy
PIRA	Provisional Irish Republican Army
PM	Prime Minister
PR	Proportional Representation
PREM	Records of the Prime Minister's Office
PSNI	Police Service of Northern Ireland
PUP	Progressive Unionist Party
RIR	Royal Irish Rangers

RTÉ	Radio Telefís Éireann
RUC	Royal Ulster Constabulary
SAS	Special Air Services
SDLP	Social Democratic and Labour Party
STV	Single Transferable Vote
TD	Teachta Dála (Member of the Lower House of the Oireachtas, or Irish Parliament)
UDA	Ulster Defence Association
UDR	Ulster Defence Regiment
UFF	Ulster Freedom Fighters
UK	United Kingdom
UN	United Nations
US	United States of America
UUC	Ulster Unionist Council
UUP	Ulster Unionist Party
UUUC	United Ulster Unionist Council
UVF	Ulster Volunteer Force

Chronology of Key Events in British–Irish Relations and Northern Ireland, 1920–2007[1]

1920	**December**	Government of Ireland Act (UK) creates a devolved parliament and government for Northern Ireland within the UK.
1921	**7 July**	Truce declared between British government and IRA.
	6 December	British and Irish delegates sign the Anglo-Irish Treaty.
1922	**7 January**	Anglo-Irish Treaty approved by the Dáil by a margin of sixty-four to fifty-seven.
	March	IRA splits into pro- and anti-treaty factions, leading to Irish Civil War.
	11 September	Dáil Éireann opens.
1923	**27 April**	IRA declares ceasefire to end Irish Civil War.
1926	**16 May**	Former Sinn Féin President Eamon de Valera leads a split from Sinn Féin to form Fianna Fáil.
1932	**9 March**	After 16 February general election, Fianna Fáil forms government with Irish Labour.
1933	**9 September**	Fine Gael party established by members of Cumann na nGaedheal.
1937		New Irish constitution changed name from Irish Free State to Éire (Ireland) and established claim to jurisdiction over the entire island of Ireland and its territorial seas.
1938	**25 April**	Anglo-Irish agreement on trade, finance and the return of the 'treaty ports' to Irish jurisdiction.

---

1 Sources for the Chronology: Foster, R. F. , *Modern Ireland 1600–1972* (London: Penguin, 1988) pp. 613–19; Bew, Paul and Gillespie, Gordon, *Northern Ireland: A Chronology of the Troubles 1968–1993* (Dublin: Gill and Macmillan, 1993); Conflict Archive on the Internet, 'A Chronology of the Conflict', compiled by Melaugh, Martin, (http://cain.ulst.ac.uk/othelem/chron.htm) 9 May 2007.

1939	**2 September**	Irish government announced its intention to remain neutral in the event of war.
1948	**18 February**	Fine Gael-led coalition formed by J.A. Costello after 3 February Irish general election.
	21 December	Republic of Ireland Act removed Ireland from the Commonwealth.
1949	**2 June**	Ireland Act (UK) declared Northern Ireland Parliament's right to approve any change to Northern Ireland's status as part of UK.
1951	**30 May**	Fianna Fáil regained power after Irish general election.
1954	**6 April**	Flags and Emblems Act (NI) prohibited display of Irish 'tricolour'.
1955	**14 December**	Republic of Ireland joined UN.
1956	**12 December**	IRA began 'Operation Harvest'.
1959	**17 June**	Eamon de Valera elected President of Ireland.
1963	**25 March**	Terence O'Neill succeeded Lord Brookeborough as PM of Northern Ireland.
1965	**14 January**	Irish Taoiseach Sean Lemass and Northern Ireland Prime Minister Terence O'Neill met in Belfast.
	14 December	Anglo-Irish Free Trade Agreement signed.
1966	**10 June**	Sean Lemass replaced by Jack Lynch as Irish Taoiseach.
1967	**January**	NICRA established.
	11 December	Lynch and O'Neill met in Belfast.
1968	**8 January**	Lynch and O'Neill met in Dublin.
1969	**4 January**	People's Democracy march attacked by loyalists at Burntollet Bridge.
	28 April	Northern Ireland Prime Minister Terence O'Neill resigned and was replaced by James Chichester-Clark.
	13 August	After July riots in Derry/Londonderry, Irish Taoiseach Jack Lynch requested UN intervention and warned of possible Irish intervention in Northern Ireland.
	14 August	British army sent to Northern Ireland 'in aid of the civil power'.

1970	**11 January**	IRA split into Provisional IRA and Official IRA.
	6 May	Irish cabinet ministers Neil Blaney and Charles Haughey dismissed and charged with conspiracy to import arms.
1971	**6 February**	First British army soldier (Gunner Robert Curtis) killed by PIRA.
	20 February	Brian Faulkner succeeded Chichester-Clark as NI PM.
	9 August	Internment introduced in Northern Ireland, leading to severe escalation of violence (See Appendix, Figure 3).
	5 October	Ian Paisley formed Democratic Unionist Party.
1972	**30 January**	Thirteen killed by British army during banned civil rights march in Derry/Londonderry.
	2 February	British embassy attacked and burned in Dublin.
	24 March	UK parliament suspended Northern Ireland parliament and introduced direct rule from Westminster.
	7 July	NI Secretary William Whitelaw held secret talks with PIRA in London.
1973	**1 January**	UK and Ireland joined European Economic Community.
	8 March	A Northern Ireland referendum was held on the constitutional status as a part of the United Kingdom. On a turnout of 57 per cent, 98 per cent of voters supported the status quo. Most nationalists abstained from the 'border poll' on the grounds that it was only in Northern Ireland rather than in both jurisdictions on the island.
	20 March	UK White Paper on constitutional proposals for Northern Ireland proposed power-sharing and an Irish dimension.
	10 April	Northern Ireland Assembly Bill introduced at Westminster.
	28 June	In elections to the Northern Ireland Assembly, candidates supporting power-sharing and an Irish dimension won fifty-two seats against twenty-six opposed.
	21 November	The Northern Ireland Executive was formed consisting of six 'Faulkner Unionists', four SDLP, and one Alliance member, plus four non-executive

	27 November	Following IRA pub bombings in Guildford, Woolwich and Birmingham, the British government introduced the Prevention of Terrorism (Temporary Provisions) Bill, which was debated and became law by 29 November.
	22 December	The IRA announced a temporary ceasefire from 22 December until 2 January 1975.
1975	**17 January**	The IRA announced an end to its extended ceasefire.
	10 February	The IRA announced a renewed ceasefire to facilitate further talks with persons representing (indirectly) the British government.
	1 May	Elections were held for a Constitutional Convention for NI. The UUUC won 54.8 per cent of the seats. Since they were opposed to power-sharing, the convention collapsed by the autumn, was re-convened in February 1976 but failed to reach agreement and was dissolved formally on 5 February 1976.
1976	**1 January**	The British government announced the ending of 'special category status' for prisoners convicted of terrorist offences. IRA prisoners immediately protested against the introduction of 'criminalization' and began a 'blanket protest' on 14 September.
	5 April	James Callaghan succeeded the resigning Harold Wilson as Labour PM.
1979	**3 May**	After the British general election, Margaret Thatcher became PM of a Conservative government.
	27 August	IRA attacks killed eighteen British soldiers at Warrenpoint, Co. Down and Lord Louis Mountbatten and three others off the coast of Sligo.
	25 October	NI Secretary Humphrey Atkins invited the UUP, DUP, SDLP and APNI to a constitutional conference to discuss a political settlement. The talks lasted from 7 January 1980 to 24 March 1980 but failed to reach a consensus.
	7 December	Charles Haughey replaced Jack Lynch as Taoiseach. Lynch had resigned on 5 December.
1980	**27 October**	Seven republican prisoners began a hunger strike in protest against the ending of 'special category status'.

	8 December	Following a summit between the British PM Margaret Thatcher and Irish Taoiseach Charles Haughey, the two leaders issued a communiqué declaring the two governments' intention to conduct a series of studies considering the 'totality of relationships' between the two states.
	18 December	Republican hunger strikes called off temporarily.
1981	**1 March**	Bobby Sands, IRA leader in the Maze Prison, began a new hunger strike to protest against the ending of 'special category status'. Ten republicans, including Sands, died on hunger strike by 20 August 1981.
	6 November	Irish Taoiseach Garret FitzGerald and British PM Margaret Thatcher held a summit in London and announced the establishment of the Anglo-Irish Intergovernmental Council which would facilitate meetings between the two governments.
1985	**15 November**	Irish Taoiseach Garret FitzGerald and British PM Margaret Thatcher signed the Anglo-Irish Agreement which established the consent principle for any change in the status of Northern Ireland (based on the wishes of a majority of voters living there), created the Anglo-Irish Intergovernmental Conference and established the principle of power-sharing as a condition for the return of devolved government to NI.
1988	**11 January**	Secret discussions took place between SDLP leader John Hume and SF President Gerry Adams. The meetings lasted until 30 August 1988.
1991	**30 April**	NI Secretary Peter Brooke initiated discussions among the four main constitutional parties in Northern Ireland. Preliminary discussions in what became known as the 'Brooke/Mayhew' talks began.
1992	**29 April**	NI Secretary Patrick Mayhew (Brooke's successor) announced the recommencement of political talks among the four main constitutional parties in NI.
	10 November	The 'Brooke/Mayhew' talks ended after unionists protested at the recommencement of work by the Anglo-Irish Intergovernmental Conference.
1993	**24 April**	The IRA exploded a massive bomb at Bishopsgate in London, causing an estimated £350 million in damages. On the same day, John Hume, leader of

the SDLP, and Gerry Adams, leader of Sinn Féin, issued their first joint statement.

4–11 September The IRA held an unofficial ceasefire believed to coincide with the visit of an Irish-American delegation led by former Democratic congressman Bruce Morrison.

15 December The British and Irish governments issued a joint declaration from 10 Downing Street, London. The 'Downing Street Declaration' adjusted the consent formula for any change in Northern Ireland's status and invited paramilitaries into talks on condition of verifiable ceasefires.

1994 **29 January** US President Bill Clinton granted a visa to SF President Gerry Adams to address a peace conference in New York. The British government protested strongly.

31 August The IRA announced a 'complete cessation of military activities'.

13 October The Combined Loyalist Military Command (CLMC) announced a ceasefire of all loyalist paramilitary organizations on the condition of the maintenance of the IRA ceasefire.

1 December US President Bill Clinton appointed George Mitchell, former Senate majority leader, as a 'special economic advisor' on Ireland.

1995 **22 February** The British and Irish governments published jointly 'A New Framework for Agreement' and the British government published 'A Framework for Accountable Government in Northern Ireland'. Combined, the 'Framework Documents' outlined a power-sharing government for Northern Ireland and substantial cross-border bodies connecting the two jurisdictions on the island.

7 March In Washington, NI Secretary Patrick Mayhew outlined three pre-conditions (hereafter 'Washington Three' conditions) before Sinn Féin would be accepted into talks: a willingness to 'disarm progressively'; agreement on a method of decommissioning; and a start to the process.

1996 **24 January** The International Body on Arms Decommissioning, led by US Special Envoy George Mitchell, issued its report. It proposed a set of six principles on non-violence, elections for a negotiating forum,

		simultaneous talks and paramilitary decommissioning and security reforms.
	9 February	The IRA ended its ceasefire with a massive explosion at South Quay in the London Docklands, killing two people and causing hundreds of millions of pounds in damages.
	30 May	Elections were held for the Northern Ireland Forum.
	10 June	Talks began at Stormont, chaired by George Mitchell, including British PM John Major, Irish Taoiseach John Bruton and the main parties, apart from Sinn Féin (excluded by the governments) and DUP (self-excluded).
1997	**1 May**	Tony Blair became British PM after Labour won general election with a substantial majority of 147.
	20 July	IRA reinstated its ceasefire after contacts with British government.
	9 September	Sinn Féin signed the Mitchell Principles on non-violence, a pre-condition for entry into multi-party talks.
	7 October	Substantive multi-party talks resumed at Stormont, Belfast, after sixteenth months of procedural wrangling.
1998	**10 April**	Good Friday Agreement signed at Belfast.
	22 May	The Good Friday Agreement was supported by 71.12 per cent of voters in a referendum in Northern Ireland and by 94.39 per cent in the Republic, indicating 85.46 per cent support on the island of Ireland.
	25 June	Elections held for the new Northern Ireland Assembly.
	15 August	Omagh bombing by 'real' IRA (splinter from IRA) killed twenty-nine people and an unborn child.
1999	**29 November**	Nominations to the Executive of the new NI Assembly took place, with UUP leader David Trimble named as First Minister and SDLP deputy-leader Seamus Mallon named as Deputy First Minister.
2000	**11 February**	NI Assembly suspended because of lack of agreement on paramilitary arms decommissioning.
2001	**23 October**	The first act of IRA decommissioning was confirmed by the Independent International Commission on Decommissioning.

2002	**14 October**	NI Secretary John Reid suspended devolved power-sharing amidst allegations of Sinn Féin spying at Stormont.
2003	**April**	British and Irish governments announced formation of Independent Monitoring Commission to scrutinize paramilitaries and assess government fulfilment of implementation obligations.
	21 October	UUP leader David Trimble rejected the IRA's third act of decommissioning because of a lack of transparency.
	26 November	The DUP and Sinn Féin emerged as the largest parties from the NI Assembly elections.
2004	**8 December**	Deal between DUP and Sinn Féin failed over the DUP demand for published photographic evidence of weapons decommissioning.
2005	**28 July**	IRA statement declared war is over.
	26 September	IICD head General John de Chastelain confirmed that IRA had decommissioned all remaining arms.
2006	**13 October**	St Andrews Agreement reached between British and Irish governments and the main NI parties on a schedule for the restoration of the GFA.
2007	**28 January**	Sinn Féin held a special Ard Fheis (party conference) to approve a motion giving the party's ruling executive authority to declare support for the new Police Service of Northern Ireland.
	7 March	In elections to the NI Assembly the DUP and Sinn Féin again emerged as the dominant parties.
	26 March	DUP and Sinn Féin jointly announced agreement on a restoration of GFA institutions by 8 May.
	8 May	DUP leader Ian Paisley accepted nomination as First Minister and Sinn Féin deputy leader Martin McGuinness accepted nomination as Deputy First Minister as power is restored to the GFA institutions.

Acknowledgements

I have accumulated many debts during the long gestation of this book. I began the research as a PhD student at the Government Department of the London School of Economics and Political Science in 1989. I am deeply indebted to my supervisor, Professor Brendan O'Leary, for his supervision and his suggestions to expand the scope from political violence to the wider political relations between Britain and Ireland. His encouragement and friendship have been invaluable and prove that coercion and conciliation can be useful forms of supervision, if not good strategy for conflict regulation.

In addition, numerous politicians, officials, 'activists' and academics across both islands have offered their time and thoughts, both on and off the record, between the early 1990s and 2007. Particular thanks must go to Professor Sumantra Bose, Professor Richard Bourke, Professor D.G. Boyce, Dr Peter Catterall, Dr Bruce Cauthen, Dr John Coakley, Dr W.H. Cox, Professor Patrick Dunleavy, Dr Jonathan Githens-Mazer, Professor Adrian Guelke, Dr John Hutchinson, Dr Eric Kaufman, Seamus Kelters, Dr Michael Kerr, Dr Bill Kissane, Professor John McGarry, David McKittrick, Dr Sean MacDougal, Dr Jonathan Moore, Professor Richard Nobles and Professor Ken Young.

I feel extremely fortunate to have had enjoyed the love and encouragement of a wonderful family. My parents Des and Terry O'Duffy deserve great thanks for their love and support over the years, along with Anne, Gavan and Siobhan, the O'Duffys in Monaghan and the O'Connors and Slatterys in Tipperary, the Heydens in London, Ambrosis in Argentina and the late Anny Chaponnais.

True friends of an academic are those not embarrassed to keep asking about the long-overdue manuscript. I would like to thank the following for their friendship, support and patience: Rob Dickinson, Sean Foy, Christophe Galez, Ambreen Hameed, Duncan Ivison, Jon Kipphoff, Pete Lewenstein, the late F.W. Molloy, Gilles Mordant, John O'Neill, Richard Pratt, Sharon Rigby, Peter Spencer, Tim Stainton, Daniel Thorold, Jon Ward, Marcus Williams, David Williams and Tim Wright.

I am extremely grateful to Lisa Hyde of Irish Academic Press for her enthusiasm and support for the project. Andrew Lynch and Aonghus Meaney both provided important and timely editorial interventions. All remaining errors and omissions are my responsibility.

Earlier versions of some chapters have been published previously. An earlier version of Chapter 2 was published in an article co-written with Jonathan Githens-Mazer in *Commonwealth and Comparative Politics,* 40, 2 (2002), pp.120–45, published by Frank Cass. Chapters 5 through 8 build on work published in two articles in *Nations and Nationalism*, 5, 4 (1999) and 6, 3 (2000), published by Cambridge and the Association for the Study of Ethnicity and Nationalism. Some data presented in Chapters 4 through 7 were published in a chapter, 'Containment or Regulation? The British Approach to Ethnic Conflict in Northern Ireland', in McGarry, John and O'Leary, Brendan (eds), *The Politics of Ethnic Conflict Regulation* (Routledge, 1993). Analysis of data on deaths and parliamentary debate in Chapters 4 through 7 was published in a chapter, 'The Price of Containment: The Effect of Violence on Parliamentary Debate on Northern Ireland 1964 to 1993', in Catterall, Peter and MacDougal, Sean (eds), *Northern Ireland in British Politics* (Macmillan, 1996). Some analysis of data on political violence presented in Chapters 4 through 6 was published in an article, 'Violence in Northern Ireland 1969 to 1994: Sectarian or Ethno-National?' in *Ethnic and Racial Studies*, 18, 4 (1995), pp. 740–72, published by Routledge.

I have been fortunate to teach in the Department of Politics at Queen Mary, University of London since 1997, under the headships of Professors Diana Coole, Wayne Parsons and Raymond Kuhn (twice). Along with other fantastic colleagues, they have provided a stimulating and collegial atmosphere for scholarship. The Departmental Secretary, Jasmine Salucideen and Departmental Administrator, Dr Monika Nangia, both deserve special mention for their assistance. I would like to thank Ed Oliver, Cartographer at Queen Mary, who produced the map of Protestants in Ireland, 1911. I am also grateful to the many undergraduate and graduate students who have helped me develop and refine analytical approaches to this and other conflicts. As Adjunct Professor at the University of Notre Dame's London Programme since 1994 I have benefited greatly from the interaction with students on my course on conflict regulation and from interaction with the Rev. Professor Paul Bradshaw, Dr Gill Gregory, Dr Laura Holt, Dr Cornelius O'Boyle, Isobel Stromboli, Professor Tom Swartz and Steve Whitnall. I would also like to thank the librarians and staff at the following libraries and institutions: British Library of Political and Economic Science, British Library, Irish National Archives (Dublin), Linen Hall Library (Belfast), Newshound (John Fay), Notre Dame Library (London), Queen Mary Library, Public Records Office (Kew).

Brendan O'Duffy
London, May 2007

Introduction
Pikes and Politics, Guns and Government

In June 1798 the newly appointed British Viceroy of Ireland, Marquis Cornwallis, wrote to the Duke of Portland concerning the state of the rebellion in Ireland and his strategy for ending it:

> The accounts that you see of the numbers of the enemy destroyed in every action, are, I conclude, greatly exaggerated; from my own knowledge of military affairs, I am sure that a very small proportion of them only could be killed in battle, and I am much afraid that any man in a brown coat who is found within several miles of the field of action, is butchered without discrimination...
>
> I shall immediately authorize the General Officers in the different districts which have been the seat of warfare, to offer (with certain exceptions) to the deluded wretches who are still wandering about in considerable bodies, and are committing still greater cruelties than they themselves suffer, the permission of returning quietly to their homes, on their delivering up their arms and taking the oath of allegiance, and I shall use my utmost exertions to suppress the folly which has been too prevalent in this quarter, of substituting the word Catholicism instead of Jacobinism, as the foundation of the present rebellion.
>
> I have, &c.,
>
> CORNWALLIS[1]

Similar concepts were re-visited in 1923 following the formal end of hostilities between supporters and opponents of the Anglo-Irish Treaty (1921). That treaty granted dominion status for the twenty-six-county 'Irish Free State', gave formal recognition to the devolved government of Northern Ireland that had been legislated in the Government of Ireland Act (1920) and authorized a Boundary Commission to determine the border separating the two entities. A proposal was made by the defeated anti-treaty forces to place their arms and ammunition in secure bunkers, to be monitored by a neutral party, including members of the Catholic clergy. The offer was made conditional on the pro-treaty side disavowing of their treaty obligation for elected officials to pledge an oath of allegiance to the British crown. Such was the sanctity of the oath of allegiance to the crown to the recently negotiated treaty (the oath was also the central point of contention in the treaty debates) that the offer was refused by the provisional 'Free State' government and the proposed trade of arms for oath was quietly abandoned. Instead of a systematic handover or surrender, weapons were left in the hands of the combatants, either greased by careful owners or in most cases left to rust. Some romantic nationalists might assert that, like the blood of martyrs, the organic treatment of the implements of violence fertilized subsequent cycles of violence. Others might regret the lack of resolve on the part of civic authorities to smite the opponents of the state.

Whatever the merits of these opposing views, it is hard to deny that since the ceasefires of 1994 and throughout the negotiation of the Good Friday Agreement in 1998 and its partial implementation thereafter, the related issues of paramilitary weapons, policing and de-militarization have been central obstacles to a durable settlement. The question of paramilitary weapons decommissioning caused the breakdown of the first ceasefire in 1996, and was a central issue leading the British government to suspend the power-sharing institutions of the Good Friday Agreement (1998) five times between 2000 and 2003. Paramilitarism, policing and the criminal justice system were the most contentious issues separating Sinn Féin and the Democratic Unionist Party in their negotiations over a resumption of power-sharing from 2004 to 2007.

As these examples attest, the implements and organization of violence are ultimate indicators of state legitimacy and therefore symbols of agreement on constitutive national sovereignty. For example, in Cornwallis' view (above) the 'deluded wretches' holding out against the British army could not be held responsible for being caught up in the Jacobin-inspired[2] uprising, though their leaders certainly could. By extension, Ireland could be subordinated to the empire with the Act of Union (1800) in a manner that overturned the precedent that limited Westminster sovereignty over Ireland (based on the repeal of the 'Declaratory Act' (1720) in 1782 and the 'Renunciation Act' of 1783). As Nicholas Mansergh has emphasized, while 'the influence of constitutional conceptions upon practical politics should not be exaggerated... Nonetheless, in this particular instance the dispute about the ultimate validity of the Act of Union, and consequently the extent to which it was morally as well as legally binding, underlined the wide gulf that existed between English and majority-Irish psychological attitudes to the 1800 settlement...'[3] In 1923, for the Provisional government led by William T. Cosgrave, the ratification of the Anglo-Irish Treaty by the Dáil established its democratic legitimacy, while the British threat of a return to war if the treaty (and the oath in particular) were violated, prevented a deal on decommissioning on anti-treaty arms. The absence of closure on the question of weapons was an indication of unrequited national legitimacy, both for the Irish Free State and for the new Northern Ireland government. As developed in Chapters 2 to 4, the failure to regulate conflict through principles and processes of national consent perpetuated violent politics.

In this light the progressive solution to the latest 'guns for government' crisis is revealing. The Provisional Irish Republican Army (IRA) announced on 28 July 2005 that it 'formally ordered an end to the armed campaign'[4] and then on 26 September satisfied the British and Irish governments, international observers, a Catholic priest and Protestant minister that it had put its remaining weapons 'beyond use'. These moves were made in exchange for commitments by the British government to de-militarize Northern Ireland, follow through on police and judicial reforms, and ensure the full implementation of the Good

Friday Agreement. This exchange represents a form of 'levelling' that was unthinkable to the British governments in 1800 and 1921. What these diachronic comparisons of the conception of weapons and proponents of violence reveal is a levelling of the status of opposing nationalisms as the basis of state legitimacy.[5] The British–Irish relationship has evolved to constitute agreement on a process of national self-determination and on the governing principles of consensual (power-sharing) and liberal-national civil and political rights. While formal, constitutive sovereignty resides with Britain over a part of the island of Ireland, other aspects of sovereignty (defined below as 'regulative') have been transformed into a bi-national architecture in which a productive and relatively stable exchange relationship has been created. At the same time, it will be argued that the trading of guns for government has provided bountiful exchanges of strategic and symbolic goods. Far from appeasement,[6] the ability of British and Irish governments to trade implements of violence with republican and loyalist 'extremists' has produced substantial commitments to constitutional politics. Sinn Féin and the Provisional IRA have accepted partition as a valid expression of unionist self-determination and power-sharing, and have (conditionally) recognized the legitimacy of the reformed police and judicial services of Northern Ireland. The political parties associated with loyalist paramilitaries have also accepted the mechanism of self-determination, power-sharing and the Irish dimension. The historic deal reached in March 2007 between Sinn Féin and the DUP to share power in Northern Ireland, in the North–South Ministerial Council and British–Irish Council, was a product of national status agreement between Irish and British peoples and governments.

In this work I argue that an understanding of the dynamics of the conflict requires an understanding of the historical legacies of Irish and British relations, both at the elite and popular levels. In particular I will develop an analytical framework (borrowing from sociological, social-psychological, political science and international relations) that improves our understanding of two fundamental relationships: first, the relationship between physical-force and constitutional movements (both challenging and defending national interests and the state); and secondly, the relationship between challenging movements and the state policies or strategies for managing conflict, with particular emphasis on the role of national status conceptions and their constitutional forms. These dynamics are central to contemporary debates not only on conflict regulation in Northern Ireland but also to the transformation of violent into constitutional politics in comparable ethno-national conflicts in Israel and Palestine, India, Pakistan and Kashmir, Sri Lanka, Cyprus, and Lebanon, where one or more external states have national sovereignty disputes over territory, governance, and civil, cultural rights of individuals and 'identity' groups.[7]

In developing an analytical framework to study relations between national-ism and conflict regulation, I am of course indebted to the considerable historical scholarship on Ireland, Britain and Northern Ireland. I have also carried out primary analysis of British and Irish state papers and parliamentary debates and have conducted interviews with officials and elected representatives in Britain, the Republic of Ireland and Northern Ireland. But the main goal is not political history but to contribute to the study of conflict and conflict regulation within the traditions of comparative political and social sciences. These approaches generally agree on the sixteenth and seventeenth century origins of conflict, though they disagree on relative priority of economic, political and cultural factors. I specifically attempt to build on the work of my PhD supervisor, Brendan O'Leary, and also John McGarry, whose work distinguishes between endogenous (internal e.g. social, political, economic) and exogenous (external, e.g. international) causes and their implications for conflict regulation.[8] Similar appreciation of the multi-dimensionality of conflict is found in the work of the late John Whyte, and from a post-modernist perspective, in the work of Joseph Ruane and Jennifer Todd;[9] from a structuralist perspective in the work of Paul Bew, Peter Gibbon and Henry Patterson,[10] and from an international relations perspective in the works of Paul Arthur[11] and Adrian Guelke.[12] While differing considerably on the priority of structural, institutional and cultural factors, they all recognize the importance of British and Irish relations and the centrality of opposing claims to national self-determination, as well as more localized sources of conflict between nationalists and unionists in Northern Ireland. However, none of these approaches attempts to analyze systematically the relationships between (popular and elite) conceptions of nationalism, state legitimacy and political violence.

THE PLAN OF CAMPAIGN

Chapter 1 develops a generalizable analytical framework that allows for the specification of causality between elite conceptions of conflict and popular acceptance of nation-state configurations. Chapter 2 begins with an analysis of the negotiation and implementation of the Anglo-Irish Treaty, paying particular attention to the mutual perceptions of national status 'with and within' the British state. In Chapters 3 and 4 the analysis of the residual effects of contested national status are demonstrated by analyzing the political effects of partition on Irish government policy towards Britain and Northern Ireland in the post-Second World War era. The 'unresolved questions' of national self-determination were central factors shaping policy for the Irish government and for the Northern Irish government from the early 1960s. The combination of the Irish nationalist imperative (as codified in Articles 2 and 3 of the Irish constitution), unionist insecurity as a 'double minority' and British reluctance to intervene in the face of internal nationalist reform demands all contributed directly to the escalation of violence and the re-opening of the Irish question. The primary importance of British–Irish status relations on conflict and its regulation are demonstrated in Chapters 5 through 7 through a systematic analysis of negotiations over constitutional relations, institutional design and implementation in the Sunningdale (1973), Anglo-Irish (1985) and British–Irish/Good Friday Agreements (1998) respectively. In tracing the evolution of intergovernmental relations, and specifically the vertical integration of British–Irish 'bi-nationalism' at the state, governmental and societal levels, I demonstrate how the two governments have been able to establish parameters for conflict regulation that have encouraged both Irish nationalists (including militant republicans) and unionists (including militant loyalists) to moderate opposing maximalist demands for self-determination in exchange for consensual processes of national self-determination, power-sharing government, border-transcending institutions and political and civil rights protections. The concluding chapter considers these developments both in the historical context of British–Irish relations and in the comparative study of ethno-national conflict regulation.

To develop a comparative framework for the analysis of nation- and state-building we need to first consider how the legitimation of governmental and constitutional authority is grounded in conceptions of national self-determination. In the next chapter I try to bring the nation back into state theories by showing how insights from the philosophical and empirical study of political violence interact with theories of social exchange, nationalism and the state.

Notes

1. Marquis Cornwallis to the Duke of Portland, 28 June 1798, reproduced in Killen, John (ed.), *The Decade of the United Irishmen: Contemporary Accounts 1791–1801* (Belfast: Blackstaff, 1997) p. 143.
2. The French revolutionary movement led by Robespierre that attempted, through a reign of terror from 1793 to 1794, to impose a centralized, democratic national republic based on popular sovereignty.
3. Mansergh, Nicholas, *The Irish Question 1840–1921*, 3rd Edition (London: Allen and Unwin, 1975) p. 321.
4. IRA statement 28 July, 2005.
5. See Brendan O'Leary's analysis of the transformation of the IRA in the context of British–Irish conflict regulation and state-craft, 'Looking Back at the IRA: Constitutional Mission Accomplished?', in Heiberg, Marianne, O'Leary, Brendan and Tirman, John (eds), *Terror, Insurgencies and States: Ending Protracted Conflicts* (Philadelphia, PA: University of Pennsylvania Press, 2007).
6. Patterson, Henry, 'From Insulation to Appeasement: the Major and Blair Governments Reconsidered', in Wilford, Rick, *Aspects of the Belfast Agreement* (Oxford: Oxford University Press, 2001).
7. See for example Wolff, Stefan, *Disputed Territories: The Transnational Dynamics of Ethnic Conflict Settlement* (Oxford: Berghahn, 2003); Bose, Sumantra, *Contested Lands: Israel–Palestine, Kashmir, Bosnia, Cyprus and Sri Lanka* (Cambridge, MA: Harvard University Press, 2007); Coakley, John (ed.), *The Territorial Management of Ethnic Conflict* 2nd Edition (London: Frank Cass, 2003).
8. O'Leary, Brendan and McGarry, John, *The Politics of Antagonism: Understanding Northern Ireland* 2nd Edition (London: Athlone, 1996); see also McGarry, John and O'Leary, Brendan, *Explaining Northern Ireland: Broken Images* (Oxford: Basil Blackwell, 1995); McGarry, John (ed.), *Northern Ireland and the Comparative World* (Oxford: Oxford University Press, 2001); McGarry, John and O'Leary, Brendan, *The Northern Ireland Conflict: Consociational Engagements* (Oxford: Oxford University Press, 2004).
9. Ruane, Joseph and Todd, Jennifer, *The Dynamics of Conflict in Northern Ireland: Power, Conflict and Emancipation* (Cambridge: Cambridge University Press, 1996); and their edited collection *After the Good Friday Agreement* (Dublin: University College Dublin Press, 1999).
10. Bew, Paul, Gibbon, Peter and Patterson, Henry, *Northern Ireland 1921–1994: Political Forces and Social Classes* (London: Serif, 1995).

11. Arthur, Paul, *Special Relationships: Britain, Ireland and the Northern Ireland Problem* (Belfast: Blackstaff, 2000).
12. Guelke, Adrian, *Northern Ireland: the International Perspective* (Dublin: Gill and Macmillan, 1988).

1

Political Violence and Nation-State Legitimacy

Resistance to your acts was necessary as it was just; and your vain declaration of the omnipotence of parliament, and your imperious doctrines of the necessity of submission, will be found equally impotent to convince or enslave your fellow subjects in America.

"Non dimicare et vincere" their victory can never be by exertions. Their force would be most disproportionately exerted against a brave, generous and united people, with arms in their hands and courage in their hearts: – three million of people, the genuine descendants of a valiant and pious ancestry, driven to those deserts by the narrow maxims of a superstitious tyranny...Are the brave sons of those brave forefathers to inherit their sufferings as they have inherited their virtues?[1]

Lord Chatham (William Pitt 'The Elder')
20 January, 1775

Tony Blair said he recognized our frustrations. He said: "You guys' (sic) problem is you don't have guns."[2]

Mark Durkan (Leader, Social Democratic and
Labour Party)

While it is common to identify violence and force as, respectively, illegitimate and legitimate manifestations of coercive power,[3] such definitions are indeterminate since they require further judgment on the legitimacy or authority of the state, within which violence occurs, or against which violence is directed.[4] Hannah Arendt distinguished *power*, 'the human ability not just to act but to act in concert', from *authority*, where power is vested in persons and the hallmark of which is the 'unquestioning recognition by those who are asked to obey; neither coercion nor persuasion is needed,' and *violence*, 'which is distinguished by its instrumental character...designed and used for the purpose of multiplying natural strength...'[5] Central to Arendt's distinctions among power, authority and violence is the concept of popular consent. Whereas violence

does not depend on numbers or opinions, but on implements...it is the people's support that lends power to the institutions of a country [read: 'state'], and this support is but the continuation of the consent that brought the laws into existence to begin with. Under conditions of representative govern-ment the people are supposed to rule those who govern them. All political institutions are manifestations and materializations of power; they petrify and decay as soon as the living power of the people ceases to uphold them.[6]

Yet, Arendt, like many other thinkers who consider the origins of state legitimacy, fails to ask the prior question: who are *the people*, from whom consent is granted? Likewise, Max Weber's widely cited definition of the state as 'a human community that (successfully) claims the monopoly of the legitimate use of physical force within a given territory'[7] provides little insight into the criterion of legitimacy of the political unit itself, i.e. the state. Instead, Weber, and the vast majority of scholars who have analysed the concept of political legitimacy, reveal a statist bias by focusing on components of legitimacy at the regime and government levels,[8] while taking for granted state legitimacy: 'the justification of the political unit itself'.[9]

BRINGING THE NATION BACK IN TO STATE THEORY

A range of political theorists and scientists offer more contingent theories of the state. Claus Offe, for example, has argued that within any polity '[t]he horizontal phenomena of trust and solidarity are preconditions for the "vertical" phenomenon of the establishment and continued existence of state authority... this means that before citizens can recognize the authority of the state, they must first mutually recognize each other as being motivated by trust and solidarity'.[10] Michael Mann has contributed a more elaborate theory of the state that explicitly builds on Weber's institutional approach. In rejecting materialist, pluralist and elitist approaches, Mann develops a polymorphous theory that emphasizes the complex interactions among ideological, economic, military and political forces of the modern era.[11] Mann stresses the economic and military determinants of states and state-society relations in his comparative analysis of western European cases and the United States, while emphasizing the contingent nature of state power, and specifically (via Weber) the vertical relationship between elites and institutions at the centre and 'parties' (in the general sense i.e. factions), social classes and status groups (e.g. castes) sharing a state's territory.[12] In elaborating Weber's theory, Mann produces a contingent conception of the state as one that is composed of a 'differentiated set of institutions and personnel embodying centrality... to cover a territorially demarcated area over which it exercises *some* degree of authoritative, binding rule-making, backed up by *some* organized physical force.[13] Thus his theory rejects an overly coherent conception of the state, emphasizing instead the structured but dynamic relations among clusters of networks of bureaucratic and party elites, the military, economic producers and consumer groups and various social and civic interest groups.

In developing Weber's incomplete theory of the state Mann has undoubtedly improved our understanding of the sources of social, political and economic power, state capacity and inter-state relations. But in building on Weber's theory the state-centred approaches tend to discard an important motivational element:

the 'societalization' process in which communal solidarity is developed by parties, classes and status groups, all of whom 'necessarily presuppose a comprehensive socialization, and especially a political framework of communal action, within which they operate'. Further, Weber argued that

> societalization (even when it aims at the use of military force in common) reaches beyond the frontier of politics. This has been the case in the solidarity of interests among the Oligarchs and among the democrats in Hellas, among the Guelfs and among the Ghibellines in the Middle Ages, and within the Calvinist party during the period of religious struggles ... [T]heir aim is not necessarily the establishment of new international political, i.e. territorial, dominion. In the main they aim to influence the existing dominion.[14]

Elsewhere, Weber defined the nation as an extended ethnic community, based not usually on common economic interest but on a more diffuse set of common interests and motivations that amount to a 'community of sentiment [elsewhere a 'sentiment of prestige'[15]] which would adequately manifest itself in a state of its own'.[16] In this view, there is nothing deterministic about class, status or cultural forms of solidarity. Weber recognized, for example, that language was not deterministic in shaping either national aspirations nor explaining nation-state stability. While a Swiss nation was cohesive despite linguistic pluralism, Anglicization did not undermine Irish national opposition to Britain, nor explain why Alsatian prestige was grounded in French rather than German symbolism.[17] What matters is the relationship between and among various ethnic, class and political identities and interests. Thus, as students of ethnic or ethno-nationalist conflict recognize, where class, religion, and ethnicity are parallel and reinforcing, conflict over control of state institutions and constitutional relations between and among nations is more intense.[18]

Anthony Smith and his 'ethno-symbolist' school (including John Hutchinson and Jonathan Githens-Mazer) as well as 'perennialists' like John Armstrong and Adrian Hastings have developed the most comprehensive analyses of the ideational forces that bond solidary groups in pursuit of social, economic and political power and authority. For these opponents of the modernist (or constructivist) explanations, nation- and state-building are profoundly shaped by pre-modern solidary alignments based on perceived, extended kinship groups or *ethnie:* a named unit of human population sharing myths and memories of collective historical experiences, a shared culture (including religion, language and customs) with a sense of solidarity and subjectively-felt entitlement to a specific territory or homeland. These approaches are careful to distinguish their theories from those of either biological or cultural 'primordialists' who assert that *ethnies* and nations are extended kinship groups linked to some pre-existing biological or cultural community. Instead, ethno-symbolists and perennialists argue that pre-modern ethnic and proto-nationalist identities and interests shape modernization as much as they are shaped by modernization. There is little doubt, for example, that Gaelic culture in Ireland was an important obstacle to Anglicization of language, religion and politics.

For example, John Hutchinson, drawing on the work of Michael Richter, has emphasized the development of a Celtic–Christian synthesis from the introduction of Christianity by St Patrick in the fifth century AD. This synthesis was responsible for solidifying the Gaelic language as religious scholars standardized the language by transforming it from oral to written form. These processes were 'ethnogenic' in that important myths based on the Ulster and Fenian cycles were chronicled, along with the *brehon* legal code, poetry, genealogies of Irish kingdoms – including that of Irish high king Brian Boru – and literary productions such as the eighth-century *Book of Kells* that represented Ireland's status as a bastion of Christianity.[19] However mythical, these oral and literary cultures limited the prospects for Anglicization and religious reformation.

If, as Mann and others recognize, power is distributed territorially to lower-order representative bodies and local councils and vertically between state, industrial elites and socially based networks of interest, then the Smithians emphasize Weber's ethnicist strand and the independent role of myths, memories and symbols as the sinews of solidary bonds linking different classes, interests and status groups. The most enduring and successful ethnic and national groups tend to possess at least the following two conditions: a well-developed written vernacular language, usually codified as a scriptural language (Latin-based languages of Europe, Arabic in the Muslim empire stretching from the steppes of Asia to the Iberian peninsula (and north Africa); and a demotic *ethnie* (usually also defined in part by religion, such as the Catholic Irish ethos of 'faith and fatherland' from the late sixteenth century, Catholic Franks, Calvinist Protestant New English in North America and Ireland, Calvinist Dutch Afrikaaners in southern Africa (contemporary South Africa), Jewish Zionists in Palestine (and contemporary Israel) and so forth. For both Smith and Hastings, religion plays a particularly important role in sanctifying origin myths (e.g. Clovis in France) as well as in interpreting military victories and defeats as divinely pre-destined. Miroslav Hroch adds a third pre-condition for predicting durable nationalist movements: institutions or traditions of ancient statehood. These were important in explaining the strength of national movements among Poles, Magyars, Norwegians, Czechs and Croatians during the nineteenth century, but were also important in Ireland from at least the fourteenth century.[20]

By synthesizing cultural and political theories of nationalism we can offer a counter-argument to those who have approached the subject of conflict and political violence from a statist perspective. For instance, Conor Cruise O'Brien, who has written extensively on political violence in Ireland and elsewhere, fails to question the underlying legitimacy of the 'democratic state' by denying the validity of analyses that take 'something like [a position of] neutrality between a democratic state and its armed internal enemies'.[21] Yet at the same time O'Brien adopts a relativist attitude towards the subject by stating: 'When I speak of the defence of democracy, I am not of course in any way defending those colonial wars which have been waged by democracies in conditions where democracy is for home consumption, not for export.'[22] Ireland and Northern Ireland clearly are not included in his list of colonial wars.

O'Brien, in the civic nationalist tradition, avoids consideration of the relationship between nationalism and state legitimacy. Instead, he takes for granted the legitimacy of '*the* democratic system' and asserts vaguely that 'people who live in democratic states know what that version means in practice to them'.[23] Paul Wilkinson, who has also written on Ireland and political violence generally, shares this statist bias in his attempt to correct the imbalance in liberal thought towards individual rights, democracy and participation 'at the cost of any attention to obligations, duties, law, authority and order'.[24] He argues that:

> It can never be right for minorities – however intensely they may desire to realise particular aims or to redress specific grievances – to use violence to try to coerce the majority or the government into submitting to their demands... And if persuasion through the ballot box, lobbying and peaceful demonstration ultimately fails to win the minority's objectives, then, according to the tested principles of liberal democracy, they must abide by the democratic decision of the majority.[25]

By defining proponents of violence as 'minorities' Wilkinson presumes agreement on the national basis of state legitimacy and ignores the possibility that minorities in one state, like Catholics/nationalists in Northern Ireland, could consider themselves *nationalist* minorities seeking re-unification with the Irish state, or that the majority Protestants/unionists could fight to defend the union with Britain. By extension, O'Brien and Wilkinson offered draconian prescriptions for any group that uses violence to challenge state legitimacy. For Wilkinson: 'to be effective a liberal state must not foster civil violence: it must conquer it'.[26] Likewise for O'Brien: 'the best way for a democracy to deal with what is called political violence is to set aside its supposedly political character and concentrate on its criminal aspect as an armed conspiracy'.[27] These are more than just academic debates. As an Irish Labour TD, O'Brien became Minister for Posts and Telegraphs and was instrumental in strengthening Section 31 of the Broadcasting Act which banned members of Sinn Féin and the Provisional Irish Republican Army from the airwaves.

Charles Townshend's magisterial analysis of political violence in Ireland and Northern Ireland since 1848 does address the fundamental relationship between violence and state legitimacy, but does so tautologically:

> The *result* of all this [political violence]... was to restrict the legitimacy of the British government of Ireland. The state was widely perceived there as a mere relation of forces rather than a higher juridical or ethical entity. The extent to which it visibly rested on force undermined its claim to the monopoly of force, and its claim that violent resistance was illicit... [T]he negativity of attitudes to the state and of nationalist political orientation... clearly legitimized the use of force.[28]

For Townshend, political violence by rebellious, pre-modern, half-conquered natives undermined the legitimacy of the British state.[29] Professor Max Beloff adopted a similar line of argument regarding Northern Ireland:

> [T]he ultimate tragedy, in many of these situations, is that the disorder which sporadic terror promotes makes harder the curing of the genuine ills of a country which, no doubt, deserve attention... [T]o take the Northern Ireland case, a country (sic) which already suffers from heavy unemployment and under-development is not going to attract capital if it cannot guarantee life and limb to the capitalist.[30]

All of these approaches reject a relativist approach to political violence, but in so doing fail to question the underlying legitimacy of the state, as affected by popular and elite conceptions of national self-determination.

NATIONAL SELF-DETERMINATION

Taking a relativist view of the legitimacy of the state is not enough to explain the dynamics of conflict nor prescribe approaches to conflict regulation. For this we need to consider the evolution of the ideological underpinning of the modern international system to evaluate the relationship between violent and constitutional politics.

With others,[31] Walker Connor has proposed that since the French and American revolutions the fundamental source of state legitimacy is national self-determination: the degree to which the nation, a 'named people', is realized in the form of a state.

> Nearly everywhere, it proved to be the equating of *the people* with *my people*, that is to say, with *my nation*, that was to breathe life into the otherwise sterile concept of popular sovereignty... Once the nation has been substituted for the people, it is the national group that becomes the final arbiter in determining whether the state or states in which it resides is to be perceived as legitimate or illegitimate.[32]

The confluence of national self-awareness (e.g. 'we the people') and popular sovereignty ('the people shall rule') form the foundations of state legitimacy in western liberal thought. Yet, such a claim begs an obvious question: if national self-determination is the foundation of state legitimacy, why are there so few true nation-states, i.e., states where the nation and the state coincide? The answer is that most ethno-national groups, while insisting on some form of right to national self-determination, are willing to settle for less than outright independence.[33] More importantly, certain ethno-national configurations can achieve hegemony sufficient to preserve borders and constitutional order for extended periods. Michael Keating's analysis of stateless peoples, such as Scots, Catalans and Quebecois, questions whether the unitary, civic nation-state was merely an aberration between the plural sovereign conceptions that defined the early modern period and the multi-level governance and pooled sovereignty that defines contemporary Europe and Canada. Keating emphasizes the importance that contemporary constitutional Scottish and Irish nationalists place on ancient constitutional rights over defined territories based on national consent. Modern Scottish nationalist histories interpret the Declaration of Arbroath (1320) as an assertion of the rights of the Scottish people against absolutism of either the English or Scottish kingdoms. Contemporary recognition of such rights was provided in the 1953 case, *MacCormick* v. *Lord Advocate*, in which the 1707 Act of Union was held to be superior law to any act of the union parliament.[34] Similarly, Irish nationalist historians and constitutional nationalist politicians contest both the fact and implications of 'conquest' and 'consent' theories of English or British sovereignty over Ireland. Seventeenth-century lawyers argued, for example, that Magna Carta was ratified in a distinct form for the Irish kingdom and also that it explicitly recognized the rights of a separate parliament.[35] These arguments remain forceful precisely because of their ability to integrate social conceptions of solidarity, both ethnically in terms of language rights and conceptions of a national homeland, as well as civically in terms of nation-state sovereignty.

For the moment it is important just to emphasize that the relationships between ethnicity, nationalism and the state should be treated as variables rather than conceptual, institutional or constitutional absolutes. John Hutchinson and Anthony Smith, for example, both develop syntheses of primordial and modernist explanations of ethnicity and nationalism by arguing that modern historical processes such as universalist scriptural religions, empire expansion, inter-state warfare, mercantile trade, migration and industrialization do not simply lead to the construction of new nations but instead usually lead to syncretic processes in which older *ethnie* are often transformed (Gaelic and Old English in Ireland), sometimes eradicated (Carthaginians by Romans) but rarely, *pace* Eric Hobsbawm and Benedict Anderson, are new nations simply invented or imagined without being rooted in some form of pre-modern ethnic attachment.[36] John Hutchinson argues that surviving nations require 'embedded institutions' like official churches; constitutional, political, legal (including law enforcement) institutions that act as custodians of older ethnic cultures, like Basque autonomy rights grounded in historic recognition of rights of *fueros,* or Quebec autonomy and sovereignty claims based on the primacy of the founding confederation of English and French Canada. Hutchinson also emphasizes the popular reception of ethnic ideas when confronted by calamities such as war, revolutions and natural disasters (e.g. plague or famine), particularly in frontier regions like Britain and Ireland, Russia and its numerous frontiers, the Ottoman empire and its Slavic, Macedonian and Greek frontiers where adjacent *ethnie* have violently and repeatedly confronted imperial or colonial projects.[37]

In response to Mann's arguments concerning the institutional effects of warfare on the construction of national identity and patriotism, Hutchinson argues that pre-modern ethnic and proto-nationalist repertoires of myths, memories and symbols act as interpretive frameworks that reinforce ethnic and national sentiments at the popular level, separate from state institutions. For example, both Gaelic *brehon* and Anglo-Norman antiquarians interpreted the

Elizabethan 'conquest' of the late sixteenth century in ways that reinforced Gaelic and 'Old English' conceptions of identity and conceptions of ancient constitutional and ecclesiastic rights. Irish antiquarians emphasized the Milesian (Gaelic) origins of the Stuart clan in the hope that the Stuart monarchy would represent a Britannic regnal union that was specifically opposed to the constitutional subordination to the English parliament.[38] Following Oliver Cromwell's campaign in Ireland (1649 to 1652), Irish poets compared the plight of Gaelic and Anglo-Irish royalists, who were banished to Connacht and Clare, with the exodus of the Israelites, thus predicting that temporary defeat would be followed by national liberation.[39] Equally, as Colin Kidd has observed, the need for an ethnic foundation for contemporary political power led the intelligentsia of the Protestant new English settlers from the second half of the seventeenth century to justify conquest by appropriating for their own the Gaelic constitutional history and Old English (Anglo-Norman) ecclesiastical heritage.[40] Alternatively, during the Home Rule 'crisis' of 1912–14, unionists in Ulster justified their defiance of Westminster legislation granting Home Rule as a violation of the contractual relationship established between Scottish and English colonial settlers and the crown in the seventeenth century.[41]

The objective in this study is not to adjudicate between the opposing ethno-national and civic-national constitutional claims but instead to demonstrate the formative impact of these contests on the development and reinforcement of opposing constitutional traditions, especially as they have been used to legitimate violence. In doing so, I draw on Christopher McCrudden's distinction between the 'pragmatic empiricist approach, which is traditionally British',[42] and the constitutional idealist approach which is more prevalent in continental Europe, Canada and the United States. In the pragmatic empiricist tradition, 'authoritative constitutional structures *evolve,* they are seldom *made*'.[43] Trial and error are the hallmarks of policy-making and constitutional engineering. 'Solutions are what works and what lasts. Institutions should therefore operate flexibly, learn from the past and develop to suit the conditions of their time.'[44] By contrast, the constitutional idealist tradition begins with a core set of ideals based on 'values which political and legal institutions are required to promote'.[45] It is no coincidence that constitutional idealism developed in former British colonies in direct response to imperious constitutional engineering. Whether in opposition to monarchic or parliamentary assertions of sovereign imperialism, these colonies asserted rights of autonomous decision-making and limits to either monarchic prerogative or Westminster parliamentary sovereignty.[46] In this respect Ireland was no exception. The timing and extent of violence was directly related to the viability of constitutionalism to uphold and promote 'national' rights. And the perception of justice deriving from these exchanges shaped directly national stereotypes and status conceptions of the 'other'. State-building attempts were limited by pre-modern ethnic alignments, by the polarizing effects of the Protestant reformation, and the variability of upward mobility offered at the governmental and societal levels. These contests then shaped national identities and perceptions of justice that underpinned subsequent conflict.

It is difficult to dispute that all the major constitutional reform efforts, whether successful or not, were achieved by movements which were 'militantly' nationalist, in the sense of having an army to back demands with the threat of force. The most important constitutional precedents for Irish nationalists – the repeal of the Declaratory Act (1720) in 1782, and the Renunciation Act of 1783, removing Britain's right to legislate for Ireland in matters within the jurisdiction of the newly restored Irish parliament – both resulted from the pressure of constitutional appeals backed by the explicit threat of violence by the mainly Protestant Volunteer movement. Alternatively, the unionist/loyalist defence against the passage of Home Rule from 1912 to 1914 combined parliamentary opposition with the mobilization of the Ulster Volunteers and made explicit threats of violent resistance that threatened a wider British civil war. For Irish nationalists, Daniel O'Connell's use of the implicit threat of violence, achieved by corralling proto-nationalist and agrarian groups within the Catholic Association, was decisive in achieving Catholic Emancipation in 1829. Likewise, constitutional appeals backed by the implicit threat of violence were responsible for substantial land reform between 1881 and 1903, and for prising open the franchise and moving the British parliament to vote for Home Rule in 1893 and 1912. The success of Irish nationalists in achieving dominion status for twenty-six counties in 1921 was a result of open rebellion, combining militant republican and erstwhile constitutional nationalists between 1917 and 1921. Likewise, unionists' abilities to threaten civil war by coalescing with British unionists and key sections of the army were responsible for blocking the implementation of Home Rule from 1912, and then effectively delimiting the territorial boundary of the Irish Free State between 1920 and 1921. 'Ulster could not be coerced' was the bedrock of the Conservative–Liberal wartime coalition government's policy towards Ireland.

In sum, violent politics was culturally and institutionally normalized during the proliferation of national consciousness and during the establishment of the constitutional relations between Britain and Ireland. This is not an argument for mere relativism, nor is it an attempt to justify or rationalize violence. Instead, I will attempt to show more positively in Part II how an understanding of the political cultures of opposing nationalisms can lead to the prescription of strategies for conflict regulation sufficient to achieve and retain popular national consent. I will assert that the historical pattern of challenges, defences and regulatory policies reveal consistent behavioural patterns that can inform negotiation and constitutional and institutional design and thereby contribute to the theory and practice of conflict regulation.

STATE STRATEGIES FOR REGULATING ETHNO-NATIONAL CONFLICT

John McGarry and Brendan O'Leary have identified two broad strategies employed by states in their response to communal and/or ethno-national demands: 'difference-eliminating' and 'difference-managing'. Difference-eliminating strategies include forced population transfers, genocide, partition and/or secession, and integration and/or assimilation. Difference-managing[47] strategies include consociationalism, cantonization and/or federalism, third-party intervention and hegemonic control. All of these strategies have been attempted in Ireland throughout the course of the past three centuries, with the debatable exception of genocide.[48]

For the analysis of political violence and nationalism it is useful to simplify further the McGarry–O'Leary taxonomy according to the criterion of consent, which I identified above as the distinguishing characteristic among authority, power and violence.[49] Consensual strategies for conflict regulation include both difference-eliminating strategies, such as agreed secession and integration/assimilation, as well as all of the difference-managing strategies undertaken mutually and voluntarily. At the other extreme are strategies based on the concept of 'control', defined by Ian Lustick as: 'the emergence and maintenance of a relationship in which the superior power of one segment is mobilized to enforce stability by constraining the political actions and opportunities of another segment or segments'.[50] Broadly conceived, control strategies can include both difference-eliminating as well as difference-managing strategies, as long as they are *not* based on consensual agreement among the constituent communal or ethno-national groups. Thus, control strategies can include forced population transfers, genocide, forceful integration/assimilation, partition, third-party intervention, imposed federalism and/or cantonization.

If consensus and control represent poles of a spectrum of voluntarism, then the intermediate category, 'confused', represents strategies which either combine aspects of consensus and control or represent partial, irresolutely applied versions of one or the other. Partial autonomy agreements such as 'Grattan's parliament' of 1782, the partition of 1921 and the 'coercive consociationalism' of the Anglo-Irish Agreement (1985)[51] are all examples of strategies that are neither controlling nor consensual. Confused strategies can oscillate between what McCrudden has described as pragmatic and principled constitutionalism. They have three common features: first, they include security policies which define challenges to state authority as neither criminal (clearly illegitimate) nor as acts of war (potentially legitimate); secondly, they are intended to reform social, economic, and/or political aspects of the conflict rather than the constitutional status of the state; lastly, they tend to lead to 'settlements' which are non- or minimally consensual: they exclude significant communal or ethno-national groups from the process of agreement. All aspects of a confused strategy can also be combined, either statically, as in the policy of 'light railways and heavy punishment', or in succession, as in the alternating policies of 'coercion and conciliation' as described by L.P. Curtis as the mode of Conservative–Unionist governance in the last quarter of the nineteenth century[52] or as displayed in the alternating fits of security and political initiatives by Conservative and Labour governments in Northern Ireland from 1969 to 1993. Thus, I conceive of 'confused' in a literal sense as the joining or succession of different strategies, which either contradict their intended purpose or represent partial adjustments that are insufficient to cross the threshold into either consensus or control. Confused policies are not necessarily the product of muddled thinking among leaders, although they may well be. They are more often products of constraints imposed by ethno-national politics, limited institutional capacity, and/or exogenous geo-political factors, such as inter-state wars or economic crises. To understand the impact of state policies on nationalism we need to specify the dynamics of interaction, studying the motivation and justification for response or action. The dynamics of these relations can be understood as forms of exchange relations.

Exchange theory and state-society relations

Economic, political and social psychological applications of exchange theory emphasize the importance of status recognition on the quality of exchange relations between social groups, ethno-nations and states. For exchange theorists like Willer et al. the influence exerted by super-ordinates in exchange experiments is mediated by emotional responses after previous negative interactions with a super-ordinate.[53] Antagonism resulting from perceptions of unjust status hierarchies offsets both power (equivalent to control) and influence (equivalent to consent). In these experiments the influence that one actor has over another or others is largely determined by the degree to which status is mutually recognized and accepted. Enhanced and mutually perceived status in turn has a positive effect on acceptance of power differentials, as recognized by Weber in his study of status groups.

Similarly, normative theorists of nationalism tend to argue that nationally plural states require status agreement through rights of self-determination that achieve an equilibrium of consensus on the territorial and personal (or communal) relations between or among nations within a given state. Status-confirming self-determination processes enhance individual and collective perceptions of upward mobility, particularly for national elites, but also in terms of wider social conceptions of democratic representation, equitable systems of justice, accountable law enforcement and policing, multi-cultural or explicitly multi-national language and education policies. Plural conceptions of nationalism offer rewards that can compensate subordinate or co-ordinate constituents within or among states. The antithesis predicts that the unwillingness or inability of a super-ordinate to offer rewards to subordinates would produce resentment or enmity.

Social exchange theorist Linda Molm described a common pattern of super-ordinate behaviour as '"nattering": unsystematic responses expressing displeasure and irritation, but without following through with any real costs and without risking more serious confrontation'.[54] Nattering results from the super-ordinate's inability or unwillingness to offer reward to compensate a subordinate, who then pesters until it produces flails of annoyance. Only when the pestering reaches a systemic and intolerable level is the super-ordinate moved to address fundamental sources of antagonism. This equilibrium process is very similar to Zartman's conception of a hurting stalemate in civil and inter-state wars as well as the dominant interpretations of the coercion–conciliation policies toward Ireland throughout the nineteenth and early twentieth centuries.

Consider Thomas Pakenham's characteristic (Anglo-Irish) overview of the British response to Irish claims for national recognition:

> ...the second Irish war of independence of 1919–21 not only failed to win a united Ireland, but resulted in a return to a form of self-government in Ulster that had already proved disastrous in [17]'98. Forty years later the stench of history is overpowering. Catholics have remained poor, politically powerless, and alienated from government. Stormont has maintained Protestant ascendancy as stoutly as the Dublin Parliament. Successive British Governments have decided to let well alone, dodging the attacks of the Left with the same tactics Pitt used against Fox – Ireland is an Irish responsibility.[55]

Michael Keating, quoting Maitland, has argued that the 'British problem in Ireland' that has prevented the achievement of either control or consent has been the 'lack of a theory of authority between absolute dependence and absolute independence'.[56] In fact, this confusion between Ireland's status as colony and kingdom goes back much further, at least to the beginning of Henry VIII's reign when the first attempts were made to impose English common law throughout Ireland. These attempts provoked revolts by Anglo-Norman (Old English) barons against 'composition' of land (for revenue collection) and the enforcement of Anglican conformity.[57] Similarly, both Gaelic Irish and Old English combined during the 1640s in a 'confederacy' that sought a dominion status that would protect their interests in land and religion (Catholicism) from the Puritan-dominated English parliament. It is the centrality of these constitutional goals that leads Ó Siochrú, following John Elliott and others,[58] to argue that the Irish confederacy represented a form of 'corporate' or 'national' constitutionalism led by legal scholars and practitioners defending the rights and liberties of a particular community that included both Gaelic and Old English.[59] This community may not have been explicitly nationalist in the sense of seeking sovereign statehood, but it was national in asserting autonomy for Ireland within the Westminster system and, moreover, a form of autonomy that was a compact, conditional on the consent of representatives of the Irish people, and which constitutionally entrenched protection for sufficient political autonomy to strengthen ecclesiastical, political and tenurial rights.[60] After the 'Glorious Revolution' of 1688 led by William of Orange restored Protestant ascendancy in both England and Ireland, similar arguments were made by members of the ascendancy in Ireland – notably William Molyneaux and Jonathan Swift – who felt that England's pragmatic, reactive approach to governance in Ireland was inimical to ascendancy interests.[61] The constitutional and emotional precedents set by the legislative responses to these demands will be explored in the next chapter. For now it is sufficient to consider the theoretical implications of exchange theory for the study of conflict and conflict regulation.

Empirically, consensus and control represent equilibrium states in which stability[62] is achieved either because a regime or government representing a dominant segment monopolizes the control of the legitimate use of force, or because authority is consensually grounded, either to a power-sharing government, to the constituent units of a new cantonal or federal structure, or within a newly independent state. It follows that the intermediate category, confusion, should be associated with high levels of instability, as apparently understood by the Duke of Cumberland when he justified his draconian repression of the Jacobin rising in Scotland in 1745 by arguing that 'an ill-judged lenity [is] the greatest cruelty' to compare his treatment with the more timorous treatment of the 1715 rising.[63] Such a prediction is consistent with several notable studies of the relationship between the levels of government or regime repression and subsequent levels of political violence. A series of studies on different aspects of repression–reaction patterns have supported the existence of an 'inverted U' relationship between repression and political violence.[64] These studies have found that low levels of repression are associated with low levels of instability, high levels of repression are also associated with low levels of instability as massive force *temporarily* quells dissent, while medium levels of repression are associated with high levels of instability because they are enough to provoke opposition, but insufficient to suppress violence.

The logic of this relationship can be applied to the relationship between conflict regulation strategies and anti-state political violence. If we accept that low levels of repression are logical corollaries of 'consensual' conflict regulation strategies, that high levels of repression are corollaries of 'control' strategies, and that medium levels of repression are corollaries of 'confused' strategies, then we can hypothesize that the relationship between coercion and consent is normally distributed, like a bell-curve. The trick is to explain the balance of forces producing the equilibrium. As the conflict regulation literature readily attests, consensus is the most difficult stage to achieve in deeply divided societies with deep ethnic (including linguistic and religious) cleavages. When such cleavages produce territorially concentrated 'peoples' with conceptions of rights to autonomy on a 'homeland', we have an 'ethno-national' conflict.[65] Since the combination of popular ethnicity and territorial politics usually involves contests over sovereignty and may, as in Ireland, involve one or more competing sovereigns, these conflicts involve a higher level of complexity to internal, non-territorial minority conflicts and usually require that consent is underpinned by agreement at the state, governmental and societal levels. In the absence of attention to the vertical links between these levels of authority, control may be easy for powerful states to implement, but difficult to maintain over time because of the political, military and economic costs associated with the suppression of ethno-national movements.[66]

To explain the constancy of pattern and organized response according to core national principles (both civic and cultural), we need to ask whether other forms of currency can be manipulated in the settling of a conflict. This is where Linda Molm's findings have implications for conflict regulation, in particular the idea that subordinates need to be compensated for their lower status. State- and nation-building is centrally concerned with the success of reward power (economic, cultural, political, ideological) rather than naked coercion. A common theme among the pantheon of modernist scholars, from Weber to Anderson, is the centrality of status recognition, especially as this affects security of land tenure, political rights and constitutional authority. For Benedict Anderson, the trigger point in the conversion of Latin American *colons* from potentially imagined nations (united as reading publics due to print capitalism) into actual national movements was their perception of status inferiority and lack of upward mobility within the imperial system.[67] Ernest Gellner describes a similar phenomenon in his description of separatist nationalism as an elite-led response to the absence of upward mobility in states where an ethnic group does not have access to institutional power or education in the dominant tongue. To take a comparable case to Ireland, the national integration of Scotland into Great Britain is often explained by the maintenance of access to higher office and the related recognition of national sovereignty in legal code, education and administration.[68]

In Ireland, the access to 'place' for Catholics was restricted by law (during the 'penal era' from 1691 until 1829 when emancipation granted the right of Catholics to sit in the Westminster parliament) and then by competition with the loyal Protestant ascendancy. From the second half of the nineteenth century, as Catholic nationalist elites saw opportunities to enter the state administration, there emerged strata of ecclesiastics, soldiers and administrators who saw possibilities for upward mobility within the Irish administration of the empire state. These strata of upwardly mobile Irish (mostly Catholic but also including significant sections of Protestant and Presbyterian society) underpinned the Home Rule 'movement' from the 1870s to around 1914,[69] and provided the bedrock of support for the Anglo-Irish Treaty of 1921 that entrenched Ireland's status as a dominion of the British empire. Crucially, the conditional loyalty to the empire state was consistently demonstrated by the radicalization of nationalism that followed constitutional failures to enhance status symmetry, and were interpreted with reference to the previous historical experience of nation and state-building within the empire. Opposed to this group of aspiring integralists were strata of lower-ranking officials, educators etc. eventually aligned with small-holding tenant farmers, all of whose limited prospects within the empire state conditioned their loyalty and, after the failure of constitutional reform, combined to form cultural nationalist, separatist revivals.[70] The slide to militant republican separatism from 1912 to 1918 cannot be explained without recognizing the conditional nature of Irish loyalty to the British empire, and the antecedent experience of imperious constitutionalism.[71]

Where my approach differs from these broadly instrumentalist interpretations is its emphasis on nationalism as an ideology shaped by early modern and modern experiences of constitutionalism, as well as the materialist and instru-mentalist motives identified by modernist scholars of nationalism. Such a synthesis is consistent with theories of ethno-nationalism that distinguish between the non-rational goals and rational means used to achieve them.[72] It is also consistent with the social movement theorists' emphasis on group cohesion as a necessary, if not sufficient, condition of movement success. With others, Charles Tilly has increasingly emphasized the role of 'networks of trust' such as those provided by kinship, religion, ethnicity and class in explaining the social cohesion necessary for sustained collective action.[73] The most promising explanations of Islamic radicalism and suicide terror also combine network theory and nationalist theory to explain the motivation and solidarity of these new global networks.[74]

Critics of societal-level explanations of challenges to state authority (including collective violence and revolutions) argue that insufficient attention is paid to the independent capabilities of the state and state elites to respond to, or even control, the mobilization of challengers to state authority.[75] Hannah Arendt typified this view when she asserted: 'Revolutionaries do not make revolutions! The revolutionaries are those who know when power is lying in the street and when they can pick it up. Armed uprising by itself has never yet led to a revolution.'[76] These approaches recognize the variability of the strength of challenges to state authority, but they emphasize the importance of elite-level politics, and in particular the structural and institutional sources of power within and between militarily and industrially modern states.[77]

In the following analysis of the dynamics of the relationship between Irish nationalism and the British state, we will try to 'bring the nation back in' to theories of the state to analyze the dynamics of nation-state relations as exchange relations. Beginning with the negotiations of the Anglo-Irish Treaty in 1921 we will analyze the effects of contested national status on the negotiation and implementation of constitutional agreements, the impact of status contests on the politics of Northern Ireland from 1921 to 1972 and then the evolution of British–Irish intergovernmental conflict regulation from 1985 to the present.

Notes

1. From speech to House of Lords, 20 January, 1775, quoted in Adolphus, John, *The History of England: From the Accession of King George the Third to the Conclusion of the Peace in 1783, Volume II* (London: T. Cadell, Jun. and W. Davies, 1802) pp. 201–2.
2. O'Doherty, Malachi, 'Durkin's Push for Irish Unity', *Fortnight,* Issue 407 (October), 2002.
3. See Wilkinson, Paul, *Terrorism and the Liberal State* (London: Macmillan, 1977) p. 23; Cf. Gilmour, Ian, *Riot, Risings and Revolution: Governance and Violence in Eighteenth-Century England* (London: Hutchinson, 1992) p. 2.
4. Arendt, Hannah, *On Violence* (London: Allen Lane, 1970) pp. 143–51.
5. Arendt, *On Violence* pp. 143–5.
6. Ibid. pp. 152, 140, emphasis added.
7. Weber, Max, *From Max Weber: Essays in Sociology*, Translated, edited and with an introduction by Gerth, H.H. and Mills, C.W (eds) (Oxford: Oxford University Press, 1946) p.78.
8. Connor defines regime-legitimacy as 'the propriety or rightfulness of the rule of a particular individual, clique, or administration' and governmental legitimacy as the propriety or rightfulness of 'a particular form of government and with its corresponding ideology and institutions, regardless of the individuals who momentarily occupy its key positions'. See his article, 'Nationalism and Political Illegitimacy', *Canadian Review of Studies in Nationalism,* Vol. VIII, No. 2 (1984) p. 205.
9. Ibid. pp. 202–7; see also Jackman, Robert W., *Power Without Force: The Political Capacity of Nation-States* (Ann Arbor, MI: University of Michigan Press, 1993) pp. 25–36; Lustick, Ian, *Unsettled States, Disputed Lands: Britain and Ireland, France and Algeria, Israel and the West Bank–Gaza* (Ithaca: Cornell University Press, 1993) pp. 1–6.

10.   Offe, Claus, 'Democratic Welfare State in an Integrating Europe', in Greven, M.T. and Pauly, L.W. (eds), *Democracy Beyond the State? The European Dilemma and the Emerging Global Order* (Oxford: Rowman and Littlefield, 2000) p. 67.
11.   Mann, Michael, *The Sources of Social Power: Volume II, The Rise of Classes and Nation-States 1760–1914* (Cambridge: Cambridge University Press, 1993).
12.   Mann, *The Sources of Social Power: Volume II*, p. 58.
13.   Mann, *The Sources of Social Power: Volume II*, p. 55, emphasis added.
14.   Weber, *Essays in Sociology*, p. 195.
15.   Ibid. p. 171.
16.   Ibid. pp. 176–7.
17.   Ibid. p. 177.
18.   Horowitz, Donald, *Ethnic Groups in Conflict* 2nd Edition (Berkeley, CA: University of California Press, 2000) Chs. 4–5.
19.   John Hutchinson, *Nations as Zones of Conflict*, p. 27
20.   Ellis, Steven G., *Tudor Ireland: Crown, Community and the Conflict of Cultures 1470–1603* (London and New York: Longman, 1998) p. 250; see also Richter, Michael, *Medieval Ireland: The Enduring Tradition* (Dublin: Gill and Macmillan, 1988). For a comparative European perspective see Hroch, Miroslav, 'National Self-Determination from a Historical Perspective', in Periwal, Sukumar (ed.), *Notions of Nationalism* (Budapest: Central European University Press, 1995) pp. 78–9; see also Keating, Michael, *Plurinational Democracy: Stateless Nations in a Post-Sovereignty Era* (Oxford: Oxford University Press, 2001) Ch. 2.
21.   O'Brien, Conor Cruise, *Herod: Reflections on Political Violence* (London: Hutchinson, 1978) p. 76.
22.   Ibid. pp. 76–7.
23.   Ibid. pp. 24–5, emphasis added.
24.   Wilkinson, Paul, *Terrorism and the Liberal State* (London: Macmillan, 1977) p. 4
25.   Ibid. p. 40. The only exceptions where Wilkinson accepts the legitimacy of armed resistance to state authority is a situation where a minority represses a majority and disallows constitutional challenges to state authority. He cites South Africa during apartheid as an example but does not consider it as comparable to the Stormont era.
26.   Ibid. p. 40.
27.   O'Brien, *Herod* p. 80; see also Clutterbuck, Richard, *Britain in Agony: The Growth of Political Violence* (London: Faber, 1978); and O'Doherty, Malachi, *The Trouble with Guns: Republican Strategy and the Provisional IRA* (Belfast: Blackstaff, 1996).
28.   Townshend, Charles, *Political Violence in Ireland: Government and Resistance since 1848* (Oxford: Clarendon, 1983) pp. 412–13, emphasis added.
29.   Ibid. pp. 47–8.
30.   Beloff, Max, 'Terrorism and the People', in Beloff, Max (ed.), *Ten Years of Terrorism: Collected Views* (London: Royal United Services Institute for Defence Studies, 1979) p.118.
31.   See Keating, *Plurinational Democracy* Ch. 1; Gellner, Ernest, *Nations and Nationalism* (Oxford: Blackwell, 1983); for discussions of the evolution of the concept of sovereignty, see Shinoda, Hideaki, *Re-examining Sovereignty: From Classical Theory to the Global Age* (London: Macmillan, 2000).
32.   Connor, Walker, 'Nationalism and Political Illegitimacy', *Canadian Review of Studies in Nationalism*, Vol. VIII, No. 2 (1984) p. 210.
33.   Connor, Walker, *Ethnonationalism: The Quest for Understanding* (Princeton, NJ: Princeton University Press, 1993) pp. 81–4.
34.   Keating, *Plurinational Democracy*, p. 37.
35.   Keating, *Plurinational Democracy*, p. 37; drawing on Kidd, Colin, *Subverting Scotland's Past: Scottish Whig Historians and the Creation of an Anglo-British Identity, 1689–c. 1830* (Cambridge: Cambridge University Press,1993); and Morrill, John, 'The Fashioning of Britain', in Ellis, Steven G. and Barber, Sarah (eds), *Conquest and Union. Fashioning a British State, 1485–1725* (London: Longman, 1995).

36. Smith, Anthony D., *The Ethnic Origins of Nations* (Oxford: Blackwell, 1986); Hutchinson, John, *Nations as Zones of Conflict* (London: Sage, 2004).

37. Hutchinson, *Nations as Zones of Conflict*.

38. Kidd, Colin, *British Identities before Nationalism: Ethnicity and Nationhood in the Atlantic World, 1600–1800.* (Cambridge: Cambridge University Press, 1999) p.156.

39. Ó Mealláin, Fear Dorcha 'An Díbirt Go Connachta' (Exodus to Connacht), translated and reproduced in Ó Tuama, Seán and Kinsella, Thomas (eds), *An Duanaire 1600–1900: Poems of the Dispossessed* (Portlaoise, Ireland and St Paul, MN: Dolman, 1981) pp. 104–9.

40. Kidd, Colin, *British Identities before Nationalism: Ethnicity and Nationhood in the Atlantic World, 1600–1800* (Cambridge: Cambridge University Press, 1999) pp. 162–77.

41. Miller, David W., *The Queen's Rebels: Ulster Loyalism in Historical Perspective* (Dublin: Gill and Macmillan, 1978) pp. 62–6; see also Carty, Anthony, *Was Ireland Conquered? International Law and the Irish Question* (London: Pluto, 1996) Ch. 5.

42. McCrudden, Christopher, 'Northern Ireland and the British Constitution', in Jowell, Jeffrey and Oliver, Dawn (eds), *The Changing Constitution* Third Edition (Oxford: Clarendon, 1994) p. 323.

43. Ibid. p. 325.

44. Ibid. p. 325.

45. Ibid. p. 326.

46. Canny, Nicholas and Pagden, Anthony (eds), *Colonial Identity in the Atlantic World, 1500–1800* (Princeton, NJ: Princeton University Press, 1987).

47. McGarry, John and O'Leary, Brendan (eds), *The Politics of Ethnic Conflict Regulation* (London: Routledge, 1993) Ch. 1.

48. Irish and British accusations of genocide begin with the 1641 Catholic uprising against English and Scottish planters in Ulster and were countered, both temporally and mythically, by Irish accusations of genocide by Oliver Cromwell in 1649.

49. Esman, Milton, *Ethnic Politics* (Ithaca, NY: Cornell, 1994) Ch. 9.

50. Lustick, Ian, 'Stability in Deeply Divided Societies: Consociationalism versus Control', *World Politics* Vol. 31, No.3 (1979) p. 328.

51. O'Leary, Brendan and McGarry, John, *The Politics of Antagonism,* pp. 220–41.

52. Curtis, L.P., *Coercion and Conciliation in Ireland 1880–1892: A Study in Conservative Unionism* (Princeton, NJ: Princeton University Press, 1963).

53. *Willer, D., Lovaglia, M.J. and Markovsky, B., 'Power and Influence: A Theoretical Bridge', in Willer, D. (ed.), Network Exchange Theory (Westport, CT: Praeger, 1999) p. 239*

54. Patterson, Gerald R., *Coercive Family Process* (Eugene, OR: Castalia, 1982). For applications of exchange theory to political processes see, for example, Lawler, Edward J. 'Power Processes in Bargain', *Sociological Quarterly* No. 33 (1982) pp. 17–34; see also Lawler, Edward J. and Yoon, Jeongkoo, 'Power and the Emergence of Commitment Behavior in Negotiated Exchange', *Sociological Theory,* Vol. 11 (1993) pp. 268–90; Lawler, Edward J. and Yoon, Jeongkoo, 'Commitment in Exchange Relations: Test of a Theory of Relational Cohesion', *American Sociological Review,* Vol. 61 (1996) pp. 89–108.

55. Pakenham, Thomas, *The Year of Liberty: The Bloody Story of the Great Irish Rebellion of 1798* (London: Panther Books, 1972) pp. 405–6.

56. Keating, *Plurinational Democracy,* pp. 39–40; citing Maitland, F.W., 'Translator's Introduction', in Gierke, Otto, *Political Theories of the Middle Age* (Cambridge: Cambridge University Press, 1900) p. x. n.1.

57. Ellis, Steven, *Ireland in the Age of the Tudors 1447–1603: English Expansion and the End of Gaelic Rule* (London: Longman, 1998) Chs. 9–11.

58. Elliott, John, 'Revolution and Continuity in Early Modern Europe', *Past and Present,* 42 (1969) pp. 35–56.

59. Ó Siochrú, Micheál, *Confederate Ireland 1642–1649: A Constitutional and Political Analysis* (Dublin: Four Courts, 1999) pp. 237–8.

60. Foster, R.F., *Modern Ireland 1600–1972* (London: Penguin, 1989) pp. 161–3.
61. Lustick defines stability as 'the continued operation of specific patterns of political behaviour, apart from the illegal use of violence, accompanied by a general expectation among the attentive public that such patterns are likely to remain intact for the forseeable future'. See Lustick, 'Stability in Deeply Divided Societies', p. 325.
62. Ian Gilmour, *Riot, Risings and Revolution: Governance and Violence in Eighteenth-Century England* (London: Pimlico, 1992) p. 129.
63. Gupta, D.K., Singh, H. and Sprague, T., 'Government Coercion of Dissidents: Deterrence or Provocation?', *Journal of Conflict Resolution,* Vol. 37, No. 2 (1993) pp. 301–39. See also Dudly, Ryan and Miller, Ross A., 'Group Rebellion in the 1980s', *Journal of Conflict Resolution,* Vol. 42, No. 1 (1998) pp. 77–96; Finkel, Steven E., Muller, E.N. and Opp, K-D., 'Personal Influence, Collective Rationality, and Mass Political Action', *American Political Science Review,* Vol. 83, (1989) pp. 885–903.
64. Lijphart, Arend, *Democracy in Plural Societies* (New Haven: Yale University Press, 1977); Horowitz, Donald, *Ethnic Groups in Conflict,* 2nd Edition (Berkeley, CA: University of California Press, 1999).
65. See Jackman, Robert, *Power Without Force: The Political Capacity of Nation-States* (Ann Arbor, MI: University of Michigan Press, 1993) pp. 36–8.
66. Anderson, Benedict, *Imagined Communities: Reflections on the Origins and Spread of Nationalism* (London: Verso, 1983) Ch. 4.
67. McCrone, David, *The Sociology of Nationalism: Tomorrow's Ancestors* (London: Routledge, 1998) pp. 129–35; Poggi, Gianfranco, *The Development of the Modern State* (London: Hutchinson, 1978) p. 100.
68. Jackson, Alvin, *Home Rule: An Irish History* (London: Weidenfeld and Nicholson, 2003); see also Kissane, Bill, *Explaining Irish Democracy* (Dublin: University College Dublin Press, 2001); Paseta, Senia, *Before the Revolution: Nationalism, Social Change and Ireland's Catholic Elite, 1879–1922* (Cork: Cork University Press, 1999).
69. Garvin, Tom, *Nationalist Revolutionaries in Ireland* (Oxford: Clarendon, 1987) Ch. 3; Hutchinson, John, *The Dynamics of Cultural Nationalism,* Ch. 8; and *Nations as Zones of Conflict,* pp. 83–4, 89.
70. Githens-Mazer, Jonathan, *Myths and Memories of the Easter Rising: Cultural and Political Nationalism in Ireland* (Dublin: Irish Academic Press, 2006).
71. Hutchinson, John, *Nations as Zones of Conflict* (London: Sage, 2005); see also Connor, Walker, *Ethnonationalism,* pp. 65–86, 195–209. For a critique of instrumentalist and materialist explanations of nationalism, see Smith, *Nationalism and Modernism,* Ch. 3.
72. Tilly, Charles, *Trust and Rule* (New York and Cambridge: Cambridge University Press, 2005).
73. Gurr, Ted and Goldstone, Jack, 'Comparisons and Policy Implications', in Goldstone, Jack, Gurr, Ted and Moshiri, Farrokh (eds), *Revolutions of the Late Twentieth Century* (Boulder, CO: Westview, 1991) pp. 126–8, 301–5; Tilly, Charles, *From Mobilization to Revolution* (Reading, MA: Addison-Wesley, 1978) pp. 62–8; Zimmerman, Ekkart, *Political Violence, Crises, and Revolutions: Theories and Research* (Boston, MA: Schenkman, 1983) p. 321.
74. For example, Sageman, Marc, *Understanding Terror Networks* (Philadelphia, PA: University of Pennsylvania Press, 2005); Pape, Robert A., *Dying to Win: The Strategic Logic of Suicide Terrorism* (New York: Random House, 2005); Roy, Olivier, *Globalised Islam: The Search for a New Ummah* (London: Hurst, 2004).
75. For example, see Lustick, Ian, *Unsettled States, Disputed Lands;* Nordlinger, Eric, *On the Autonomy of the Democratic State* (Cambridge, MA: Harvard University Press, 1981); Skocpol, Theda, *States and Social Revolution* (New York: Cambridge University Press, 1979) pp. 24–33; Evans, P.B., Rueschmeyer, D., Skocpol, T. (eds), *Bringing the State Back In* (Cambridge: Cambridge University Press, 1985). For attempts to synthesize societal- and state-level forces see Esman, *Ethnic Politics*; see

also Migdal, Joel, *State in Society: Studying How States and Societies Transform and Constitute one Another* (Cambridge: Cambridge University Press, 2001).

76. Arendt, Hannah, *Thoughts on Politics and Revolution: A Commentary* (Orlando, FL: Harcourt, Brace, Jovanovich, 1970) p. 206.

77. See Mann, *The Sources of Social Power, Volume II;* see also Tilly, Charles et al (eds), *The Formation of National States in Western Europe* (Princeton, NJ: Princeton University Press, 1975); Tilly, Charles, *Coercion, Capital and European States,* AD 990–1990 (Oxford: Blackwell, 1990).

Part I:
Semi-Sovereignty
and
Semi-Constitutionalism

Prologue to Part I

The power of political structures has a specific internal dynamic. On the basis of this power, the members may pretend to a special 'prestige', and their pretensions may influence the external conduct of the power structures. Experience teaches that claims to prestige have always played into the origin of wars ... The realm of 'honour', which is comparable to the 'status order' within a social structure, pertains also to the interrelations of political structures.

Max Weber[1]

Sometimes we underestimate the influence of symbolism on the political process. Students of Irish politics ignore this at their peril. Our history is replete with conflict centring on the question of symbols.

Paul Arthur[2]

In his history of the United Irish uprising of 1798, Thomas Pakenham (Lord Longford) characterized Britain's approach to Ireland thus: 'For four hundred years they nibbled at Ireland. And still by the reign of Elizabeth [I] she was only half digested – part colony, part dependency, part nation, a source of more weakness than wealth for Church and Crown, and a prey to each successive enemy of Britain.'[3] In the following brief sketch of British–Irish relations only the broadest patterns of governance and resistance will be outlined to emphasize the effects of incomplete conquest on the development of national identities and national conceptions of state legitimacy.

Tudor and Stuart governance of Ireland from the early sixteenth to the end of the seventeenth century was characterized by attempts at centralizing authority and establishing conformity to both Protestantism and English common law. In practice a series of reactive policies alternated between fits of assimilation and colonization, and coercion and conciliation. Elizabeth I's *Pacata Hibernica* (1603)[4] did produce a lasting, though patchy, ethnic frontier as the flight of the Gaelic earls (Tyrone and Tyrconnell) in 1607 allowed the crown to sponsor the plantation of six Ulster counties by Scottish and English settlers. Insufficient settler numbers left many Gaelic Irish Catholics in place, though generally marginalized on religious grounds and in terms of the quality of land in their possession. A rebellion against the planters in 1641 precipitated a second attempted conquest by Oliver Cromwell which was more successful in terms of land reclamation and the sponsorship of settlement, but which was then partially reversed after the restoration of the monarchy in 1660. Control was achieved only by the end of the seventeenth century, following the decisive victory in 1690 of William of Orange over the Catholic James II at the Battle of the Boyne. Penal Laws against Catholics and

Presbyterian 'dissenters' allowed the 'new English' settlers to become the 'Protestant ascendancy', owners of over 85 per cent of land who also maintained privileged access to administrative and professional careers.[5]

Most scholars of Irish history, society and politics recognize that status contests were also constitutive of national identity and conceptions of state legitimacy. To take the most glaring example, the statue of Oliver Cromwell stands proudly at Westminster as a symbol of Protestant faith and parliamentary sovereignty, yet in Ireland Cromwell is remembered more for his attempted ethnic cleansing through his invitation for Irish Catholics to go to 'Hell or Connaught'. More subtly and immediately, the legacy of governance under the Protestant ascendancy produced an alliance in the early 1790s between Catholic and Presbyterian 'men of no property' whose shared conceptions of injustice against the ascendancy and their English sponsors temporarily transcended the 'settler-native' cleavage to produce a militant Irish republican rebellion in 1798.[6]

It was precisely the threat of such an alternative basis of national state legitimacy that led the British government to respond to the United Irish uprising with the Act of Union (1800) which re-united the two kingdoms (Great Britain and Ireland) under a single legislature and a single executive based at Westminster. As noted in the Introduction, Westminster sovereignty over Ireland had been limited in 1782 by the repeal of the Declaratory Act (1720) and the passage of the Renunciation Act (1783), which granted significant legislative autonomy to the restored Irish parliament. To overturn these acts the British government reminded the ascendancy of their vulnerability and offered cash payments of £7,000 per seat, selective peerages and promises of freer trade under the union to persuade a majority of 158 against 115 to dissolve the Irish parliament.[7] The coercive or at least 'semi-constitutional' means by which the Irish Act of Union was passed contributed to the perpetuation of violent politics by undermining Irish conceptions of British constitutionalism.

LEGACIES OF FORCE: IRISH NATIONALISM VERSUS BRITISH UNIONISM

It is common in political and historical treatments of nineteenth- and early twentieth-century Ireland to contrast competing physical-force and constitutional nationalist traditions. The former were intent on using force to achieve Irish independence and fomented uprisings in 1798 (United Irishmen), 1848 (Young Ireland), 1867 (Fenian, Irish Republican/Revolutionary Brotherhood, IRB) and 1916 (neo-Fenian, IRB). Constitutional nationalists generally requested reforms within the union, including the Catholic Association (which secured Catholic Emancipation – the right for Catholics to sit in the Westminster parliament – in 1829) the Repeal movement (which requested, unsuccessfully between 1834 and 1847, the repeal of the Act of Union (1800) and the restoration of a subordinate Irish parliament) and the Home Rule campaign for legislative autonomy sponsored by the Irish National League and then the Irish Parliamentary Party from 1882 to 1914.

The politics driving this cyclical conflict have been analysed as a conflict between the emerging Irish demos and the conservative forces of the landed Protestant ascendancy, for whom the union became the safeguard of its economic, social and political status. Liberal unionist and revisionist nationalist interpretations of the constitutional history of British–Irish relations in the modern era both emphasize the potential for the Irish demos to be integrated into the British empire state of the late nineteenth century.[8] Alvin Jackson has argued in his history of Home Rule that the combination of upward mobility through the Irish party and administrative systems, would, along with sufficient safeguards of unionist interests, have integrated constitutional nationalism into the British state, if Home Rule had been legislated for swiftly and resolutely.[9] Similarly, R.F. Foster has emphasized that the ascendancy of militant republicanism was caused not by any substantial continuity with previous nationalist imperatives, but mainly by the external emergency of the First World War.[10]

These interpretations are certainly right to emphasize the potential construction of Irish national loyalty to the British empire. But we can also ask why, despite the potential for upward mobility through democratic channels, and following the transfer of land ownership from the Protestant ascendancy to Irish farmers, there remained such reservoirs of separatist nationalism. In their stress on contingency these historical approaches ignore the impact of continuity of the bi-national conflict as represented by symbiosis of physical-force and constitutional nationalist and unionist traditions. Indeed, it is now generally accepted that the symbiosis of physical force and constitutional nationalist traditions was the *leitmotif* of challenges to British governance under the union.[11] To take two examples; Daniel O'Connell's Catholic Association was avowedly constitutional in its demands for Catholic Emancipation but his movement was also able to wield the implicit threat of agrarian and proto-nationalist violence if justice was not done.[12] When offering advice to Isaac Goldsmid, parliamentary spokesman for the Jewish Emancipation movement in England, O'Connell emphasized: 'You must I repeat *force* your question on the Parliament. You ought not to confide in English liberality. It is a plant not genial to the British soil. It must be *forced*. It requires a *hot-bed*.'[13] Moreover, O'Connell subsequently promoted the need to repeal the union *not* on the rights of self-determination for the Irish nation, but instead on the failure of the English nation to extend equal rights to Catholics in Ireland since the Reformation.[14] Similarly, the Irish National League and the Irish Parliamentary Party, both led by a Protestant, Charles Stewart Parnell, sought the restoration of an Irish parliament to guarantee Irish rights within the empire. Parnell was willing to make more explicit threats of violence to underpin his constitutional reform campaign, using agrarian violence and moral force inter-changeably to support land reform during the Land War from 1880–2 and regularly warning that the 'hillside men' or 'Captain Moonlight' (agrarian bandits) would out-flank his moderate movement if land reform and Home Rule were not granted.[15] Parnell's National League emerged from the Irish Land League, which had made Ireland barely governable from 1880 to 1882. The Land League itself was a 'new departure' in Irish nationalist politics that brought together former Fenian militants whose rebellion for outright independence had been repressed in 1867 with constitutionalists seeking a restoration of the Irish parliament.[16]

Equally, unionist mobilization against Home Rule in both 1886 and 1892–3 was swift, militant and endorsed by English Conservatives like Randolph Churchill when he declared: 'Ulster at the proper moment will resort to the supreme arbitrament of force; *Ulster will fight, Ulster will be right.*'[17] As 'unionists', most Protestants in Ireland felt a conditional loyalty to the empire and her government. Rebellion was considered legitimate against any party, movement or government that threatened to tamper with the sacrosanct bond between Ireland and Britain. Given the decline of the southern Protestant ascendancy following Catholic Emancipation, the disestablishment of the (Protestant) Church of Ireland, electoral reform and then land reforms of 1903–9, unionism increasingly became Ulster unionism as their territorial concentration in the four north-east counties of Ulster became the most effective protection for Protestantism and its manifest spiritual, economic and political benefits.[18]

The centrality of violence to the constitutional politics of the nineteenth and early twentieth centuries, and the bi-national conflict it represents, are clear evidence of the continued fluidity of nation-state relations between Britain and Ireland. Thus most of the historians who emphasize the viability of the Home Rule project up to the summer of 1916 and the marginality of radical republicanism also concede that Irish loyalty to the United Kingdom was conditional and fluid.[19] This conditionality is represented most clearly by John Redmond, the leader of the Irish Parliamentary Party, who argued in 1905 that the

> Act of Union has no binding moral or legal force. We regard it as our fathers regarded it before us, as a great criminal act of usurpation carried by violence and fraud, and we say that no lapse of time and no mitigation of its details can ever make it binding upon our honour or our conscience.[20]

Given the legacy of violent politics and contested state legitimacy, it is easy to understand why supporters of moderate constitutional nationalism gravitated towards extremism when the Westminster parliament suspended the Home Rule Bill on 15 September 1914 in the face of threatened violence from Ulster unionists and imminent war on the continent.[21] The Easter Rising of 1916 may have been launched by a small cabal of radical nationalists but the exhaustion of constitutional nationalist tactics, the demonstrable success of unionists in using violence to defeat Home Rule and the over-reaction by a British state in patriotic war mode led to a tipping away from constitutionalism towards support for physical-force tactics to achieve outright independence. The catalysts for this tip towards radicalism are generally recognized as the British government's decision to execute fifteen leaders of the Easter Rising (and later, Roger Casement), followed by the threat to impose conscription in Ireland. However, there is also substantial evidence that the tip had begun in 1913 and 1914 as the Home Rule Bill was delayed by both parliamentary and paramilitary unionism.[22] Other scholars go further and draw links between movements supporting Irish national self-determination, such as Sinn Féin (founded in 1905), and the continued importance of the Irish Revolutionary Brotherhood (IRB) within the Gaelic Athletic Association and Gaelic League.

Even if these were marginal to the established Irish Parliamentary Party, they did represent parameters of Irish self-determination that were shaped by collective perceptions of national justice to limit the flexibility of the IPP in negotiating relations within the empire. Jonathan Githens-Mazer has thoroughly documented and analyzed the catalyzing process after the rising, demonstrating that pre-existing ethnic and national myths, memories and symbols of Irish subordination to British rule were central to the discourse of intellectuals, governing elites and the masses in supporting a radical shift from moderate constitutional nationalism within the empire to radical republicanism demanding sovereignty and territorial integrity.[23]

Only by recognizing the continuity of this bi-national conflict can we understand how, within two years of the Easter Rising, Ireland was polarized between Irish nationalists seeking full independence and Ulster unionists determined to use any means to protect the union. In the Westminster election of 1918, Sinn Féin, led by Eamon de Valera, won seventy-three of 105 Irish seats on a ticket supporting sovereign independence. Unionist parties won twenty-six seats, including twenty-three of thirty seats in the six counties that became Northern Ireland.[24] Sinn Féin refused to take its seats at Westminster and established Dáil Éireann as an independent Irish parliament. It used its electoral mandate as a declaration of war against Britain. After nearly three years of war from 1919–21, delegates from the self-declared Irish Republic and the British government agreed to a truce and negotiations to determine relations between Ireland and Britain and within Ireland between unionists and nationalists. In a long correspondence with Lloyd George, de Valera attempted to gain prior recognition of Ireland's independence, to which British Prime Minister Lloyd George responded:

> The geographical propinquity of Ireland to the British Isles is a fundamental fact. The history of the two islands for many centuries, however it is read, is sufficient proof that their destinies are indissolubly linked. Ireland has sent members to the British Parliament for more than a hundred years. Many thousands of her people during all that time have enlisted freely and served gallantly in the Forces of the Crown. Great numbers, in all the Irish provinces, are profoundly attached to the Throne. These facts permit of one answer, and one only, to the claim that Britain should negotiate with Ireland as a separate and foreign power.

To which de Valera replied:

> In Ireland's case, to speak of her seceding from a partnership she has not accepted, or from an allegiance which she has not undertaken to render, is fundamentally false, just as the claim to subordinate her independence to British strategy is fundamentally unjust. To neither can we, as the representatives of the Nation, lend countenance.[25]

This fundamental sovereignty dispute over the Act of Union was resolved neither before nor during negotiations. The British government was negotiating on the basis of a settlement *within* the empire, while the Irish plenipotentiaries were negotiating on the basis of a settlement *with* the empire, Northern Ireland

– temporarily – exempted. The British insistence on imperial integrity may well have been the maximum allowable given the strength of Conservative Unionists within the post-war coalition government. Nevertheless, by comparing the status recognition accorded to the two nations in Ireland (Catholic/nationalist and Protestant/unionist) with and within the British empire we can assess the extent to which mutual exchange relationships, what international relations theorists call 'compacts of coexistence',[26] were developed and their impact on demotic and elite conceptions of nation-state legitimacy.

NATIONS, STATES AND STATUS

To begin to operationalize our conceptual model of national status in inter-governmental relations we need first to consider the emergent norms under-pinning the international state system at the time of the negotiations which established the treaty relationship between Britain and the Irish Free State and the boundary between the Irish Free State and Northern Ireland.

Modern constitutionalism presumes a hierarchical division between *constitutive sovereignty* – the legal authority to govern – and 'regulative sovereignty' – the rules regulating 'antecedently existing activities'.[27] In Blackstone's classical conception, constitutive sovereignty was the imperial parliament's

> uncontrollable authority in making, enlarging, retraining, abrogating, repealing, reviving and expounding of laws, concerning matters of all possible denominations, ecclesiastical, or temporal, civil, military, maritime or criminal; this being the place where that absolute despotic power, which must in all governments reside somewhere, is entrusted by the constitution of these kingdoms. All mischiefs and grievances, operations and remedies, that transcend the ordinary course of the laws, are within the reach of this extraordinary tribunal. It can regulate or new model the succession of the crown ... alter the established religion of the land ... change and create afresh even the constitution of the kingdom and of parliaments themselves ... It can, in short, do everything that is not naturally impossible.[28]

For Sørensen, the constitutive sovereignty 'is based on the legally recognised constitutional independence of the state, which is a legal, absolute, and unitary condition ... [and] which has remained fundamentally unchanged since it became the dominant principle of political organisation in the seventeenth century'.[29]

Modern political theorists question the assumptions of a restricted, hierarchical set of authorities and argue instead that sovereignty is best conceived as an open system of relative powers (causal) and authority (normative) which are shifting and concentric rather than static and hierarchical. Republican and federalist theories from the seventeenth century, for example, emphasized the diffuse nature of authority (sanctioned power) and advocated systems of governance that purposely separated authorities and prevented absolute or ultimate authority by dividing power territorially (federation), institutionally (through the division of the legislative, judicial and executive branches of government) and constitutionally (through adherence to the 'rule of law' as established by a constitution).[30] The principle of dividing sovereignty which characterized the United Provinces of the Netherlands, the location of ultimate sovereignty in the 'crown in parliament' following the English 'revolutions' of the seventeenth century and the creation of the federated United States all represented significant adjustments away from the classical Hobbesian notion of absolute sovereignty. They also reflected wider and deeper demands for consent and participation in legislative and executive processes, on the basis of nationalist claims to self-determination.

In international relations theory, the dominant Grotian or 'internationalist' tradition emerged by the turn of the nineteenth century as a compromise between the realist tradition – grounded in classical conceptions of state sovereignty – and contractarian (constitutional) bases of authority – grounded in civic and/or ethnic conceptions of nationalism as constitutive criteria of statehood. The Grotian tradition therefore places primacy on the grounding of state authority and responsibility in the institutions of their particular society,[31] but accepts 'the Hobbesian premise that sovereigns or states are the principal reality in international politics'.[32] This tradition could not solve the type of dispute between the Irish nation and the British state, as represented by the de Valera–Lloyd George correspondence (above). On the one hand, the American and French revolutions had set precedents which supported Rousseau's principle of 'national sovereignty', in which ultimate sovereignty resides not simply in the aggregation of individual members of a society (or nation) but in the nation itself, as a reified collective will, over and above the individuals' sovereignty. Broad agreement existed on the principle of majority rule as the fairest system for determining popular will, but only subsequent to agreement on the constitution itself as the ultimate arbiter of power. Axiomatically, the principles of state sovereignty and primacy of constitutionalism and the rule of law did not extend to relations between or among recognized nation-states. By extension, there was no agreement on the criteria of membership or on processes of external self-determination.[33]

Confusion was heightened by the elevation of the relative status of the nation in constituting sovereignty as developed by the League of Nations after the Paris Peace Conference (1919). In attempting to develop a positive international legal order, US President Woodrow Wilson argued that 'no nation should seek to extend its polity over any other nation or people, but that every people should be left free to determine its own polity, its own way of development, unhindered, unthreatened, unafraid, the little along with the great and powerful'.[34] These positivist aspirations may have been useful justifications for the dismantling of the defeated Austro-Hungarian and Ottoman empires, but they were clearly problematic for victorious empires like Britain. Immediately in the British case, and gradually in the western European context, the attempt to establish a universal, positivist basis in international law gave way to a *de facto* hierarchy of sovereignties. As Shinoda has noted, Dicey's distinction between legal and political sovereignty was extended to the inter-state sphere in the sense that 'great power' sovereigns were held in higher esteem than 'semisovereign' entities like Bulgaria or other colonies or dependencies (like Ireland). Anthony Carty has demonstrated, for example, that British officials and statesmen did not recognize Ireland as an independent sovereign state, despite the evolution of the Commonwealth from the 1930s, and despite the treaty relations established between Britain and Ireland.[35] The dominant strands of British constitutional theory maintained clear objections to the universalist assumptions behind the principle of equality of nations, as embodied in the post-war League of Nations. As Shinoda notes, the 'presupposition of the existence of separate equal nations was too artificial for British lawyers like [William O.] Manning, who agreed with Dicey's principal distinction between legal and political sovereignty. In Shinoda's view, 'Dicey's theory of sovereignty at once explains the imperial principle of sovereignty in the "international" field and the democratic and national principle of sovereignty in the domestic field'.[36]

Ireland's status between kingdom and colony would expose the tension between these two conceptions. As developed in the British empire, the distinction between imperial and national sovereignty allowed for the granting of dominion status to the newly federated six colonies of Australia (1901) and to the confederation of the Provinces of Canada (Ontario and Quebec), New Brunswick and Nova Scotia in 1867. These precedents were instrumental in proposing the pluralization of sovereignty in the form of legislative autonomy (Home Rule) for Ireland as debated between 1886 and 1920[37] and as a model for the Irish Free State's dominion status established with the Irish Free State Constitution Act of 1922.

Thus while the League of Nations attempted to define conditions (not rights) under which national self-determination could be exercised, the British constitutional tradition delimited any such exercise as being within the purview of its imperial parliament. As a result, the British imperial tradition prevailed over Ireland's plea for sovereign recognition at the Paris Peace Conference in 1919. Both the US and French governments placed the primacy of unanimity within the 'committee of four' – particularly the importance of Britain as an ally – above the domestic Irish–American or 'international' considerations of the Irish leaders.[38] For de Valera, as President of Sinn Féin, the failure to secure Irish recognition risked their status as national leaders. In Longford and O'Neill's words, 'If the statesmen in Paris refused to receive him and the other Irish representatives, it would be clear to the world that all their altruistic professions were no more than a wartime ruse to delude their own people.'[39]

Left unresolved, perhaps necessarily, was what George Sørensen has described as the 'core aspect of regulative sovereignty', i.e. specific rules or criteria for deciding changes in the constitutive basis of the state, including the territory and constitution. As the lynchpin in the compact between constitutive sovereignty and regulative sovereignty, these aspects were central to the negotiations and implementation of the Anglo-Irish Treaty. The resulting quality of the British–Irish and British–Irish–Northern Irish exchange relationships can be analyzed according to degrees of parity in elite and popular conceptions of these aspects of sovereignty.

2

Coercing Agreement: The Anglo-Irish Treaty and its Discontents

I have always been strongly of the view that you could not [coerce Ulster] without provoking a conflict which would simply mean transferring the agony from the South to the North, and thus unduly prolonging the Irish controversy, instead of settling it.

D. Lloyd George, British Prime Minister,
14 December 1921.[40]

Fianna Fáil is a slightly constitutional party. We are perhaps open to the definition of a constitutional party, but before anything we are a Republican party. We have adopted the method of political agitation to achieve our end because we believe, in the present circumstances, that method is the best in the interests of the nation and of the Republican movement, and for no other reason...Our object is to establish a Republican Government in Ireland. If that can be done by the present [constitutional] methods we have, we will be very pleased, but, if not, we would not confine ourselves to them.

Sean Lemass, Fianna Fáil TD,
21 March 1928[41]

The obverse of Lloyd George's explanation of the settlement was, of course, that the rest of Ireland could be coerced into accepting both dominion status and partition. Lloyd George's 'settlement' led to the deaths of 2–3,000 in the Irish civil war (1922–3); agony was transferred from the South to the North, and eventually led to the deaths of more than 3,500 people between 1969 and 2000. These legacies may have been preferable to the likely civil war between Irish nationalists and Ulster unionists had the latter been subordinated to a Dublin parliament. But the following analysis of conflict regulation suggests that more benign scenarios were conceivable and achievable.

The characteristic pattern of coercion and conciliation, the failure to implement Home Rule in 1914, quasi-military policing, quasi-political status for republican prisoners, all contributed to the perpetuation of violent politics by indicating that the state was moveable under force and that constitutionalism was bound by British national and imperial interests. The British government temporarily extricated itself from the conflict because it could use the threat of force to insist on a deal which preserved Ireland's place within the empire, while allowing Ulster unionists to exempt themselves and substantial territory from the terms of the settlement. War-weary English and Irish publics both accepted the Anglo-Irish Treaty as a deliverer of peace. But the ability to control violence is precisely what Lloyd George did better than his Irish counterparts in the treaty negotiations.

When British Prime Minister David Lloyd George was attempting to sustain the coalition between his Liberal Party and the Conservatives over the Irish question, he was tempted to justify both 'talking to murderers' (the IRA) and granting Home Rule to Northern and 'Southern Ireland' (as they were then conceived by British elites) by emphasizing the failure of reactive responses based on alternate bouts of coercion and concession. Lloyd George considered using Sir Edward Bulwer-Lytton's views to impress on his Conservative coalition partners:

> This quick alternation of kicks and kindness, this coaxing with the hand and spurring with the heel, ... allowing the justice of complaint, and yet stifling its voice – of holding out hopes and fears, terror and conciliation ... is a system that renders animal and human beings alike, not tame but savage, is a system that would make the most credulous people distrustful and the mildest people ferocious.[42]

Most telling for its resonance with the findings of exchange theorists, Bulwer-Lytton interprets the long-term effects on conceptions of justice: 'I fear ... a sullen, bitter, unforgiving recollection, which will distrust all our kindness and misinterpret all our intentions; which will take all grace from our gifts; which will ripen a partial into a general desire for a separate legislature, by a settled conviction of the injustice of this ... '[43]

The Irish delegation to talks convened in London by Lloyd George was given a mandate to negotiate for recognition of the right to choose its own government and to preserve the territorial integrity of the island. The ideological basis of this 'republican' mandate was firmly ingrained in the constitutional perspectives of national leaders, though with variation on the thresholds of the extent and pace of unified independence considered acceptable and capable of averting civil war among Irish nationalists. Arthur Griffith, the pivotal figure in the Irish delegation, based his 'sister kingdom' theory of the British–Irish relationship on the constitutional precedents set by the repeal of the Declaratory Act (1720) in 1782 and the Renunciation Act of 1783, granting a devolved Irish parliament and thereby, for Griffith, recognizing the sovereignty of a separate Irish kingdom. With others, Griffith had concluded that the negative Irish experience with British constitutionalism had established a right to form its own all-Ireland parliament. For Griffith, the recognition of national status was paramount in justifying the republic:

> We do not feel ourselves to be a colony but a nation. It is much more than a question of administration and economics. There is an intense national feeling. The people of Tyrone think of their poets and warriors as living people not as you do of King Alfred as dead. You may think it foolish but you must take account of that sentiment in making a settlement ...[44]

Griffith's 'sister kingdom' theory sat somewhere between the more doctrinaire republican views of de Valera, which insisted on recognition of Ireland as an independent state, and the more pragmatic 'stepping stone' approach of Michael Collins who, after intensive weeks of negotiations with the British, was willing to accept dominion status within the empire (equivalent to Canada) and then evolve towards full independence.[45] The agreed strategy holding together this spectrum of views was based on the principle of 'external association' in which a sovereign Irish state would enter into a contractual, treaty-relationship *with* the British empire. The strategy was to leverage an insistence on territorial unity of the island to achieve external, sovereign recognition. The hegemonic conception of the principles of unity and independence were recognized as such by British officials with the best perspective of Irish elite thinking, such as Sir Alfred Cope of the Irish Office.[46]

The absolute nature of territorial sovereignty was the strongest card in the Irish delegation's hand, not least because of the violation of the territorial integrity and rights of small nations that had been a central justification of western involvement in the First World War.

Going into the negotiations, Lloyd George was fully aware of the weakness of his government's hand on the territorial unity issue (the Ulster question) and felt that the British government and public would only support a continuation of war on the question of Ireland leaving the empire: 'Men will die for Throne and Empire. I do not know who will die for Tyrone and Fermanagh.'[47] But he did know that many Protestants in Ulster would fight for the latter. A status hierarchy that favoured unionist over nationalist aspirations meant that Lloyd George had already conceded the principle of partition to the combined forces of Irish (particularly Ulster) unionists and English Conservatives. The Government of Ireland Act (1920) created a separate parliament for Northern Ireland based initially on the six 'plantation' counties of Antrim, Armagh, Down, Fermanagh, Londonderry and Tyrone.

To counter the pre-emptive partition, the Irish delegation attempted to secure a mechanism for establishing the border between the South and North in a way that would guarantee eventual Irish reunification. Towards this end, they insisted on a guarantee in advance from Ulster Unionist leader James Craig to accept what the Irish delegation understood as the mandate of the proposed Boundary Commission: a decision-making procedure based on local plebiscites which would have guaranteed, as a minimum, the transfer of the two counties with Catholic majorities – Fermanagh and Tyrone – to the South.[48] Having failed to achieve these two concessions they declared their intention to return to Dublin to consult with the Dáil. At this point Lloyd George famously held up two letters and, according to Austen Chamberlain, stated:

> I have to communicate with Sir James Craig to-night. Here are the alternative letters which I have prepared, one enclosing Articles of Agreement reached by his Majesty's Government and yourselves, and the other saying that the Sinn Féin representatives refuse to come within the Empire. If I send this letter it is war, and war within three days. Which letter am I to send?[49]

Why the ultimatum? The ostensible reason was that Lloyd George had promised James Craig that he would be informed of the outcome of the negotiations before the re-opening of the Northern Ireland parliament (6 December). But the bottom line was that Craig and the unionists could not be coerced into accepting the Irish delegates' interpretation of the terms of the Boundary Commission mandate and they could plausibly bring down the government with the support of their Conservative allies. Lloyd George was acutely aware of the vulnerability of his position on 'essential unity'[50] and privately had assured Craig that the Boundary Commission would at least preserve the six-county status quo, which unionists considered the minimal territorial entity sufficient for economic and political viability. Given these constraints, the coalition government was only united on the principle of removing the Irish question from British politics and this goal could be achieved with a combination of deception (on the terms of the Boundary Commission) backed by the explicit threat of force.[51] The option most likely to avoid a serious split in Ireland – external association with a partition plan based on local plebiscites – required both a concession on the unity of the empire and the coercion of Protestant/unionists in Ulster.[52]

Given their uncertainty on the question of territorial integrity and their mandate as plenipotentiaries, the Irish delegation was committed to achieving what they could justifiably sell as a recognition of national independence, hence their commitment to the principle of 'external association': a voluntary relationship *with* the British empire based on recognition of Ireland as an independent state, associated with the empire for matters of common interest such as defence and foreign relations and recognizing the British monarch as the head of the association, rather than as head of the Irish state.

The Irish assertion of a degree of parity as an external partner or associated state was not, however, acceptable to Britain's coalition government (Liberal–Conservative) or to the British public because of the implications for the diminution of the empire. Lloyd George insisted on Ireland's place *within* the empire: 'All my colleagues would share my view of this document [Irish draft reply setting out 'external association']. If they are not coming into the empire, then we will make them.'[53] This view of civic nation-building within empire was expressed, most naturally, by King George V when opening the first Northern Ireland parliament on 22nd June 1921:

> The eyes of the Empire are on Ireland today – that Empire in which so many nations and races have come together in spite of ancient feuds, and in which new nations [Northern Ireland] have come to birth within the lifetime of the youngest in this hall.

Then, without a hint of irony, the supremacy and benevolence of the imperial parliament was exalted and sovereignty asserted in the most personal and possessive terms:

> [T]he Parliament of the United Kingdom has in the fullest measure provided

the powers; for this the Parliament of Ulster (sic) is pointing the way. The future lies in the hands of my Irish people themselves.[54]

These words were drafted by South African General J.C. Smuts, who was also called on by Lloyd George to try to whittle away at the Irish extremes of republic and unity. In a letter to de Valera, Smuts compared the situation in Ireland to that of South Africa in the Boer War, and suggested that de Valera's republican and unificatory ideals should be put aside in order for him to accept the British offer of dominion status. In addition, Smuts insisted to de Valera that Ulster must be left alone, and dealt with separately, thus assigning an equality of status to the north of Ireland that, in de Valera's republican outlook, must have been inconceivable. Furthermore, Smuts goes on to say:

> I know how repugnant such a solution must be to all Irish patriots, who look upon Irish unity as a *sin qua non* of any Irish settlement. But the wise man, while fighting for his ideal to the uttermost, learns also to bow to the inevitable. And a humble acceptance of the facts is often the only way of finally overcoming them. It proves so in South Africa, where ultimate unity was only realised through several stages and a process of years; and where the Republican ideal, for which we had made unheard of sacrifices had ultimately to give way to another form of freedom ...

> As to that form of freedom, here to you are called upon to choose between two alternatives. To you, as you say the Republic is the true expression of national self-determination. But it is not the only expression; and it is an expression which means your final and irrevocable severance from the British League. And to this, as you know, the Parliament and people of this country (sic Britain) will not agree ...

> A history such as yours must breed a temper, and outlook, passions, suspicions, which it is most difficult to deal with. On both sides sympathy is called for, a generosity, and a real largeness of soul. I am sure the English and Irish peoples are ripe for a fresh start. The tragic horror of recent events, followed so suddenly by a truce and fraternising all along the line, has ... created a new political situation.[55]

In this view, which must have been approved by Lloyd George, neither the core regulative element of sovereignty (self-determination) nor the core constitutive element (territorial integrity) was offered. Winston Churchill revealed, unwittingly, but presciently, the lack of recognition of either aspect of national sovereignty when he tried to underline the inevitability of unity by declaring that Smuts was in the process of offering Rhodesia inducements to enter the South African Union. Rhodesia is now not only separate from South Africa but itself fractured into Zambia and Zimbabwe.

The record of the cabinet meeting of 10 November 1921 is particularly instructive on the impact of national status on conceptions of sovereignty. First,

Lloyd George described to the coalition cabinet how the Irish delegation had conceded the principle of the republic: 'They hauled down the Republican flag and adopted the flag of the Empire.'[56] Consciously or not, Lloyd George elided the distinction insisted on by the Irish delegates between external association (with) and internal membership of (within) the British empire: 'They [the Irish] wanted "Association with the Empire". Carson [unionist leader] wanted "within the Empire" [as did the British government]... '[57] 'They are simple; they have none of the skill of the old nationalists; these men are not accustomed to finessing; they mean to come in and work *with* the Empire.'[58]

But Ireland could not be both *in* the empire and working *with* the empire. Indeed, the contradiction in this last clinching argument went unnoticed within the cabinet because of the hegemonic conception of empire and strategic unity across the Liberal–Conservative spectrum. But it is centrally important because, wilfully or not, Lloyd George had misrepresented the Irish delegation's conception of the outer limits of a deal which would secure popular and elite consent among Irish nationalists. Moreover, the ethno-centric basis of British status conceptions was evident in Lloyd George's condescending attitude towards the delegates as well as his justification for partition. When Griffith claimed that Ulster unionist resistance to coming in to an all-Ireland parliament was predicated on British support, Lloyd George replied:

> We are only behind them to this extent that we cannot allow civil war to take place at our doors which would embroil *our own* people. It would be bad enough if we could bring down a fire curtain between us. There is nothing we would like better than that they should unite with you.[59]

By denying the substance of the Irish conceptions of national self-determination, the final deal proposed was considered by the Irish delegation to be unsatisfactory. They then attempted to make the negotiations break on the question of the national territory, specifically Ulster, and threatened to return to Dublin to consult with the full Irish cabinet.[60] Given his side's self-professed weakness on Ulster, Lloyd George abandoned the consent principle and exerted power, famously threatening war 'within three days'. Under duress, undermined by tactical negotiating mistakes[61] and convinced by a conscious ruse that the treaty would deliver 'essential [territorial] unity',[62] the Irish delegation signed and eventually precipitated a civil war in Ireland.

That the Anglo-Irish Treaty was based on force rather than consent affected profoundly the British–Irish relationship, government within the Irish Free State (later Republic) and Northern Ireland, precisely because it reflected divergent national status conceptions.[63] In terms of our classification of approaches to conflict regulation it was coercive, based on majoritarian domination within Northern Ireland and a coercive maintenance of the empire's territorial, strategic integrity. The constitutional status of the Free State and Northern Ireland were undermined by the fraudulent basis of the treaty, with particular regard to the mandate of the Boundary Commission.[64]

The degrading effects of the status barriers and their nationalist content on exchange relations were immediately evident in the negotiations over the treaty's implementation.[65] British officials warned that the Irish draft constitution, which attempted to re-assert the principle of external association, was tantamount to a negation of the previous treaty, and that it was now up to the representatives whether or not they could deliver the terms they had agreed. Collins insisted that he would not have English common law forced upon the Irish, to which Lloyd George responded that the Provisional Government could abolish certain laws. Moreover:

> it was a question between Republican and Monarchical Institutions. Acts of the State in Ireland must run in the name of the Crown. This was the Monarchy in the British Commonwealth. The Crown was a mystic term which, as they well knew, in the British Commonwealth stood for the power of the people.[66]

Griffith countered that the crown had long stood for something else in Ireland, and that it was regarded as a 'symbol of tyranny', whereas Collins said that in Ireland no-one would accept a system where Sir Edward Carson (unionist leader) would sit in judgement of Irish [law] suits. British officials made assurances that the Free State would be justly treated in the Commonwealth, and the only tangible effect of this dominion status would be that the Irish role in international affairs would be handled by the British Foreign Office. In doing so, Lloyd George compared the positions of Canada and Ireland, citing arguments developed among the dominions at international conferences. Quite tellingly, however, Collins countered by stating that 'distance protected Canada from British aggression. Ireland must have in her constitution safeguards which would give her the guarantees which distance secured to Canada.'[67]

A similar attempt was made to earn status equivalence with regard to territorial unity. For Collins, to accept a partition in principle required a reflexive right for northern nationalists, thus asserting the primacy of the rights of Irish people on the existing territory, albeit with a secondary right recognized for *some* Ulster unionists – those in the four north-eastern counties. Acceptance of unionist consent was conditional: 'We cannot allow solid blocks who are against partition in the North of Antrim, through a part of Derry and part of Armagh to Strangford Lough. If we are not going to coerce the NE corner, the NE corner must not be allowed to coerce.' (see map p. 44)[68] The British reaction was that if the Provisional Government had wanted safeguards in the constitution they should have negotiated them within the treaty. This points exactly to the effects of coercion because it was precisely that threshold of external association, and the asked-for specificity on the Boundary Commission – neither the design of simpletons – over which the Irish delegates had been coerced at the end of the treaty negotiations.

Disagreement persisted on the meaning and legality of the fundamental issues at the heart of the treaty and the constitution until the British–Irish Treaty of 1999 and arguably beyond to the extended crisis of executive formation in Northern Ireland. From 1922 until 1932, the pro-treaty Provisional Govern-

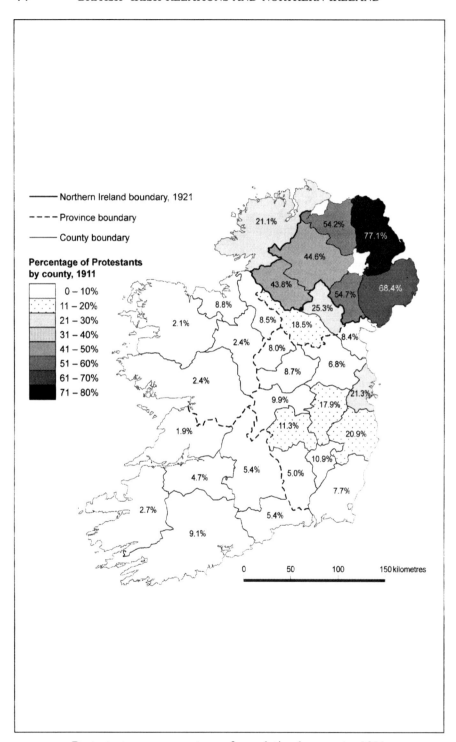

Protestants as a percentage of population by county, 1911

ments formed by Cumann na nGaedheal interpreted their role in the Common-wealth as having satisfied the core criteria of national self-determination, especially after Ireland's admittance to the League of Nations in 1923.[69] But over the course of this period, and not least because of the degradation of relations resulting from the collapse of the boundary commission, opposition to the treaty grew, leading to the rise of Fianna Fáil from the remnants of anti-treaty Sinn Féin, again led by de Valera, committed to the original republican ideals of full independence and unity.[70]

PROVISIONAL GOVERNMENT

We may have to bow our heads for a time to the enforced partition of our country by a foreign Power, but the sanction of our consent that partition can never have. We deny that any part of our people can give away the sovereignty or alienate any part of this nation or territory. If this generation should be base enough to consent to give them away, the right to win them back remains unimpaired for those to whom the future will bring the opportunity.

Eamon de Valera, Sinn Féin President,
10 December 1925[71]

The central dilemma for Irish governments since the civil war in their attempt to monopolize the legitimate use of force is that the Anglo-Irish Treaty was signed and ratified by leaders who were united on the two related principles enunciated by Wolfe Tone in 1793: 'to assert the independence of the country and to unite the whole people of Ireland'.[72] The preamble to the Irish Free State Constitution Act, 1922 declared that the constituent assembly [which] sat 'in the confidence that the National life and unity of Ireland shall thus be restored, hereby proclaims the establishment of the Irish Free State (otherwise called Saorstát Éireann)...' Michael Collins, whose pivotal position within the IRA and IRB was crucial to the ratification of the treaty, famously described it as offering 'freedom, not the ultimate freedom that all nations desire and develop to, but the freedom to achieve it'.[73] In sum, the civil war between pro-treaty and anti-treaty forces was about means rather than ends.

The means and ends of the treaty are also significant for an understanding of state legitimacy. Neither Conor Cruise O'Brien[74] nor Tom Garvin treats as significant the threat of force in the signing of the Anglo-Irish Treaty. Garvin quotes Cardinal Logue as representing the majority view of anti-treaty mobilization as 'a wild and destructive hurricane spr[u]ng from such a thin, intangible, insubstantial vapour'.[75] Collins' subsequent denial that the threat of force was decisive should be weighed against his need to support the ratification of the treaty from a position of strength. These views elide the significance of force as the final arbiter used by the British government both in the treaty negotiations and also in the negotiations over the Free State constitution in the summer of 1922. As a result of this *fait accompli*, the opportunity to develop a consensual nationalist position or compromise was denied. In 1922, the fragmentation of the nationalist bloc into pro-and anti-treaty sub-blocs created an opportunity for the British government literally to force the inclusion of the treaty terms in the new Free State constitution. During negotiations over the drafting of the Free State constitution, Churchill warned Collins in June 1922: 'You will find that we are just as tenacious on essential points – the Crown, the British Commonwealth, No Republic – as de Valera and Rory O'Connor, *and we intend to fight for our points*.'[76] This warning was embellished to undermine the attempt by Collins and de Valera to form a coalition between pro- and anti-treaty members of Sinn Féin for the election of the Provisional Government in June 1922. Since such a coalition would almost certainly be based on de Valera's principle of 'external association', Churchill told the cabinet that the 'more the fear of renewed warfare was present to the minds of the electors, the more likely were they to go to the polls and support the treaty'.[77] The threat of force achieved its intended result and contributed directly to the drift towards civil war, the emergence of which was by no means certain.[78]

Though the anti-treaty IRA's seizure of the Four Courts in Dublin and the assassination of Sir Henry Wilson, Unionist MP and former Chief of Imperial General Staff (1918–22), were the actual triggers of the civil war, the tipping point came with the failure of constitutionalism to address the core of the conflict. Churchill had presented an ultimatum in the Commons on 26 June, arguing that the British government would 'resume full liberty of action in any direction that may seem proper'[79] if the pro-treaty forces did not face down the occupiers of the Four Courts. As a result, Kevin O'Higgins justified the attack, using British artillery, against an anti-treaty IRA unit occupying the Four Courts as follows: 'Had we not taken this step this Parliament would not have met and the very existence of the Parliament was at stake...[W]e anticipated by a couple of hours the creation of conditions... which would have brought back the British power – horse, foot, artillery and navy.'[80]

The reliance on the implicit threat of British military intervention, and British weapons, reflected the absence of agreement on constitutive sovereignty. Nevertheless, politically, the pro-treaty side achieved a clear electoral mandate from the June 1922 election (in which pro-treaty candidates outnumbered anti-treaty candidates by ninety-two to thirty-six) and formed a Provisional Government. In December 1922 the Dáil passed the constitution establishing Saorstát Éireann (the Irish Free State). Confronted with civil war, the Provisional Government passed draconian emergency legislation to establish military courts, suspended *habeas corpus*, and extended the use of capital punishment. In total, the Free State government executed seventy-seven anti-treaty prisoners between November 1922 and June 1923. In addition, approximately 13,000 suspects were interned during that period. The death toll for the civil war has been estimated at between three and five thousand.[81] The financial costs amounted to nearly £50 million, which Garvin has estimated as one-quarter of the gross national product of the day.[82]

In addition to the human suffering and financial loss, a significant cleavage in Irish party politics was perpetuated based on support or opposition to the treaty, particularly over the questions of national status and territorial unity. For the anti-treaty side the status of the state, not to mention the government, formed in 1922 was *provisional*. The anti-treaty forces did not sue for peace but instead announced a 'suspension of offensive' for 30 April 1923 which read:

1. In order to give effect to the decision of the government and Army Council embodied in attached Proclamation of this date, you will arrange the suspension of all offensive operations in your area from noon Monday, April 30.
2. You will ensure that – whilst remaining on the defensive – all units take adequate measures to protect themselves and their munitions.
   Signed,
   Frank Aiken, IRA Chief of Staff.

De Valera's addendum to the above message stated that 'military victory must be allowed to rest *for the moment* with those who have destroyed the Republic'.[83]

As a result of this ambiguous conclusion, Cumann na nGaedheal, the pro-treaty party, remained the largest party in government from 1923 until 1932, but was challenged almost continuously by republican proponents of physical and moral force. A *coup d'etat* was threatened in 1924 by a faction of 'old IRA' within the Free State army that had formed the 'IRA organization' in order to press the Cosgrave government to fulfil Michael Collins' pledge to use the Anglo-Irish Treaty as a stepping stone to 'unity and complete independence'.[84] This threat was faced down but it was followed by a large number of small-scale attacks against representatives of the Free State government from 1924 through 1931.

The ambiguous truce that ended the Irish civil war was outlined in the Introduction as an example of lingering status contests where the oath of allegiance to the crown prohibited the Free State government from monopolizing legitimate violence. A further blow to the Free State government's status came with the collapse of the Boundary Commission in 1925, with W.T. Cosgrave, President of the Executive Council, having to admit that the Irish delegates to the treaty negotiations had been purposely misled over the criteria to be used for deciding the border.[85] In Cosgrave's view, the denial of the popular consent to inhabitants of the border counties was a negation of the assurances given to the Irish delegates that had been crucial elements in their ultimate decision to sign the treaty.[86] Recognizing the potential damage to governmental legitimacy, Cosgrave refused to put the Boundary Agreement to a referendum, citing the civil war state of emergency as justification for the withdrawal of a plebiscite. The legitimacy crisis deepened in 1928 when the Free State government removed the constitutional provision for referenda to prevent Fianna Fáil's attempt to remove the oath of allegiance.[87]

Thus, Garvin emphasizes the success in the 1920s of the main pro-treaty party, Cumann na nGaedheal (led by W.T. Cosgrave) in negotiating a change in the oath to one of 'fidelity' (rather than the more subordinate 'allegiance') which grammatically levels the status of the two nations. Cosgrave's government was able to demonstrate some incremental constitutional progress towards autonomy *within* the British empire. Achievements such as 'O'Higgins' comma' elevated the status of Ireland within the title of the monarchy[88] and the accession of Ireland to the League of Nations in 1923 demonstrated the pro-treaty government's interest and capability to seek status parity with other dominions *within* the empire. Such pressure led Kevin O'Higgins, Minister for Justice and External Affairs, to attempt to entice the British government to consider a dual monarchy relationship which, though rejected by the British, reflected O'Higgins' concern to elevate Ireland's international legal status. Indeed, O'Higgins had previously recognized the impact of Ireland's coerced inclusion in empire:

> It [the Commonwealth] has been called a league of free nations. I admit in practice it is so; but it is unwise and un-statesman-like to attempt to bind any such league by any ties other than pure voluntary ties... I quite admit in the case of Ireland the tie is not voluntary... the status is not equal.[89]

The centrality of national status-seeking to internal party competition has been documented by John Regan, who argues that Cumann na nGaedheal, while leading a counter-revolution against republican purity, eventually 'failed to address a deeper and still popular demand for tangible progress on the issues of national sovereignty and social justice which Fianna Fáil had – as evidenced in the two 1927 elections – tapped into'.[90] By 1932, according to Regan, the demotic base of Fianna Fáil's mandate for republican status-seeking was well established: 'Fianna Fáil in 1932 transcended the status of political organisation to become a mass political movement on O'Connellite, Parnellite and revolutionary Sinn Féin models.'[91] Pro-treaty Cumann na nGaedheal's achievements were considerable in stabilizing democratic norms but they were insufficient to head off Fianna Fáil's semi-constitutional republicanism which governed, alone and in coalition from 1932 until 1948, all the while underpinned by the imperative to achieve parity *with* rather than within empire.[92]

In contrast to the tenuous legitimacy of the first Free State government and the persistence of 'irregularism', from 1932, Fianna Fáil was able to absorb the vast majority of the IRA 'organically', while using emergency powers to suppress the recalcitrant. The majority of the estimated 30,000-strong IRA supported Fianna Fáil and played an important role in the party's electoral success in 1932.[93] Fianna Fáil in government was able to manage internal dissent, even control it because it monopolized popular support for nationalist status-seeking. Most importantly, the anti-treaty Fianna Fáil became the dominant party of government by delivering constitutive and regulative sovereignty from the British empire. Upon forming a coalition government with Labour in 1932, de Valera immediately began dismantling the Anglo-Irish Treaty by making significant changes to elements of constitutive sovereignty. The oath of allegiance to the crown was abolished. Payments of land annuities to the British government were suspended, sparking a trade war. The emergency powers that established the military courts were abolished and remaining IRA prisoners were released. By 1937 de Valera's government enacted (through referendum) a new constitution, *Bunreacht na hÉireann*, asserting national sovereignty over external affairs (Article 1) and laying claim to sovereignty over the whole island of Ireland:

> **Article 2:** The National territory consists of the whole island of Ireland, its islands and the territorial seas.
>
> **Article 3:** Pending the reintegration of the national territory, and without prejudice to the right of the Parliament and Government established by this Constitution to exercise jurisdiction over the whole of that territory, the laws enacted by that Parliament shall have the like area and extent of application as the laws of Saorstát Éireann and the like extra-territorial effect.

While these reforms did not satisfy the army council of the IRA, who demanded nothing less than the complete 'sovereignty and unity of the Irish Republic...',[94] Fianna Fáil had demonstrated that constitutional republicanism could achieve tangible, if limited, progress towards these goals, albeit at the expense of strained relations with both Britain and Northern Ireland.

Revisionist interpretations of the evolution of the Irish policy toward unification tend to emphasize that the anti-treaty side, particularly de Valera, came to accept the primacy of constitutional politics and the futility, even counter-productivity, of attempting to coerce unionists into ending partition, or indirectly, to use force to encourage Britain to end partition.[95] While undoubtedly true, these interpretations arguably confuse ends and means. Even if interpreted as cynical opportunism, the use by de Valera of independence and unity as negotiating leverage reveal the demotic and elite consensus on these aspects of national legitimacy. For example, Garvin observed that the pro-treaty side was dominated by leaders who had a taste of state power, experience in public administration or civic professions, implying a sell-out by pragmatists for state power, in an ethnically-cleaner twenty-six-county unit modelled along British constitutional lines. But the rise of pragmatists to the higher ranks of government could as easily be interpreted as a form of instrumentalism in which the state apparatus serves nationalist goals. The following section explores such an interpretation of the evolution of British–Irish relations in the inter-war years.

RE-ESTABLISHING CONSENT: THE ANGLO-IRISH TREATY OF 1938

The distinction between Ireland's relationship with and within empire became acutely significant by December 1937 when, with ominous signs of war looming over the continent, the British Prime Minister Neville Chamberlain invited de Valera to London to negotiate outstanding treaty items: the control of key Irish ports, munitions production and the settlement of the 'trade war' over agricultural tariffs which began with Fianna Fáil's refusal to pay land annuities.[96] The position of the British representative to Ireland, C.L. Maffey, represents the hegemonic conception of Ireland among British officials in the

Dominions Office. In a memo, under the heading: 'What we really need from Eire now and in the future', Maffey wrote: 'We no longer want to govern or administer Eire. We have had enough of that and are well quit of it. What we need is to restore the strategic unity of *our* island group. Nothing else matters.'[97]

The assumption of possession reveals the hierarchical bias. Ireland would have to remain within the British empire in order for imperial sovereignty to underpin jurisdiction over Irish ports or airspace. This position, which fit within the British interpretation and implementation of the Anglo-Irish Treaty of 1921, was clearly at odds with the Irish position as expressed since Fianna Fáil came to power in 1932 and established in Article 1 of the 1937 constitution. Maffey, for one, was in no doubt that forceful assumption of power to respond to or pre-empt a German invasion would be resisted forcefully and popularly in Ireland.[98] The Irish position was that any new Anglo-Irish agreement required the fundamental exchange of an end to partition and the return of ports to Irish sovereignty in exchange for free trade and a substantial defence pact. And northern nationalists clearly expressed their opposition to a deal on trade and defence that did not include an end to partition.[99] In one exchange Maffey recorded de Valera arguing: 'It was no use asking the people in Ireland to fight on behalf of freedom when freedom was denied in a portion of Ireland owing to the influence of an uncompromising minority [unionists in Northern Ireland].'[100]

The clash between the British conception of the justice of a subordinate power relationship and the Irish conception of the justice of a consensual exchange relationship was apparent in the Anglo-Irish negotiations that began in 1938. The British government's initial argument was that its forces should have an automatic right to defend ports belonging to a dominion of the British empire. De Valera, by contrast, emphasized the justice of a consensual exchange relationship between two sovereign states. He asserted that 'the claim of Eire to the Defended Ports rested primarily on the doctrine of National Sovereignty. As the Irish people saw it, the presence of British detachments in these ports was nothing less than an act of aggression.'[101] Admitting that Ireland did not have the naval or air capabilities to defend the ports from such an act, de Valera attempted to reassure the British while emphasizing the principle of consent: '[t]he natural direction in which to look for such assistance would be from the Government of the United Kingdom. That Government in its turn would be more secure for the purposes of the emergency if the help which they extended to Eire had been freely asked for by the Government of Eire.'[102] British Prime Minister Neville Chamberlain countered that 'the fear was not that the Irish would not defend the ports, but that they would not allow the ports to be made available to the UK forces'.[103]

Despite the unresolved disagreement on partition, the 1938 treaty did represent an elevation of the status of the Irish Free State by Britain in the recognition of Irish sovereignty over the disputed ports. In exchange, de Valera gave private assurances of co-operation in the event of war. In addition, the trade war was resolved with a free trade agreement and a final settlement of the outstanding land annuities with a one-off payment from Ireland of £10 million.

This figure represented only one-tenth of the sum calculated by the British Treasury as owed by the Irish for the buy-out of the mainly Protestant landlord class at the beginning of the century. Interestingly, the British Treasury accepted this diminished sum with an equanimity supporting the primacy of status and exchange relations over pure economic rationale. According to Foster, 'strong conciliatory arguments were advanced from (of all places) the British Treasury – to the effect that Ireland had the moral advantage after centuries of oppression, and the chance of "a new chapter" was worth some financial generosity.'[104]

For de Valera the treaty was a political and diplomatic success (he later called it his greatest achievement) that removed all remaining sources of antagonism between Britain and Ireland 'except partition'.[105] De Valera emphasized that the cumulative effects of his government's constitutional reforms created a focus on the remaining issue of partition and the evolution of views of British officials reveals the impact of the partition issue as diplomatic leverage. While disdainful of de Valera's opportunistic and rhetorical use of partition for domestic politics – 'ignorance, distorted history and the inoculation (sic) of hate in school and church have produced this sorry harvest, and Mr. de Valera is the slave of his own Frankenstein'[106] – reports to the cabinet also reported his belief in the depth of popular attachment to both neutrality[107] and ending partition: 'It is not a side-issue or a faked issue . . . men will fight and die for it.'[108]

The outbreak of a new IRA campaign in 1939 was evidence of the tensions de Valera needed to manage within the broad republican family. With the outbreak of war the IRA declared that 'the present crisis caused by the intervention of Germany and Italy, and the success of their campaign, makes our job easier. The enemies of England are, by that fact, the friends of Ireland.'[109] The Irish government response demonstrated the value it placed on maintaining mutual exchange relations with Britain. The Fianna Fáil government had moved to ban the IRA in 1936 and brought in the Offences Against the State Act in 1939 to establish military courts for the trial of IRA suspects. During the war the government interned more than 500 IRA activists, executed six IRA members and allowed three hunger strikers seeking political status to die.[110] Once again, as Joseph Lee has emphasized, violence exposed the debates over state legitimacy. 'De Valera was regularly taunted with reneging on his own earlier persona . . . [but] regularly replied that the constitution of 1937 had invested the state with a new legitimacy and 'there were no longer any obstacles in the way of any section to utilising constitutional means'.[111]

The British government may have been comforted by Ireland's exercise of internal sovereignty but the outbreak of war elevated the strategic necessity of controlling sea routes and airspace. British officials, ministers and advisors considered various schemes whereby Ireland could be induced to end its position of neutrality in exchange for a British commitment to end partition. But for de Valera, this defence of national sovereignty was more fundamental than the achievement of Irish unity itself. This position was established in his speech to *Seanad Éireann* (the Irish Senate) in February 1939:

Suppose we were to get unity in the country provided we were to give up the principles that are here in this first Article of the Constitution – the "sovereign right of the nation to choose its own form of Government, to determine its relations with other nations, and to develop its life, political, economic, and cultural, in accordance with its own genius and traditions" – I would not sacrifice that right, because without that right you have not freedom at all ... [I]f by sacrificing [the right to national freedom] we were to get a united Ireland and that united Ireland was not free to determine its own form of Government, to determine its relations with other countries, and, amongst other things, to determine, for example, whether it would or would not be involved in war..[112]

One element of constitutive sovereignty (sovereign recognition as a republic) could not be traded for another (territorial unity). Now, this could be dismissed as obfuscation hiding deeper fears of the difficulties in swallowing nearly one million Protestants into a state whose constitution recognized the special status of the Catholic Church.[113] Equally, it has been argued that de Valera's rejection of Churchill's offer was based on the possibility, in 1941, that Hitler's Germany would be victorious.[114] But considering the status-value of the prize of unity, the re-absorption of more than half a million northern Catholics, and the potential long term economic advantages, it would be simplistic to assume that de Valera's anti-partitionism was merely rhetorical. Moreover, the dismissive view of the importance of unity dismisses what exchange theorists call the 'audience costs' of losing influence among other states, and domestic perceptions of impotence by flying kites that never take wind.[115]

The British side remained resolute in asserting that unity was not a British responsibility, but a matter for mutual self-determination for the nations recognized, unilaterally, in the Government of Ireland Act (1920), the Anglo-Irish Treaty (1921) and the 'boundary agreement' of 1925. British Prime Minister Neville Chamberlain's private view was that ultimately there would have to be a united Ireland just as there was a united Canada, but this aim would have to be realized by a very different road to that by which Mr de Valera and his colleagues were approaching it.[116] It was for the South to entice the North into a consensual unity. This 'benevolent detachment' of British elites persisted from the inter-war period to the present, even evolving as the agreed basis for self-determination in the Good Friday Agreement (1998). Yet, despite the subsequent cultivation of this 'consent principle', the problem in 1940 was that none of the treaties it then relied on could be safely regarded as consensual.

While unionist fears of absorption into a Catholic, agrarian state were strengthened by the Catholic basis of the 1937 constitution and Fianna Fáil's economic protectionism, the assumption of the rectitude of partition as a reflection of 'sufficient consensus' suggests not a neutral arbiter position but a three-tiered hierarchy. In formal terms, as Paul Arthur has emphasized, the dominion status of the Irish Free State was more independent than the devolved government of Northern Ireland. But in terms of national self-determination, Northern Ireland's 'non-coercible' status was shown to be above that of the Irish

Free State. The latter's claim to territorial re-unification was accepted as an aspiration but dismissed as a responsibility of the British government. So, for example Sir Eric Machtig, Permanent Under Secretary in the Foreign Office suggested to Foreign Secretary Anthony Eden in 1940 that:

> One day the North and the South will be amalgamated . . . [t]he process of peaceful union would be carried out by negotiations between the North and the South. We should stand remote from that. But we must compel the North to talk. We must make it plain to them that they do not hold a blank cheque from us . . . The fear is that, *as always hitherto*, politics will force us to accept once more the dictation of the Orange clubs . . . [117]

This recognition that the extreme defenders of unionism had previously set the limits of British territorial withdrawal and, moreover, that Britain needed to compel Northern Ireland to talk, contrasts sharply with the claim to 'benevolent detachment' regarding partition. Loyalty to crown and empire remained the decisive condition for recognition of the legitimacy of self-determination.

Ending Irish neutrality required a change to constitutive sovereignty that was held by Irish elites and public to be at least as important as territorial unity. Even if de Valera may have been tempted to consider such an exchange, the domestic political risk of abandoning or significantly modifying Irish neutrality required that the exchange – reunification – was a certainty rather than a probability. But because of the British government's hierarchical view of the status of rights of self-determination and the strategic importance of 'loyal Ulster', there was little chance that any British government could or would force unionists to accept unification. According to de Valera's official biographers, the offer from Churchill did not give 'equal holds':[118] 'Ireland would be involved in the war and the ending of partition would be no more than a half promise over which Belfast would have the full right of veto. Redmond had responded to this kind of promise in 1914, but de Valera was not likely to do so in 1940.'[119] Winston Churchill, as Prime Minister in the war-time coalition exemplified this view when considering new proposals for the neutrality–unity exchange, arguing that the problem was de Valera's unwillingness to demonstrate 'true loyalty to Crown and Empire', as well as the impossibility of forcing unionists to accept re-unification.[120] In response to General Hubert Gough's proposal for an Anglo-Irish agreement proposing exchange of neutrality and rejoining of Commonwealth for Irish unity, Churchill's hand-written note in the margin makes it clear that coercion of Northern Ireland was impossible: 'He [Gough] seems to have forgotten the Curragh Mutiny.'[121]

The re-enforcement of the three-tiered hierarchy was revealed in Churchill's letter to Northern Ireland Prime Minister Sir Basil Brooke at the close of the war:

> We have travelled a hard and darksome road to victory in Europe, and at every turn in this memorable journey the loyalty and courage of Ulster have gleamed before the eyes of man . . . Ulster enabled us to keep our Atlantic life-

line open, and saved Ireland from becoming a battle-ground in which many powerful forces might have been involved. A strong, loyal Ulster will always be vital to the security and well-being of our whole Empire and Commonwealth.[122]

Such warmth contrasted with the chill of Anglo-Irish relations brought by de Valera's official expression of condolences following Hitler's death and Churchill's scathing remarks against the Irish stance on neutrality during his victory speech.[123]

CONCLUSION

Ireland may at last and in truth become the land of the 'United Irishmen' if her leaders are brave enough and wise enough to be loyal to *her highest good*. If they fail through weakness or false optimism (as the English have so often failed in recent years) the future, I fear, will be as tragic as the past.

W.K. Hancock[124]

It is no coincidence that the achievement of semi-sovereignty correlated with the evolution of 'slightly constitutional' politics. The absence of constitutive sovereignty meant that conceptions of national status and their constitutional manifestation were central to both internal governmental authority as well as external relations with and within the British empire. As Paul Arthur has noted, the piece-meal, pragmatic approach to British foreign policy meant that 'Ireland, obsessional and single-minded, made the running. Britain adapted to a policy of adjustment.'[125] This is not to suggest that national status questions regarding full independence and territorial unity were necessarily more powerful than economic and strategic concerns such as defence costs arising from participation in war, or economic costs associated with Irish unification. These were undoubtedly significant factors for any government, especially one attempting to pursue a form of economic autarky as pursued by Fianna Fáil in the inter-war years.[126] Nor am I suggesting that any British or Irish government since 1921 could or should have coerced unionists in Northern Ireland into accepting unity. Instead, a more modest claim is that conceptions of national status have been decisive in the politics of both parts of Ireland and between Britain and both parts of Ireland. While it is commonly argued that de Valera reinforced partition by promoting his narrow, populist vision of the Republic, both domestically and internationally, these arguments pay insufficient attention to the imperatives of national status-seeking by elites and the public.

As the next chapters show, national status is also central to the regulation of conflict. Relative parity creates potential for mutual exchanges instead of one-sided exertions of power associated with control regimes and overly rigid, statist, 'nationalising' projects as developed in Northern Ireland since 1921. British imposition of partition and the lack of implementation of important safe-guards exemplified one-sided 'problem dividing' rather than either power-dividing (through federalism) or power-sharing (through institutional representation of ethnic or national communities). Instead, the approach raised expectations of re-unification among Irish nationalists in both jurisdictions, eroded unionist confidence in British guarantees of union and perpetuated the siege mentality that was used to justify suppression of the Catholic minority in Northern Ireland. While this may have been a better result than the likely war between unionists and nationalists, the evidence presented here suggests that officials and leaders were aware of the need for benevolent 'engagement' rather than detachment.

Notes to Prologue to Part I and Chapter 2

1. Weber, *Essays in Sociology,* pp. 159–60.
2. Arthur, Paul, *Special Relationships: Britain, Ireland and the Northern Ireland Problem* (Belfast: Blackstaff, 2000) p. 82.
3. Pakenham, *The Year of Liberty,* pp. 29–30.
4. 'Literally "Hibernian (or Irish) Peace"', the title of chapter 1 of J.C. Beckett's *The Making of Modern Ireland 1603–1923* (London: Faber and Faber, [1966] 4th Edition, 1981).
5. Connolly, S.J., *Religion, Law and Power: The Making of Protestant Ireland 1660–1760* (Oxford: Clarendon, 1992) p. 13.
6. Elliott, Marianne, *Partners in Revolution, the United Irishmen and France* (New Haven: Yale University Press, 1982).
7. Bartlett, Thomas, *The Fall and Rise of the Irish Nation* (Dublin: Gill and Macmillan, 1992); Elliott, Marianne, *Wolfe Tone, Prophet of Irish Independence* (New Haven and London: Yale University Press, 1989); Whelan, Kevin, *The Tree of Liberty: Radicalism, Catholicism and the Construction of Irish Identity* (South Bend, IN: University of Notre Dame Press, 1996).
8. Watson, J. Steven, *The Reign of George III 1760–1815* (Oxford: Clarendon, 1960) p. 400.
9. Maume, Patrick, *The Long Gestation: Irish Nationalist Life, 1891–1918* (Dublin: Gill & Macmillan, 1999); Jackson, Alvin, *Home Rule: An Irish History 1800-2000* (London: Weidenfeld & Nicolson, 2003; Paseta, Senia, *Before the Revolution: Nationalism, Social Change and Ireland's Catholic Elite, 1879-1922* (Cork: Cork University Press, 1999).
10. Jackson, Alvin, *Home Rule,* pp. 171–4.
11. Foster, R.F., *Modern Ireland 1600–1972* (London: Penguin, 1988) p. 461.
12. Jackson, Alvin, *Home Rule: An Irish History 1800–2000* (London: Weidenfeld & Nicolson, 2003).
13. O'Ferrall, Fergus, *Catholic Emancipation: Daniel O'Connell and the Birth of Irish Democracy* (Dublin: Gill and Macmillan, 1985) pp. 3–4; Jenkins, Brian, *The Era of Emancipation: British Government of Ireland, 1812–1830* (Kingston, Ont: McGill-Queen's University Press, 1988) pp. 87, 161; Bartlett, Thomas, *Fall and Rise of the Catholic Nation,* pp. 333, 340–2.
14. Quoted in MacDonagh, Oliver, *O'Connell: The Life of Daniel O'Connell 1775–1847* (London: Weidenfeld and Nicolson, 1991) p. 269, emphasis in original.
15. Carty, Anthony, *Was Ireland Conquered? International Law and the Irish Question* (London: Pluto, 1996) pp. 60–5.
16. Valente, Joseph, 'The Manliness of Parnell', *Éire-Ireland,* Volume 41:1&2, (Earrach/Samhradh / Spring/Summer 2006) pp. 64–121.
17. Moody, T.W., *Davitt and Irish Revolution 1846–8* (Oxford: Clarendon, 1981) pp. 248–87.
18. Quoted, with emphasis in original, in Churchill, Randolph S., *Winston S. Churchill 1874–1965, Volume I, Youth, 1874–1900* (London: Heinemann, 1966) p. 71.
19. Fitzpatrick, David, *The Two Irelands 1912–1939,* pp. 20–5.

20. Jackson, Alvin, *Home Rule*, p. 172; citing Bew, Paul, *Ideology and the Irish Question: Ulster Unionism and Irish Nationalism, 1912–1916* (Oxford: Oxford University Press, 1994) pp. 144–52; Maume, Patrick, *The Long Gestation*, p. 171.
21. Quoted in Mansergh, Nicholas, *The Irish Question, 1848–1921*, p. 245.
22. For an explanation of the radicalization of Irish nationalism that emphasizes the legacy of popular and elite conceptions of national justice, see Githens-Mazer, Jonathan, *Myths and Memories of the Easter Rising* (Dublin: Irish Academic Press, 2006).
23. Githens-Mazer, *Myths and Memories of the Easter Rising* Fig. 4 and 5, citing Intelligence Reports, 1914–16 CO 903/19 PRO Kew; see also Fitzpatrick, David, *Politics and Irish Life 1913–1921* p. 96; Jackson, Alvin, *Home Rule: An Irish History, 1800–2000* (London: Weidenfeld & Nicolson, 2003) pp. 134–5.
24. Githens-Mazer, Jonathan, *Myths and Memories of the Easter Rising*.
25. O'Leary and McGarry, *The Politics of Antagonism*, Table 2.2.
26. Official Correspondence relating to the Peace Negotiations. Part Two: Correspondence arising from the conversations at London between President de Valera and the British Prime Minister, 13 August 1921.
27. Bull, Hedley, *The Anarchical Society: A Study of Order in World Politics* (London: Macmillan, 1977) p. 31.
28. See Shinoda, *Re–examining Sovereignty; see also* Sørenson, George, 'Sovereignty: Change and Continuity in a Fundamental Institution', *Political Studies,* 47(1999) pp. 590–604.
29. Blackstone, William, *The Sovereignty of the Law, Selections from Blackstone's "Commentaries on the Laws of England"*, pp. 36, 71, quoted in Morris, Christopher W., *An Essay on the Modern State* (Cambridge: Cambridge University Press, 1998) p. 179.
30. Sørensen, 'Sovereignty: Change and Continuity in a Fundamental Institution', *Political Studies,* Special Issue: Sovereignty at the Millennium, Vol. 47, No. 3 (1999) p. 593.
31. The classic work is Hamilton, Alexander, Madison, James and Jay, John, *The Federalist Papers* (London: New English Library, 1961).
32. Bull, Hedley, *The Anarchical Society* (London, Macmillan, 1977) p. 27.
33. Ibid. p. 26.
34. Ibid. p. 29.
35. Quoted in Halévy, Daniel, *President Wilson* (London: John Lane, 1919) p. 269.
36. Carty, Anthony, *Was Ireland Conquered? International Law and the Irish Question* (London: Pluto, 1996) pp. 163–6. Carty cites *Moore v. The Attorney General of the Irish Free State* (1935) as the authoritative legal decision on the constitutional position of Ireland as a Dominion of the Empire.
37. Shinoda, *Re–examining Sovereignty,* p. 52.
38. Kendle, J.E., *Ireland and the Federal Solution: The Debate over the United Kingdom Constitution, 1870–1921* (Kingston and Montreal, Canada: McGill-Queen's University Press, 1989) pp. 12–15; see also Jackson, Alvin, *Home Rule: An Irish History, 1800–2000* (London: Weidenfeld & Nicolson, 2003) p. 28.
39. Mansergh, Nicholas, *The Irish Question 1840–1921* (London: Allen & Unwin, 1975) pp. 299–305.
40. Longford, Earl of and O'Neill, Thomas P, *Eamon de Valera* (London: Hutchinson, 1970) p. 93.
41. H.C. Fourth Series, vol. 149, col. 38, 14 December 1921.
42. Dáil Debates, 22: 1615, 21 March 1928.
43. Quoted in Jones, Thomas, *Whitehall Diary, Vol. III, Ireland 1918–25* (London: Oxford University Press, 1971) pp. 158–9.
44. Ibid. p. 159.
45. Quoted in Jones, *Whitehall Diary,* p. 132.
46. Regan, John M., *The Irish Counter-Revolution 1921–1936: Treatyite Politics and Settlement in Independent Ireland* (Dublin: Gill and Macmillan, 1999) pp. 5–16, 44–5.
47. Jones, *Whitehall Diary,* pp. 99–102.
48. Ibid. p. 110.

49. The concept of 'essential unity' is elaborated in Pakenham, Frank (Lord Longford), *Peace by Ordeal* (London: Sidgwick & Jackson, 1972) pp. 221, 228, 258, 273. The Irish delegates were led to believe that the Boundary Commission would be governed principally by the desires of the local populations in areas under consideration. The effect of such a popular plebiscite would, the Irish delegates believed, re-unite the counties with Catholic/nationalist majorities – Fermanagh and Tyrone. The remaining four-county Northern Ireland would be economically unviable, or so it was hoped, and would therefore have little choice but to accept reunification. See also Dangerfield, George, *The Damnable Question: A Study in Anglo-Irish Relations* (London: Quartet, 1979) p. 339; Pakenham, *Peace by Ordeal*, pp. 132–6.

50. Pakenham, *Peace by Ordeal*, p. 239.

51. Jones, *Whitehall Diary*, p. 111.

52. Boyce, D.G., *The Irish Question and British Politics 1868–1986* (London: Macmillan, 1987) p. 65.

53. On Chamberlain's idea for 'Home Rule all-around' see Mansergh, *The Irish Question 1840–1921* pp. 179–87. On federalism in the Irish context see Kendle, J.E., *Ireland and the Federal Solution: The Debate over the United Kingdom Constitution, 1870–1921* (Kingston and Montreal, Canada: McGill-Queen's University Press).

54. Jones, *Whitehall Diary*, p. 170.

55. Ibid. p. 79.

56. Letter from Smuts to de Valera, 4 August 1921 [UK] Dominions Office (DO) 1119/1038 PRO, Kew.

57. Jones, *Whitehall Diary*, p.160.

58. Ibid.

59. Ibid.

60. Jones, *Whitehall Diary*, p. 129.

61. Pakenham (Lord Longford), *Peace by Ordeal* (London: Sidgwick & Jackson, 1972) pp. 236 ff.

62. There were two tactical blunders which undermined the Irish delegation's 'Ulster card': first, Arthur Griffith had privately agreed by letter to Lloyd George that the Boundary Commission was an acceptable formula for dealing with the vexed problem of territorial integrity. Therefore, when the Irish delegation were trying to break the negotiations on the absence of a guarantee from unionist leader James Craig as to the mandate of the Boundary Commission, Lloyd George revealed Griffith's prior pledge to accept the Boundary Commission *in principle*. Second, George Gavan Duffy verbally stated in the late stages of negotiation that the real barrier to a deal was the principle of empire, rather than territorial unity. The combination of these two positions undermined the Irish delegates' opportunity to make the negotiations break on territorial integrity (Ulster). See Dangerfield, *The Damnable Question*, pp. 333–9; see also Regan, J.M., *The Irish Counter-Revolution*, pp. 20–2.

63. Pakenham, *Peace by Ordeal*, pp. 132–6; 221, 228, 258, 273. For the international legal implications of the treaty see Carty, *Was Ireland Conquered?*, pp. 135–9.

64. The centrality of the forceful conclusion to the treaty and its subsequent implementation is also emphasized by John Regan in *The Irish Counter-Revolution*, p. 377.

65. Carty, *Was Ireland Conquered?*, pp. 135–41.

66. Diary of Negotiations, 27 May 1922, CAB 2111/257, PRO, Kew.

67. Very Secret Memorandum of Interview between PM, Mr. Griffith and Mr. Michael Collins held in the Cabinet Room, 10 Downing St., 1 June 1922, CAB 211/257, PRO, Kew.

68. Ibid.

69. Quoted in Jones, *Whitehall Diary*, p. 131; also quoted in Townshend, *Political Violence in Ireland*, p. 382.

70. Garvin, Tom, *1922: The Birth of Irish Democracy* (Dublin: Gill and Macmillan, 1996) pp. 132–51; see also Regan, *The Irish Counter-Revolution*, pp. 146–8.

71. Ibid. 242–3.

72. 10 December 1925, quoted in O'Brien, *Herod: Reflections on Political Violence.* (London: Hutchinson, 1978) p.131.
73. Quoted in MacDermot, Frank, *Tone and his Times* (Dublin: Anvil, 1980) p. 182; cf. O'Brien, *Herod,* p. 229.
74. Coogan, Tim Pat, *The Man who Made Ireland: The Life and Death of Michael Collins* (Niwot, CO: Roberts Rinehart, 1992) p.301.
75. O'Brien, *Herod*, pp. 24–39, 128–140.
76. Garvin, *1922: The Birth of Irish Democracy,* pp. 61–2.
77. Extract from Sir Neville McReady's 'Annals of an Active Life', published in the *Irish Times* 3 Feb. 1965 as reproduced in NA 96/6/12, Dublin. McReady was British Commander in Chief in 1922.
78. Younger, Carlton, *A State of Disunion* (London: Fontana, 1972) p.146.
79. Garvin, *1922: The Birth of Irish Democracy,* pp. 51–62.
80. Macardle, Dorothy, *The Irish Republic,* 2nd Edition, (Dublin: Irish Press, 1957) p. 771.
81. Ibid. p. 785.
82. Garvin, *1922: The Birth of Irish Democracy* p. 101; Hopkinson, Michael, *Green Against Green: The Irish Civil War* (Dublin: Gill and Macmillan, 1988) p. 273; Lyons, F.S.L., *Ireland Since the Famine* (London: Fontana, 1973) pp. 467–8; Neeson, E., *The Civil War, 1922–1923* (Dublin: Poolbeg, 1969) p. 291.
83. Garvin, *1922: The Birth of Irish Democracy,* p.164.
84. Quoted in O'Clery, Conor, *Phrases Make History Here: Political Quotations in Ireland 1867–1987* (Dublin: O'Brien, 1987) p. 84, emphasis added.
85. Quoted in Munger, Frank, 'The Legitimacy of Opposition: The Change of Government in Ireland 1932', *Contemporary Political Sociology Series,* Vol. 1, No. 06-006 (1975) p. 29; see also Valiulis, Maryann, *Almost a Rebellion* (London: Tower, 1985).
86. Keogh, Dermot, *Twentieth-Century Ireland: Nation and State* (Dublin: Gill and Macmillan, 1994) pp. 23–7; Macardle, *The Irish Republic*, pp. 903–23.
87. Carty, *Was Ireland Conquered?*, p. 140.
88. Munger, 'The Legitimacy of Opposition', pp. 20–1; Lyons, *Ireland Since the Famine* (1973) pp. 476–9.
89. O'Higgins successfully negotiated a change in the official title of the monarch from 'of Great Britain and Ireland and of the British Dominions beyond the seas' to 'of Great Britain, Ireland, and the British Dominions beyond the seas'. The added comma was meant to symbolize a degree of status symmetry *within* empire, but actually only restored the *status quo ante* of the Act of Settlement (1701). See Fitzpatrick, David, *The Two Irelands, 1912–1939* (Oxford: Oxford University Press, 1998) p. 150.
90. Quoted in Carty, *Was Ireland Conquered?*, p. 84.
91. Regan, *The Irish Counter-Revolution*, pp. 276, 295–6.
92. Ibid. p. 307.
93. Ibid. pp. 305–17; Fitzpatrick, *The Two Irelands,* pp. 150–1; Fanning, Ronan, *Independent Ireland* (Dublin: Helicon, 1983).
94. Patterson, Henry, *The Politics of Illusion: A Political History of the IRA* (London: Serif, 1997) pp. 53–61.
95. Quoted in Coogan, *The IRA*, p. 94.
96. Garvin *1922: The Birth of Irish Democracy,* pp. 182, 194; Arthur, *Special Relationships* p. 89.
97. See Canning, Paul, *British Policy Toward Ireland 1921–1941* (Oxford: Oxford University Press, 1985).
98. Memo from Maffey to Machtig, 3 June 1940, DO 130/10 f. 18,1. PRO Kew.
99. Ibid.
100. Bowman, John, *De Valera and the Ulster question 1917–73* (Oxford: Oxford University Press, 1989) pp. 174–5.
101. Memo from Maffey to Machtig, 3 June 1940, DO 130/10 f. 18, 3 PRO Kew.
102. Proceedings of Conference Between Representatives of the United Kingdom and Éire, CAB 27/164 I.N. Series, p. 24, PRO Kew.

103. Ibid. p. 25.
104. Ibid. p. 25.
105. Foster, *Modern Ireland*, p. 553.
106. Bowman, *De Valera and the Ulster Question,* p. 182–3.
107. Proceedings of Conference Between Representatives of the United Kingdom and Éire, CAB 27/164 I.N. Series, p. 2, PRO Kew.
108. Memo from Maffey to Machtig, 3 June 1940, DO130/10, f20, 1, PRO Kew.
109. Memo from Maffey to Eden, 17 January 1940, DO 130/10, PRO Kew.
110. IRA activities, A12/1, NAI.
111. Lee, *Ireland, 1912–1985: Politics and Society* (Cambridge: Cambridge University Press, 1989) pp. 222–3; Keogh, Dermot, *Twentieth-Century Ireland: Nation and State* (Dublin: Gill and Macmillan, 1994) p.110.
112. Lee, *Ireland, 1912–1985,* p. 223.
113. Quotation from 'The Unity of Ireland: Partition Debated in Seanad Éireann', Official Reports, 9 February 1939 (Dublin: The Stationery Office) p. 10.
114. Lee, *Ireland 1912–1985,* pp. 201–6.
115. Bowman, *De Valera* pp. 223–31; see also Fisk, Robert, *In Time of War: Ireland, Ulster and the Price of Neutrality, 1939–45* (London: Andre Deutsch) pp. 160–73.
116. Fearon, James D., 'Domestic Political Audiences and the Escalation of International Disputes', *American Political Science Review* Vol. 88, No. 3 (1994) pp.577–93; Doron, Gideon and Sened, Itai, *Political Bargaining: Theory, Practice & Process* (London: Sage, 2001) p.149.
117. Cabinet Conclusions, 17 January 1938, CAB 27 I.N.C. (38), 198, PRO Kew.
118. Machtig to Eden, undated, DO 130/10, PRO Kew.
119. In the sense of 'playground' exchanges between children who only exchange marbles, for example, once the giver and receiver have equal holds on the items to be exchanged.
120. Longford, Earl of and O'Neill, Thomas P., *Eamon de Valera* (London: Hutchinson, 1970) p. 366.
121. Hand-written comment by Churchill, in response to letter from Minister of Labour, Ernest Bevin to Churchill, 18 June 1940, PREM 4/53/2, PRO, Kew. Bevin proposed the creation of an all-Ireland 'joint Defence Council' and 'that we should enter into an agreement with Ireland. That there should be a statement, that we are willing to accept a new constitution on the basis of a united Ireland at the end of hostilities'. Churchill's scrawl in the margins suggests that he 'can't be a party to the coercion of Ulster to join the Southern counties; but I am much in favour of their being permitted. The big [problem] with this is de Valera showing true loyalty to Crown and Empire.' For a contrasting view, see Bowman, *De Valera and the Ulster Question*, pp. 223–30.
122. Hand-written comment by Churchill to letter from Gough, 9 December 1941, PREM 4/53/4 PRO Kew.
123. Letter from Churchill to Brooke, 12 June 1945, PREM 4 53/1 PRO Kew.
124. Hoppen, K.T. *Ireland since 1800: Conflict and Conformity* Second Edition (London: Longman, 1999) p. 204.
125. 'The Effect of the War on Ireland's Destiny as a European Nation – Reflections by an Australian', 16 May 1940, PREM 4/53/2, PRO Kew. Hancock was the author of the *Survey of British Commonwealth Affairs, Volume I: Problems of Nationality 1918–1936* (Oxford: Oxford University Press, 1937).
126. Arthur, Paul, *Special Relationships*, p. 94. Arthur cites David Vital's analysis of Britain's 'piecemeal approach to foreign policy', in Vital, David, *The Making of British Foreign Policy* (London: Allen and Unwin, 1968) p. 99.
127. Lee, J.J. *Ireland 1912–1985,* pp. 195–201.

3

Gone but not Forgotten:
The Legacy of Violent Politics, 1922-1969

> I should call to mind the sacrifices we have so recently made in agreeing to self-government and consenting to the establishment of a Parliament for Northern Ireland. Much against our wish, but in the interests of peace, we accept this as a final settlement... If there exists an equal desire for peace on the part of Sinn Féin, they will respect the status quo in Ulster, and will refrain from any interference with our Parliament and rights, which under no circumstances can we admit.
>
> Sir James Craig, Northern Ireland PM (reading letter to British Prime Minister David Lloyd George)[1]

> No Irishman, no supporter of national self-determination admitted the right of any Irish minority to secede from Ireland... [It is] abundantly clear that our claim extends to every inch of Irish soil and that nothing less will satisfy the Irish people.
>
> John A. Costello, Irish Taoiseach[2]

If the Anglo-Irish Treaty was an admission of failure by the British state to monopolize the legitimate use of force in Ireland, the partition of the island and the creation of Northern Ireland was an attempt to retain sovereignty over the remaining parts of Ireland where such control could safely be devolved from Westminster. The shape of the partition was designed to maximize the area of Northern Ireland controlled by the Protestant/unionist majority while minimizing the threat posed by the Catholic/nationalist minority. Initially, British imperial interests were safeguarded by the Free State's membership of the Commonwealth and the oath of allegiance to the crown sworn by members of the Oireachtas. British strategic interests were protected by the control of all Irish ports until 1938. Yet as important as these imperial symbols and strategic safeguards were, the acceptance of their gradual erosion at the hands of successive Irish governments lends support to the argument that the overriding concern was to remove the Irish question from British politics, while maintaining the commitment to Northern Ireland's union with Great Britain.[3]

In this chapter I argue that the pragmatic and ambivalent approach to imperious constitutionalism guaranteed that the Ireland question would become the Northern Ireland question and that its politics would be violent. This explanation differs from those that emphasize the institutional, structural and cultural sources of conflict *in* Northern Ireland, though these are all recognized as important factors affecting the form of governance and the types of opposition that emerged.[4] Instead of a Northern Ireland focus, most comparative political science and international relations approaches recognize the Northern Ireland conflict as, in Paul Arthur's view, 'Anglo-Irish relations writ small'.[5] Indeed, the IRA's campaign to destabilize the new Northern Ireland government was, as Charles Townshend has argued, a direct result of the ambiguous and coercive handling of partition and dominion status. Collins' authorization in June 1922 of the assassination of Sir Henry Wilson, formerly Chief of the Imperial General Staff (CIGS) and newly elected Westminster MP from North Down, appears to have been an attempt to maintain IRA unity in the face of the split over the 1921 treaty. This assassination and other violence in turn reinforced the unionist militarization of their 'sub-state' and Catholic alienation from it.[6]

CONTROL BY PROXY

The direct causal effects of this form of 'remote control' can be seen most clearly in the implementation of the Government of Ireland Act (1920). As with the Boundary Commission (discussed in the previous chapter), the priority of stabilizing unionist domination led to pragmatic over principled constitutionalism and, in this case, procedural rather than substantive minority rights protections. As Brigid Hadfield has explained, the sovereign authority to govern Northern Ireland as vested in section 75 of the Government of Ireland Act, was offset by

> Westminster's desire for non-involvement in Northern Ireland affairs, a constitutional convention that it would not legislate for Northern Ireland without the latter's (full-blooded or half-hearted) consent and a ruling in 1923 of the Speaker of the Westminster House of Common that no question could be asked there on matters transferred to the Northern Ireland Parliament.[7]

Thus the terms of the treaty, meant to compensate Catholics/nationalists in Northern Ireland, were allowed to lapse. The first test of sovereign authority set a precedent for the exercise of hegemonic control. In 1922 the British Governor to Northern Ireland attempted to assert the crown's authority[8] to reserve the bill passed in the Northern Ireland parliament to change the electoral system for local elections from proportional representation to the plurality, first-past-the post, system. The British government was moved to intervene because the proportional representation electoral system was designed as an important safeguard for the nationalist minority. The unionist government threatened to resign if the bill was reserved and, despite protests from the Provisional Irish government, the bill was eventually given royal assent. This reserve authority was never exercised again. Similarly, the proposed Council of Ireland, meant to bring legislators together from the two jurisdictions, lapsed by 1925 into a hopeful plea to 'avoid friction which might mar or retard the further growth of friendly relations between the said Governments and peoples'.[9] Legislation meant to disallow discrimination on the grounds of religion was framed and interpreted by the (UK appointed) Northern Irish Supreme Court[10] in ways that failed to prevent systematic discrimination against Catholics.[11] On the contrary, as Brigid Hadfield has recognized, the judicial framework allowed Prime Minister Craigavon[12] to claim a 'Protestant Parliament and a Protestant state' – in response to de Valera's establishment of a special place for the Catholic Church in the 1937 constitution.[13] Furthermore, the ambivalent position of the Irish Free State (Republic from 1949) towards reunification – in which successive Irish governments accepted the *de facto* existence of Northern Ireland while claiming *de jure* authority over the entire island – contributed to unionists' sense of vulnerability and led to renewed cycles of alternation between constitutional and physical-force republicanism on both sides of the border.

For an explanation of the perpetuation of violent politics, the Northern Ireland control strategy had at least three implications.[14] First, hegemonic control produced what Patrick Buckland called a 'factory of grievances'[15] which underlined for the nationalist community the futility of constitutional means for the pursuit or defence of its interests. Secondly, the hegemonic fortress legitimized the use of force to defend the *Protestant* state against internal and external enemies. Finally, control limited the efficacy of constitutional republicanism in the South by highlighting the stranded plight of Catholics/nationalists in Northern Ireland, thereby perpetuating physical-force republicanism as a competitor within the field of Irish nationalism.

FUNCTIONAL (NATIONAL) INTEGRATION

By the early 1960s the successive failures of constitutional and physical-force nationalism produced a familiar series of revisions or 'new departures' among Irish nationalists. The re-ascendance of Fianna Fáil in the Republic, and the modernization of its policies under the influence of the erstwhile 'slightly-constitutional' republican Sean Lemass did not, by any means, vitiate the *de jure* claim to unity: Lemass declared in 1962 that EEC membership would make partition 'an anachronism that all sensible people will want to bring [to] an end'.[16] These integrationist views on Irish unity were apparent in Fianna Fáil's formation of a constitutional committee, chaired by Lemass, which attempted to make the Irish constitution more attractive to unionists by proposing to adjust the claim to sovereignty over the island of Ireland to an aspiration for unity and by removing the articles referring to the special position of the Catholic Church.[17] These reforms were premature given the weight of traditional anti-treaty and Catholic influences within the party. But the promotion of unity was undoubtedly used opportunistically by Fianna Fáil to regain power in 1957, and the party still sought re-unification as a primary by-product of economic interdependence with Great Britain and Northern Ireland, within the European Economic Community.[18] An illuminating biographical note from the Foreign Office to the British Prime Minister reveals, in addition to deep cultural prejudice, the British understanding of Lemass's functionalist integrationism:

Mr. Lemass seems to have little of the typical Irishman in his make-up despite his revolutionary record [e.g. active in 1916 rebellion; elected as Sinn Féin TD in 1924; and Fianna Fáil from 1926; of 'Jewish Background'...]. He is sensible, courageous and cool-headed, a man of affairs with his feet on the ground...

He believes in the inevitability of the reunification of Ireland and probably thinks that in time economic factors such as membership of the E.E.C. or an Anglo-Irish Free Trade Area will help to bring it about. He finally took the firm action necessary to end the border outrages, and follows a policy of co-operation at all levels with Northern Ireland.[19]

Lemass's interest in functional integration as a means to promote re-unification was revealed in his meeting with Prime Minister Terence O'Neill in 1965 when he expressed the view that 'Irish Republican authorities had it in mind to extend and accelerate Free Trade area arrangements which existed between the Republic and Ulster (sic). They wished to be quite separate from the Free Trade Area between the UK and the Republic and they contemplated that the speed at which tariffs were dismantled would be faster.'[20] This view runs contrary to Henry Patterson's claim that Lemass's anti-partitionist integrationism was mainly an attempt to insulate his government from criticism over domestic economic policy.[21]

In any case, there was an asymmetrical pay-off for the British who faced big risks by pushing economic, social and political reform on reluctant unionists. Therefore, the default policy of 'benevolent detachment' was maintained. A confidential memo to the Prime Minister from the Commonwealth Secretary suggested, after noting the thawing of Anglo-Irish relations and warm relations between Lemass and O'Neill:

Looking to the future it would probably be desirable that partition should be brought to an end and we can even look forward to the day when a reunified Ireland would join the Commonwealth. Nevertheless, our position is governed by the Ireland Act, 1949, ...our Ambassador in Dublin strongly advises, therefore, that we should do our best to show Mr. Lemass that, *even if we did share his ambition to see partition ended*, we should only harm the prospects of doing so were we to attempt to intervene, and we believe that the interests of both North and South are best served by continuing, but benevolent detachment on our part.[22]

THE LIMITS OF FUNCTIONAL INTEGRATION

Functional integrationists believed that economic inter-dependence among nation-states of Europe would produce 'spill-over' in the form of technocratic governing institutions needed to regulate trade and markets. The European Coal and Steel Community had by 1958 evolved to the European Economic

Community with a Council of Ministers, Commission, Advisory Parliament and a Court of Justice, and had stabilized French–German relations. However, the limits of functional integrationism are equally evident in the pattern and extent of European integration. Indeed, the ambitious attempt to create a political union alongside an economic union has been limited by the same issue at the heart of the conflict in and over Northern Ireland: nationalism. The European Union has been dominated by intergovernmental co-operation between and among the nation-states of Europe, rather than any progressive evolution towards a shared European identity underpinning a European supra-national state.

In Ireland, the centrality of the national question and its resulting border dispute meant that functional integration was limited by diametrically opposing goals regarding the border: the Irish government was seeking to remove the border while the Northern Ireland government was trying to strengthen it.

Initially it appeared that Lemass had an exchange partner when Captain Terence O'Neill succeeded the retiring Lord Brookeborough as Unionist Prime Minister in 1963. O'Neill was the first non-landed Prime Minister of Northern Ireland and shared Lemass's emphasis on economic modernization, including infrastructure development, to attract inward investment. A climate of unionist revisionism was also encouraged by the successful use of internment on both sides of the border against the IRA's border campaign (1956–62) and the IRA's public abandonment of the armed struggle in 1962.

The 'liberal unionist' view projected by O'Neill believed that the post-war British consensus based on the provision of universal access to health, housing and higher education could cultivate British, civic nation-building in Northern Ireland among the first generation of Catholic graduates. [23] Early indications were promising. The traditional, rural-based Nationalist Party came under pressure from a younger generation of activists, organized in a group called National Unity and then the National Democratic Party, to end its policy of abstention from Stormont. On 3 February 1965 the Nationalist Party announced that it would take its place at Stormont as the official opposition, while assuring that 'our fidelity to the united Ireland ideal remains unaltered by this decision'. [24] Those constitutional nationalists who did not have faith in the ability or willingness of the Nationalist Party to replace its goal of a united Ireland with reforms within Northern Ireland bypassed Stormont and appealed directly to the Labour government in London. The two primary organizations, the Campaign for Social Justice (CSJ, founded 1964) and the London-based Campaign for Democracy in Ulster (CDU, founded 1965) concentrated on exposing injustices such as discrimination in employment and housing allocation, the gerrymandering of electoral boundaries, property qualifications for voting in local elections, and the repeal of the draconian Special Powers Act. In February 1967 the leaders of the CSJ formed the Northern Ireland Civil Rights Association (NICRA) as a province-wide organization to pursue reformist goals. NICRA quickly became an umbrella organization comprised of the original moderate Catholic/nationalist reformers, representatives of the trade union movement, as well as a significant number of republican activists. [25] The organization was composed of eighteen local civil rights committees and membership was inclusive. In October 1968, a more radical civil rights movement named Peoples' Democracy (PD) was formed by student activists at Queen's University Belfast. PD's manifesto echoed that of NICRA but went further by demanding a commitment to full employment, land redistribution, the repeal of the Special Powers Act, and a united Ireland, albeit one reformed along radical socialist lines.[26] Both NICRA and PD were specifically committed to pursuing their goals non-violently, although PD's definition of, and commitment to, non-violence was less clear-cut.

A similar process of revision had occurred within the IRA as the narrow and socially conservative militarism, which had failed abjectly in the border campaign, was rejected in a new departure towards a wider social and economic radicalism. Cathal Goulding led this new departure, under the intellectual influence of revolutionary Marxist Roy Johnston. Through front organizations such as the republican clubs and the Wolfe Tone societies, the IRA encouraged its members to get involved in local civil rights campaigns,[27] just as the IRB had infiltrated the Gaelic League and GAA during its lean times in the 1890s. As an internal IRA document advised:

> The achievement of democracy and civil rights will make the way open for linking the economic demands to the national question. Those who see the former as an end in itself... insofar as they comprise the present leadership of the NICRA... may be expected to lose interest as rights are gained. They must then be replaced by more consistent people.[28]

Indeed, as Richard English has shown, civic-republican ideas inspired by Wolfe Tone were developed by southern nationalist academics Desmond Greaves and Anthony Coughlan, and propagated through the Wolfe Tone societies. The civic republican argument was that unionists were pawns in the game of British imperialism and that a staged strategy of undermining Stormont through moral force would force British intervention. Unionist resistance against British reform demands would then, so the argument went, remove the scales from eyes and make unionists realize their interests (material and ideational) were best served in a socialist republican Irish state. As with the previous new departures, this one caused a split within the IRA. A series of publicity attacks in the Republic culminated in the bombing in March 1966 of Lord Nelson's pillar in Dublin.[29] This faction would go on to form an important element of the Provisional IRA, which would emerge in January 1970. For example, the leader of the 1966 schism, Richard Behal, later became 'foreign affairs' officer of Provisional Sinn Féin.[30]

While these schisms were not yet crystallized, the resurgence of both traditional and socialist republicanism, and especially the latter's 'entryist' strategy regarding the civil rights movement, demonstrated the continued salience of the national question and the limits of potential for civil rights reforms to answer that super-ordinate question. For example, Richard Rose's 'loyalty survey', taken in the summer of 1968 at the height of O'Neillism and before the outbreak of civil unrest, revealed that even in these favourable circumstances only 33 per cent of Catholics supported the constitution of Northern Ireland, while 34 per cent were opposed, and 32 per cent were undecided.[31] In the same survey, 56 per cent of Catholics wanted the border abolished,[32] exactly the proportion of the nationalist vote given to Sinn Féin in 1955 that had sparked the border campaign (Operation Harvest) the following year.

Within the cyclical context of the politics of partition, the unravelling should not have been surprising. Terence O'Neill expressed his fears to the British government that by 1966 the IRA had re-grouped to force levels equivalent to 1956.[33] The conflict over national identity and its constitutional expression could not be separated from the sincerely held desire for moderate social, economic and political reforms. The unwillingness of both the British and Irish governments to face the core national questions contributed directly to the re-escalation of violent politics.

THREATS TO HEGEMONY: REVISIONIST UNIONISM

The resurgence of both traditional and socialist variants of republicanism naturally limited O'Neill's room for manoeuvre within unionism. Traditional unionist interests were threatened when the British Labour government and the nationalist minority began to exert pressure to integrate the latter into the state as equal citizens.[34] Whether O'Neill was actually committed to the degree of reform needed to satisfy minority grievances is debatable. Paul Arthur has argued that O'Neill was more interested in 'the politics of the flamboyant gesture',[35] while Bew et al. emphasize the threat posed to O'Neill by the election of Wilson's Labour government in 1964 with sympathies towards promoting a united Ireland.[36] What is clear is that O'Neill's reformist stance fragmented the unionist bloc because reform threatened the basis of hegemonic control within the Protestant state. Without active support from Westminster or a sufficient liberal base within the Unionist Party, O'Neill was stranded.

O'Neill's gestures to the nationalist minority and especially to Dublin were interpreted as a sell out or 'Lundyism'[37] in local parlance, especially since republican involvement in the civil rights movement was well known, though exaggerated.[38] Two important organizations quickly developed in response to the threat of 'O'Neillism'. In 1966, the Reverend Ian Paisley established the Ulster Constitution Defence Committee (UCDC) with a vigilante wing known as the Ulster Protestant Volunteers (UPV), whose constitution stated:

> The Ulster Constitution Defence Committee and the Ulster Protestant Volunteers which it governs is one united society of Protestant patriots pledged by all lawful methods to uphold and maintain the Constitution of Northern Ireland as an integral part of the United Kingdom as long as the United Kingdom maintains a Protestant Monarchy and the terms of the Revolution Settlement.[39]

The second group to emerge in 1966 was the Ulster Volunteer Force (UVF), which took its name from the unionist army raised in 1912 by Edward Carson to fight Home Rule. Led by Gusty Spence from the Shankill Road in Belfast, the UVF represented the extreme loyalist section of the unionist community: largely working-class and devoted members of the Orange Order who mirrored the republicans of the nationalist community in their determination to fight for the protection of their interests. In response to republican activity surrounding the events of the fiftieth anniversary of the 1916 Rising, the UVF declared war against the IRA and promptly killed two innocent Catholics. Spence was convicted of both murders and sent to prison for life.[40] The UVF then went underground but its small band of leaders retained a considerable supply of weapons. More importantly, the re-emergence of the UVF signalled that a significant section of working-class Protestants would be willing to take up arms in opposition to either republicans or the modernizing politicians who threatened to undermine unionist hegemony.

While the UPV and UVF were fringe elements in 1968, they were clearly representative of a much larger section of the unionist community determined to defend its national interests. In Rose's loyalty survey, a bare majority, 52 per cent of Protestants, claimed that they would approve of 'any measures' to keep Northern Ireland a Protestant country i.e., as Rose interprets, to maintain 'a Protestant monopoly of power in the regime'. Moreover, of these 52 per cent, the majority (58 per cent) approved 'any measures' to 'defend Protestant ways'.[41]

Given the polarized divisions within both nationalism and unionism it is difficult to imagine how any government at Stormont could have managed reform. What about the sovereign? While the CDU effectively gained the attention of Labour MPs at Westminster from 1965 through 1967, the parliamentary convention prohibiting discussion of issues under Stormont's jurisdiction prevented this approach from forcing O'Neill to confront more than surface reform. Unionists at both Stormont and Westminster vehemently denied the existence of discrimination, and argued that the civil rights campaign was a mere extension of the traditional nationalist tactic of subversion through protest. As the Northern Ireland Home Affairs Minister William Craig proclaimed at Stormont:

> It [the Nationalist Party] is in my view a party depending on a sense of grievance, completely lacking in positive policies for the advancement of the country or even the people it purports to represent. The smear, denigration and agitation tactics which it so readily adopted are weapons of destruction ...

> All this has got to stop; *there is not the slightest excuse for such activity* ... The Government intend to see that the rule of law prevails and political advantage or any form of embarrassment, intimidation or threat shall not deter us. A law-abiding community is a necessary base to sustain and expand the great social and economic advance that Northern Ireland is enjoying. All men of goodwill should realize this and rally to the support of law and order.[42]

With the constitutional reform process blocked at both Stormont and Westminster, both the NICRA and PD escalated their tactics by taking their campaign to the streets. From the summer of 1968 through the autumn of 1969 a series of demonstrations and marches were organized which challenged directly Protestant/unionist hegemony. The details of the marches from Coalisland to Dungannon, within the walled city of Derry/Londonderry, in Armagh, Newry and from Belfast to Derry/Londonderry are well documented.[43] All of the marches were either banned outright or severely restricted from Protestant/unionist areas and all ended violently as the marchers defied the bans and were met by a combination of the police and counter-demonstrations led by the Reverend Ian Paisley and Major Ronald Bunting.

The pattern of escalation leading up to the fateful Apprentice Boys march of 12 August 1969 should have been a sufficient indicator of the degree to which the conflict had evolved beyond the boundaries of a civil rights campaign into a 'traditional' confrontation between nationalists and unionists. In April 1969, James Callaghan, Home Secretary in the Wilson government, expressed a flawed, though prescient, analysis of the government's predicament:

> The nature of the problem with which we are dealing is not ephemeral. There is a desire to secure basic constitutional rights which I think everyone in the House believes should exist in Northern Ireland. If they are not conceded, there follows the basic desire to protest. This has brought the backlash of violence, which is escalating. *The pattern in which we are moving is one in which grievances produce protest, protest produces violence and violence is followed by counter-violence.* Attitudes are frozen into immobility. This is succeeded by more violence. The end of that road would be the complete collapse and breakdown of relations between the communities and the collapse of the system of government under which they are living. We are only in the early stages of that journey along that road, but it is imperative that, although our voice may not be heard much on the other side of the Channel, the united voice of Westminster should express itself loudly and clearly against any further progress along that path to hell.[44]

The British assumption that equal citizenship would solve the unrest was wishful thinking, encouraged by the chimera of tranquillity sustained since the Irish question was removed from British politics. At least three factors stand out which indicate that O'Neill's government was incapable of preventing the moderate elements within both the unionist and nationalist blocs from being marginalized by extremists from each side. First, the marches demonstrated the inadequacy of the security forces in a situation of communal antagonism. The televised beatings of peaceful marchers (including Westminster MP Gerry Fitt and several visiting colleagues), the indiscriminate use of water canons during the first NICRA–DHAC (Derry Housing Action Committee) march in Derry/Londonderry on 5 October, 1968, and RUC rampages through the Bogside all led directly to serious rioting and the attempted micro-secession of the nationalist Bogside into what was called 'Free Derry'.[45] With a total strength of just over 3,000 in 1968 the RUC was severely tested by the escalation of street violence. More importantly, the unsuitability of the entirely Protestant B

Specials for crowd and riot control duties in Catholic areas meant that the RUC was acting with a backup unit that was reviled by the nationalist community. In turn, the initial unwillingness of Northern Ireland Home Affairs Minister William Craig to sanction the use of the B Specials provided justification for the mobilization of groups of loyalist 'defenders' such as Paisley's UPV and John McKeague's Shankill Defence Association (SDA).[46]

Because of the begrudging pace of reforms, radical factions came to dominate both NICRA and PD by the end of 1968. Following the events in Dungannon in June, when a peaceful NICRA march was met with a Paisley-led counter-demonstration, the republican members of the NICRA executive convinced the more moderate members to conduct a march in Derry/Londonderry on 5 October in association with the republican-dominated DHAC.[47] While Purdie is careful to emphasize that the republican influence within NICRA was far from controlling, it is clear that the decision to adopt confrontational tactics was a purposeful attempt to provoke a crisis that would either force O'Neill into going further and faster towards reforms (the moderates' agenda) or would allow the IRA to revive its struggle.[48]

Some reforms were granted in November, 1968: the Derry/Londonderry corporation was replaced by a nominated commission; the company vote was abolished; an ombudsman was appointed to monitor complaints made against local and state government; a (voluntary) points system was established for the allocation of public housing; and a review of the Special Powers Act was commissioned. However, those groups which were willing to meet O'Neill half way in 1966 or 1967 were now out-flanked by those whose appetite for more substantial reform was only whetted by O'Neill's quick response to the first episodes of trouble: instability appeared to work for both reformers and radicals. The PD leadership became convinced that NICRA's significant bourgeois contingent had capitulated too easily when in December it agreed to O'Neill's request for a ban on marches as an act of good faith following the government's reform programme. To press its demands, PD organized a march from Belfast to Derry/Londonderry commencing on 1 January 1969. At Burntollet, on 4 January, 200 loyalists – including off-duty members of the B-Specials – attacked the march, armed with stones and cudgels.[49]

O'Neill called an election in February 1969 to seek a reform mandate and face down the ultras within his party. From a total of thirty-nine Unionist MPs, Official and Independent Unionists who were definitely 'pro-O'Neill' took twenty-seven seats (twenty-four Official and three Independent), while the anti-O'Neill Unionists took ten seats and three were undecided.[50] In twenty-three head-to-head contests, anti-O'Neill candidates edged pro-O'Neill candidates by twelve seats to eleven.[51] Instead of a reform mandate, the election result gave impetus to the ultra-loyalists to step up the pressure against O'Neill. Between March and the end of April a team of bombers composed of members of the UPV and the UVF caused explosions at an electricity installation at Castlereagh, the Silent Valley reservoir in Co. Down, and an electricity sub-station at Portadown.[52] The UPV's *Protestant Telegraph* claimed that the explosions were the work of the IRA and, though they were in fact placed by loyalists, the obfuscation succeeded in tipping enough public pressure against O'Neill, who resigned on 28 April 1969.

COERCION AND CONCILIATION REVISITED

> When it comes to asserting the integrity of this province against attack, moderation must go hand in hand with the mailed fist.
>
> Roy Bradford, Unionist (Stormont) MP[53]

O'Neill's successor, James Chichester-Clark, was in a difficult position, to put it mildly. He won the internal leadership contest within the Official Unionist Party by only one vote. He faced, simultaneously: pressure from Westminster to continue reforms, a potential mutiny within the Unionist Party led by William Craig, an ongoing revolt from Paisley's loyalists, an increasingly militant minority revolt led by the civil rights movement and a security force which was both weak in number and partisan in composition. Lacking leverage or reward power, his response was an unimaginative combination of coercion and conciliation, the hallmark of an unravelling control strategy. 'Non-traditional' marches and counter-demonstrations were banned under the Special Powers Act. Two conciliatory reforms followed: first, an amnesty was granted to all persons charged and/or convicted of public order crimes between October 5 1968 and May 5 1969. This freed Paisley and Bunting, who were in custody after the Newry incident, and rescinded charges against the RUC members as well as Stormont MPs Ivan Cooper and Eddie McAteer and Westminster MPs Gerry Fitt and Bernadette Devlin. Second, after meeting with Wilson and Callaghan on 21 May, Chichester-Clark announced that legislation would be brought forward to reform local government elections and the allocation of public housing.

Neither of the two concessions addressed the deeper causes of the conflict, and after a brief pause it escalated in a manner consistent with a confused conflict regulation strategy. Although the early level of violence was insufficient to change policy, violence had been sufficiently rewarding for both loyalists, who had successfully brought down O'Neill, and for the more radical factions within the civil rights movement, who had forced the government to concede the first substantial reforms. Police violence then exacerbated polarization: shortly after the death of a 42-year-old Catholic taxi driver, Sam Devenney, who died of injuries inflicted by the RUC after a riot in the Bogside, nationalist MP Gerry Fitt declared in the House of Commons:

> If the Unionist Government – I am now making the most serious statement that I have ever made and I make it in the full knowledge of where I am speaking – can exist only by having the draconian Special Powers Act to support it, by denying social justice to the 40 per cent minority in Northern Ireland, by discriminating in jobs and houses, if that Government can exist only by having all these standards to support it, that Government has the right

to be overthrown. It is the moral duty of anyone who believes in Christianity and of anyone who believes in social justice to overthrow such a structure, which can exist only with such legislation to protect it.[54]

The radicalization of nationalist and unionist politics was not simply the product of bad governance, economic competition, primordial nationalism or religious sectarianism. Instead, the shift from constitutional to violent politics is best explained as a cascade from the remnants of the coerced Anglo-Irish Treaty: opposing British and Irish claims to sovereignty over Northern Ireland and a failure to implement even the minimum safeguards meant to make partition more palatable, particularly to the nationalist minority in Northern Ireland. Despite awareness of the need for creative safeguards and re-configurations of sovereignty, contested inter-state relationships provoked unionist fears, southern nationalist opportunism and northern nationalist grievance. The next two chapters analyze the British and Irish governments' search for answers to this question, showing how the opposing claims to sovereignty affected their willingness and ability to intervene as conflict regulators.

Notes

1. Quoted in N.I.H.C., vol. 1, col. 49, 20 September 1921.
2. *Dáil Debates,* 117:3, 5 July 1949.
3. Boyce, D.G., *The Irish Question and British Politics 1868–1986* (London: Macmillan, 1988), p.65; Lustick, *Unsettled States* pp. 237–8; Buckland, Patrick, *Ulster Unionism and the Origins of Northern Ireland 1886–1922* (Dublin: Gill and Macmillan, 1973) p. 125.
4. Structural analyses of Northern Ireland include Bew, Paul, Gibbon, Peter and Patterson, Henry, *Northern Ireland 1921–1996: Political Forces and Social Classes* (London: Serif, 1996); Farrell, Michael, *Northern Ireland: The Orange State* (London: Pluto, 1980). For a survey and critique of internal explanations see McGarry, John and O'Leary, Brendan, *Explaining Northern Ireland: Broken Images* (Oxford: Blackwell, 1995) Chs 5–7.
5. Arthur, *Special Relationships*, p. 2.
6. Townshend, *Political Violence in Ireland,* pp. 381–8.
7. Hadfield, Brigid, 'The Northern Ireland Constitution', in Hadfield, Brigid (ed.), *Northern Ireland: Politics & the Constitution* (Buckingham: Open University Press, 1992) p. 3.
8. Section 12(2) of the Government of Ireland Act (1920) authorized the Governor to reserve a Bill instead of granting Royal Assent. Ibid., p. 3.
9. Ireland (Confirmation of Agreement) Act 1925, as quoted Ibid.
10. Boyle, Hadden and Hillyard claimed in 1970 that fifteen of the twenty high court judges appointed between 1922 and 1970 were 'openly associated' with the Ulster Unionist Party. Boyle, K., Hadden, T. and Hillyard, P., *Law and State – The Case of Northern Ireland* (London: Martin Robinson, 1984) p. 12.
11. O'Leary and McGarry, *The Politics of Antagonism,* pp. 112–19.
12. Formerly Sir James Craig.
13. Hadfield, 'The Northern Ireland Constitution', p. 4.
14. O'Leary and McGarry, *The Politics of Antagonism,* Ch. 3.
15. Buckland, Patrick, *The Factory of Grievances: Devolved Government in Northern Ireland 1921–39* (Dublin: Gill and Macmillan, 1979).
16. Quoted in O'Clery, Conor, *Phrases Make History Here: Political Quotations in Ireland, 1867–1987* (Dublin: O'Brien Press, 1987) p. 117.

17. The suggested wording of the new articles was:
Article Two: The Irish Nation hereby proclaims its firm will that its territory be re-united in harmony and brotherly affection between all Irishmen.
Article Three: The laws enacted by the Parliament established by this Constitution shall, until the achievement of the nation's unity shall otherwise require, have the like area and extent of application as the Laws of the Parliament which existed prior to the adoption of this Constitution. Provision may be made by law to give extra-territorial effect to such laws. *Report of the Committee on the Constitution,* Prl. 9817 (Dublin: Stationery Office, 1967).
18. Lee, *Ireland 1912–1985,* pp. 367–9.
19. Briefing Note on Lemass, Dec. (no specific date), 1965, PREM 13/982, PRO Kew.
20. Notes of Downing St. meeting between Lemass and PM Harold Wilson, 26 July 1965, PREM 13/982, PRO Kew; see also Patterson, Henry, 'Sean Lemass and the Ulster Question 1959–65', *Journal of Contemporary History,* Vol. 34, No. 1 (1999) pp. 145–59; Lyne, Thomas, 'Ireland, Northern Ireland and 1992: The Barriers to Technocratic Anti-Partitionism', *Public Administration,* Vol. 68 (1990) pp. 417–33.
21. Patterson, 'Sean Lemass and the Ulster Question', p. 156.
22. Memo from Commonwealth Secretary (Arnold Smith) to Wilson, 22 July 1965, PREM 13/983 (37/65), PRO Kew.
23. The impact of the Labour–Conservative consensus on the provision of universal welfare entitlements on Northern Ireland politics is highlighted by Patrick Buckland, *A History of Northern Ireland,* pp. 106–8; see also Brendan O'Leary and John McGarry, *The Politics of Antagonism,* pp 157–9.
24. Quoted in O'Clery, *Phrases Make History Here,* p.119.
25. Cameron, D.S.C (Lord), *Disturbances in Northern Ireland: Report of the Commission appointed by the Governor of Northern Ireland* (Hereafter 'Cameron Report') (Belfast: Her Majesty's Stationery Office, 1969) pp. 77–9.
26. Ibid., p. 124; Purdie, *Politics in the Streets,* pp. 219–43.
27. Kelley, Kevin J., *The Longest War: Northern Ireland and the IRA* (London: Zed, 1988) pp.84–90; Patterson, Henry, *The Politics of Illusion: A Political History of the IRA* (London: Serif, 1997) pp. 126–7; Purdie, *Politics in the Streets,* p.125.
28. Quoted in Bob Purdie, *Politics in the Streets,* p. 129. Purdie is quoting an extract from *An tOglach (The Volunteer),* a secret IRA publication. This and other extracts were read aloud in Stormont by William Craig in June 1968 in an effort to support claims that the IRA was using the civil rights movement as a front for its programme to unite Ireland.
29. A small group of IRA volunteers, led by Richard Behal, refused to accept the new departure and went on a small bombing spree in the Republic in opposition to both the Goulding faction and Lemass's friendlier relations with both O'Neill and the UK government. The group attacked a British torpedo boat in Waterford harbour in August 1965, then blew up a telephone exchange in Kilkenny in February 1966, before blowing up Nelson's column in Dublin in March. See Kelley, Kevin, *The Longest War: Northern Ireland and the IRA* (London: Zed, 1988) pp. 89–90.
30. Ibid., p. 90.
31. Rose, Richard, *Governing Without Consent* (London: Faber, 1971) p.189.
32. Ibid., p. 213.
33. N.I. Home Secretary (Craig) estimated IRA numbers as approximately 3,000 activists and supporters. O'Neill claimed in a letter to Labour Home Secretary Frank Soskice that IRA preparations were equivalent to 1956; RUC claimed there were thirty-four training sessions in the South and requested that Wilson put pressure on the Irish government to clamp down on the IRA. O'Neill to Soskice, 4 April 1966, PREM 13/980, PRO Kew.
34. Frank Wright, *Northern Ireland: A Comparative Analysis* (Dublin: Gill and Macmillan, 1987) pp. 184–200.
35. Arthur, Paul, *Government and Politics of Northern Ireland* (London: Longman, 1984) p. 93.

36. Bew, Gibbon and Patterson, *Northern Ireland 1921–1996,* pp. 176–8; Farrell, *The Orange State*, pp. 240–3; O'Leary and McGarry, *Politics of Antagonism,* pp.162–5.
37. Robert Lundy was the Governor of Londonderry who attempted to surrender to the forces of the Catholic King James II in 1689 during the siege of Londonderry.
38. Nelson, Sarah, *Ulster's Uncertain Defenders: Protestant Political, Paramilitary and Community Groups and the Northern Ireland Conflict* (Belfast: Appletree Press, 1984) pp. 49–53.
39. Quoted in Cameron Report, pp. 118–19.
40. Spence was released in 1997 and lent important weight to the UVF's support for the Good Friday Agreement (1998).
41. Rose, *Governing Without Consensus,* p. 192.
42. N.I.H.C., vol. 70, cols 1022–3, 16 October 1968.
43. Farrell, *The Orange State,* pp. 239–56.
44. H.C. 5th Series, vol. 782, col. 320, 22 April 1969, emphasis added.
45. Cameron Report, pp. 71–6.
46. Nelson, *Ulster's Uncertain Defenders*, pp. 87–93.
47. Purdie, *Politics in the Streets,* pp. 138–58.
48. Patterson, *The Politics of Illusion,* pp. 126–7.
49. Cameron Report, p. 46
50. Flackes, W.D. and Elliott, Sydney, *Northern Ireland: A Political Directory 1968–88* (Belfast: Blackstaff, 1989) pp. 303–4.
51. Farrell, *The Orange State,* p. 254.
52. Bruce, Steve, *The Red Hand* (Oxford: Oxford University Press, 1992) pp. 30–1.
53. N.I.H.C., Vol. 803, Col. 206, 3 July 1970; cf. Rose, *Governing Without Consensus,* pp. 108–9.
54. H.C. 5th Series , vol. 782, col. 306, 22 April, 1969.

4

From Civil Rights to Civil War: 1966–1972

There are two Germanies, two Koreas, two Indias, two Vietnams, two Palestines, even, God help us, two Cypruses, and, at the moment, two Nigerias ... I have enumerated these other cases of, oppression if you like, partition if you like; but can anyone point to one in which there has been so little effusion of blood as there has been in Ireland since that Treaty?

Quintin Hogg, Conservative MP[1]

... [I]t was not until heads were broken in Londonderry that the attention of the British Press, public and Parliament was focused on Northern Ireland. It was not until violence again erupted in Derry and other parts of Northern Ireland this weekend that the Unionist Chief Whip announced the possibility of universal suffrage in local government elections, a principal plank in the civil rights campaign.

Paul Rose, Labour MP[2]

The cycles of violence produced by the confused intervention created new challenges to the regulation of old conflicts, exposing the issues that had been fudged in the Government of Ireland Act (1920) and the Anglo-Irish Treaty (1921). This chapter analyses the dynamics of the slide from civil rights protests to civil war and considers the implications for the more general understanding of relationships between nationalism and statehood (including territoriality); governance in contested nation-states (including policing, security, counter-insurgency policies) and political and social mobilization. Above all, it will focus on the legacy of the national status conflicts and the effects of contested British–Irish relations on the escalation of conflict.

BRITISH AND IRISH ELITE PERCEPTIONS OF THE PROBLEM

Given what appeared to be obvious splintering and out-flanking within both nationalist and unionist blocs during the escalation of civil rights protest in 1968 and 1969, how did the governments respond to this escalation? The dominant view within the British Labour government was that Northern Ireland was expendable as a constituent territory of the United Kingdom, but only by agreement between both parts of the island. But consensual re-unification appeared to officials as a distant prospect given unionists' political, social (including religious) and economic antagonism towards Irish reunification. Given these obstacles, the risks for Britain in pushing for reunification were, in Lustick's terms, 'regime-threatening': potentially causing 'civic upheavals, violent disorders and challenges to the legitimate authority of governmental institutions...'[3] Of course there were differences in approach among British government departments: the Dominions Office was naturally more inclined to maintain good relations with the Irish government while the Home Office was more inclined to leave well enough alone and sustain or at least placate unionist governments.[4] Northern Ireland remained, in Paul Arthur's view, a 'sideshow' useful for deflecting attention from more proximate interests such as the sterling crisis.[5]

The contrast between the British government's public and private justifications of non-intervention exemplified the confused approach. Then Home Secretary James Callaghan later recalled: 'There was not at that stage any real long-term planning: we were living from hand to mouth and making policy as we needed to.'[6] In April 1969 he told the Commons:

> The Government's approach has sprung from the simple conception that these problems are most likely to be solved successfully and permanently if the people of Ireland (sic) solve them. They have the institutions. They have a Parliament and a Government. The Government are supported by some, rejected by others.[7]

Privately, the government's first priority was to avoid a backlash from Protestant loyalists. As Callaghan emphasized to the cabinet:

> [O]ur whole interest was to work through the Protestant government. The Protestants are the majority and we can't afford to alienate them as well as the Catholics and find ourselves ruling Northern Ireland as a colony.[8]

Violence filled the vacuum created by these contradictory positions. From 14 August the number of British troops increased from the standing figure of 2,500 to 4,000 on active duty and by the beginning of September 6,000 British troops had been brought to Northern Ireland. Eight civilians were killed on the night of 14/15 August and 145 civilians and four RUC members were wounded.[9] While the violence merely reinforced the segregation of Derry/Londonderry, in Belfast it led to the largest forced population movement in Europe since the Second World War. Between July and the end of October 1969, approximately 1,820 families (83 per cent of which were Catholic, representing 5.3 per cent of all Catholic households in Belfast) were forced out of their homes as loyalists attempted to ethnically cleanse parts of west and north Belfast.[10] At least 170 homes and sixteen factories were destroyed by fire on the night of 14/15 August alone.[11]

As violence escalated, the Irish government shifted from its functional integration approach to more overt and opportunistic pressure for constitutional change. For example, the approach since the mid-1960s of seeking 'an adequate marriage settlement' for the 'Northern Ireland daughter',[12] and using the joint

British–Irish bid for EEC membership to lubricate the integrationist mechanism,[13] shifted to a more confrontational approach. On 13 August the Irish Prime Minister, Jack Lynch, declared that the Irish government could 'no longer stand by and see innocent people injured and perhaps worse'. He also threatened to call for a UN peace-keeping force, announced the mobilization of 2,000 reserves of the defence force and the establishment of field hospitals along the border. Most tellingly, he declared that since

> the reunification of the national territory can provide the only permanent solution for the problem, it is our intention to request the British Government to enter into early negotiations with the Irish Government to review the present constitutional position of the 6 counties of Northern Ireland.[14]

By late 1969 and the spring of 1970 Irish officials were advising government that the 'short-term policy of doing nothing to rock the boat while privately making our views known to London and insisting on reforms has been successful but it is not enough by itself. The vital necessity of local government reform is still under examination... *but thereafter the whole field of policy in relation to the North remains to be decided.*'[15] A careful balance was attempted between pressuring the British government and antagonizing it. This tension was revealed in the Irish government's deliberations over its approach to the UN, where the Irish government had to avoid recognizing the British claim to sovereignty over Northern Ireland to emphasize partition as the root cause of conflict.

> [T]actically it might be inadvisable to include in the Memorandum any references to the right of Self-determination or similar political concepts. The most appropriate title for the item would seem to be 'The Situation in the North of Ireland' which has the advantages of avoiding the use of provocative terms such as Six Counties as well as making it more difficult for the British to argue that under Article 2.7 of the charter, the UN had no right to intervene in matters which are essentially within the jurisdiction of any State. This would preclude our spokesman in the course of the debate from relating the present crisis in the North to the root cause from which it springs, namely, the unnatural division of our country and urging the resolution of that problem.[16]

The outcome of these deliberations followed a familiar pattern. The absence of an intergovernmental relationship and the statist bias of the international legal position meant that Irish governments had limited means of advocating on behalf of the nationalist minority or pursuing Irish unity. A semi-constitutional conduit followed. While it is extremely doubtful that Lynch was prepared to launch an invasion, a group of Irish cabinet members, including Neil Blaney and future Taoiseach Charles Haughey, were later accused of supplying funds and attempting to procure arms for neighbourhood 'defence committees' which inevitably included members of the IRA.[17] Charges against Blaney were dropped and Haughey was acquitted. Nevertheless, strong suspicions survived that members of the Irish government not only supplied arms and money to groups in the North, but that they specifically encouraged a split to weaken the Marxist wing (which became the Official IRA) and favour the physical-force wing which became the Provisional IRA (PIRA).[18]

It is likely that the split within the IRA would have occurred without intervention from the Republic, but the unauthorized actions of members of the Irish government had several important effects: Fianna Fáil's push undoubtedly encouraged the PIRA in their strategic calculations as to the efficacy of violence in moving the conception of the Northern Ireland 'problem' into a tip towards a British consideration of Irish unity. It also created (or revealed) a schism within Fianna Fáil that lasted, in some views, for two decades.[19] In turn, the Republic's ambiguously bellicose posture helped the British government justify its intervention, not as a neutral arbiter, but 'in aid of the civil power' i.e., the Stormont government.

Even if the Wilson government was inclined to promote eventual unity, in the short term it viewed the Irish government's confrontational defence of Catholics in Northern Ireland as counter-productive. Lynch repeatedly emphasized to Wilson in their meeting in London on 30 October 1968 that 'the basic cause of the situation in Northern Ireland was Partition', to which Wilson replied that '"banging of the drum" would only make conditions worse than they were and would be of little help to the Taoiseach's co-religionists, whose problems in Northern Ireland were recognised by him [Wilson].'[20]

INTERVENTION: THE MICRO-MANAGEMENT OF CIVIL DISORDER

The first tentative steps towards engagement and the ambiguous goals of the intervention reflected the British government's continued reluctance to intervene in Northern Ireland. Following the riots of August 1969 the British army was sent in under Clause 75 of the Government of Ireland Act[21] to intervene 'in aid of the civil power'. In October, the government moved to placate nationalist grievances against the excesses committed by the Protestant-dominated Ulster Special Constabulary or 'B Specials' by disbanding it. Its replacement, the Ulster Defence Regiment (UDR), was a regiment of the British army and therefore controlled, ultimately, from Westminster.[22] While the RUC was nominally under the direction of the army's General Officer Commanding (GOC), in fact it retained separate, and from the army's point of view, totally inadequate, intelligence-gathering networks. Thus the central lesson from counter-insurgency studies – that civil and military commands be integrated – was not applied.[23]

The absence of forethought reflected the unanimous opinion within the Wilson cabinet that the intervention of troops was a temporary expedient to simply 'restore order'. On the ground the situation appeared different, as urban frontiers – 'no-go' areas – provided challenging terrain. After a quick baptism in the intricacies of street fighting in Northern Ireland, the GOC, LG Sir Ian Freeland, was asked by the Stormont cabinet how long it would take for his men to 'repossess' the Bogside. He replied, 'three hours to take over and about three years to get out again'.[24] This ten-fold underestimate underlines shrouded views produced by decades of benevolent detachment.

The British government's response was also an attempt to apply another classic counter-insurgency strategy: the separation of militant extremists from their social base through the intentional combination of coercion and conciliation. The Downing Street Declaration (19 August 1969, not to be confused with the 1993 Declaration) declared on one hand that troops would be withdrawn once law and order was restored, and on the other hand recognized the legitimacy of most of the civil rights movement's demands, declaring that local government elections would be held under 'one man one vote' and hinting that the B Specials would be phased out. This particular strategy was clearly influenced by 'relative deprivation' theories, which happened to be the orthodox explanation for public disorder and political violence in the advanced democracies.[25] An economic development programme published in 1970 stated that the 'root cause' of civil unrest could be solved by reducing unemployment and improving housing.[26] This report was in turn influenced by the Cameron Commission's findings, which described the early disorders as a result of 'a sense of resentment and frustration at the failure of representations for the remedy of social, economic and political grievances'.[27] While there is little doubt that grievances did produce frustration, the return of militant republicanism and militant loyalism were also revivals of opposing national projects. Unlike the civil rights movement in the United States, where challenges did not extend to nation-state legitimacy and territorial boundaries, the Northern Ireland conflict remained predicated on opposing self-determination claims.

By the spring of 1970 the Labour government realized that the conflict had escalated beyond the reform agenda of the civil rights movement, towards a state-level conflict over contested sovereignty. Yet a complacent approach to state-craft is evident:

> Although it was impossible to forecast the future course of events with any accuracy, it was clear that the whole Irish problem was once more on the move and that there would be pressure for fundamental changes *going far beyond what was at present contemplated*. In these circumstances, it was important to get a dialogue going with the Government of the Irish Republic after the reports [Cameron and Hunt] had been published... Nevertheless, if there were to be any prospect of a final solution, relations between the North and South of Ireland, and between the South and the United Kingdom must be lifted to a different plane. As things stood at present this was likely to take a long time.[29]

Was it thinkable for the British government to achieve at least temporary control? Callaghan warned Chichester-Clark that a long-term commitment of British troops would be 'all or nothing',[30] meaning the suspension of Stormont and the introduction of direct rule from Westminster.[31] Thus while the Wilson government was aware of the dangers of an ambiguous and partial intervention, and also aware that the conflict had escalated beyond the civil rights demands, the pattern of policy-making was still reactive and reluctant. The effects on moderate unionism and nationalism were devastating.[32]

For many in the unionist establishment and among the loyalist grass-roots, the intervention of the army and the diplomatic concessions to nationalists were treated as a forced capitulation to the combined civil rights/republican movement. The publication of the Cameron report in September and the Hunt Report in October magnified loyalist anger. Cameron essentially upheld the validity of the grievances enunciated by the civil rights movement over gerrymandering, discrimination in both housing allocation and public sector employment, and the absence of universal suffrage in local government.[33] He also condemned the lack of discipline within, and composition of, the RUC and the UDR. The Hunt report recommended that the RUC be disarmed and the B Specials stood down, to be replaced by the Ulster Defence Regiment under the command of the British army.[34]

With clear echoes of the Home Rule emergencies and the perceived need for forceful resistance against British apostasy, loyalist rioting intensified in September and October of 1969. By the spring of 1970, unionist hardliners were separately organizing their opposition to Chichester-Clark, who in March was forced to expel five MPs from the Unionist Party, including William Craig and Harry West, for failing to support the government on a no-confidence motion.[35] In April, Paisley entered constitutional politics by winning a by-election in O'Neill's former Bannside constituency, while another anti-Chichester-Clark candidate, the Rev. William Beattie, won the South Antrim seat in another by-election. Paisley repeated his success in the June Westminster election by taking the North Antrim seat.

The famous pictures of British soldiers being served tea by women in nationalist areas represented a false dawn as the belated and partial reforms could not stem the radicalization in both communities. In several areas, army officers negotiated with local defence committees and had barricades removed, but the majority of the barricades remained until the middle of September. The army's first major project, the construction of a corrugated steel and barbed wire 'peace line' separating the Falls Road and Shankill Road may have separated rioters but it also reinforced the segregation of West Belfast into Catholic/nationalist and Protestant/loyalist sections. Behind the barricades the IRA was regrouping. The split within the IRA between Marxists and doctrinaire republicans was accelerated by the violence of August. In Belfast the IRA was caught unprepared both organizationally and militarily when called on to defend nationalist areas. When street violence erupted the IRA had been noticeably absent, except for a few scattered individuals who were able to mobilize arms. Ridiculed in their own community with slogans such as 'IRA = I Ran Away', the expanding core of IRA members in Belfast formed the nucleus of the Provisional IRA (PIRA).

The radicalization of a substantial minority of the nationalist community demonstrated how reactive and piecemeal intervention exposed underlying sources of national conflict. The motive of neighbourhood defence quickly transformed, according to Richard English, into a 'pride in resistance' and then retaliation against what many nationalists felt were aggressive policing and army tactics. English also recognizes that PIRA military and political strategy became dominant over the Official IRA because the former more effectively responded to local grievances *and* traditional republican, Catholic, anti-British and anti-imperial ideologies.[36] Thus the complaints over unjust policing resonated with the more general non-recognition of the legitimacy of government at Stormont. Emergent republican leaders like Gerry Adams justified physical-force tactics as necessary responses to failed constitutionalism and moral force protests of the Nationalist Party and the civil rights movement respectively. Republican heroes and martyrs were recalled from the United Irishmen of the 1790s through the Fenian/IRB uprisings of the 1860s and the revivalists of 1916. Finally, the political programme published as *Éire Nua* in 1971 emphasized not only the right of self-determination of the Irish nation, but proposed a form of government for the island based on a federation of the four 'ancient' provinces of Ulster, Munster, Connaught and Leinster. Whether these proposals were influenced directly by the confederacy of the 1640s is uncertain. But it is clear that dominant conception of Irish national rights of self-determination underpinned challenges both to 'British imperialism' and the entities produced by partition: the Irish Free State and Northern Ireland. A selective interpretation of history demonstrated to the IRA leaders that terrorism had been successful in driving the British out of Palestine, Cyprus and, most recently, Aden. The PIRA's initial target of thirty-six soldiers was based on the number of British soldiers killed in Aden in 1967 believed to have precipitated British withdrawal. The pedigree of both British loyalist and Irish republican ideas in no way determined political and paramilitary responses but they help explain their resonance in a time of emergency.

MAUDLING THROUGH: MEDIUM-DOSE REPRESSION AND RADICALIZATION

Wilson's Labour government was unexpectedly defeated in the general election of June 1970 and a new Conservative government was formed, with a majority of only thirty in the House of Commons and Edward Heath as Prime Minister. The Conservatives, with Reginald Maudling as Home Secretary, were faced with the choice of attempting to implement reforms through a weakened Stormont government, or to impose direct rule. They opted to continue the Labour policy of detached intervention for several reasons. First, the traditional links within the 'Conservative and Unionist party' made them less likely to revoke Stormont's powers. Second, while they were in agreement with Labour about the need to address nationalist minority grievances they considered street violence as a 'law and order' problem that could only be met with a clear reassertion of British sovereignty, both to settle the unionist government and to counter the Irish government's attempt to internationalize the conflict. As opposition leader, Heath had met Irish Tanaiste (Deputy Prime Minister) and Minister for Foreign Affairs Frank Aiken and had warned against the negative intergovernmental relations stemming from what Heath described as 'Éire's interference in British affairs'.[37] After a British–Irish summit in September 1971 in London, the Conservative Prime Minister Ted Heath told the Irish Taoiseach Jack Lynch that he could not accept that anyone from outside the United Kingdom could participate in meetings to promote the political development of any part of the United Kingdom.[38] Such statements were meant to edify the unionist government but they also reflected the Conservatives' more 'integralist' conception of Northern Ireland's place in the union.

The continuation of confused intervention limited moderates' abilities to compete against ultras in both nationalist and unionist communities. The core of moderate nationalist leaders from the civil rights movement responded to the growing ascendance of the republican movement by forming the Social Democratic and Labour Party (SDLP) in August of 1970.[39] The diverse composition of the party, which included Gerry Fitt and Paddy Devlin from the Northern Ireland Labour Party (NILP), Austin Currie of the Nationalist Party, prominent civil rights activists John Hume, Ivan Cooper and Paddy O'Hanlon and Paddy Wilson of Republican Labour, emphasizes the threat posed by the PIRA to the nationalist middle ground. But the antagonism generated by the army's offensive approach forced the moderate nationalists into symbiotic relations with the republican movement in opposition to security policy, particularly the Special Powers and Criminal Justice Acts.[40]

Following the anti-army riots of 1970, the PIRA stepped up its offensive. Resources began to flow into the movement in the form of radicalized recruits from Derry/Londonderry, Belfast and traditional rural havens such as south Armagh. It was estimated that the PIRA's manpower increased from 100 or so in June 1970 to roughly 800 by December (600 in Belfast, 100 in Derry/Londonderry and 100 elsewhere in Northern Ireland).[41] Arms, explosives and money were flooding in from the Republic and the US where NORAID and other Irish-American groups were encouraged by the PIRA's resurrection of militant tactics.[42] The monthly total of explosions increased steadily from the beginning of 1971 (see Figure 1), the vast majority of which can be attributed to the PIRA, even though they did not begin to claim responsibility for explosions until the second half of 1971.[43]

PIRA violence and the continued existence of 'no-go' areas in Derry/Londonderry and Belfast created pressure within the unionist bloc for more draconian security initiatives. In February 1971, thirteen people were killed, including the first British soldier (Gunner Curtis), and two RUC constables, as riots erupted in Ballymurphy and Ardoyne. A PIRA bomb meant for the army killed five BBC technicians in Tyrone. In March, the PIRA lured three 17-year-old Scottish soldiers from a pub in Ligoniel, a suburb of Belfast, shot each in the back of the head and left their bodies on a country road. These killings surpassed another symbolic threshold as the hardline unionists demanded the re-introduction of internment. However, Chichester-Clark believed, on army advice, that a quick fix of repression would be counter-productive in the already polarized climate. While he declared that Northern Ireland was 'at war' with the PIRA, he knew that it would be an extended campaign rather than a decisive battle. To meet the immediate demand he went to London to ask for 3,000 more troops and when he received only 1,300 he resigned. His successor, Brian Faulkner, attempted to maintain the middle ground by stocking his cabinet with a mix of hardliners and moderates while offering the SDLP indirect participation in government through a committee system to oversee legislation in the lower house of Stormont. Consideration would also be given to restore proportional representation in local elections.[44] The SDLP expressed interest but the logic of escalation intervened in July when the army shot two Catholic youths, Seamus Cusack and Desmond Beattie, in Derry/Londonderry. Witnesses denied the army's claim that the two were either gunmen or bombers. The SDLP demanded an inquiry into the shooting and when the unionist government declined they walked out of Stormont for an indefinite period and attempted to establish 'multiple sovereignty' by calling a nationalist assembly at Dungiven, Co. Derry/Londonderry.[45]

The SDLP walkout was an important conflict regulation failure. Until that moment there was balanced competition between the SDLP and the PIRA for control of the significant minority, wavering between tacit support for rioters and active support for constitutional initiatives.[46] By the spring of 1971 the Provisionals' offensive was destabilizing but it did not enjoy unbridled support across the nationalist community. The early own goals, mistakes and callous killings would not have been tolerated for long if the SDLP had been able to demonstrate progress in achieving significant constitutional reform. The radical nationalist argument that Faulkner's committee system was 'too little too late', while accurate, misses the wider point that Faulkner could not have offered a more substantial constitutional reform package even if he wanted to, because of the out-flanking pressure within the unionist bloc.

Only the British government could have insisted on a root and branch approach to the crisis, but this required addressing the core constitutional issues of nationalism and sovereignty. Privately, consideration was given to involving the Irish government in a form of joint-sovereignty over Northern Ireland. A report to the British cabinet by the Central Policy Review Staff in September 1971 proposed that defeating the IRA and restoring law and order was a 'negative aim, however desirable' because it 'has no positive content unless it masks a hopeless desire to return to the status quo ante'.[47] A clear indication of the possibility of regime-contraction followed:

> The fact that Northern Ireland is constitutionally part of the United Kingdom is no more or less relevant in terms of political realism than the fact that Algeria was part of metropolitan France...if the six counties ceased to be British...the net saving to public expenditure would be considerable.[48]

Cabinet Secretary Burke Trend's accompanying memo was more guarded, accepting that to let Ulster go totally in the sense of expelling it from the UK is, presumably, unthinkable *in the current climate*. But is it less unrealistic to think in terms of an arrangement which would give Dublin not complete control over Ulster (sic), but at least more effective say in its administration? [S]ooner or later, all the parties will be driven to the negotiating table. It will be both more honourable and more economic to go there sooner rather than later.[49]

Prescient remarks. But was Trend's approach viable? On balance, the answer from the cabinet to the pregnant question posed by the CPRS was negative. Despite recognizing that Faulkner was unable to deliver a form of power-sharing acceptable to the nationalist minority,[50] the inclination of Prime Minister Ted Heath and Home Secretary Reginald Maudling was first to establish law and order and then consider more constitutive questions.

The insistence of the British government on distancing itself from the source of the conflict encouraged the Stormont government to use draconian powers. Heath and Maudling were hesitant to undermine the new Faulkner government because they knew that if Faulkner fell, hardliners like William Craig were waiting in the wings. Emphasizing the threats faced from all sides, Faulkner asked in mid-July for permission to introduce internment in exchange for a ban on the Apprentice Boys parade in Derry/Londonderry. Heath resisted initially, but agreed to a trial run on 23 July when 2,000 troops were mobilized in an 'intelligence gathering' operation in republican areas. Finally, even after the army expressed its reservations about both the timing and extent of the planned operation, and in the face of stern opposition from the Irish Taoiseach, Heath agreed to allow the internment operation to proceed on 5 August.

There were at least four significant problems with 'Operation Demetrius', as the internment swoop was labelled. All have implications for counter-insurgency aspects of conflict regulation. First, the scale of the operation was a classic example of the folly of 'medium dose' repression. Some 346 men were arrested on the morning of 9 August (although 116 were released within forty-eight hours). The operation was neither small enough to be acceptable politically to the nationalist community nor large enough completely to immobilize the republican organization. Considering the estimates of the size of the PIRA at 800 and OIRA at 200, the arrest of 350 still left a fair share of militants, not to mention the new recruits inspired by such a draconian sweep.[51] Secondly, attempts to isolate militant republicans from their social base were offset by the decision not to intern loyalist paramilitaries for fear of destabilizing the unionist government.[52] Thirdly, the operation was based on flawed intelligence, partly because the PIRA was a rapidly growing and changing organization and partly because of the strained relationship between the army and the RUC. As a result, the list of suspects was outdated, and many of those arrested were retired rebels who had been active in the 1940s and 1950s; one suspect from Armagh had been dead four years.[53] The practice run on 23 July, necessitated by the intelligence gaps, had tipped off the Provisional leadership, most of whom avoided arrest.

The British government was soon revising its initially positive assessment of internment as violence escalated and criticism mounted from the Irish government over the treatment of detainees and the lack of Protestant/loyalist internees.[54] Reginald Maudling made the curious claim in his memoirs that internment improved the security situation but poisoned the political situation because of the unanimity of Catholic/nationalist opposition.[55] In fact the security situation had deteriorated immediately to new levels of intensity, as shown in Figure 2, with an average of 2.8 deaths per month in the 18 months preceding internment, increasing over ten-fold to 34.3 deaths per month in the following 18 months. Apart from the street violence associated with riots, the sharp increase in the number of explosions demonstrated that the Provisional command structure was still intact. On 5 September they boldly issued a demand for a truce.[56]

While their offensive began before internment, it is indisputable that internment allowed it to turn an offensive into a campaign because it united the nationalist community in opposition to Stormont. The nationalist reaction echoed the rise of Sinn Féin following the execution of the leaders of the Easter Rising in 1916, and again following the internment of Sinn Féin leaders and subsequent force-feeding of hunger-strikers. By October, 26,000 families were on a rent and rates strike; the nationalist areas of Derry/Londonderry and Belfast were sealed off by barricades; an organization called the Northern Resistance Movement (NRM) was formed by PD in cooperation with the Provisionals, while NICRA was effectively under the control of the OIRA.[57] Nationalist politicians of various hues became united as 'anti-unionists'; hundreds resigned from local government positions and public appointments. The alternative assembly at Dungiven failed after two sessions because the basis for any moderate nationalist response was obliterated by the ascendancy of the Provisionals.[58]

The escalation of PIRA violence led directly to the fragmentation of the unionist bloc as loyalists mobilized in response to both the PIRA escalation and Faulkner's Unionist Party that had, in their view, lifted their thumb. In September the Ulster Defence Association (UDA) was formed as a unifying organization for the myriad neighbourhood defence associations that had sprung up since internment. By the beginning of 1972 the UDA had roughly 40,000 members and was closely linked to the powerful Loyalist Association of Workers (LAW).[59] Former members of the B Specials formed the Ulster Special Constabulary Association (USCA) in April, 1971 with a membership of roughly 10,000 (including members who had joined the new UDR). In December of 1971 the UVF took its first major offensive action by planting a bomb in McGurk's pub in Belfast, killing fifteen Catholic/nationalist civilians. It is indicative of the degree of polarization that had taken place that Faulkner, whose internment strategy had led directly to an upsurge of violence, was being criticized by Paisley and William Craig as too soft on republicans. Paisley, with lawyer Desmond Boal, formed the Democratic Unionist Party in September 1971 to oppose the Ulster Unionist Party while Craig began to mobilize grassroots opposition to Faulkner.

The Conservative government's response to the fragmentation of the unionist bloc was to reassert Westminster sovereignty over law and order, eliminate the 'national question' with a border poll and then establish a devolved power-sharing government for Northern Ireland.[60] The release of state papers from this era reveals familiar, pragmatic and reactive policy-making. A report, 'Northern Ireland: Contingency Planning', presented to the government in July 1971, considered three primary options, reflecting the spectrum from coercion to consent.[61] The coercive option of radical social engineering by population transfer and re-partition was ruled out. At the other extreme, an inclusive process, including talks with the Provisional IRA and more formal cooperation with the Irish government, was also ruled out because it was believed that formal contacts with either would undermine Faulkner's fragile hold on unionist government. The intermediate option was to harass the PIRA and OIRA leaderships while pressuring unionists and moderate nationalists to accept power-sharing along the lines of Faulkner's committee system.

'Soldiering on' was counterproductive. The number of internees increased from the initial run of 346 to 924 by April 1972. Troop levels had been increased from 6,000 to 14,000 and the army began to take a more offensive posture against rioters and suspected accomplices, killing twenty-nine civilians in the five months between August 1971 and January 1972. When the Heath government finally offered a peacemaking initiative in October 1971, in the form of a green paper, the SDLP was in no position to sell it to the nationalist community because the PIRA campaign was in full swing. In any case, the initiative was insubstantial because it largely repeated the committee offer made by Faulkner in June.

Perhaps the most damaging development, one rarely emphasized by commentators on this eventful period, was the breakdown of bi-partisan agreement on 'benevolent detachment'. This shift meant that the Labour opposition at Westminster now viewed the *status quo*, rather than Irish re-unification, as 'regime-threatening'. In response to the Conservatives' failure to either keep or make peace, Labour opposition leader Harold Wilson broke ranks in November by issuing a proposal for a united Ireland (within fifteen years) in exchange for the Republic joining the Commonwealth,[62] a clear u-turn from his 1969 declaration that the 'responsibility for affairs in Northern Ireland is entirely a matter of domestic jurisdiction'.[63] Wilson's unilateralism went even further in March 1972 when he held secret talks with PIRA leaders, just after the bombing of the Abercorn restaurant, which had killed two and injured over 100. The talks led nowhere, but the PIRA was bolstered by its success in bombing its way to such high-level negotiations and rationalized that it could see out the Conservative government with an escalation of violence, then invite a succeeding Labour government to implement its re-unification policy.[64]

The disastrous internment policy set the stage for what could be interpreted as a conspiracy towards a British entrance strategy to impose direct rule. In a cabinet meeting on 1 December 1971, the Prime Minister summed up the meeting with a chilling warning that if the army could repress the PIRA and create a breathing space for a new political initiative, 'we might come to a point where we might have to run the risk of precipitating a situation in which direct rule becomes inevitable', despite unionists' attachment to Stormont.[65] The crisis created by 'Bloody Sunday' on 30 January 1972 did, intentionally or not, create such a pretext. On 30 January 1972 NICRA organized a march in Derry/Londonderry. Northern Ireland Home Secretary William Craig banned the march but the organizers ignored the ban. The army knew that the NICRA leadership was by then dominated by members of OIRA, so it planned to sweep up the leadership during the march. The Parachute Regiment was specifically drafted in for the operation. The dispute over the initial act of provocation goes on to this day, but the result was that the members of the Parachute Regiment opened fire on the demonstrators, killing thirteen unarmed civilians. Lord Widgery's investigation into Bloody Sunday, which exonerated the soldiers and laid most of the blame on the organizers of the illegal march, was the last straw for Stormont as the reaction reverberated around the world. In Dublin a crowd of more than 20,000 burned down the British embassy, while in the Commons, MP Bernadette Devlin physically assaulted the Home Secretary Reginald Maudling. Faulkner was called to Westminster and told that all security powers were to be taken away. He resigned and on 24 March 1972 the government at Stormont was prorogued.

CONCLUSION

The similarity in the evolution of strong nationalist symbiosis between 1912 and 1918 and the civil rights period is not coincidental. In both cases, the seemingly irresolvable clash over national status was avoided in favour of a partial 'solution'. In this case the conflict was wishfully interpreted as one based primarily on socio-economic grievances (by Labour government and moderate unionists) or, alternatively, as a question of law and order (by both the Conservative government and more hard-line unionists). The slide to civil war demonstrates the direct relationship between nationalism and state legitimacy as the core conflict over sovereignty re-emerged and eclipsed the subsidiary problems of minority rights and security policies. In particular, these events demonstrate how reactive and partial intervention exacerbated internal fragmentation within the nationalist and unionist communities by demonstrating to the challengers that the state was only moveable and defensible by force. Instead of separating extremists from their social base, the confused intervention drove recruits into the PIRA and united the wider nationalist community in opposition to Stormont. In turn, the failure to achieve a decisive level of control during 1968 and 1969 contributed to unionist fragmentation and loyalist counter-violence against nationalists. Finally, the polarization strained British–Irish intergovernmental relations as the Fianna Fáil government felt compelled to internationalize the conflict both diplomatically through the UN and through covert, un-sanctioned gun-running by members of the Irish government.

The next chapter develops the implications of these policy failures for the theory and practice of conflict regulation through power-sharing.

Notes

1. H.C. 5th Series, vol. 782, col. 313, 22 April 1969. Quintin Hogg later became Lord Hailsham of St. Marylebone.
2. H.C. 5th Series, vol. 782, col. 313, 22 April 1969. Paul Rose was chairman of the Campaign for Democracy in Ulster (CDU) from 1965 to 1973.
3. Ian Lustick, *Unsettled States, Disputed Lands*, p. 45. For Lustick, the status of a national territory that has achieved the 'ideological hegemony' stage represents a non-negotiable conception where 'hegemonic beliefs prevent the question of the future of the territory from occupying a place on the national political agenda'. The conception of a territory in the 'regime stage' means that 'a government interested in relinquishing the area finds itself more worried about civic upheavals, violent disorders, and challenges to the legitimate authority of governmental institutions than with possible defections from the governing coalition or party'. Finally, the conception of a territory in the 'incumbency stage' means that the contest over the integrity of that territory is fought as political bargaining and coalition formation within the confines of 'normal' party politics.
4 See Arthur, *Special Relationships,* pp. 23–4.
5. Ibid., p. 53.
6. Ponting, Clive, *Breach of Promise, Labour in Power 1964–1970* (London: Hamish Hamilton, 1989) p. 340.
7. H.C., 5th Series, vol. 782, col. 320, 22 April 1969.
8. Crossman, Richard, *The Diaries of a Cabinet Minister, Vol. III: Secretary of State for Social Services, 1968–70* (London: Hamilton, 1977) p. 622.
9. Scarman, (The Hon.) Mr Justice, 'Violence and Civil Disturbances in Northern Ireland in 1969, Report of Tribunal of Inquiry', Cmnd. 566 (Hereafter 'Scarman Report') (Belfast: Her Majestey's Stationery Office, 1972); A British army officer's view is provided by Michael Dewar, *The British Army in Northern Ireland* (London: Arms and Armour, 1985) p. 33.
10. John Darby, *Conflict in Northern Ireland: The Development of a Polarized Community* (Dublin: Gill and Macmillan, 1976).
11. Scarman Report, Ch. 1.
12. The *Irish Times* 2 January 1998.
13. 'Partition: Government Policy', 29 December 1969–23 April 1970, 2000/6/101, INA.
14. 'Statement by the Taoiseach', Mr J. Lynch, 13 August 1969, as reproduced in 'Partition: Misc. Correspondence, Resolutions', 2000/6/150, INA.
15. 'Report to Taoiseach and Cabinet by Eamon Gallagher on trip to Derry', 29 March 1970, emphasis added.
16. 'Partition: Government Policy August 1968–August 1969', 2000/6/657, INA.
17. The Central Citizens Defence Committee (CCDC) was led by Jim Sullivan of the Official IRA but, like McKeague's SDA, it also included many members who were unaffiliated with any paramilitary organization such as MPs Paddy Devlin (NILP) and Paddy Kennedy (Rep. Lab.) as well as the local priest, Canon Padraig Murphy. Flackes and Elliot, *Northern Ireland: A Political Directory,* p. 95.
18. Subsequent evidence, including a statement made by Lynch (in a letter to *Irish Independent* journalist Bruce Arnold sent in the early 1990s) claimed that a second reason for sending the army to the border was to stifle or even attack republican sympathizers sending arms and supplies from Co. Monaghan as reported in Brian Dowling, 'Lynch planned military push against republicans', *Irish Independent,* 8 January 2000.
19. Scott Bowman 'The roots of the arms crisis not found yet', The *Irish Times,* 15 January 2000.
20. 'Religious tolerance in Ireland', 99/1/99, INA.
21. Clause 75 of the *Government of Ireland Act* (1920) states:
   Notwithstanding the establishment of the parliament of Northern Ireland or of anything contained in this Act, the supreme authority of the parliament of the United

Kingdom shall remain unaffected and undiminished over all persons, matters and things in Northern Ireland and every part thereof.

22. Rose, *Governing Without Consent*, pp. 130,139–51.

23. Hamill, Desmond, *Pig in the Middle: The Army in Northern Ireland 1969–84* (London: Methuen, 1985) pp.51–67; see also Newsinger, John, *British Counterinsurgency: From Palestine to Northern Ireland* (Basingstoke: Macmillan, 2002).

24. Quoted in Hamill, *Pig in the Middle*, p. 24.

25. The classic study is Gurr, Ted, *Why Men Rebel* (Princeton, NJ: Princeton University Press, 1970).

26. Cunningham, Michael, *British Government Policy in Northern Ireland, 1969–1989: Its Nature and Execution* (Manchester: Manchester University Press, 1991) p. 40.

27. 'Cameron Report', p. 55.

28. By the end of 1969 the death toll reached fifteen, which included the deaths of one member of the RUC and twelve civilians, of which six were Catholic and six were Protestant. Injuries to the security forces alone increased from 379 in 1968 to 765 by the end of 1969. The total of 765 injuries broke down into 711 to RUC and 54 to the army. Royal Ulster Constabulary, 'Chief Constable's Report, 1993'.

29. Cabinet minutes, Cab 128/46, 1970.

30. 'Contingency planning for maintenance of law and order, including military assistance and possible legislation to suspend constitution; part 3', PREM 13/2843, PRO Kew.

31. 'Civil disturbances in Londonderry, October 1968', PREM 13/2841, PRO Kew.

32. Wright, Frank, *Northern Ireland: A Comparative Analysis* (Dublin: Gill and Macmillan, 1987) pp. 210–11.

33. 'Cameron Report', p. 64.

34. Hunt, Baron (Chairman), 'Report of the Advisory Committee on Police in Northern Ireland', Cmd. 535 (Hereafter 'Hunt Report') (Belfast: Her Majesty's Stationery Office, 1969).

35. The five MPs expelled from the Unionist Party by Chichester-Clark were William Craig, Harry West, Desmond Boal, John McQuade and Norman Laird.

36. English, Richard, *Armed Struggle,* pp. 120–31; see also Bishop, Patrick and Mallie, Eamonn, *The Provisional IRA* (London: Heinemann, 1987) p. 140; Mac Stíofáin, Seán, *Memoirs of a Revolutionary* (Edinburgh: Gordon Cremonesi, 1975) p. 143.

37. 'Partition: Government Policy August 1968–August 1969', 200/6/657, INA.

38. Quoted in O'Clery, Conor, 'Why Sunningdale Failed', *Irish Times,* Special Section: The Path to Peace, 24 February 1999, p.2.

39. McAllister, Ian, *The Northern Ireland Social Democratic and Labour Party: Political Opposition in a Divided Society* (Basingstoke: Macmillan, 1977) pp. 29–35.

40. Ibid., pp. 97–113.

41. Buckland, *A History of Northern Ireland,* p.145.

42. NORAID, the Irish Northern Aid Committee, was established in New York in 1969 as a 'relief agency' for the families of activists engaged in the 'war' against the British. Holland has estimated that NORAID provided £5 million pounds to PIRA/PSF between 1969 and 1987. Holland, Jack, *The American Connection: U.S. Guns, Money, and Influence in Northern Ireland* (New York: Viking, 1987).

43. Bishop and Mallie, *The Provisional IRA,* pp. 165–75.

44. Cunningham, *British Government Policy in Northern Ireland,* pp. 44–5.

45. McAllister, *The Northern Ireland Social Democratic and Labour Party,* pp. 104–6.

46. Bishop and Mallie, *The Provisional IRA*, pp.171–2.

47. Bowcott, Owen, 'Heath was Urged to Share Ulster with Dublin', *The Guardian* 1 January 2002. Bowcott summarizes the report of the Central Policy Review Staff, submitted to the cabinet on 3 September 1971.

48. Ibid.

49. Ibid., quoting memo by Sir Burke Trend, accompanying CPRS Report.

50. 'Situation in Northern Ireland', 27 July to 9 September 1971, CAB 164/879, p. 2, PRO Kew.

51.   The army considered several options based on its estimate of the quality of its intelligence and the predicted effect in disabling the organizational capability of the PIRA. The first option was only to round up roughly thirty known leaders, the second was to round up everyone that appeared on any of the various lists (more than 500 altogether). The third was a compromise between the two in which the largest list was pared down to around 350. See Hamill, *Pig in the Middle: The Army in Northern Ireland 1969–84* (London: Methuen, 1985) pp. 55–67.

52.   Draft letter, Heath to Lynch, 8 August 1971, 15/478/8, PRO Kew. The initial reassurance that internment would be a balanced policy against paramilitaries from both communities was deleted (struck through).

53.   Hamill, *Pig in the Middle,* p. 60.

54.   'Situation in Northern Ireland', 18 August, 1971, CAB 164/879, PRO Kew.

55.   Maudling, Reginald, *Memoirs* (London: Sidgewick and Jackson, 1978) p. 185.

56.   The Provisionals' five-point demand included: 'an end to the British forces' campaign of violence; the abolition of Stormont; a guarantee of non-interference in the election of a 9 county Parliament (*Dáil Uladh*); the immediate release of detainees; compensation for those who had suffered from British violence', quoted in Deutsch, R. and Magowan, V., *Northern Ireland: A Chronology 1968–73* (Belfast: Blackstaff Press, 1973) pp. 124–5.

57.   Farrell, *The Orange State,* p. 285.

58.   McAllister, *Northern Ireland Social Democratic and Labour Party,* pp. 112–13.

59.   Bruce, *The Red Hand: Protestant Paramilitaries in Northern Ireland* (Oxford: Oxford University Press, 1992) pp. 49–50, 80–1.

60.   Maudling, *Memoirs,* pp.186–7.

61.   'Northern Ireland: Contingency Planning' 22 July 1971, PREM 14/1010, PRO Kew.

62.   H.C., Fifth Series, vol. 826, col. 1586, 25 November 1971.

63.   Quoted in *The Times* (London) 20 August 1969.

64.   Bishop and Mallie, *The Provisional IRA,* pp. 215–17.

65.   Heath's summary of Cabinet meeting, 1 December 1971, CAB 130/522 p. 13, PRO Kew.

5

From Confusion to Power-Sharing:
the Twin-Tracks to Sunningdale

We speak for the overwhelming majority of the House of Commons so recently elected, that we will not negotiate on constitutional or political matters in Northern Ireland with anyone who chooses to operate outside the established constitutional framework, with non-elected, self-appointed people who are systematically breaking the law and intimidating the people of Northern Ireland – their fellow citizens and our fellow citizens within the United Kingdom.

Harold Wilson, British Prime Minister, 25 May 1974[1]

We need a new vision that will end the old quarrels ... It is either that or return to the old instability with the periodic violence, death and destruction.

John Hume, SDLP Deputy Leader, October 1973[2]

[I]f the British Government were to misjudge the situation and tried to impose a settlement that was clearly unreasonable... then it would be simply impossible for responsible politicians to hold the line and the result would not only be a farcical regional parliament but a disastrous crash into politics by force.

Brian Faulkner, Ulster Unionist Party Leader, 23 November 1972[3]

The fall of Stormont and the re-ascendance of violent politics signalled the failure of the containment strategies adopted by both the British and Irish governments since 1921. The year 1972 was the most violent of the current phase of conflict as 467 people were killed. In the vacuum of authority left by the fall of Stormont, paramilitary groups (both republican and loyalist) openly challenged the monopoly of the legitimate use of force. The same monopoly was still being contested in early 1974 when the 'established constitutional framework' referred to by Wilson above, was launched with the 'Sunningdale' power-sharing executive and assembly. The power-sharing agreement was the most balanced and ambitious conflict regulation strategy attempted by a British government in Ireland since the Home Rule era. Nevertheless, the power-sharing experiment met a similar fate to that of Home Rule: it was suspended amidst threats and deeds from unionists fearful of ascendant Irish nationalism.

This chapter attempts to explain the failure of Sunningdale by emphasizing the contradictions of the twin-track approach, which attempted to defeat terrorists on one track while encouraging moderate nationalists and unionist parties in Northern Ireland to share power on the other. By developing a framework (adapted from Ian Lustick) for analyzing intergovernmental status relations, I demonstrate how the avoidance of the opposing sovereignty claims over Northern Ireland cascaded downwards to impact negatively on nationalist–unionist relations there. This interpretation differs from those that emphasize the internal, Northern Ireland dimensions of the conflict.

COUNTER-INSURGENCY AS CONFLICT REGULATION

Frank Kitson, whose *Low Intensity Operations: Subversion, Insurgency and Peacekeeping* became something of an unofficial manual for the British army in Northern Ireland during the 1970s, emphasized the need to co-ordinate four main elements of counter-insurgency:

- Co-ordination among security agencies and their government
- A conducive 'political atmosphere', created by successful propaganda that de-legitimizes unconstitutional activity
- Intelligence gathering machinery that is sufficiently coordinated to be complementary to security and propaganda policies (above) but sufficiently decentralized to penetrate an insurgent organization at ground level.
- Rule of law that balances the maintenance of constitutional safeguards (such as *habeas corpus)* against proximate threats to physical security.[4]

In the last chapter we saw how the absence of a unified command and medium-dose repression had backfired. In this chapter we can assess elements of the other three strands of the doctrine. Indeed, the 'twin-track' approach pursued by the British government was, consciously or not, an attempt to integrate these four elements. To summarize, one track emphasized security and legal measures to defeat or substantially degrade the PIRA (and, by extension, reduce loyalist retaliation). The other track combined propaganda, reform and persuasion to cultivate support for power-sharing among Northern Ireland's nationalist, unionist and non-aligned politicians.

The Northern Ireland case allows us to test this theory under the particular circumstances of the British–Irish relationship. Charles Townshend, in a historical overview, summarized the imperialist dilemma as follows: 'Ireland still seem[ed] to be at once too metropolitan to permit the colonial-style departures from the "British way" which might allow some sort of forcible pacification, and too colonial to compel adhesion to British standards.'[5] As we have seen, the confused conflict regulation approach was nothing if not the 'British way' of suppressing dissent. It had the hallmarks of quasi-judicial and quasi-military strategies adopted in the nineteenth and early twentieth centuries to combat agrarian and republican violence. The conflict was defined as neither a war nor criminal behaviour, but as an 'emergency' situation which required 'special' legislation. The crucial error in this 'twin-track' strategy, stemming from the unwillingness to face the conflicting national questions, was to assume that the militants within each bloc could be suppressed to facilitate a constitutional settlement. This view, which ignored the considerable official advice going to the British governments, stemmed ultimately from the wishful thinking that the conflict was over Northern Ireland, rather than between Britain and Ireland.

TWIN-TRACK ON BRITTLE RAILS

The first Secretary of State for Northern Ireland, William Whitelaw, attempted to use the interim period between the imposition of direct rule and negotiations with Northern Ireland leaders to 'get on top of the gunmen', and to create a space for the ascendance of moderates from each communal bloc.[6] First, internment was modified to 'detention' under the Detention of Terrorists Order (1972) that introduced an element of quasi-judicial scrutiny to the executive's role in the detainment of suspects.[7] Second, the Diplock Report,[8] published in December 1972, was commissioned specifically to devise a judicial apparatus which would replace internment with a system which would be less overtly provocative, and more politically acceptable to moderate nationalists who were boycotting negotiations while internment was in effect. Lord Diplock, and English judge and Law Lord, recommended that normal jury trials for terrorist-related offences be suspended because of the widespread intimidation of witnesses and jurors, and replaced with single-judge, no-jury courts which became known as 'Diplock' courts. Diplock also recommended that the admissibility of confession evidence be widened; that the RUC and army be given wider powers of arrest; and that schedules of terrorist offences and proscribed organizations be devised. All of these recommendations were subsequently incorporated into the Emergency Provisions Act (EPA, 1973).[9] Third, under pressure caused by a hunger strike being waged in Crumlin Road jail by forty republican prisoners who demanded political status, and desperate to create a breathing space for the besieged army, Whitelaw announced that both republican and loyalist prisoners would be given '*special* category status', which meant that they would be allowed to wear civilian clothing, to have more liberal visiting arrangements and more food parcels. The PIRA interpreted these concessions as *de facto* political status and called off the hunger strike.[10] Whitelaw and his successors would pay a high price for granting political status to republican and loyalist prisoners, but at the time, the short-term gain of placating both the PIRA and the SDLP appeared to outweigh the long-term risks of legitimizing the republican movement and succumbing to the tactic of the hunger strike.[11]

Finally, secret channels of communication were opened up with both the Official and Provisional IRA as the violence escalated following internment.[12] Whitelaw used his powers of review to reduce the number of internees from 924 in March to 243 by the middle of August 1972 (see Figure 3). The secret negotiations led to a ceasefire (a 'truce' from the PIRA's point of view) which lasted from June 26 to July 8, during which time secret talks were held in London between Whitelaw and the PIRA leadership, including Gerry Adams and Martin McGuinness, then in their twenties. However, the Provisionals did not go to London to negotiate but rather to present an ultimatum to the UK government, the essence of which was 'declare your intention to withdraw by 1975 or the war goes on'. They also asked for recognition of the right of the Irish people as a whole to decide the constitutional future of Ireland,[13] an end to internment, the release of all political prisoners, and the immediate withdrawal of the British army to barracks. Whitelaw rejected the package of demands with only formal hesitation and two days after the PIRA leaders returned to Northern Ireland the ceasefire was over. Whitelaw considered himself fortunate that the PIRA was content with political status for its prisoners and believed that it could have done much more political damage if it had at least strung the discussions along with a glimpse of flexibility.

> I was extremely fortunate over this incident. If, as a result of deciding in favour of a secret exploratory meeting, I had become involved in further discussions with the IRA leaders, I would eventually have landed myself in great difficulties. Clearly those ought to have been the IRA tactics. As it turned out, by returning to violence almost at once, they presented me with a considerable advantage. They proved that they were intransigent and that it was the British Government who really wanted an end to violence.[14]

Similarly, Gerry Adams has admitted that the Provisionals lacked negotiating skills and handled the talks badly. 'I think,' Adams reflected in 1993, 'that we would be more mature ... I think I would be able to handle it better.'[15]

M.L.R. Smith has emphasized that the PIRA did not make more out of the negotiations because 'careful evaluation of the utility of armed force has just not been an historical pre-requisite for IRA action'[16] and that the success of the militants in the internal debates[17] revealed a dearth of 'real strategic reasoning behind all the havoc'.[18] Yet the PIRA had seen their campaign succeed in bringing down Stormont, then force Labour (in opposition) to propose a timetable for unity, achieve political recognition for its prisoners, and have its leaders to London for talks. It was by no means clear that violence had outlived its strategic utility. Therefore, the British conflict regulation strategy of encouraging the competition between militants and constitutionalists was counter-productive because it encouraged the PIRA to believe that violence was working, which then undermined the likelihood of a compromise of its demands.

The militants prevailed in the internal PIRA debate that followed the failed negotiations. They had killed sixteen British soldiers in June leading up to the ceasefire; they killed seventeen more in July and nineteen in August. On Friday, 21 July the IRA placed three large car bombs in Derry/Londonderry and twenty-two bombs throughout the city of Belfast, the results of which added to the litany of symbolic watersheds and became known as 'Bloody Friday'. In Belfast, six civilians were killed in the Oxford Street bus station as people sought cover there following warnings of car bombs in nearby streets. On 21 July alone, nine people were killed, seven civilians and two Welsh guards. The month of July 1972 was the bloodiest in the current phase of conflict as republican paramilitaries killed forty-four people, including nineteen members of the security forces and twenty-two civilians. Loyalists responded by killing nineteen civilians and an Ulster Defence Regiment (UDR) soldier.

In response to the PIRA escalation the army was given the green light to go on the offensive. The goal of Operation Motorman was first to 'clear out certain nests of vipers',[19] by removing the barricades which marked the boundaries of the no-go areas in Derry/Londonderry and Belfast; second, to 'establish a continuing presence in all hard areas to dominate both IRA and Protestant extremists. This would neutralize their ability to influence events until a political settlement had been achieved.'[20] Seven extra battalions were drafted in for the exercise and the total strength of the security forces was increased by over 12,000 to stand at 29,411, approaching the force-strength of the mid-seventeenth-century Cromwellian campaign.

While it is clear that the counter-offensive disrupted the PIRA's ability to organize openly, to move armaments and engage the army, its status as an occupying force was entrenched. The number of British soldiers killed by the PIRA did drop significantly from July 1972 to January 1973, then rose through the first half of 1973 and then dropped again through 1975 (see Figure 4). Under the new provisions of the EPA the number of detainees increased back to the pre-ceasefire levels so that by the end of 1973 there were 547 republicans and forty-seven loyalists in custody, and 1,414 persons had been charged with terrorist-related offences.

Nevertheless, the PIRA was sufficiently well-equipped and organized to go underground, regroup and continue its offensive, albeit with a switch in emphasis back to commercial targets in urban areas, including mainland Britain from March 1973, and security force targets in rural and border areas.[21] Bombs per day declined only slightly from 3.8 per day in 1972 to 2.7 per day through 1973.[22]

By forcing the British army to take the offensive, the PIRA was able to regain a large degree of political legitimacy as defenders in the republican strongholds. The army began running undercover intelligence operations with soldiers trained by the Special Air Services (SAS).[23] The number of houses searched in Northern Ireland more than doubled from 17,262 in 1971 to 36,617 in 1972 and doubled again in 1973 to 74,556.[24] The nationalist community was disproportionately subjected to internment: from 1971 through 1976 there were two loyalists interned for every death attributed to loyalist paramilitaries, compared to thirty-five for every death attributed to republicans (calculated from data in Figure 3 above). The high profile of the army made it look once again like an occupying force and the gradual revelation of undercover operations confirmed that it was at war against the militants rather than acting as a neutral arbiter. Hamill described the 'Catch-22':

A great deal of the Army's success was due to better information and intelligence, and a lot of this was gathered by close contact, using intensive patrolling and searching. At the same time, these constant searches, both on the streets and in homes, were perhaps the biggest single bone of contention amongst the Catholics which contributed to their dislike of the Army.[25]

The opportunity to encourage the PIRA to moderate its absolutist demands was wasted because the British conflict regulation strategy was inconsistent, reactive and geared towards containment rather than stable regulation.

The same events that encouraged the PIRA to keep bombing encouraged the majority of the unionist community to believe that the British state was capitulating to republican violence. As in 1912, the result was the development of strong symbiosis in opposition to what they perceived as movement toward a united Ireland and a diminution of Protestant/unionist control within Northern Ireland. The link between constitutional and physical-force movements was personified by William Craig who, throughout 1972, was able to mobilize militant support for his Vanguard movement while remaining a member of the Unionist Party. In March 1972, just a week before Stormont was prorogued, Craig warned a mass meeting in Belfast: 'If the politicians fail it will be our job to liquidate the enemy.'[26] In an attempt to prevent out-flanking by maintaining a broad front, Faulkner brought Craig into the party's policy-making apparatus, where he was directly involved in the formation of the party's call for a return to devolved control over security which was presented at the Darlington Conference in September.

When the British government ignored unionist pleas and presented an outline for an internal power-sharing arrangement and an 'Irish dimension', or institutional role for the Irish Republic,[27] the threats became more explicit. The UVF underlined the threat of a backlash in December 1972 by exploding two car bombs in Dublin that killed two civilians and injured hundreds more. The bombing was timed to influence a vote in the Dáil on an amendment to the Offences Against the State Act to widen the power of the courts to convict suspected terrorists based solely on the Garda's suspicion that someone was a member of a proscribed organization. Following the bombing, which was initially believed to be the work of the PIRA, the cross-party resistance to the draconian judicial measures vanished and the amendment was passed.

In sum, during this period, both republican and loyalist paramilitary groups challenged the British government's monopoly of the legitimate use of force. The success of their respective challenges was due not only to their organizational preparedness but, more fundamentally, to the confused conflict regulation strategy that wavered between control and consent. The narrow coercion and conciliation strategy towards the PIRA convinced their leaders that violence was working. This result exacerbated the competition with the SDLP and encouraged the formation of strong symbiosis between unionist leaders and loyalist paramilitaries who became convinced that violence was justified in defence against the PIRA and against concessions by the British government to nationalists.

The degree to which violence was successful in imposing the Northern Irish question on reluctant Westminster governments is revealed in Figure 5. Between 1964 and 1974, the r-square correlation between the number of deaths resulting from political violence and the amount of debate on Northern Irish political and constitutional matters was .91 (out of 1.0), meaning that *ceteris paribus*, 91 per cent of the variance in debate was accounted for by the death rate. This figure specifically excludes debate on matters of security and violence, which we would normally expect to correlate with deaths.

The symbiotic nationalist alliance, combining moral and physical force, had succeeded in shifting the British conception of the status of Irish nationalist claims. As the next section shows, the Irish government suddenly became involved in the negotiation of a constitutional settlement that confronted once again the opposing claims to sovereignty.

NEGOTIATING SUNNINGDALE: EXCLUSION AND ASYMMETRICAL SOVEREIGNTY

Despite the limited success of the security track, the British government moved steadily to promote power-sharing between nationalists and unionists as the main element of the political track. The sequence of developments along this track will first be outlined to indicate the priorities that shaped policy, followed by a more detailed analysis of British–Irish intergovernmental relations and their impact on conflict regulation before and after the Sunningdale Agreement.

The British government's first priority was, revealingly, to remove the political salience of the border. As Conservative Home Secretary Reginald Maudling recalled: 'There was no prospect whatever of a long-term solution to the political problem *in* Northern Ireland so long as the minds of the politicians and the politically conscious were wholly absorbed with the issue of the Border.'[28] Maudling added: 'The only hope I could see for the future was the creation of a united community *in* Northern Ireland which the Republic would be prepared at least to let live.'[29]

But the near consensus within the nationalist community was that the state-level problem could not be separated any longer from the issues of reform in Northern Ireland, as indicated by the near unanimous nationalist boycott of the border poll. While Catholic/nationalist rejection of the border poll did remind British leaders that an 'Irish dimension' was integral to any settlement, the ethos and structure of the Sunningdale Agreement was still weighted towards an internal Northern Ireland settlement, rather than balanced in a way which reflected the competing claims to sovereignty by Britain and Ireland. The British government's summary of its consultation process could detect only one nexus of consent: 'Whatever their views on sovereignty and citizenship, most of those consulted (although not all) have favoured the restoration of some kind of devolved institutions of government in Northern Ireland.'[30] Furthermore:

> It may be said that these proposals leave much unresolved; and so they do. But it would require either exceptional vision or exceptional foolhardiness to forecast the future development of relationships involving North and South in Ireland, the United Kingdom, and the British Isles and Europe. *But there is much which can usefully be done to defeat terrorism by concerted action throughout Ireland, and to serve the economic and social interests of all the people, North and South.*[31]

The absence of attention to the fundamental nationalist causes of the conflict was directly related to the exclusionary policy of consent towards national self-determination. Could a more inclusive approach have been developed? Perhaps. If we consider the evolution of thinking within the Irish Fianna Fáil government we can at least assert that the border issue could not have been so easily wished away had that government been involved in negotiations. With the escalation of violence, Irish officials' conceptions of the problem had shifted from the reformist, governmental-level emphasis on political and civil rights in Northern Ireland to the state-level question of partition itself. Following the fall of O'Neill in 1969 and the splintering of unionism, the Irish government had shifted towards a policy of applying pressure on the British government to promote Irish unity. For example, Irish Finance Minister George Colley agreed with John Hume's advice prior to a tri-partite summit with the British and unionist governments, that the Irish should ask for official clarification on British objections to Irish unification, to which the SDLP and Fianna Fáil government could respond.[32] While such a traditional approach would certainly have hardened unionist opposition to Irish government involvement in negotiations, it would also have forced the British government to consider root causes of conflict.

Any pressure that might have developed towards confronting the opposing sovereignty claims was eased on 1 March 1973 when Fianna Fáil, who failed to secure a majority in the Irish election of 28 February, was replaced by a Fine Gael–Labour coalition. With a majority of only one seat, and a decisively less 'republican' ethos, the prospects were diminished for evolving a conflict regulation process that was inclusive of core national sovereignty issues – and parties and movements representing those issues. Any prospect of drawing the republican movement into a negotiated settlement was nullified, as the new Irish government intensified draconian security measures aimed at de-legitimizing the IRA.

Without considering the underlying reasons for the fixation with the border, a 'border poll' was organized on 8 March 1973 in an attempt to remove the issue of partition from the process and clear the way for an internal power-sharing deal. The result of the poll was a foregone conclusion as the vast majority of the nationalist electorate rejected it as a valid expression of self-determination. On a turnout of less than 60 per cent, 591,820 supported Northern Ireland's place as part of the United Kingdom against only 6,463 who supported Irish reunification.

The next stage was an election on 28 June 1973 for seats in a new Northern Ireland Assembly. Held under Single Transferable Vote (STV), Faulkner's pro-agreement unionists ('Official' Unionist Party) won only a minority of unionist assembly seats (twenty-one firmly supporting power-sharing while twenty-seven wavered or were firmly against).[33] The nationalist SDLP secured a more substantial mandate within the nationalist bloc, securing 22.1 per cent of the overall vote and securing nineteen assembly seats. Still, the results and the strength of the IRA campaign demonstrated that there was a considerable minority of nationalists who supported the Provisional IRA's maximalist push for a British withdrawal. Combined, the pro-agreement representatives of the unionist and nationalist communities gained forty of the eighty Northern Ireland Assembly seats, while the cross-community Alliance Party (eight seats) and Northern Ireland Labour Party (one seat) added to the pro-agreement side.

The result was the evolution of a British-led process, geared initially towards devolved power-sharing in Northern Ireland, followed by a belated side-payment to nationalists in the form of a Council of Ireland linking Northern Ireland and the Irish Republic. The Conservative British and Fine Gael–Labour Irish governments both believed in an exclusionary approach in which a security offensive against the militants could create an opening for constitutional politicians to negotiate a devolved power-sharing arrangement. Francis Pym, the Northern Ireland Secretary appointed on 2 December, outlined this exclusionary approach in the Commons:

> Throughout these difficult years it has always been said that a solution lay in a vigorous two-pronged approach: a vigorous onslaught against the terrorists, coupled with political advance. That political advance will shortly be a reality, and it must be the earnest hope, desire and indeed, expectation that everyone will now give the new constitution the chance it truly deserves and stand up straight for Northern Ireland . . . [34]

There had been considerable political advance among moderates in terms of the acceptance of the principle of power-sharing, enhanced rights protections and some form of Irish Dimension. But substantial portions of each community opposed these parameters. Competition within the nationalist bloc continued because the core sovereignty issues were excluded, and therefore the framework of negotiations was unacceptable to militant nationalists, represented by the Provisional IRA.[35] The unionist middle was fragmented because the fall of Stormont amidst paramilitary violence led many unionists to lurch towards more extreme 'loyalist' parties such as Vanguard and Ian Paisley's Democratic Unionist Party (DUP). The tipping effect away from pro-agreement unionism was increased when the British government reneged on its commitment given in the power-sharing white paper that the negotiation of the Sunningdale Agreement would include the 'leaders of elected representatives of Northern Ireland opinion'. Instead, the leaders of Vanguard and the DUP were excluded from the negotiations, and immediately formed an anti-power-sharing alliance, the United Ulster Unionist Council (UUUC). Moreover, the broken bi-partisanship was sustained through the negotiating process. In June 1973, Labour Shadow Foreign Secretary James Callaghan remarked that Britain would be 'reconsidering' its position if the power-sharing assembly was 'sabotaged', warning that 'Britain cannot bleed forever'.[36] Despite these ominous signs, the agreement was incorporated into the Constitution of Northern Ireland Act (1973) and the executive was installed on 1 January 1974 with Faulkner as Chief Executive and Gerry Fitt of the SDLP as Deputy Chief Executive.[37]

Michael Kerr has argued that the sequencing of the political process towards Sunningdale reflected a necessary degree of 'creative ambiguity' in order to encourage moderates from each community to move gradually towards compromise on core issues.[38] The sequencing of the political process leading to Sunningdale does lend some support to this idea, but only if we accept the premise that the conflict is a Northern Ireland rather than British–Irish one. If, as I have argued, it is the latter, then the creative ambiguity thesis needs to be considered in terms of relationships between governments of sovereign states with, in this case, competing claims to sovereignty over Northern Ireland.

THEORIZING INTERGOVERNMENTALISM

To gauge the ability and willingness of each government to deliver vital side-payments to compensate for status asymmetry, I adapt Ian Lustick's classification of thresholds for state-building and state-contraction to the British–Irish intergovernmental relationship (see Figure 6). For Lustick, the status of a national territory that has achieved the 'ideological hegemony' stage represents a non-negotiable conception where 'hegemonic beliefs prevent the question of the future of the territory from occupying a place on the national political agenda'.[39] The conception of a territory in the 'regime stage' means that 'a government interested in relinquishing the area finds itself more worried about civic upheavals, violent disorders, and challenges to the legitimate authority of governmental institutions than with possible defections from the governing coalition or party'.[40] Finally, the conception of a territory in the 'incumbency stage' means that the contest over the integrity of that territory is fought as political bargaining and coalition formation within the confines of 'normal' party politics.

To adapt this threshold classification to British–Irish conflict regulation I have made two adjustments to the scheme. First, the exchange relations of the British and Irish governments will be plotted according to a second, vertical dimension that signifies the hierarchy of sovereign status with regard to negotiations and international relations.[41] How, for example, did British governments and officials in relevant ministries conceive of the Irish state's constitutional relations with Britain and Northern Ireland? I specify that intergovernmental negotiations which centre on *mutual* adjustment to core constitutional claims to sovereignty take place above the state-level threshold, whereas negotiations which commit only a particular government to an agreement take place above the government-level threshold. In Figure 6 both Labour and Conservative British governments are placed above the state-level because they are governments of a state (the United Kingdom of Great Britain and Northern Ireland) with internationally recognized sovereignty over Northern Ireland. Both Fianna Fáil and Fine Gael–Labour Irish governments are plotted above the government-level because, while the constitution of their state laid claim to sovereignty over the island of Ireland, this claim was not recognized by Britain or the international community.

A second modification to Lustick's scheme is the explicit differentiation between government and opposition parties where these represent realistic challenges to and restraints on governmental bargaining, especially where proponents of violence see strategic advantage in the policies of governmental opposition parties. Breaks in bi-partisanship among the largest parties in Britain and Ireland had important effects on the strategic thinking of out-flanking paramilitary groups and more extreme 'constitutional' parties. Thus in Figure 6 the placement of the British Labour opposition (1970–4) in the 'incumbency stage' reflects its support, in principle, for a process leading to a united Ireland. As noted, the broken bi-partisanship was a significant fillip for the Provisional IRA because they were led to believe that a future Labour government would deliver a united Ireland. Equally, the lack of bi-partisanship between Fianna Fáil in opposition (1973–7) and the governing Fine Gael–Labour coalition was a significant factor in limiting the latter's ability to offer concessions to unionists.

The relationship between the sovereignty question and internal bloc fragmentation is apparent if we consider the relative status of the two governments during the Sunningdale period. Article 5 of the Sunningdale Communiqué declared that: 'The Irish Government fully accepted and solemnly declared that there could be no change in the status of Northern Ireland until a majority of the people of Northern Ireland desired a change in that status.' This declaration was an attempt to address the conflicting sovereignty claims entrenched in each state's constitution. Thus the Irish declaration reflected only the current Fine Gael–Labour government's position. It did not commit the Irish government to the constitutional change required to eliminate the claims to sovereignty, as expressed in Articles 2 and 3 of the constitution. Therefore, the Irish government of the day was merely recognizing, for its own part, Northern Ireland's place as a part of the United Kingdom. The fact that this status hierarchy reflected the international legal position is of secondary concern for the test of exchange theory. What matters are the empirical effects of the opposing national conceptions of the hierarchy.

The empirical effects of this status hierarchy were immediately apparent. Without the political mandate to rescind or amend Articles 2 and 3, the Irish government could only offer a weaker guarantee to unionists by agreeing that the Council of Ireland would decide policy by unanimity and by an Irish government commitment to 'hand over or try' suspected terrorists. When the Irish Supreme Court declared in January 1974 that the Sunningdale Agreement did not abrogate *de jure* claim to sovereignty over the entire island of Ireland (*Boland v. An Taoiseach*), unionists feared that unreconstructed republicanism would legitimize physical-force republicanism of the IRA and, in the context of an ambiguous Council of Ireland, would, as one member of the SDLP had boasted, 'trundle the North into a united Ireland'.[42] Two of the principal Irish negotiators at Sunningdale (Garret FitzGerald of Fine Gael and Conor Cruise O'Brien of Irish Labour) believed that Faulkner's pro-agreement support was undermined by the absence of an explicit recognition of Northern Ireland's place as part of the United Kingdom.[43]

Moreover, the ambiguity of the powers and decision-making mechanisms of the Council of Ireland severely undermined Faulkner's position because they could, especially in the context of the Boland decision, be interpreted as an embryonic all-Ireland government. To complicate matters still further, the Conservative government called and lost a snap election in February 1974 to face down striking miners in Britain. Unionist opponents of the power-sharing agreement, whose election slogan, 'Dublin is only a Sunningdale away' won eleven out of twelve Westminster seats from Northern Ireland (see Figure 7). With brutal irony, the eleven anti-agreement Ulster Unionist MPs refused the Conservative whip, denying Heath a majority and allowing Harold Wilson to form a minority Labour government.

Despite Labour's conception of the Northern Ireland problem in opposition, the Irish government's inability to solidify regime-contraction (by changing Articles 2 and 3) meant that the two sovereigns retained asymmetrical conceptions of core sovereignty principles. The new minority Labour government was faced more directly with a regime-level threat of civil war and the Irish coalition government could not offer the level of constitutional adjustment required to satisfy unionists. As a result, support for anti-agreement forces within both communities grew. Unionists were clearly worried about Wilson's conception of Northern Ireland as expendable, as expressed in Lord Hunt's description of Wilson's approach to conflict regulation: Wilson believed that

> if only you could find the right gimmick or solution or whatever, this would solve it – you'd do it at a stroke, one bound and *we're free* ... By feeling that there was a sort of golden key – that if only you could find the right constitutional solution everyone would agree with it – he didn't allow sufficiently for the really considerable mistrust and fears and apprehensions on both sides of that community.[44]

Meanwhile, the IRA was bolstered by Labour's questionable resolve. In April 1974 Defence Secretary Roy Mason said: 'Pressure is mounting on the mainland to pull out the troops; equally, demands are being made to set a date for withdrawal.'[45] The power-sharing executive collapsed in May 1974 following a two-week strike by the Ulster Workers' Council (UWC), aligned with the UUUC (described below).

Could the slide away from support for the Sunningdale Agreement have been halted? In his thorough and perceptive analysis of the agreement, Michael Kerr has emphasized that the Council of Ireland was the decisive threat that drove unionists to reject the agreement.[46] This factor was more important than unionist opposition to power-sharing with nationalists in Northern Ireland. If the Irish government had made more of an effort to delete or amend Articles 2 and 3 of the Irish constitution and if the SDLP had been more sensitive to Faulkner's needs for concession on the Council of Ireland, then Faulkner would have been able to hold the unionist middle ground. But the magnitude of these 'ifs' represents more fundamental factors. Both the weakness of the Fine Gael–Labour coalition and the inability of the SDLP to accept a diminution of the Council of Ireland were results, not causes, of the prior national issues. As Kerr's own analysis demonstrates, Articles 2 and 3 were deeply-held representations of unrequited nationalism, as was the dominance of the nationalist strand of the SDLP that insisted on a Council of Ireland with executive powers.

An intergovernmental approach, grounded in the national history of conflict, offers a more persuasive and parsimonious explanation of the failure of Sunningdale. Given the contested claim to sovereignty between Britain and Ireland and the centrality of the issue of partition to both nationalists and unionists in Northern Ireland, it is clear that a minimum condition for stable intergovernmental bargaining was the elevation of the Irish government to the state-level, equal in status as the British government with regard to mutual adjustments to constitutional claims to sovereignty. In all of the rounds of negotiations devising and implementing Sunningdale from 1973 to 1974, core-sovereignty issues (particularly unionist insistence on achieving a change to Articles 2 and 3) were critical to the balance of power within the unionist bloc. Faulkner's bottom line in the Sunningdale negotiations (6–9 December 1973) was that his party's acceptance of a Council of Ireland would require as an exchange the amendment of Articles 2 and 3 of the Irish constitution. Then in March 1974 Faulkner's pro-agreement assembly group decided that the Council of Ireland would only be implemented in exchange for changes to Articles 2 and 3.[47] But the Fine Gael–Labour coalition could not offer such an exchange, even though it was 'thinkable', because of the likelihood that the Fianna Fáil opposition would be able to defeat any attempt to put Articles 2 and 3 to a referendum. While such an approach may have been feasible between 1965 and 1968, the cycle of violence from 1969 raised the salience of the core national issues. A symmetrical exchange of constitutional claims to sovereignty would have required reciprocal changes in the British constitutional claims to sovereignty. But the British government was seeking a solution to the conflict *in* Northern Ireland rather than a fundamental constitutional change. Therefore, in neither the British nor the Irish polity did a clear opportunity exist to make the exchange of core sovereignty claims the foundation of a settlement. As a result, the process was necessarily exclusive of significant portions of each main community and could not reasonably be interpreted as an expression of national self-determination.

For the British Conservative government, at least from 1972 to 1974, the idea of core sovereignty adjustments in the direction of regime contraction was conceivable, but with regime-threatening implications as demonstrated by loyalist mobilization against the Provisional IRA and the growth of anti-agreement unionism. Additionally, the ideological attachment to 'law and order' constrained Conservative conflict regulation, as exemplified most poignantly in the Sunningdale negotiations by Heath's rigid position on maintaining Westminster control over security[48] and his reneging on his previous assurance to end internment. The failure or inability to deliver this vital side-payment to the SDLP meant that, contrary to Garret FitzGerald's subsequent view,[49] the SDLP had to emphasize the importance of the Council of Ireland to compete politically with republicans North and South. This radicalization in turn contributed to the tipping of support away from pro-agreement unionists.

Having assumed responsibility for maintaining the security powers that were denied the power-sharing executive, neither the Conservatives nor the subsequent Labour government showed any determination to, in Pym's words, 'stand up straight for Northern Ireland' by enforcing the Sunningdale Agreement.

THE UWC STRIKE: THE MORAL FORCE OF LOYALISM

[The British government] will not be intimidated or blackmailed into departing from the Constitution Act or from its avowed intention of proceeding with the Sunningdale agreement
NI Secretary Merlyn Rees[50]

Given Wilson's public sympathy for Irish re-unification, unionist uncertainty of the resolve of the new *minority* Labour government to maintain the union, combined with doubt in the ability of the army to defeat republicanism, a majority of unionists supported the UUUC, which was both clearly committed to the union and, through its symbiotic links with the paramilitaries, apparently capable of defending it. The result of the February election undermined the legitimacy of the power-sharing executive and made its components more hesitant to continue to compromise. Faulkner attempted to weaken the Council of Ireland by having it implemented in two stages, first as a Council of Ministers with very limited consultancy roles and only later as a council with a parliamentary tier. But the SDLP was in no position to weaken the Council of Ireland because internment was still in effect and Pym had not kept his promise to release a significant number of detainees.

The UUUC, in some ways mimicking the successful trade union strategy in Britain, incorporated trade unions into a new Ulster Workers' Council (UWC). Like the Land League, the original UVF and the later stages of the civil rights movement, the groundswell of opposition to the established constitutional authority enabled proponents of constitutional and physical-force means to coalesce. The UWC recruited skilled workers from key sections of industry and public works, including, most decisively, the power stations. They also established links with the Ulster Army Council (UAC), formed in December 1973 to unite the leaders of the UDA (including the UFF), the UVF, the Ulster Special Constabulary Association (USCA, made up of former B-Specials) and the Red Hand Commandos (RHC).[51] On the political front, the UWC brought together all of the constitutional anti-Sunningdale forces, including, after an initial period of hesitation, Paisley, Craig and West. Just before the strike, the UAC had warned: 'If Westminster is not prepared to restore democracy, that is, the will of the people made clear in an election, then the only way it can be restored is by a *coup d'etat*'.[52] While matching republican levels of killing, loyalists also maintained barricades and road-blocks to prevent workers from getting to work. On the fourth day of the strike the UVF, without claiming responsibility, detonated three car bombs, two in Dublin and one in Monaghan town, killing thirty-three people.[53]

Given the formation of bloc alignments, a neutral and resolute arbiter would have called for intervention in order to uphold the executive and give the moderate sub-blocs (the SDLP and Faulkner unionists) an advantage in their competition with the radicals. However, the strength of the anti-agreement unionists compared to the weakness of the power-sharing executive required just the type of forceful intervention that the British government had been trying to avoid since 1921. Echoes of the Curragh 'mutiny'/'incident' of 1914 were heard as the army was determined to avoid a two-front war and hesitant to intervene because of the lack of unionist support for the agreement.[54] Wilson then played into the hands of the UWC by making a speech in which he referred to the people of Ulster as 'spongers'.[55] Rees ordered the arrest of a few UDA men and on the tenth day the army was ordered in to man the petrol pumps. The UWC merely threatened to escalate the power-stoppages if the army intervened and on the fourteenth day of the strike Faulkner announced the resignation of the power-sharing executive.

TOWARDS CONTAINMENT: THE CONSTITUTIONAL CONVENTION AND THE 'TRUCE'

The failure of the power-sharing initiative led both the British and Irish governments to distance themselves from an active role in the conflict regulation process. Both governments agreed that a lasting settlement could only come about if the internal parties to the conflict could find common ground, an implicit recognition that neither government had a monopoly on the legitimate use of force required to ensure a constitutional settlement.[56] In June, Liam Cosgrave, the Irish Taoiseach in the Fine Gael–Labour coalition government, declared that people in the Republic 'are expressing more and more the idea that unity or close association with a people so deeply imbued with violence and its effects is not what they want'.[57] In July, Rees announced in the Commons the formation of a Constitutional Convention 'of Northern Irish people, elected by Northern Irish people, and considering the future of the Northern Irish people. We do not think it right that the Government should take a part in the Convention, or should seek to influence either its deliberations or conclusions.'[58]

Rees and others interpreted, wishfully, the mobilization of the Ulster Workers' Council as an indication of the emergence of non-sectarian, progress-ive politics. While unconstitutional politics of the sort practised by the UWC was not, as Pym had declared, 'the British way of doing things',[59] it was the reality of irrational Irish politics. Conservative MP Julian Critchley described the convention as:

> an attempt to persuade those who have recently exercised power to show responsibility, an attempt to persuade the UWC in particular – *where the*

power resides – that it is its turn to exercise a degree of responsibility. *If this is so, then it looks as if at last the problem is being returned to Ireland.* The genius of the first Lloyd George settlement after the First World War was that if the Irish were sufficiently irrational to practise murder in the pursuit of their political ideals, they should have the responsibility for it ... [60]

Bi-partisan confusion was apparent in the elision of the distinction between Rees' conception of the 'Northern Irish people' and Critchley's irrational 'Irish'.

Consistent with this bi-partisan view, Labour's 'normalization' strategy was ultimately a modification of the failed 'twin-track' approach of defeating terrorism while promoting moderates to talk, but not before an initial attempt to entice republican and loyalist extremists into a political process.

In May 1974 proscriptions of both Provisional Sinn Féin and the UVF were lifted and the last detainees were released shortly after. The PIRA leadership was then tempted into a truce after its national and international standing was undermined by the infamous pub bombings in England – in Birmingham, Woolwich and Guildford between August and November 1974 – which killed twenty-eight people and injured hundreds.[61] The PIRA announced a temporary ceasefire at Christmas 1974 and then extended it from 10 February 1975 while unofficial negotiations with representatives of the British government took place that convinced the PIRA leadership that the British government was looking for a way to withdraw.[62] Whether the government's hints at withdrawal were serious or merely a ruse to entice the IRA into a cessation of violence is a matter of continuing debate.[63] It appears that Rees saw an opportunity to strengthen the doves within the PIRA leadership and exploited it in order to reduce the level of violence prior to the Constitutional Convention. This opportunistic manoeuvre backfired because it appeared to both loyalists and unionists that the PIRA had not only bombed its way to the negotiating table after the 'mainland' atrocities, but also that the British government was considering withdrawal. Loyalist violence escalated sharply during the ceasefire and, in the absence of progress in talks with the government, the PIRA was drawn into retaliation. The talks and ceasefire did weaken the PIRA as morale and momentum waned and the security forces took advantage of the ceasefire by stepping up surveillance and the recruitment of informers. As a result of these setbacks, the southern-based leadership of Dáithí Ó Conaill and Ruairí Ó Brádaigh was eventually marginalized by a 'northern command' led by Gerry Adams, Martin McGuinness and others. Given their support for the peace process from the 1990s, it might be tempting to argue that the encouragement of this split was progressive because it encouraged these 'Northern Irish' republicans to accept a partitionist settlement. But in the late 1970s this faction represented the hawks; they quickly moved to re-structure the PIRA into a less pregnable 'cell-structure' and by 1981 had dropped the southern command's federalist *Éire Nua* proposals in favour of a 'long war' seeking a unitary, socialist Republic.

Having failed in its inclusion attempt, the Labour government reverted to a more conventional twin-track approach. On one track, an attempt was made to deny the political legitimacy of militant republicanism and loyalism by 'criminalization': the removal of 'special category status' for prisoners convicted of scheduled offences. Criminalization was combined with 'Ulsterization', which aimed to reduce the front-line role of the British army and replace it with 'police primacy' and the enhancement of the role of the locally recruited Ulster Defence Regiment. The second track – encouraging moderate nationalists and unionists to share power – was modified by removing the central arbitration role of the British government and encouraging the Northern Ireland parties to find their own means of accommodation without pressure from London or Dublin. While a thorough treatment of this period is beyond the scope of this work, we need only note that the two constitutional initiatives (a Constitutional Convention in 1975 and 1976 and the Conservative government's Constitutional Conference in 1979) both avoided consideration of an Irish dimension sufficient to interest the SDLP. Finally, as the next chapter reveals, the attempt to de-legitimize republican and loyalist paramilitaries backfired spectacularly.

CONCLUSION

The cardinal aim of our policy must be to influence Northern Ireland to solve its own problems. It is still my view that there will be a settlement only when both communities in the Province desire it, work in cooperation to rid themselves of their extremists, and of *their own free will* produce terms that are acceptable to both, with Britain at hand to urge and to nudge them forward.

James Callaghan, British Prime Minister (1976–9).[64]

The fact that Callaghan was self-evidently repeating his advice given to Labour colleagues ten years earlier reveals either a sincere conviction of the insignificance of the Irish dimension or, less charitably, a refusal to learn from past mistakes. Maybe a more instinctive approach was called for. We saw in the previous chapter that Callaghan had predicted the descent along the 'road to hell' caused by the failure of protest to secure reforms. We then saw that the first instinct of Callaghan's successor as Home Secretary, Reginald Maudling, was to address the border issue since it was so prevalent in the minds of nationalists and unionists. Then with direct rule, the first Northern Ireland Secretary, William Whitelaw, had been tempted by his first instinct to negotiate directly with the Provisional IRA. Finally, Labour Northern Ireland Secretary Merlyn Rees' first instinct was also to try to talk to the gunmen. The instincts of all of these home and Northern Ireland secretaries were therefore based on addressing first principles: the border and the relationship between nationalism and state legitimacy.

First instincts gave way to pragmatic measures as the difficulties of solving or regulating the opposing first principles of nationalists and unionists were formidable. But the unwillingness or inability to appreciate the bi-national roots of conflict contributed directly to its escalation. From 1972 to 1973 the confused twin-track strategy exacerbated competition within both blocs because initial negotiations with the PIRA convinced them that violence was working, and by extension, convinced loyalists that violence was required to defend the status of Northern Ireland. As a result, the brief opportunity to cultivate a hurting stalemate that existed in mid-1972 was lost. In the context of a hot war, pressure increased for a deal to relieve domestic and international pressure on both governments. But, in the absence of stable intergovernmental relations, the Sunningdale Agreement had to obfuscate the core national questions while leaving the (successfully contested) monopoly of legitimate force with the British government.

This period of British–Irish relations presents at least one clear implication for both counter-insurgency and conflict regulation: the attempt to co-ordinate security measures with power-sharing and other political and economic reforms is unlikely to succeed if there is a fundamental sovereignty dispute between external 'kin-states'. Instead, as Stefan Wolff and Michael Kerr have both emphasized in their comparative studies of Northern Ireland, such kin-states need, at a minimum, to reach agreement bi-laterally on mechanisms of self-determination and other subordinate parameters of power-sharing and minority rights protections in order to stabilize the aspirations and threats of internal parties to a dispute.[65] In ethno-national conflicts in particular, the absence of kin-state intergovernmental relations is likely to exacerbate conflict by focusing on security and legal approaches to treat the symptoms rather than root causes. The next chapter analyzes the foundations of a British–Irish intergovernmental relationship that has attempted, with considerable success, to confront and regulate core causes of conflict.

Notes

1. Quoted in Dewar, Michael, *The British Army in Northern Ireland* (London: Arms and Armour, 1985) p. 101, emphasis added.
2. Quoted in White, Barry, *John Hume: Statesman of the Troubles* (Belfast: Blackstaff, 1984) p. 135.
3. Quoted in *Fortnight*, 30 November 1972, p. 14.
4. Kitson, Frank, *Bunch of Five* (London: Faber and Faber, 1977) Ch. 23; see also Kitson, Frank *Low Intensity Operations: Subversion, Insurgency, Peace-keeping* (London: Faber and Faber, 1971); Eveleigh, R., *Peace-Keeping in a Democratic Society: the Lessons of Northern Ireland* (London: Hurst, 1978); Wilkinson, Paul, *Terrorism and the Liberal State* (London: Macmillan, 1977) pp. 155–8.
5. Townshend, Charles, *Britain's Civil Wars: Counterinsurgency in the Twentieth Century* (London: Faber, 1986) p.72.
6. Cunningham, *British Government Policy in Northern Ireland,* pp. 45–50; Whitelaw, William, *The Whitelaw Memoirs* (London: Aurum Press, 1989) pp. 93–4.
7. Under the Detention of Terrorists Order (1972) suspects were detained on an Interim Custody Order (ICO) approved by the Northern Ireland Secretary, for up to twenty-eight days, after which the Chief Constable had either to refer the case to a commissioner or release the suspect. This provision became incorporated into the Emergency Provisions Act (1973).
8. 'Report of the Commission to Consider Legal Procedures to Deal with Terrorist Activities in Northern Ireland' (Diplock Report), Cmnd. 5185 (London, HMSO, 1972).

9. For a critical interpretation of this legislation, see Boyle, Kevin, Hadden, Tom and Hillyard, Paddy, *Law and State: The Case of Northern Ireland* (London: Robertson, 1975); see also Hillyard, Paddy, *Suspect Community: People's Experience of the Prevention of Terrorism Acts in Britain* (London: Pluto Press in association with Liberty, 1993); see also Cunningham, Michael, *British Government Policy in Northern Ireland, 1969–1989: Its Nature and Execution* (Manchester: Manchester University Press, 1991) pp. 67–74.
10. Bishop and Mallie, *The Provisional IRA*, pp. 225–6.
11. Whitelaw, *The Whitelaw Memoirs*, p. 94.
12. Bishop and Mallie, *The Provisional IRA*, pp. 214–17.
13. The PIRA's demand for the right to national self-determination is nearly identical to that issued in the joint Sinn Féin–SDLP statement following the meeting of Gerry Adams and John Hume in April of 1993 (see Ch. 7).
14. Whitelaw, *The Whitelaw Memoirs*, p. 101.
15. Quoted in *The Guardian*, 4 December 1993.
16. Smith, M.L.R., *Fighting for Ireland? The Military Strategy of the Republican Movement* (London: Routledge, 1995).
17. For an inside account see McGuire, Maria, *To Take Arms: A Year in the Provisional IRA* (London: Macmillan, 1973) pp. 104–47.
18. Smith, *Fighting for Ireland*, p. 237.
19. Hamill, *Pig in the Middle*, p. 113.
20. Ibid., p. 115.
21. On the supplying of the IRA and the link with Libya, see Geldard, Ian and Craig, Keith, *IRA, INLA: Foreign Support and International Connections* (London: Institute for the Study of Terrorism, 1988) pp. 72–6.
22. Calculated from Irish Information Partnership, *Agenda Database*.
23. Adams, James, Morgan, Robin and Bambridge, Anthony, *Ambush: The War Between the SAS and the IRA* (London: Pan, 1988) pp. 72–3.
24. Buckland, *A History of Northern Ireland*, p. 161.
25. Hamill, *Pig in the Middle*, p. 143.
26. Quoted in Dillon, Martin and Lehane, Denis, *Political Murder in Northern Ireland* (Harmondsworth: Penguin, 1973) p. 62.
27. The proposals for power-sharing and the first public enunciation by a British government of an 'Irish Dimension' or institutional role for the Irish Republic in Northern Ireland were published in a discussion paper entitled *The Future of Northern Ireland* (London: HMSO, 1972).
28. Maudling, *Memoirs*, p. 186, emphasis added.
29. Ibid., p. 187, emphasis added.
30. Northern Ireland Constitutional Proposals, 1973, Part 1, Article 5 (a).
31. Ibid., Pt. 5, Article 115.
32. Memo from John Hume to George Colley, September 1971, 2001/43/1393, NAI.
33. Bew, Paul and Gillespie, Gordon, *Northern Ireland: A Chronology of the Troubles 1968–1993* (Dublin: Gill and Macmillan, 1993) p. 65.
34. H.C. 5th Series, vol. 866, col. 670, 13 December 1973.
35. English, *The Armed Struggle*, p. 166.
36. Quoted in Bew, Paul and Gillespie, Gordon, *Northern Ireland: A Chronology of the Troubles 1968–1993* (Dublin: Gill and Macmillan, 1993) p. 65.
37. In all, the executive was divided into seven Unionists (six with voting powers), six SDLP (four voting) and two Alliance (one voting). The decision to include four non-voting members in the executive was made as a compromise between the Unionists and the SDLP (at Hume's suggestion so that the Unionists could have a majority of voting members while the non-Unionists (the SDLP and Alliance) would have a majority of total executives. See White, *John Hume*, p. 144.
38. Kerr, Michael, *Imposing Power-Sharing: Conflict and Coexistence in Northern Ireland and Lebanon,* (Dublin: Irish Academic Press, 2006) p. 58.

39. Lustick, *Unsettled States, Disputed Lands*, p. 45.

40. Ibid.

41. Wolfgang Danspeckgruber has developed a similar conceptual scheme that differentiates between vertical dimension of authority and horizontal dimension of territoriality. See Danspeckgruber, Wolfgang, 'Conclusions', in Danspeckgruber, Wolfgang (ed.), *The Self-Determination of Peoples: Community, Nation and State in an Interdependent World* (London: Lynne Reinner, 2002) Ch. 13.

42. Bew and Gillespie, *A Chronology of the Troubles*, p. 76.

43. Kerr, *Imposing Power-Sharing*, p. 60; O'Brien, Conor Cruise, *States of Ireland* (London: Granada, 1974) pp. 302–3.

44. Quoted in Hennessey, Peter, *Muddling Through: Power, Politics and the Quality of Government in Postwar Britain* (London: Indigo, 1996) p. 261.

45. The statement (later retracted) is quoted in Bew and Gillespie, *A Chronology of the Troubles*, p. 82.

46. Kerr, *Imposing Power-Sharing*, pp. 57, 60–4.

47. Bew and Gillespie, *A Chronology of the Troubles*, p. 81.

48. Kerr, *Imposing Power-Sharing*, p. 60.

49. Ibid.

50. Quoted in Fisk, Robert, *The Point of No Return: The Strike that Broke the British In Ulster* (London: Andre Deutsch, 1975) p. 107.

51. Nelson, Sarah, *Ulster's Uncertain Defenders: Protestant Political, Paramilitary and Community Groups and the Northern Ireland Conflict* (Belfast: Appletree, 1984); Miller, David, *Queen's Rebels: Ulster Loyalism in Historical Perspective* (Dublin: Gill and Macmillan, 1978).

52. Quoted in Buckland, *A History of Northern Ireland*, p. 170.

53. Allegations of security force collusion in the UVF car-bombings have been given weight, though not proof, by the Irish Oireachtas's Joint Committee for Justice, Equality, Defence and Women's Rights *Final Report on the Report of the Inquiry into the Dublin and Monaghan Bombings* (the Barron Report) pp. 18–19.

54. Hamill, *Pig in the Middle*, pp. 152–4.

55. Bew and Gillespie, *A Chronology of the Troubles*, p. 86.

56. Cunningham, *British Government Policy in Northern Ireland*, pp.93–9.

57. Quoted in Farrell, *The Orange State*, p. 320.

58. H.C. 5th Series, vol. 976, col. 1167, 9 July 1974

59. H.C. 5th Series, vol. 866, col. 670, 13 December 1973.

60. H.C. 5th Series, vol. 976, col. 1197–8, 9 July 1974, emphasis added.

61. The best account of the PIRA's Great Britain campaign, including the miscarriages of justice which resulted, is by Chris Mullin (1987).

62. Bishop and Mallie, *The Provisional IRA*, pp. 269–79.

63. Rees claimed in a letter to *The Times* (London) on 17 July 1983 that his government had 'seriously considered' withdrawal from Northern Ireland but that the cabinet had unanimously rejected the idea. Bew and Gillespie, *A Chronology of the Troubles*, p.171. Mark Ryan quotes Rees as saying: 'We set out to con them [the PIRA] and we did.' Ryan, Mark, *War and Peace in Ireland: Britain and Sinn Féin in the New World Order* (London: Pluto Press, 1994) p. 58.

64. Callaghan, James, *Time and Chance* (London: Collins, 1987) p. 500.

65. Wolff, Stefan, *Disputed Territories: The Transnational Dynamics of Ethnic Conflict Settlement* (Oxford: Berghahn, 2003) Ch. 9; Kerr, *Imposing Power-Sharing*, Ch.8.

Part II:
The Evolution of British–Irish Intergovernmentalism

Prologue to Part II

Unionism and nationalism ... point towards quite different objectives and at the end of the day there can be only one answer to the question – is this piece of territory part of this state or that state.

David Trimble, First Minister Designate of
Northern Ireland Assembly, 9 September 1998[1]

Northern Ireland [will] be 'into or moving into a united Ireland situation' in 15 years' time.

Gerry Adams, Sinn Féin President
12 February 1999[2]

The opposing national ambitions represented by Trimble and Adams sustained a violent conflict that claimed over 3,000 lives in thirty years, from a population of just one and a half million people. According to Brendan O'Leary's calculation, on per capita terms it was among the most violent in the world from 1970 to 2000.[3] And yet despite the persistence of the opposing aspirations of Adams and Trimble presented above, majorities from both national communities and the opposing sovereigns agreed in 1998 *a process* for national self-determination (while disagreeing on the outcome). The Belfast/Good Friday Agreement (hereafter GFA) of 1998 suggests that the contest over national sovereignty has been pluralized into *potentially* manageable components, combining bi-national intergovernmentalism with federal and confederal territorial arrangements, consociational 'power-sharing' government and reflexive political and civil rights protections in the United Kingdom and the Republic of Ireland.[4] The hybrid, multi-layered design of institutions and constitutions reflects historical, social and political learning and policy network development based on bi-national principles, whose implications for the theory and practice of conflict resolution and regulation will be developed in this concluding part.

The handshake between Irish Taoiseach Bertie Ahern and Northern Ireland First Minister Designate, Ian Paisley, on 4 April 2007, and their discussions about commemorating the battle of the Boyne (1 July 1690) represented a potential reconciliation of colonial sources of conflict. As we have seen, in the aftermath of that attempted conquest, the insecurity of the settler society and their corporate leverage in stabilizing British control of Ireland led to draconian laws against the Catholic Irish population. In the present context a chance exists for both 'settler' and 'native' to reconcile their relations as ethno-nations and for the triangular British–Irish–Northern Irish relationship to be made perpendicular: with British–Irish relations 'overpinning' nationalist–unionist relations. Both sets of relations at the state and governmental level are of course themselves integrated with wider east-west relations among the devolved parts of Britain and Ireland and with Europe, at the national, supra-national and regional level.

The components of the settlement are not new: the bi-national British–Irish Treaty at the heart of the GFA is arguably a re-negotiation, if not of the Williamite conquest or the Act of Union (1800) then at least the Anglo-Irish Treaty of 1921. The North–South Ministerial Council is a third attempt at an institutionalized Irish dimension, which was originally proposed in 1920 and again in 1973 with the Sunningdale Agreement. The new Northern Ireland Assembly resurrects (and enhances) the principle of proportionality which was meant to entrench minority participation in government of the devolved Northern Ireland parliament established with the 1920 Government of Ireland Act and which was the centrepiece of the Sunningdale Agreement.

What has changed most fundamentally is the relative equalization of the status of the opposing nation-states (the United Kingdom and the Irish Republic) with regard to *de jure* and *de facto* authority in and over Northern Ireland. These relations reflected the principle of parity of esteem of the two national traditions contesting historical foundations and contemporary destinations of opposing British and Irish national projects. The rest of this prologue attempts to situate the analysis of the book within the political science and international relations (IR) literature on conflict and conflict regulation.

EXPLAINING LATE TWENTIETH-CENTURY BRITISH–IRISH RELATIONS

International relations scholarship has emphasized the transformation of British–Irish relations from one characterized by asymmetry and contested sovereignty (both over Northern Ireland and in terms of the evolution of Ireland from dominion to independent status) towards symmetry and sovereignty-pooling. With others, Paul Gillespie has emphasized several developments that have transformed British–Irish relations into a more symmetrical form of interdependence.[5] First, membership of the European Economic Community has eroded Irish economic dependence on the UK. Whereas over 90 per cent of Irish exports and 50 per cent of imports were to and from the UK in 1937, these figures were 26 and 37 per cent, respectively, by 1995.[6] Ireland's economic growth since the early 1990s was based on European regional funding, a young, well-educated population and a low corporate tax rate that encouraged multinational investment in the only English-language country within the Eurozone. By 2004 Ireland achieved near equal wealth with the UK in terms of per capita purchasing power.[7]

A political by-product of both countries' membership of the EEC/EU was to allow Irish ministers to meet with their British counterparts as equals in the context of the European Council of Ministers. Council meetings have played an important role in allowing the two governments to discreetly coordinate their policies on Northern Ireland, especially since the early 1990s.[8] More generally, European integration has transformed the essentialist and binary English–Irish opposition into a more pluralist and liberal form of nationalism, symbolized by the transformation of Irish nationalism from ethnic (anti-English) and territorial (unitary island) conceptions to subjective and voluntarist forms as enunciated in the amended Articles 2 and 3 of the Irish constitution (as explained in Chapter 8). It is suggested that the changing conceptions of Irish national identity are embedded in European notions of plural national and ethnic identities and concomitant models of pooled sovereignty and multi-level governance.

A third theme emphasized by Gillespie and other IR scholars is the impact of domestic and international events like wars, both hot and cold. The intensification of violent conflict in Northern Ireland in the early and mid 1970s is alleged to have shifted Irish elite and popular opinion from one based on unification (by consent) to priorities of stabilization and insulation of the Irish Republic from conflict that threatened to spill over the border.[9] The impact of the First and Second World Wars has been developed in previous chapters. The end of the Cold War between 1989 and 1991 is also alleged by scholars like Michael Cox to have facilitated conflict regulation by removing the republican movement's anti-imperialist justification for violence, by allowing the British government to declare it no longer had a strategic interest in holding on to Northern Ireland and by allowing the US government to co-opt the republican movement into a peace process without fear of jeopardizing the 'special relationship' between the US and UK that had been so important during the Cold War.[10]

The US dimension itself is a fourth theme, emphasized by Paul Arthur, who traced the evolution of an influential Irish diaspora (19 per cent of Americans claim some Irish ancestry) from the constitutional nationalist-supporting 'tree-tops' of the Democratic Party to the 'grass roots' supporters of traditional Irish republicanism. Arthur argues that John Hume, the SDLP Leader (from 1979 to 2001) was almost singularly responsible for cultivating a constitutional nationalist analysis to shape a bi-partisan (but especially democratic) policy towards intervention in British–Irish relations over Northern Ireland. US congressional and presidential support for the Anglo-Irish Agreement, the International Fund for Ireland and numerous informal networks of Irish-American businessmen and civil society organizations were all important facilitators of British–Irish intergovernmental symmetry that improved the prospects for conflict regulation.[11]

These insights from IR scholarship are important additions to the political and social explanations of conflict and conflict regulation. However, there remains a considerable amount of variance in the actions of British and Irish governments, their interpretation of the conflict and especially the interests and identities of the nationalist and unionist communities in Northern Ireland. For example, Gillespie cites the New Ireland Forum (1983–4) as an example of the stabilitarian and peace-seeking southern Irish establishment. Yet all three of the forum's recommendations – for re-unification, a federal/confederal Ireland or joint authority – advocated recognition of Irish sovereignty over Northern

Ireland. Similarly, Gillespie, John Coakley and others have emphasized the decline in southern Irish interest in re-unification. They cite opinion poll evidence that shows reunification as a low priority among the Irish electorate, whose support drops precipitously when asked whether they would be willing to pay more taxes to support unity.[12] Yet a consistently high proportion (between 79 and 86 per cent between 1999 and 2006) of the Irish electorate do support reunification in principle, even if it is not a high priority.[13] The combination of economic affordability and the political prize for any Irish government that achieves reunification means that international developments have not yet produced a 'post-nationalist' era in Irish politics.

Neither has Europeanization necessarily eroded nationalist or unionist preferences for their opposing nation-state destinations. Against those versions of neo-functionalism and supra-nationalism that predicted the evolution of 'supra-nationalism', the actual trajectory of European integration has facilitated and even strengthened nationalism and nation-states, even if they are increasingly interdependent. In contrast to variants of neo-realism and neo-functionalism, the liberal intergovernmentalist approach emphasizes the domestic economic and political concerns of *national* governments, in contrast to the narrow economic focus of most rational choice accounts of institutional decision-making. Moravcsik has demonstrated that states that are flexible on questions of sovereignty increase their exchange value as negotiators able to pursue and preserve *national* interests, even where significant asymmetries of wealth or geo-strategic power exist between or among nation-states.[14] Thus, Ireland's decision to open its economy to external competition in the mid 1960s with the Anglo-Irish Free Trade Agreement and then accession to the EEC were both short-term sacrifices of economic sovereignty that were calculated to enhance long-term autonomy from Britain[15] and to promote Irish reunification through functional spill-over. In sum, as the following three chapters show, both internationalization and Europeanization have created positive forms of facilitation for conflict regulation, provided models of multi-level governance and encouraged the pluralization of national identities. But plural nationalism is still nationalism and the conflict between Irish nationalism and British unionism is still the dominant political and social source of cleavage in Northern Ireland.

EXPLAINING CONFLICT AND RESOLUTION/REGULATION: CONSOCIATION VERSUS CIVIC INTEGRATION

The dominant approach to the regulation of the conflict in Northern Ireland has been, as described in the previous chapter, the promotion of power-sharing between nationalist and unionist leaders. This approach was consistent with the theory of 'consociationalism' as propagated by Arend Lijphart and others.[16] A consociational system is defined according to four main features: government by grand-coalition of leaders representing the dominant (usually) ethno-national segments of a divided society; segmental autonomy or maximum self-rule for each community; proportionality rules for inputs into government, such as proportional representation electoral system, and outputs, such as public spending or public employment; and minority veto rules that prevent majoritarian domination.

Academics working from a 'civic integration' tradition generally oppose consociation and emphasize the need to encourage a shared community *within* Northern Ireland, mainly between moderate nationalist and unionist parties (since 1973 these have been the SDLP, Ulster Unionist Party and, episodically, the DUP). The Alliance Party, given its official policy of neutrality on the union versus unity, would be the logical focal point for civic integration. Yet, the Alliance Party averaged only 7 per cent of votes in all elections in Northern Ireland between 1973 and 2005.[17] The defenders of the civic integration approach might argue that the lack of middle ground is a product of consociational priorities since the early 70s, which has rewarded ethno-national politics. Yet, because of the continuously bi-national cleavage shaping Irish nationalist versus British unionist politics in the modern era, and the sustenance of comparable Scottish and Welsh nationalist projects within a civic-integrationist British state, it is difficult to see evidence for the development of a shared Northern Ireland civic identity. Statist approaches that focus on the Northern Ireland level therefore have difficulty explaining the breakthroughs in British–Irish relations and their impact on the GFA and its implementation. While Paul Dixon correctly argues that a purely British–Irish state-level process of negotiation denies the necessity of consent from parties in Northern Ireland, his analysis ignores the centrality of contested sovereignty, the relationship between nationalism and inter-governmentalism, and lightly dismisses the feasibility of multi-level governance as the basis for conflict regulation.[18] By suggesting that there are only two approaches to governing ethno-nationally divided societies – consociational and civic (liberal) – Dixon and others elide the centrality of the contested national status of Northern Ireland.

Other approaches to the conflict which reject the centrality of opposing nationalisms include variants of the 'human needs' approach to conflict regulation.[19] Ruane and Todd, for example, emphasize structural causes of conflict, arguing that underlying social, economic and political forces are at least as important as national status.[20] Indeed, the multi-layered government and civic institutions, especially the elaborate 'mainstreaming' of cultural and human rights proposed in the Belfast Agreement attest to the policy-makers' recognition of a more holistic 'emancipatory' approach to conflict regulation. But Ruane and Todd's emphasis on the possibility of emancipation through the reform of the economic, social, and political structures under-emphasizes the agenda-setting and 'frame-working' of the negotiations and the structure of settlement by the British and Irish governments since the Anglo-Irish Agreement of 1985, as emphasized in different ways by O'Leary and McGarry and by two of O'Leary's students, Michael Kerr and Stefan Wolff.[21]

O'Leary and McGarry, in *The Politics of Antagonism* emphasize the role of British and Irish leaders and officials in pursing state-craft based on 'coercive consociationalism', whereby unionists have been threatened with greater Irish government involvement in the affairs of Northern Ireland if they refused to share power. Their understanding of the appropriate balance between consociationalism and civic integration, including their advocacy of plural nationalist police reform, has influenced policy makers, particularly in the British Labour Party, SDLP, Sinn Féin, and Fianna Fáil, as well as the political science of comparative conflict regulation.

As another student of O'Leary, my approach attempts to add to these plural-nationalist interpretations by specifying the dynamics of conflict and the evolution of exchange relations at the state, governmental and societal levels, with particular attention paid to the centrality of territorial and cultural aspects of nationalism, as they affect conceptions of national status and state legitimacy. The conclusions support a bi-national variant of the 'liberal inter-governmental'[22] view in which the British and Irish governments have been able to shape the preferences of the parties in Northern Ireland by cultivating a symmetrical intergovernmental relationship which can deliver important side-payments to the representatives of the nationalist and unionist communities in Northern Ireland.[23]

In this light, Paul Arthur has analyzed the dynamics of the transition from 'conflict transformation' towards 'conflict resolution', emphasizing the confrontation of the 'Anglo-Irish problem' that preceded the Northern Ireland problem, and rectification of the limits of the 1920–1 settlement that had intensified nationalist versus unionist competition in Northern Ireland by exclusion (of the Irish Free State from UK politics and of northern nationalists from Northern Ireland governance).[24] Only when British–Irish relations became normalized and constructive in the European and Atlantic contexts of complex interdependence did conflict transformation become possible because it de-couples, *to an extent*, the national from territorial conceptions of state legitimacy, allowing for various forms of *internal* self-determination based on devolution, cross-border bodies etc.

But in emphasizing the transformation of conflict away from paired antagonism, Arthur and other IR and political science thinkers underestimate the endurance of nation-state primacy based on constitutional sovereignty. Figures 8 and 9 demonstrate the consistent primary attachments to Irish nationalist and British unionist identities, respectively. As a result, as Chapters 6 to 8 show , the principle objective of all sides in negotiations has been over the mechanism for regulating national self-determination. The core side payment sought by unionists has been the perpetuation of the majoritarian process of self-determination that preserves the union as long as that is the wish of a majority in Northern Ireland. For the nationalist minority the core side payment has been a declaration of British intent to support the possibility of a united Ireland if that becomes the wish of the majority in Northern Ireland and the extension of the bi-national consent rule to the two jurisdictions on the island (meaning that people in the Irish Republic have a veto on any changes to the constitutional status of Northern Ireland); guaranteed power-sharing for any devolved government in Northern Ireland; an Irish dimension linking north and south; and equal civic and cultural rights that are constituted in a bill of rights. All of these institutions and constitutional features have been developed intergovernmentally in a way that could be described as the evolution of relations from sister kingdoms to sister republics, as the rights protections balance state authority against constitutionally entrenched protections for the Irish nationalist and British unionist *demoi* or publics.

The dynamics of the relationship between nationalism and state legitimacy will be demonstrated by focusing on the conception and regulation of political violence as well as the wider priorities and incentives of the governments and the sub-national political leaders involved in (or excluded) from negotiations. It is possible to evaluate the impact of the treatment of core sovereignty issues on the fate of the agreements and, more fundamentally, to assess the extent to which these agreements represented a 'sufficiently consensual' expression of national self-determination. The aim is to test the hypothesis that nation-states that explicitly dilute their absolute claims to sovereignty over a territory can encourage reciprocal adjustments to exclusive nationalist claims to the same territory. Focusing on the treatment of the implements of violence in chapters 7 and 8, I argue that stable intergovernmental relations between the 'matron-states' (Britain and Ireland) were pre-conditions for the negotiation of power-sharing institutions in Northern Ireland and between Northern Ireland and the Irish Republic, precisely because they reflect and address dominant national status conceptions, interests and aspirations, both historical and contemporary.

6

Cultivating a 'ripe moment': The evolution of the British–Irish Intergovernmental Approach

> Perhaps [the] comparative lack of English ethnicity is one of the abiding problems in Anglo-Irish relations: The English are not really able to understand in others what they lack in themselves.
>
> I am inclined to agree with those who say that in Anglo-Irish relations we should not let ourselves be dominated by history. We should use it to understand where we are and why we are there. But when we come to think about and work for the future, having climbed the ladder of history, we should do well to throw it away. I do not believe that, at any rate in this sphere of human affairs, history is a good guide to the future.
>
> Lord Armstrong (Cabinet Secretary, 1979–87)[25]

Armstrong's views on the role of national and ethnic history represent a subtle but profound shift in the pragmatic, statist approach that had dominated British policy-making in Ireland and Northern Ireland up to the late 1970s. As the senior cabinet official advising on Northern Ireland, Armstrong played a central role in encouraging British Prime Minister Margaret Thatcher to institutionalize relations with the Republic of Ireland in the Anglo-Irish Agreement (1985). It was precisely the pluralist understanding of nationalism that led Armstrong to recognize, like Gladstone in the 1870s, that conflict in Ireland centered on equally valid, but opposing, nationalisms and that the approach to governance had to reflect that polarity.

But the additional claim for ahistorical (or non-cultural) conflict regulation would be proven wrong by the governments that crafted the Good Friday Agreement. In throwing away the ladder of history for the Anglo-Irish Agreement, the two governments failed to address their opposing claims to sovereignty. Only after historical origins of conflict were addressed *and regulated* with a new mechanism of self-determination in the Downing Street Declaration of 1993 was substantial progress made in transforming violent into constitutional politics. This chapter analyzes the evolution of the Anglo-Irish intergovernmental relationship, focusing on the governments' confrontation of the opposing self-determination issues at the core of the conflict and the *mutual* establishment of parameters for subsequent conflict regulation.

SHAKEN, NOT STIRRED

Labour Northern Ireland Secretary Roy Mason confidently reported to the Commons in June 1977 that those responsible for political violence 'have no realistic political cause and *no political or democratic backing*. The gap is widening between these criminals and the community in whose interests they claim to act. They really are being isolated.'[26] The previous year, two women, a Catholic, Mairead Corrigan, and a Protestant, Betty Williams, both from the republican Andersonstown in west Belfast, who had witnessed the killing of three children by an IRA gunman's getaway car, received the Nobel Peace Prize for their leadership of the 'peace people', a movement of Catholic and Protestant citizens against paramilitary violence.

But war-weariness did not alter a 'containment' policy because the Provisional IRA's (hereafter, 'IRA') organizational and political problems created a belief that the counter-insurgency goal of separating militants from the social base was being achieved. The IRA had suffered organizationally during 1975 and 1976, having been lulled into a morale-sapping ceasefire by a southern command that was increasingly remote from the arena of conflict, where loyalist retaliation against IRA attacks made 1976 second only to 1972 in deaths from political violence. These factors contributed to the eclipse of the southern-based leadership by the northern command (including Gerry Adams, Martin McGuinness and Ivor Bell). Adams apparently designed the cell-structure that made the IRA less vulnerable to informants and more capable of combining specialist technology, intelligence and operational planning.

This IRA was inclined to reclaim the pike staves from Armstrong's ladder of history. The transformed organization violently returned to the world stage on 27 August 1979 with two separate attacks against the crown. On that morning, off the coast of Sligo, the yacht of Lord Louis Mountbatten, the Queen's cousin and last Viceroy of India, was blown up by a thirty-pound bomb. Lord Mountbatten, Lady Dowager Brabourne, their 14-year-old grandson and a local 15-year-old local boatman were killed. In the afternoon of the same day, eighteen soldiers were killed near the border at Warrenpoint, Co. Down, when the IRA set up an ambush involving two separate bombs and machine-gunners planted along the road just over the border in the Republic.[27]

These unprecedented atrocities produced an international outpouring of hostility and acrimony towards the republican movement. Nevertheless, before the dust had even settled, politicians of all persuasions began to ride the wave of instability generated by this double atrocity. When asked whether he believed that the events of 27 August would delay a British initiative in Northern Ireland, Irish Taoiseach Jack Lynch replied to the contrary by saying: 'It might well accelerate it.'[28] Merlyn Rees, former Northern Ireland Secretary, chipped in by admitting that the IRA 'could not be defeated militarily' and that the reintroduction of internment would be a 'grave error of judgement'.[29]

These horrific rungs on the ladders of Irish and British history demonstrate why national history has to inform conflict regulation. Instead, the government continued with a twin-track approach: Atkins announced the formation of a new

Constitutional Conference, carefully clarifying that the conference would not consider changes to the constitutional status of Northern Ireland or the return of law and order powers to a devolved government.

> Responsibility for law and order in the Province, *[which] remains the Government's overriding priority in Northern Ireland*, would not be transferred... I must tell the House that political advance – or even the prospect of it – will not solve the security question, because those who are responsible for the violence in Northern Ireland will, if anything, feel that this move is a threat to them... We must be just as resolute in seeking to control violence and bring terrorism down from its present level.[30]

Not even this limited mandate could lead to any form of consensus among the constitutional parties in Northern Ireland. The Ulster Unionist Party refused to participate on the grounds that the proposals for devolved government were a repudiation of the Conservative election manifesto that had promised an integrationist approach. The DUP participated but refused to accept power-sharing at the executive level, and the SDLP participated but refused to go along with proposals which did not include executive power-sharing and an institutionalized Irish dimension.

The failure to reach any agreement among the constitutional parties, combined with the resurgence of the IRA, led both British and Irish governments to seek alternatives to the twin-track approach. Charles Haughey succeeded Jack Lynch as Taoiseach, who resigned on 5 December 1979. In his first meeting with Thatcher on 21 May 1980, Haughey played on Thatcher's security-focused agenda. He knew that Northern Ireland was a low-priority item for Thatcher but also believed that her visit to the border security posts following the Mountbatten and Warrenpoint calamities reinforced her belief in the necessity of securing formal security cooperation with the Republic. For Haughey, Northern Ireland represented an opportunity to make history. He appealed to Thatcher's historical ambition by arguing that neither leader would be remembered for launching a security initiative but that both could be remembered for achieving a lasting settlement.[31] Following the December 1980 summit, Thatcher and Haughey issued a joint-communiqué stating that future meetings would address the 'special consideration of the totality of relationships within these islands' and would discuss the formation of 'new institutional structures' that would express the uniqueness of the relationship between the UK and Ireland. While Thatcher subsequently denied approving the wording of the communiqué,[32] there is little doubt that she had been convinced of the necessity of achieving cooperation with the Republic on security. Yet the question remained as to how willing she would be to concede modifications to sovereignty sufficient to establish an Irish dimension satisfactory to nationalists North and South.

Renewed urgency in British–Irish relations was caused by the republican prisoners' hunger strikes of 1980–1.[33] It is important to note that the hunger strikes did not emerge out of thin air but were the culmination of the republican prisoners' battle for the maintenance of political status that had been phased out for new prisoners from January 1976 and for all prisoners from 1 April 1980. Thus, the hunger strikes were a tactical escalation of the ongoing war against the criminalization policy that, *pace* Wilkinson,[34] reveals the importance of considering the long-term consequences of strategies of repression. In this case, the very attempt to exert control by 'criminalizing' violence led the republican movement successfully to reassert that the conflict was about national self-determination.[35]

In the short term, the British government's reaction to the demand for political status reflected a hangover from the policy of criminalization and, by extension, the continued adherence to a confused strategy of coercion and conciliation. Thatcher was adamant that her government would not be seen to concede to the prisoners' demands: 'Above all, I would hold fast to the principle that we would not make concessions of any kind while the hunger strike was continuing. The IRA were pursuing with calculated ruthlessness a psychological war alongside their campaign of violence: they had to be resisted at both levels.'[36] Thatcher's inflexible law and order approach, exemplified by her 'crime is crime is crime: it is not political'[37] mantra before Sands' death on 5 May 1981, exacerbated anti-British hostility and provided Sinn Féin with an unexpected opportunity to develop the political wing of the republican movement, a task which the northern leadership of Adams, McGuinness and Morrison had been attempting, as yet unsuccessfully, since the truce of 1975.

In the longer term, from the point of view of both governments, the ascendance of Sinn Féin presented a clear threat to the constitutional process because it combined violent and constitutional politics in an internal republican 'new departure': the adoption of the 'long war' strategy centred on the tactics of the 'ballot box and the Armalite'.[38] The implications for a conflict regulation approach based on the twin-tracks of encouraging moderates while marginalizing extremists were disastrous. The scale of the tip away from the moderate middle-ground was first indicated by the election of Bobby Sands as MP for Fermanagh–South Tyrone in a by-election in April 1981. Sands' 30,493 votes were 1,446 more than his UUP opponent Harry West, and represented 49 per cent of the valid votes.[39] On the streets the level of rioting in the aftermath of the deaths of Sands and the nine other republican hunger strikers reached levels not seen since the early 1970s. Attacks against members of the security forces increased from 1,867 in 1980 to 9,440 in 1981.[40] The police responded with plastic bullets, which are meant to be non-lethal, but which killed eleven civilians, including four youths, between 1980 and 1986.[41] International pressure was once again brought to bear on British security policy as the European parliament issued a (non-binding) decision against the use of plastic bullets by member states, and again on 12 August 1984, following the death of Sean Downes, when the European parliament voted in favour of a motion specifically prohibiting the British security forces from using plastic bullets.[42]

Sinn Féin's electoral success continued in the aftermath of the hunger strikes with the election of Owen Carron to Sands' seat (with an increased majority) and with the election of Kieran Doherty and Paddy Agnew to seats in the Dáil.

In the longer term, Sinn Féin's electoral success levelled off, as Figure 10 indicates, to an average of 11.4 per cent (approximately 30 per cent of the nationalist vote) between 1982 and 1994 in district council, Westminster and European elections. But Thatcher's refusal to compromise on political status provided exactly the type of opportunity Sinn Féin had been searching for to strengthen its organizational machinery and maintain a limited mandate for the armed struggle.[43]

Two other remnants of the criminalization policy need emphasis: the hunger strikes, and particularly the republican campaign against prison staff, kicked off a tit-for-tat escalation between republican and loyalist paramilitaries.[44] Secondly, a series of undercover operations involving the RUC's 'E-4A', a secret, Ulsterized and SAS-trained force), were carried out to counter the IRA's *guerilla* tactics in the border areas of Tyrone, Armagh and Down.[45] On 27 October 1982 the IRA killed three RUC members with a land mine planted at Kinnego, near Lurgan, Co. Down. Two weeks later the RUC shot three unarmed IRA members at a checkpoint outside Lurgan. The three, Sean Burns, Gervaise McKerr, and Eugene Toman, were suspected of having caused the Kinnego bombing, and had been under surveillance by an undercover RUC unit.[46] The RUC members who fired the shots were tried for murder and acquitted, but the case remained unresolved after evidence emerged which suggested that the RUC was operating a shoot-to-kill policy.[47] The investigation into these and other incidents produced a considerable amount of adverse publicity as the leader of the investigation, John Stalker of the Manchester police, was the subject first of evasion by RUC officers, and then a smear campaign which eventually led to his dismissal.[48] The net effect was to add to the growing criticism of the government's anti-terrorist tactics by revealing, over a period of years, the lengths to which the security forces were forced to go in an effort to contain republican violence.

Thirdly, the legal response to the limits of forceful interrogation led to the cultivation of police informers – known locally as 'supergrasses' (from 'snakes in the grass') – from both republican and loyalist paramilitary organizations who were encouraged to testify against their erstwhile colleagues in exchange for immunity from prosecution and/or protection through relocation and a change of identity.[49] The cultivation of supergrasses has been described as a 'more discriminating form of internment',[50] and its effects were similar in the medium and long term. More than 590 people were arrested based on the evidence of seven loyalist and eighteen republican supergrasses from November 1981 to November 1983, a similar figure to the average number of internees from 1971 to 1975.[51] In the short term the supergrass system contributed to a reduction in the level of IRA activity. The new IRA cell structure was still vulnerable once penetrated by informers and this led to a temporary reduction in the capacity of the organization to respond with attacks (though the cell structure and discipline did prevent supergrasses from disrupting the IRA to the same degree as it had for the INLA, which was effectively decimated by the supergrass system).[52] In the medium term, however, the further abuse of the 'special' legal system began to embarrass the government.[53] Between 1980 and

1986, sixty-six of the seventy-five (88 per cent) appeals against convictions in supergrass trials were upheld because of an over-reliance on uncorroborated accomplice testimony.[54]

TACTICAL ADJUSTMENTS

The adverse publicity produced by the draconian security and legal tactics may have been bearable if they had been effective. They were not. With cyclical predictability, the IRA merely made tactical adjustments to maintain pressure for a more durable security arrangement. While the overall number of deaths of security force members was lower in the period from 1979 to 1986 than it was from 1969 to 1978, the shift in concentration of IRA attacks from Belfast to the border areas was significant: the proportion of security force deaths in the border area increased from 27 per cent in the period 1969 to 1978 to 51.4 per cent in the period 1979 to 1986.[55] It was this tactical adjustment which had forced the RUC into playing the IRA's game by undertaking the controversial undercover operations in the border areas and. most importantly, creating greater demand for cross-border security cooperation with the Irish government.

   In addition, the IRA adjusted to the intensified security measures by diversifying its campaign to Britain and the continent, following a 'displacement' pattern familiar to scholars of political violence. Tactically, the bombs in Britain were roughly timed to respond to political developments in Northern Ireland, although later campaigns were more open-ended and based on autonomous units. In May 1981 the IRA exploded a device at an oil refinery on the Shetland islands while the Queen was present less than half a mile away attending an official opening ceremony. In October and November 1981, following the end of the hunger strikes, the IRA exploded four devices in London, killing three people and injuring forty-two. The impact of these bombs on Thatcher's outlook was significant. After visiting the site of the worst bombing at the Chelsea barracks on 10 October which killed two people, Thatcher herself pulled a six-inch nail from the bomb out of the military coach which it struck and 'came away more determined than ever that the terrorists should be isolated, deprived of their support and defeated'.[56] Of course what she does not mention in her memoirs is that her prison policy was directly responsible for the resurgence of support for the republican movement.

FROM IRISH QUESTION TO ANGLO-IRISH PROBLEM

Violence had again forced open the constitutive sovereignty questions. The negotiating strength of the constitutional nationalist position was based on the argument that violence was a *product* rather than a *cause* of the constitutional impasse in Northern Ireland. The report of the New Ireland Forum, which had been established to provide a unified constitutional nationalist position to

combat the ascendance of Sinn Féin, expressed the nationalist view as follows:
Paragraph 4.4:

> ...The problem of security is an acute symptom of the crisis in Northern
> Ireland...Present security policy has arisen from the absence of political
> consensus...The various measures were introduced on the basis that they
> were essential to defeat terrorism and violent subversion, but they have failed
> to address the causes of violence and have often produced further violence.[57]

Therefore the instability caused by IRA violence and loyalist retaliation was
proof that Northern Ireland was, in Haughey's words, a 'failed political entity',[58]
or in the milder Fine Gael version, proof that the nationalist community was
increasingly 'alienated' from the British state. Throughout the negotiations of
the Anglo-Irish Agreement (AIA), FitzGerald emphasized the threat of Sinn
Féin's post-hunger strike ascendance, even after it became clear that the threat
of Sinn Féin displacing the SDLP as the largest nationalist party was
diminishing.[59] Furthermore, FitzGerald emphasized that nationalist alienation
could be eliminated only if the Irish government was given joint authority over
reformed policing and judicial structures which would be 'subsidiary to and
within a joint political framework'.[60] In exchange for limited joint authority, the
Irish government was willing to intensify cross-border security cooperation,
implement into Irish law the European Convention on the Suppression of
Terrorism (ECST), and offered to amend, through referendum, Articles 2 and 3
of the Irish constitution which laid claim to the territory of Northern Ireland.

Violence and the threat of violence were also of central importance to the
British negotiating position. Thatcher was clearly tempted by the Irish offer on
security:

> I started from the need for greater security, which was imperative. If this
> meant making limited political concessions to the South, much as I disliked
> this kind of bargaining I had to contemplate it. But the results in terms of
> security must come through...The best hope...seemed to lie with an Anglo-
> Irish Agreement which would acknowledge in a public way the Republic's
> interest in the affairs of the North, while keeping decision-making out of its
> hands and firmly in ours. This is what I now set out to achieve.[61]

The British government was initially willing to consider the establishment of
limited institutions of joint authority such as a Joint Security Commission and
an All-Ireland Law Commission, both of which would at least study the
possibility of formal all-Ireland institutions. However, it soon became clear that
Thatcher was unwilling to concede any form of shared executive decision-
making to the Republic, and during the negotiations both commissions were
downgraded to consultative bodies.

There were three primary developments that contributed to the hardening of
the British negotiating position, all of which were related directly to the security
situation. First, the possibility of a loyalist backlash was emphasized by the

Northern Ireland Office (NIO), which became involved in the negotiations at the stage where the practical machinations of the agreement needed to be settled.[62] The threat of a loyalist backlash was therefore influential in limiting the concessions given to the Republic to those 'saleable' to the unionist community. As Thatcher remarked following FitzGerald's purposefully exaggerated warnings of the threat of IRA instability spreading to the Republic, '... of course I shared his aim of preventing Ireland falling under hostile and tyrannical forces. But that was not an argument for taking measures which would simply provoke the Unionists and cause unnecessary trouble'.[63]

Secondly, in retaliation for the hunger strikes, the IRA bombed the Grand Hotel in Brighton during the Conservative Party conference on 12 October 1984, killing five people, including MP Sir Anthony Berry and Roberta Wakeham, whose husband John was Parliamentary Secretary to the Treasury. The bombing was also supposed to be the first in a series of bombings at English resorts planned for the summer of 1985.[64] This campaign, along with the massive 'commercial' bombs launched in Northern Ireland during 1985, was intended to disrupt the Anglo-Irish political process.[65] It was only partially successful. The renewed offensive shifted the Anglo-Irish process towards agreement on co-operative security measures.[66] The hardening continued with Thatcher's public reaction to the New Ireland Forum Report on 19 November 1984 when she dismissed each of the proposals for a unitary state, a federal/confederal formula, or joint authority by executing summarily each proposal with the phrase, 'that is out!' FitzGerald recognized that 'the political problem was being side-lined by an exclusively security-oriented approach', and his authority was severely compromised by his public humiliation at the hands of Thatcher which echoed her 'crime' mantra against the republican hunger strikes.[67]

Following the IRA's increasing success with homemade mortar technology against fortified police stations and army barracks, the sense of stalemate was intensified, forcing the two governments to confront deeper causes of conflict, increasingly aware of the need to cultivate a stable intergovernmental relationship to manage violence. In turn, the price of security co-operation for the British government was to accept the fundamental ethos at the heart of the New Ireland Forum, that violence was a product rather than a cause of conflict on the constitutional status of Northern Ireland.

NEGOTIATING THE ANGLO-IRISH AGREEMENT

In terms of the model introduced in Chapter 5 (and Figure 6), the AIA represented a shift *towards* parity of status of the two opposing sovereigns as patrons of the rights to self-determination of the two ethno-national communities in Northern Ireland (see Figure 11). Unlike the Sunningdale Agreement, the two governments did not explicitly reaffirm in the AIA the status of Northern Ireland as part of the United Kingdom. By explicitly allowing a part of the territory of the United Kingdom to secede, the British government declared itself neutral as to the relationship between Northern Ireland and Great Britain. Moreover, the British government committed itself to allow Irish unification if that became the majority wish (Article 1). While these commitments were broadly in line with the parameters of the Sunningdale Agreement, the AIA went further by establishing an Intergovernmental Conference (IGC), serviced by a permanent secretariat, staffed by British and Irish civil servants, based outside Belfast. The AIA also reaffirmed the principle that devolution of power to Northern Ireland would only happen 'on a basis which would secure widespread acceptance throughout the community' (AIA Article 4(b)) and 'with the co-operation of constitutional representatives within Northern Ireland of both traditions there' (ibid. Article 4(c)). Since the SDLP (the largest Catholic/nationalist constitutional party) was committed to achieving an 'Irish dimension' or cross-border bodies with executive powers, this section meant that both power-sharing and an Irish dimension were minimal conditions for the devolution of power to any future administration in Northern Ireland.

While these parameters for a settlement were broadly the same as Sunningdale, the AIA reiterated the parameters for a settlement that had been rejected by a majority of unionists in 1974. It portended a more symmetrical, bi-national, foundation for conflict regulation based on the institutionalized platform of co-operation between Ireland and the UK.[68] The British government had conceded the elevation of the Irish Republic from the governmental level to the threshold of the state level as a partner in conflict regulation (see Figure 11). Article 5c stated that

> If it should prove impossible to achieve and sustain devolution on a basis which secures widespread acceptance in Northern Ireland, the [Inter-Governmental] Conference shall be a framework within which the Irish Government may, where the interests of the minority community are significantly or especially affected, put forward views on proposals for major legislation and on major policy issues…' (*Agreement Between the Government of the United Kingdom of Great Britain and Northern Ireland and the Government of the Republic of Ireland*).

The British and Irish governments had agreed a process of national self-determination and institutionalized their relationship in some policy areas with regard to Northern Ireland (important *regulative* aspects of sovereignty), but the opposing constitutive claims to sovereignty over the territory of Northern Ireland remained. According to Boyle and Hadden,

> In drafting [Article 1 of the AIA] there was a conscious effort by both sides to avoid dispute on the definition of a current status for Northern Ireland… [T]he two states came to the negotiations with "different title deeds". As a result the emphasis in Article 1 is laid on the agreed conditions for any future change in the status of Northern Ireland.[69]

The avoidance of these constitutive aspects of sovereignty is instructive because it reveals core *national* differences in the conception of the status of Northern Ireland. During the negotiations of the AIA, the Irish Taoiseach (Prime Minister) Garret FitzGerald beseeched British Prime Minister Margaret Thatcher to 'understand the importance of [Articles] 2 and 3 (the Irish constitutional claims to sovereignty over Northern Ireland) and that we had to have an Agreement which would enable us to put them to a referendum as we would never satisfy the Unionists unless we removed them'.[70] But, given the strength of opposition to such a change by Fianna Fáil in opposition (still the largest single party), FitzGerald required a reciprocal *constitutive* exchange from the British government in order to have a chance of passing these core constitutional changes in a referendum. Specifically, FitzGerald wanted reformed policing and judicial structures which would be 'subsidiary to and within a joint [British–Irish] political framework'.[71] But the British government feared that the degree of shared sovereignty needed to trade for amendments to Articles 2 and 3 of the Irish constitution would be unacceptable to British Conservatives as well as Northern Ireland Unionists. Thatcher subsequently declared a minimalist view of the need to address constitutive sovereignty claims.

The response was a confused and contradictory conception of conflict regulation, aimed primarily at the exclusion and defeat of paramilitaries in order to create a space for constitutional unionists and nationalists to agree to share power in Northern Ireland. On one hand the gains in terms of establishing an intergovernmental platform are indisputable. The intentional incentive mechanism of the institutionalization of the intergovernmental relationship and the agreement on a process for self-determination in and over Northern Ireland portended the elevation of the Irish government to a more symmetrical status with the British government with regard to some regulative aspects of sovereignty. This long-term goal appears to have been a purposeful strategy pursued by the Irish Taoiseach Garret FitzGerald and the British civil servants who persuaded Thatcher to sign the AIA.[72] In practice, the Irish government did exert through the IGC considerable influence on employment legislation and some aspects of policing and security reform and improved security co-operation in border areas.[73] Indeed, the symmetrical rejections of the AIA by Irish republicans and Ulster unionists attested to the degree of balance struck by the opposing sovereigns. The reiteration of the constitutional guarantee for majority consent to any change in the status of Northern Ireland tempered unionist opposition to the AIA. While there was widespread public opposition in the form of rioting, boycott of local government and the resignation of all fifteen unionist MPs, there was significantly less overt collaboration between constitutional unionists and militant loyalists which had brought down the Sunningdale Executive in 1974.[74]

The republican movement's reaction to the AIA was also clearly influenced by the implications of British–Irish intergovernmentalism. Ed Moloney has claimed that Gerry Adams made contact with the British government as early as 1986. But international events were also important. While recognizing the challenge of intergovernmental security co-operation, the IRA was bolstered by significant arms consignments from Libya. The majority opinion within the republican movement (leadership and rank-and-file) was, as Thatcher herself declared, that force had been decisive in bringing the British government back to the negotiating table, even if, in Sinn Féin leader Gerry Adams' words, the AIA 'copper-fastened' partition.[75]

The absence of a hurting stalemate was a product of the prevailing, asymmetrical conceptions of status, as revealed by British ministers' interpretations of the AIA,[76] the primacy of security objectives and, most revealingly, by the subsequent legal disputes centred on judicial reform and extradition of suspected terrorists between British and Irish jurisdictions. In the negotiations of the AIA, FitzGerald had been led to believe that in return for the Irish implementation of the European Convention on the Suppression of Terrorism (ECST) the British government would at least consider replacing the single-judge 'Diplock' courts with three-judge courts for trials involving scheduled (i.e. terrorist) offences.[77] The Irish government delayed the implementation of the Extradition (ECST) Act from its signing in February 1986 until December 1987, hoping to pressurize the British to reform the Diplock system.[78] It was no coincidence that the British veto of the judicial reforms was followed by several notable cases in which the Irish courts refused to extradite suspected republican terrorists. It became clear that in the absence of any reform in Northern Ireland, the Irish courts would enforce the letter of the extradition agreements in order to compensate for the removal of the political offence status with safeguards in the extradition process.[79] Neither was it a coincidence that the intergovernmental relationship was least successful in managing relations involving aspects of sovereignty which were constitutive: security and judicial policies.

MUDDLING THROUGH BI-NATIONALLY

I hope the House will recall that in 1973, when those imperfect democratic structures were dismantled in Ulster, politicians were pushed to one side and the men of violence took over. I do not wish that to happen again. If there is no democracy, my colleagues and I will be pushed to one side, and the men of violence are bound to succeed because we will have been discredited in that place in which we place our trust – this House.

Ken Maginnis UUP MP[80]

In the absence of an active programme by the two governments, the local combatants remained temporarily secure in their public positions of intransigence. From the republican viewpoint the British declaration of neutrality was meaningless as long as Article 1 of the agreement maintained the 'unionist veto' on Irish unification. The republican movement was confirmed in its belief that the level and type of instability, based not just on violence but the *combination* of carefully targeted violence and political support for Sinn Féin, could push the British off the fence of neutrality and into the side of the persuaders of the merits of a united Ireland.[81] Moreover, republicans could argue that their militancy had bolstered the SDLP's case against an internal settlement.

Conversely, the leaders of the two main unionist parties could denounce the agreement, earning political points locally while allowing the second-best option of direct rule to continue. If the agreement, as Peter Robinson of the DUP stated, left the unionist community perched 'on the window ledge of the Union', he and other unionist leaders soon learned to adapt to the view from the ledge because it was certainly more attractive than the options of independence or a united Ireland which lay on the ground below. Unionist symbiosis was limited to the elite level between the Official Unionist Party (OUP) and the DUP as both parties united in an anti-agreement campaign under the banner 'Ulster Says No'. At the local government level, all eighteen unionist-controlled councils refused to conduct government business throughout much of 1986, forcing the NIO to set local rates as well as to impose fines against some of the boycotting councils. The NIO was also forced to wind up the Northern Ireland Assembly after Alliance members resigned over the unionist members' refusal to maintain the assembly's primary function of scrutinizing legislation. On 17 December 1985 all fifteen unionist MPs resigned their seats in order to force by-elections which would act as a referendum on the agreement. In the by-elections, held on 23 January 1986, unionist parties opposed to the agreement received 71.5 per cent of the valid vote,[82] but the victory was overshadowed by the loss of OUP MP Jim Nicholson's Newry and Armagh seat to Seamus Mallon of the SDLP. The by-election results were used as a mandate to launch a general strike on 3 March which brought out an estimated 200,000 people onto the streets of Belfast, and which led to severe rioting in some Protestant/unionist areas.

The willingness and ability of the RUC to contain loyalist rioting suggested that unionist elites would have to form strong symbiotic links with loyalist paramilitaries in order to make Northern Ireland ungovernable. At the beginning of 1986 it appeared that the Ulster Clubs, with a nominal membership of around 8,000, threatened to act as a bridge between constitutional and paramilitary strands of unionism. Peter Robinson of the DUP was involved in the organization of Ulster Clubs,[83] as was John McMichael, prominent UDA member and UFF leader. The Ulster Clubs were prominent in street demonstrations and the picketing of the Anglo-Irish conference at Maryfield. But since their professed aim was to protect the citizenship rights of the Ulster people *within* the United Kingdom, the Ulster Clubs and Ian Paisley's Ulster Resistance were restricted by the same 'loyalty dilemma' as unionist elites.[84]

What O'Leary and McGarry describe as a Machiavellian stroke of encouraging devolved power-sharing and acceptance of an Irish dimension in exchange for diminished British–Irish intergovernmentalism did partially succeed in its intended effect of fragmenting the unionist bloc into intransigents and potential compromisers. Molyneaux and Paisley, leaders of the OUP and DUP respectively, remained intransigently opposed to 'working' the agreement. But potential compromisers did emerge to challenge the unionist *grandees,* especially Paisley, whose anti-agreement bombast was unsupported by effective action. In 1987 Peter Robinson of the DUP, and Frank Millar and Harold McCusker of the OUP, were commissioned to form a unionist task force to produce a proposal for replacing the agreement. The resultant document, *An End to Drift*, published in July 1987, accepted that devolution based on a form of power-sharing was the most realistic option with which to replace the agreement, and that any credible negotiating position would have to be based on the threat of independence as an alternative to constitutional links with either the UK or the Republic of Ireland.[85] These proposals were played down by both Paisley and Molyneaux because threats of secession and eagerness to accept devolved government based on power-sharing were considered leaps onto the slippery slope of separation from the union which had been created by the agreement. Nevertheless, the fact that loyalist paramilitaries in the UDA were also showing signs of acceptance of the parameters of power-sharing and a bill of rights, published in their document *Common Sense* in January 1987, was an indication of movement from grassroots to elite-level towards acceptance of the principle of power-sharing.

Despite its interim success in preventing unionists from defeating the AIA – and despite Thatcher's declaration in November 1985 that 'there was no such thing as an acceptable level of violence'[86] – the asymmetrical conceptions of sovereignty, reflecting national status conceptions, precluded the type of exchanges required for more progressive conflict regulation. By the end of the decade the AIA had established a violent holding pattern. Unionists' complete rejection of the role of the Irish government in the affairs of Northern Ireland meant that, though they could not bring down the AIA, neither would they participate in negotiations over power-sharing in Northern Ireland. The leadership of Sinn Féin was slowly adapting to the new reality of British–Irish intergovernmentalism; in 1986 it ended its policy of abstention from taking seats in the Irish Dáil and opened separate dialogues with Fianna Fáil in 1986 and the SDLP in 1988. But the IRA was not convinced of Britain's neutrality and continued to see strategic advantage in escalating the conflict to 'sicken the Brits'. The failure of the two governments to confront the core sovereignty dispute sustained a significant state-legitimacy gap, which the IRA exploited violently and to which loyalists responded in kind (see Figure 12).

NEW DEPARTURE: HUME–ADAMS TALKS, I

The genesis and durability of the AIA confirmed Gerry Adams' belief that the new departure that merged the political and military within the republican bloc could only be successful if it was widened to the entire nationalist bloc, North and South. In other words, success was dependent on the achievement of an alliance with constitutional nationalism, though backed by the implicit threat of violence.[87] In 1986 Adams made secret overtures to Charles Haughey, through a Catholic priest, in which he declared that the IRA would agree a ceasefire if a future Fianna Fáil government were to make a strong commitment to Irish unity.[88] But Haughey could not risk making the type of commitment required to achieve a ceasefire because the AIA was too popular among constitutional nationalists North and South.

Given the obstacles to a new nationalist alliance, there was never any serious doubt as to the primacy of the military over the political within the republican movement. When, at its 1986 Ard Fheis, Sinn Féin passed a motion (by 429 votes to 161) to end its policy of abstention from taking seats in Leinster House (the Dáil), the decision had been pre-ordained by the IRA army council. The decision to recognize the 'partitionist' Dublin government did cause a split as Ruairí Ó Brádaigh and Dáithí Ó Conaill led a walk-out of the dissenters to form Republican Sinn Féin. However, the split was marginal because, following the delivery of an estimated 120 tons of weapons and explosives from Libya between June 1985 and September 1986, the army council was confident that the 'long war' would not be run down in favour of a political campaign.[89] As Figure 13 shows, the Libyan-supplied arms made an immediate impact: the number of IRA attacks, both shootings and bombings, increased significantly from 1986 to 1987 and continued at a high level through 1988.

The increased ferocity of the bombing campaign did strain the relationship between the political and military aspects of the movement as callous murders and IRA 'mistakes' led to an erosion of support for Sinn Féin. The IRA plumbed new depths in November 1987 with the Remembrance Day massacre at Enniskillen killing nine civilians and two former members of the security forces. Yet Enniskillen was not a 'one-off', merely the worst in a series of 'mistakes' that caused the deaths of thirty-two civilians from 1987 through 1988.

M.L.R. Smith has attributed the reckless escalation of the 'Enniskillen era' to the moribund state of strategic thinking within the republican movement, based ultimately on an 'emotional attachment to violence'.[90] True, a significant debate was occurring among republicans in light of the AIA, but there were three notable results from the political and military failures of 1987 that support a more instrumental interpretation of republican strategy than that advanced by Smith. First, there was a tactical shift by the IRA from attacks against the RUC to attacks against the army and the UDR. The IRA killed three army and eight UDR soldiers in 1987 and fourteen RUC officers, while in 1988 they killed twenty-two army, eleven UDR and five RUC members. The renewed concentration of attacks against army and UDR soldiers reflected a combination of revenge for security force 'successes' such as Loughgall and Gibraltar (both described below) and hesitancy about launching attacks with a high risk of civilian injury. Secondly, Adams attempted to repair the political damage caused by the Enniskillen debacle by entering discussions with John Hume of the SDLP in January 1988. Adams was clearly attempting to form a nationalist new departure by convincing Hume of the advantages of creating a pan-nationalist alignment opposed to cooperation with the British government on the formation of an internal power-sharing structure.[91] Thirdly, the levelling off of electoral support for Sinn Féin in the North and the nearly complete electoral marginalization in the Republic led the IRA to reassert its version of violent politics by concentrating its actions on events which had more political resonance in Britain. Apart from the shift towards army and UDR targets in

Northern Ireland, the IRA also increased the number of attacks on British army personnel outside Northern Ireland in 1988, killing three soldiers in the Netherlands, one in Belgium and one in London, where the chance discovery of a bomb factory in Clapham, south London indicated that a new British campaign was in the works. All of these elements support the interpretation that the republican leadership was essentially united in its belief that the stalemate between 'the liberation forces and the occupation forces' could be broken through a combination of 'sickening the Brits' militarily while maintaining a limited mandate for Sinn Féin within Northern Ireland.[92]

THE RETURN OF COERCION AND CONCILIATION

The continued ascendance of the militants within the republican movement created a severe test for the post-AIA cooperative security arrangements. It was immediately apparent that the Irish government was unprepared to pursue a narrow security approach at the expense of its claim to sovereignty over Northern Ireland. On the contrary, the Fianna Fáil government that came to power in March 1987 continued the Fine Gael strategy of offering security cooperation as a *quid pro quo* for the reform of the administration of justice in Northern Ireland. In negotiating the agreement's 'associated measures' FitzGerald had been led to believe that in return for the Irish implementation of the European Convention on the Suppression of Terrorism (ECST) the British government would at least consider replacing the single-judge 'Diplock' courts with three-judge courts for trials involving scheduled offences.[93] As a result, the Irish government tightened the requirements and delayed the implementation of the Extradition (ECST) Act from its signing in February 1986 until December 1987, hoping to pressurize the British to reform the Diplock system. As a result, in four notable cases (Burns, O'Reilly, Glenholmes and Ryan), the Irish courts turned down requests for extradition based on technical errors in the warrants, precipitating a crisis in the new Anglo-Irish relationship.[94]

The breakdown in co-operation exposed the contradictions in the cooperative containment exercise, and revealed once again the slavery to the confused policies of coercion and conciliation, with predictable violent results. On the one hand the British government duly implemented most of the security reforms comprising the package of 'associated measures' agreed with the AIA, including a culturally pluralist code of conduct for the RUC, joint police–army patrols in nationalist areas, and the Independent Police Complaints Commission, the repeal of the Flags and Emblems Acts (1957) that had forbidden the flying of the Irish tricolour; and some modifications to the Emergency Provisions Act.

On the other hand, these positive attempts to wean the nationalist community away from support for republicanism were more than offset by draconian legislation and intensified undercover operations. In a clear attempt to hinder Sinn Féin's electoral performance, the Elected Authorities (NI) Act, 1989 required elected representatives to declare that they would not express support for proscribed organizations or acts of terrorism, and made such expressions a civil offence. Similarly, the broadcasting ban ordered in October 1988 prohibited the broadcast on radio or television of the direct statements of any member of a proscribed organization. Both of these measures were influenced directly by the IRA's intensified campaign of violence, and specifically the Enniskillen bombing described above, as well as the killing of six soldiers by a bomb placed in their van in Lisburn in June 1988 and the bombing of an army coach at Ballygawley, Co. Tyrone on 20 August 1988 which killed eight soldiers and injured twenty-eight.[95]

The resurgence of IRA violence from the beginning of 1987 led to a more prominent role for the SAS. On 8 May 1987 the SAS ambushed an IRA unit at Loughgall, Co. Armagh as they attempted to bomb an RUC station. All eight of the IRA men were killed, including Jim Lynagh, an experienced volunteer based in Monaghan, but not before the bomb was detonated which devastated the RUC station. A civilian motorist was also killed in the crossfire. A similar ambush took place on 30 August 1988 when the SAS killed three IRA men near Drumnakilly, Co. Tyrone. This incident was alleged to be a direct act of retaliation against the Tyrone brigade following the Ballygawley massacre.[96]

The role of the SAS in the counter-terrorist campaign achieved international attention on 6 March 1988 when the SAS shot three unarmed IRA activists in Gibraltar who had been planning a spectacular reply to the SAS ambush at Loughgall.[97] Witnesses claimed that the IRA activists had been executed summarily without being given a chance to surrender. Spanish authorities failed to find sufficient evidence to prosecute but a credible documentary, *Death on the Rock*, provided evidence that the SAS was operating a shoot-to-kill policy. There was a particularly gruesome chain of fallout from the Gibraltar incident when a former loyalist paramilitary, Michael Stone, used hand grenades and a pistol to kill three mourners at the funeral of one of the IRA members killed in Gibraltar. Then at the funeral of one of Stone's victims, two off-duty soldiers drove into the funeral cortege, apparently by mistake. The two soldiers were dragged out of their car, brought to waste ground, stripped and executed by members of the IRA. Both of these incidents were recorded on film and broadcast around the world, stark indications that the AIA had changed little in Northern Ireland.

The polarized climate was intensified following the report of the Sampson inquiry in 1987, the continuation of Stalker's investigation into allegations of an RUC shoot-to-kill policy. The British Attorney General (and future Northern Ireland Secretary), Sir Patrick Mayhew, refused to prosecute a group of RUC officers despite evidence that they had conspired to pervert the course of justice. The Irish government interpreted Mayhew's declaration that prosecution was 'not in the interests of national security'[98] as a tit-for-tat response to the failure of the Irish to extradite suspected republican terrorists. This diplomatic ruckus caused a temporary suspension of the meetings between the Gardaí and the RUC, but even worse was to come. An investigation by senior British police officer John Stevens into allegations of collusion between members of the security forces and loyalist paramilitaries revealed that lists containing more than 250 names of suspected republican activists had been leaked from RUC intelligence sources to members of the UDA and UVF.[99]

CONCLUSION

The bottom line at the end of the decade was that the Anglo-Irish containment process had failed Thatcher's litmus test: neither the level of republican violence nor the core level of political support for Sinn Féin in Northern Ireland had been reduced. The successes of the Gardaí and RUC in uncovering large amounts of IRA weapons and explosives were due in large part to the fact that there were more weapons to be found after the Libyan shipments.[100] In any case, these security successes, as well as social policy successes like the passage of the Fair Employment Bill in December 1988, were largely offset by the continuation of repressive measures which galvanized support for Sinn Féin and the IRA, which in turn guaranteed a militant loyalist response.

Despite the limits of this twin-track approach, there is evidence that the bi-national intergovernmental strategy was establishing strong parameters as evidenced by the internal debates within republicanism and unionism described above and in the pattern of relations between violence and constitutional debate. Figure 14 shows a de-coupling of the two trends that had been closely related in the mid-1970s. Proponents of violence were chasing the new agenda rather than setting it. The next chapter shows how the two governments were able, after one more failed attempt at a twin-track process, to re-centre their relations on the regulation of national self-determination at the state, governmental and societal levels.

Notes to Prologue to Part II and Chapter 6

1. Quoted in The *Irish News,* 10 September 1998.
2. Quoted in The *Irish Times,* 13 February 1999.
3. The equivalent per-capita death rate in the United Kingdom would be 44,000. For a comparative analysis of the scale and nature of political violence in the post-1969 period, see O'Leary, Brendan and McGarry, John, *The Politics of Antagonism: Understanding Northern Ireland,* 3rd Edition (London: Routledge, 2007), Ch. 1, citing UN Human Security Report, 2005.
4. John McGarry's edited collection, *Northern Ireland and the Divided World: The Northern Ireland Conflict and the Good Friday Agreement in Comparative Perspective* (Oxford: Oxford University Press, 2001) contains a range of interpretations representing the main approaches to comparative conflict resolution and regulation. See also Ruane, Joseph and Todd, Jennifer (eds), *After the Good Friday Agreement* (Dublin: University College Dublin Press, 1999); Wilford, Rick (ed.), *Aspects of the Good Friday Agreement* (Oxford: Oxford University Press, 2001); Wolff, Stuart, *Disputed Territories: The Transnational Dynamics of Ethnic Conflict* (Oxford: Berghahn, 2003).
5. See also Keatinge, Patrick, 'An Odd Couple? Obstacles and Opportunities in Inter-State Political Co-operation between the Republic of Ireland and the United Kingdom', in Rea, Desmond (ed.), *Political Co-operation in Divided Societies* (Dublin: Gill & Macmillan, 1982; Fanning, Ronan, 'Small States, Large Neighbours: Ireland and the United Kingdom', *Irish Studies in International Affairs,* 9 (1998) pp. 21–9.
6. Paul Gillespie, 'From Anglo-Irish to British–Irish Relations', in Cox et al., *A Farewell to Arms?* pp. 321–2.
7. Organisation for Economic Cooperation and Development (OECD), *Selection of OECD Social Indicators: How does your country compare?* 23 February 2007 (http://www.oecd.org/country/0,3021,en_33873108_33873500_1_1_1_1_1,00.html).

8. Gillespie, 'From Anglo-Irish to British-Irish Relations', p. 322.
9. Ibid, pp. 325–7.
10. Cox, Michael, 'Rethinking the International and Northern Ireland: A Defence', in Cox et al. (eds), *A Farewell to Arms?*
11. Arthur, *Special Relationships*, Ch. 7; see also, Guelke, Adrian, 'International Dimensions of the Belfast Agreement', in Wilford, Rick (ed.), *Aspects of the Belfast Agreement* (Oxford: Oxford University Press, 2001).
12. Gillespie cites a poll for the *Irish Independent*, 31 December 1999, where 85 per cent rejected higher taxation to pay for unity.
13. In addition to the *Irish Independent* poll of 31 December 1999, see the *Sunday Business Post / Red C* poll as reported in Leahy, Pat, 'Majority Want a Nation Once Again', *Sunday Business Post*, 2 April 2006.
14. Moravcsik, Andrew, *The Choice for Europe: Social Purpose & State Power from Messina to Maastricht* (Ithaca, NY: Cornell University Press, 1998) pp. 472–501.
15. Gillespie, 'From Anglo-Irish to British–Irish Relations', p. 322.
16. Lijphart, Arend, *Democracy in Plural Societies* (New Haven: Yale University Press, 1977).
17. Calculated from CAIN, 'Political Party Support in Northern Ireland, 1969 to the Present', (http://cain.ulst.ac.uk/issues/politics/election/electsum.htm), 11 April 2007.
18. Dixon, Paul, 'Paths to Peace in Northern Ireland (I): Civil Society and Consociational Approaches', *Democratization*, 4, 1 (1997a), pp. 1–27; Dixon, Paul. 'Paths to Peace in Northern Ireland (II): The Peace Processes 1973–74 and 1994–96', *Democratization*, 4, 2 (1997b), pp. 1–25. See also Arthur, Paul, 'Anglo-Irish Relations and the Northern Ireland Problem', *Irish Studies in International Affairs*, vol. 2, no. 1 (1985) pp. 37–50 for an analysis that emphasized the primacy of the Northern Ireland dimension and pessimism concerning a British–Irish intergovernmental process.
19. Burton, John, *Conflict: Human Needs Theory* (New York: St Martin's Press, 1990).
20. Ruane and Todd, *The Dynamics of Conflict in Northern Ireland*.
21. O'Leary and McGarry, *The Politics of Antagonism*; Kerr, *Imposing Power-Sharing*; Wolff, *Disputed Territories*, Ch. 7.
22. Moravcsik, *The Choice for Europe*, pp. 18–85.
23. For example see Cox, W. H., 'Managing Northern Ireland Intergovernmentally', *Parliamentary Affairs* 40, 1(1987) pp. 80–97; Kerr, *Imposing Power-sharing*, pp. 74–6; Mair, Peter, 'Breaking the Nationalist Mould: the Irish Republic and the Anglo-Irish Agreement', in Teague, Paul (ed.), *Beyond the Rhetoric: Politics, the Economy and Social Policy in Northern Ireland* (London: Lawrence and Wishart, 1987); O'Leary and McGarry, *The Politics of Antagonism*, pp. 229–39, 327–53.
24. Arthur, *Special Relationships*, p. 180.
25. Armstrong, Robert (Lord), 'Ethnicity, the English, Northern Ireland', in Keogh, Dermot and Haltzel, Michael H., *Northern Ireland and the Politics of Reconciliation* (Washington, DC and Cambridge: Woodrow Wilson Center Press and Cambridge University Press, 1994) pp. 203–4.
26. H.C. 5th Series, vol. 934, col. 635, 30 June 1977, emphasis added.
27. Bishop and Mallie, *The Provisional IRA*, pp. 314–15.
28. Barzilay, D., *The British Army in Ulster, Volume III* (Belfast: Century Services, 1981) p. 96.
29. Flackes, W.D. and Elliott, Sydney, *Northern Ireland: A Political Directory 1968-88* 3rd Edition (Belfast: Blackstaff, 1989) p. 244.
30. H.C. 5th Series, vol. 972, col. 626, 634–5, 20 November 1979, emphasis added.
31. Collins, Stephen, *The Haughey File: The Unprecedented Career and Last Years of the Boss* (Dublin: O'Brien, 1992) p. 46.
32. Thatcher, Margaret, *The Downing Street Years* (London: Harper Collins, 1993) p. 390.
33. See Beresford, David, *Ten Men Dead: The Story of the 1981 Irish Hunger Strike* (London: Grafton, 1987). Beresford was given access to the actual communications passed between the Commanding Officers (COs) in the Maze/Long Kesh and the

leaders of Sinn Féin. More critical assessments are found in Clarke, Liam, *Broadening the Battlefield: The H-Blocks and the Rise of Sinn Féin* (Dublin: Gill and Macmillan, 1987); O'Malley, Padraig, *Biting at the Grave: The Irish Hunger Strikes and the Politics of Despair* (Belfast: Blackstaff, 1990).

34. Wilkinson, Paul, *Terrorism and the Liberal State,* pp.150–70.
35. McIntyre, Anthony, 'Modern Irish Republicanism: the Product of British State Strategies', *Irish Political Studies,* 10 (1995) p. 30.
36. Thatcher, *The Downing Street Years,* p. 390.
37. At a press conference in Saudi Arabia, Thatcher stated: 'We are not prepared to consider special category status for certain groups of people serving sentences for crime. Crime is crime is crime: it is not political.' Quoted in the *Irish Times* 22 April 1981.
38. Sinn Féin's Danny Morrison first articulated the 'ballot box and Armalite' tactical combination at the Sinn Féin Ard Fheis on 31 October 1981 in defence of the decision to contest future elections on an abstentionist platform. Morrison asked rhetorically: 'Who here really believes we can win the war through the ballot box? But will anyone here object if, with a ballot paper in one hand and the Armalite in the other, we take power in Ireland?' Quoted in *An Phoblacht/Republican News,* 5 November 1981; see also O'Brien, *The Long War,* pp. 116–17.
39. The total number of votes was 62,818, including 3,280 spoiled votes.
40. Royal Ulster Constabulary, 'Chief Constable's Report', 1989.
41. Irish Information Partnership, *Agenda Database* (London: Irish Information Partnership, 1989) Table B-21.
42. Bew and Gillespie, *Northern Ireland: A Chronology of the Troubles,* pp.163, 179–80.
43. Interview with Jim Gibney, Sinn Féin Ard Chomhairle member, Belfast, 8 August 1998.
44. The IIP classifies eleven of the twelve deaths as being the responsibility of 'unknown republicans' while the killing of David Teeney was claimed by the INLA.
45. Interview with former E-4A commander, London May 2004. E-4A was the name of the section of the RUC Special Branch that controlled the separate Headquarters Mobile Support Units (HMSUs). See also, Urban, Mark, *Big Boys' Rules: The Secret Struggle Against the IRA* (London: Faber and Faber, 1992) pp. 46–7, 151–86; Holland, Jack and Phoenix, Susan, *Phoenix: Policing the Shadows* (London: Hodder & Stoughton, 1996) pp. 77–9.
46. Bell, J. Bowyer, *The Irish Troubles: A Generation of Violence 1967–1992* (Dublin: Gill and Macmillan,1993) p. 653.
47. Murray, R., *The SAS in Ireland* (Dublin: Mercier, 1990) pp. 274–97. In May 2001 the European Court of Human Rights found the security forces guilty of failing to uphold the rights of the IRA members.
48. Stalker, John, *Stalker* (London: Harrap, 1987).
49. Greer, Steven, 'The Supergrass System in Northern Ireland', in Wilkinson, Paul and Stewart, A.M. (eds), *Contemporary Research on Terrorism* (Aberdeen: Aberdeen University Press, 1987) pp. 518–19.
50. Urban, Mark, *Big Boys' Rules: The Secret Struggle Against the IRA* (London: Faber and Faber, 1992) p. 134.
51. Greer, Steven, 'Supergrasses and the Legal System in Britain and Northern Ireland', *The Law Quarterly Review,* April (1986) p. 230.
52. Bell, J. Bowyer, *The Irish Troubles: A Generation of Violence 1967–1992* (Dublin: Gill and Macmillan, 1993) pp. 735–6.
53. Korff, Douwe, *The Diplock Courts in Northern Ireland: A Fair Trial?* (Utrecht: Netherlands Institute of Human Rights, 1984).
54. Calculated from Greer, Steven, *Supergrasses: A Study in Anti-terrorist Law Enforcement in Northern Ireland* (Oxford: Clarendon, 1995) Appendix C.
55. My calculation of deaths by location is based on the geographic breakdown used by the Irish Information Partnership, *Agenda Database* (London: IIP, 1989) Section B-2. The results in terms of deaths to army and security forces as a whole correspond closely

with the results of Murray, R. 1982 'Political Violence in Northern Ireland 1969–77', in Boal, F.W. and Douglas, J. (eds), *Integration and Division: Geographical Perspectives on the Northern Ireland Problem* (London: Academic, 1982) pp. 318–23.

56. Thatcher, *The Downing Street Years*, p. 393.
57. *Report of the New Ireland Forum* (Dublin: Stationery Office, 1984) pp. 18–19, emphasis added.
58. Arnold, Bruce, *Haughey: His Life and Unlucky Deeds* (London: Harper Collins, 1993) p. 166.
59. FitzGerald, Garret, *All in a Life: An Autobiography* (Dublin: Gill and Macmillan, 1991) p. 529.
60. Ibid., p. 504.
61. Thatcher, *The Downing Street Years*, pp. 385, 397–8.
62. FitzGerald, *All in a Life*, pp. 510–16.
63. Thatcher, *The Downing Street Years*, p. 401.
64. The IRA planned a summer bombing blitz of English resorts starting in July 1985 but the bombing team was arrested following the Brighton bombing after the Special Branch lifted a fingerprint from Patrick Magee, one of two IRA men who planted the bomb in the Grand Hotel. See Bishop and Mallie, *The Provisional IRA*, pp. 423–30.
65. O'Brien, *The Long War*, p.133.
66. Thatcher, *The Downing Street Years*, p. 399.
67. FitzGerald, *All in a Life*, p. 519.
68. Arthur, Paul, 'Anglo-Irish Relations and Constitutional Policy', in Mitchell, Paul and Wilford, Rick (eds), *Politics in Northern Ireland* (Boulder, CO: Westview, 1998) pp. 251–4; See also Cox, W. Harvey, 'From Hillsborough to Downing Street – and After', in Catterall, Peter and McDougall, Sean (eds), *The Northern Ireland Question in British Politics* (London: Macmillan, 1996); O'Leary and McGarry, *The Politics of Antagonism*, pp. 238–9.
69. Hadden, Tom and Boyle, Kevin (eds), *The Anglo-Irish Agreement, Commentary, Text, and Official Review* (London: Sweet and Maxwell, 1989) p. 26.
70. Quoted in Cochrane, Feargal, *Unionist Politics and the Politics of Unionism since the Anglo-Irish Agreement* (Cork: Cork University Press, 1997) p. 25.
71. FitzGerald, Garret, *All in a Life*, p. 504.
72. See also Arthur, *Special Relationships*, pp. 251–2; O'Leary and McGarry, *The Politics of Antagonism*, pp. 237–9; Cox, W. Harvey, 'Managing Northern Ireland Intergovernmentally', *Parliamentary Affairs*, 40, 1 (1987) pp. 82–3, 90–7; Shannon, William V. 'The Anglo-Irish Agreement', *Foreign Affairs*, Spring (1986) pp. 849–70.
73. Interview with former British army officer, London, 12 November 2006.
74. Aughey, *Under Siege*, pp. 75–7.
75. Interview with Jim Gibney, Sinn Féin, Belfast, 8 August 1998; see also Adams, Gerry, *Free Ireland: Towards a Lasting Peace* (Dingle: Brandon, 1995) pp. 105–9, 174, 188–90.
76. O'Leary and McGarry, *The Politics of Antagonism*, pp. 221–5; Cochrane, *Unionist Politics*, pp. 26–7.
77. FitzGerald, *All in a Life*, p. 554.
78. Cunningham, *British Government Policy in Northern Ireland*, pp. 207–8.
79. In four notable cases (Burns, O'Reilly, Glenholmes and Ryan), the Irish courts turned down requests for extradition based on technical errors in the warrants. For a critical legal analysis see Hogan, G. and Walker, C., *Political Violence and the Law in Ireland* (Manchester: Manchester University Press, 1989) pp. 300–2.
80. H.C. 6th Series, vol. 87, col. 812, 26 November 1985.
81. Adams, *Free Ireland*, pp. 107–9.
82. Anti-agreement unionist candidates won 418,230 votes from a total of 584,988 valid votes.
83. The Ulster Clubs emerged from the United Ulster Loyalist Front (UULF) formed in the summer of 1985 to oppose the re-routing of loyalist parades.

84. Aughey, *Under Siege*, pp. 75–7.
85. Ibid., pp. 176–82.
86. Quoted in H.C. 6th series, vol. 87, col. 747, 26 November 1985.
87. Interview with Gerry Adams, Sinn Féin President, Belfast, 3 June 2005; see also Adams, *Free Ireland*, pp. 196–8.
88. Michael Lillis, Irish official (involved in negotiation of the Anglo-Irish Agreement), *BBC Panorama*, broadcast 30 January 1995.
89. An idea of the type of weapons secured by the IRA from Libya can be gleaned from the armoury captured aboard the *Eksund* off the coast of France in October 1987. The shipment consisted of 150 tons of arms, including: surface-to-air missiles, rocket-propelled grenade launchers, approximately six tons of Semtex plastic explosive, detonators, machine guns, assault rifles and more than one million rounds of ammunition. Geldard, Ian and Craig, Keith, *IRA, INLA: Foreign Support and International Connections* (London: Institute for the Study of Terrorism, 1988) p. 76. See also O'Brien, *The Long War*, pp. 127–32.
90. Smith, *Fighting for Ireland*, p.192; a similarly dismissive view of the IRA's strategic capacity is presented in McGladdery, Gary, *The Provisional IRA in England The Bombing Campaign 1973–1997* (Dublin: Irish Academic Press, 2006).
91. Adams, Gerry, 'Why I talked to John – By Gerry' in *Fortnight* (Belfast) January 1988, pp. 6–7.
92. O'Brien, *The Long War*, pp. 152–3.
93. FitzGerald, *All in a Life*, p. 554.
94. Hogan and Walker, *Political Violence and the Law in Ireland*, pp. 300–2. The *quid pro quo* between judicial reform and Irish extradition had been operative since the mid-1970s when bipartisan support emerged in the Republic for an all-Ireland court to handle terrorist-related crime. Warner reports that out of a total of seventy-six applications by the RUC for extradition of suspects from the Republic between 1971 and 1980, forty-five or 59.2 per cent were refused; thirty-four of these (44.7 per cent of all applications) were refused on the grounds the alleged offence was political. See Warner, Bruce, 'Extradition Law and Practice in the Crucible of Ulster, Ireland and Great Britain: A Metamorphosis?', *Conflict Quarterly*, 7 (1987) pp. 57–92.
95. Other coercive measures included the Criminal Evidence (NI) Order 1988 which restricted the right to silence of those accused of terrorist offences. Amnesty International found evidence that the removal of the right to silence contributed to the strengthening of interrogation methods. See Amnesty International, *Human Rights Concerns* (London: Amnesty International, 1991).
96. Bell, *The Irish Troubles*, pp. 756–7.
97. Adams, James, Morgan, Robin and Bambridge, Anthony, *Ambush: The War Between the SAS and the IRA* (London: Pan, 1988) pp. 132–67.
98. Stalker was taken off the investigation in June 1986 and suspended from his job as Deputy Chief Constable of Greater Manchester Police over trivial allegations of connections to known criminals. His dismissal was subsequently overturned and appears to have been an attempt to hinder his investigation of the RUC. See Stalker, John, *Stalker* (London: Harrap, 1988). His replacement in the investigation, Colin Sampson of the West Yorkshire Police, presented a (unpublished) report to the government in January 1988 that found evidence to prosecute top RUC officers for perverting the course of justice, though no evidence of an official shoot-to-kill policy was found. See Amnesty International, *Political Killings in Northern Ireland* (London: Amnesty International, 1994) pp. 9–11.
99. For the context and fallout see Amnesty International, *Political Killings*, pp. 23–9; McKittrick, David, *Endgame: The Search for Peace in Northern Ireland* (Belfast: Blackstaff, 1994) pp. 156–71; McKittrick, David, *Dispatches from Belfast* (Belfast: Blackstaff, 1989) pp. 168–9.
100. Between January 1986 and March 1988 the Gardaí searched between 25,000 and 50,000 houses in the Republic and seized large quantities of arms in counties

Roscommon, Sligo, Donegal, Dublin, Meath, Limerick and Cavan, most of which were parts of the estimated 120 tons of weapons and explosives delivered to Ireland from Libya between June 1985 and September 1986. See Bell, *The Irish Troubles,* p. 730: O'Brien, *The Long War,* p. 129.

7

Forever is a Long Time:
The 'Permanent' Eclipse of Violent Politics?

Great Britain and Ireland should 'upon the first day of January, which shall be in the year of our Lord 1801, *and for ever*, be united into one kingdom, by the name of the "United Kingdom of Great Britain and Ireland".
                          Act of Union (1800, emphasis added)

I'm not hung up on a particular word. I am hung up on the concept of [the ceasefire] being permanent. I don't mind if it is said that 'the armed struggle is over', 'the days of violence are gone for good'. But I do need to know that violence is ended for good and it isn't a temporary ceasefire.
                 John Major, British Prime Minister, 31 August 1994[1]

None of us can say two or three years up the road that if the causes of the conflict aren't resolved that another IRA leadership won't come along. Because this has always happened...The history of Ireland is filled with phases of armed struggle and then of quiet, and then reprised phases of armed struggle.
              Gerry Adams, Sinn Féin President, 26 September 1994[2]

Actions are more compelling than words...I am now prepared to make a working assumption that the ceasefire is intended to be permanent.
                John Major, British Prime Minister, 21 October 1994[3]

THE LIMITS OF ANGLO-IRISH CONTAINMENT

At the signing of the Anglo-Irish Agreement Margaret Thatcher stated: 'I went into this agreement because I was not prepared to tolerate a situation of continuing violence...we must break the cycle of violence...'[4] Yet, the cooperative containment embodied in the AIA failed in its two principal aims of marginalizing proponents of violence and encouraging a devolved power-sharing administration. Instead, a new cycle of violence alternated with the halting process of negotiations among the constitutional parties. The successive phases in the next cycle of conflict followed a familiar pattern as that which led to the AIA: increased violence produced a security crisis; the failure of the security response led to new momentum for a political solution; the failure of an internal political solution produced a new vacuum which was filled by proponents of violence. By the end of 1993, the failure of successive Northern

Ireland secretaries to make significant progress on a devolved power-sharing arrangement, combined with an escalation of violence in Northern Ireland and Great Britain, produced threats to stability that were converted by the British and Irish leaders into an opportunity for a new Anglo-Irish strategy published as the Joint Declaration (or Downing Street Declaration) of 15 December 1993. In principle, this strategy moved beyond containment to address the fundamental causes of the conflict: the British and Irish states' competing claims of sovereignty over Northern Ireland. By extension, the two governments acknowledged publicly that proponents of violence would have to be included, rather than marginalized in order to negotiate a settlement. By recognizing that violence was a product rather than a cause of failed conflict regulation, the two governments positioned themselves to make a durable constitutional settlement. This chapter explains how the Joint Declaration came to be made and its implications for British and Irish conflict regulation.

TOWARDS A HURTING STALEMATE

He [Peter Brooke] is fond of recalling the story of how when he visited his ancestral homestead in Co. Cavan in 1966 a local man recognised him as a Brooke – though his family had left the area 300 years before. 'I think patience has to be exercised,' he said. 'And the episode with the old man in Mullagh – if a memory lasts as long as that – you've got to work with the grain of the wood.'[5]

Irish Taoiseach Charles Haughey made the first explicit recognition of the existence of a hurting stalemate in 1989 when he announced that the New Ireland Forum would be re-convened if republican paramilitaries committed themselves to peace. This was followed in October 1989 by a meeting of nationalist and unionist parties from both parts of Ireland, and including proxy-representation for Sinn Féin, at Duisburg, West Germany. The incipient new departure was met, coincidentally, by the arrival of the new, more historically-grounded thinking of Peter Brooke as Northern Ireland Secretary. In an interview to mark his first one-hundred days in office on 3 November 1989, and just three weeks after the IRA killed ten army bandsmen with a bomb at the Deal barracks in Kent, Brooke admitted that the IRA could not be defeated militarily.[6] Shortly after, Brooke used the 'Cyprus analogy' to hint that British governments had recognized and eventually negotiated with 'terrorists' in other colonial wars; and declared that the British government had 'no selfish strategic or economic interest in Northern Ireland'.[7] A secret channel of communication was re-opened in 1990, producing a dialogue between Sinn Féin's Martin McGuinness and an intermediate on behalf of the British government.[8] The dialogue remained secret until November of 1993 and centred on Sinn Féin's demands for a British commitment to inclusive negotiations and the British government undertaking a commitment to act as 'persuaders' for a united Ireland in exchange for a definitive end to IRA violence.[9] Here the republican movement was attempting to use the combination of violence and political leverage to affect the state-level conception of the conflict by securing a commitment from the British government to act as persuaders for a united Ireland, a commitment the British knew would produce violent loyalist resistance.

While tentatively using the secret dialogue to explore the republican movement's willingness to accept a negotiated settlement, the balance of thinking among those government ministers shaping Northern Ireland policy was that constitutional parties could reach agreement to effectively marginalize the IRA. Failing that, a return to internment was contemplated by some ministers, despite the debacle of its last implementation in 1971.[10] Thus, despite the tentative overtures to the republican movement, the Brooke–Mayhew talks beginning in 1991 (after a year of procedural wrangling) were a return to an exclusive process based on marginalizing extremists while promoting agreement among moderates. And while the three-stranded structure of the talks reaffirmed the central parameters of power-sharing in Northern Ireland (Strand 1); a North–South dimension (Strand 2) and the British–Irish intergovernmental level (Strand 3), the analysis of the negotiating positions of the British and Irish governments reveal persistently opposed approaches to conflict regulation, as indicated by divergent conceptions of the 'negotiability' of constitutive and regulative aspects of sovereignty.

Both governments stressed the necessity of the consent of a majority in Northern Ireland to any change in the constitutional status. But they differed widely on the need to compensate the Catholic/nationalist minority in Northern Ireland for the denial of their own separate right of self-determination. Both the Irish government and the SDLP agreed that such compensation required a substantial North–South body with executive powers which, far from diminishing the Irish sovereignty claim, would in some ways fulfil Article 3 of the Irish constitution by creating a means for extending Irish jurisdiction on an all-island basis. The Irish government would only be prepared to contemplate changes to Articles 2 and 3 if they were transcended in this way by all-Ireland bodies with executive powers, as well as significant reforms in Northern Ireland itself to promote 'parity of esteem' between nationalists and unionists. The Irish government defended this position by declaring that

> 'the essence of the nationalists' identity is that they are Irish and not British. They aspire to participate in a wider Irish political system no less strongly than Unionists assert the claim to have their British identity expressed in a British system.'[11]

The British government and both main unionist parties, by contrast, were seeking to *remove* rather than transcend the Irish constitutional claims. The British government supported the unionist position seeking explicit recognition of Northern Ireland's status as part of the United Kingdom and, by extension, the recognition of the right of the people of Northern Ireland to self-determination. The divergent conceptions of the sovereignty adjustments required for conflict regulation were demonstrated by the British government's belief that the Irish government's removal or amendment of Articles 2 and 3 would lead to a reciprocal gesture from unionists, in the form of agreeing to share power in a devolved Northern Ireland administration. According to Conservative Prime Minister John Major, 'Dublin disappointed us by holding back from agreeing to amend Articles 2 and 3.'[12] Sir Patrick Mayhew, Brooke's successor as Northern Ireland Secretary, believed that SDLP leader John Hume had prevented an internal power-sharing assembly being agreed in the negotiations of 1991–2, because it was balanced toward the Northern Ireland level, rather than the degree of all-Ireland integration agreed in the New Ireland Forum, and which was central to the Hume–Adams principles which were being developed from 1990.[13]

The view that changes to Articles 2 and 3 were a *quid pro quo* for unionist acceptance of power-sharing *in* Northern Ireland reflected the continuation of an asymmetrical conception of sovereignty status. Effectively, the British government was encouraging a reciprocal exchange at the 'government' rather than 'state' level, i.e. between the Irish government and Northern Ireland unionists rather than between the Irish Republic and the United Kingdom. Not only did the Irish government insist that changes to its sovereignty claim could only be considered in the context of a strengthened Irish dimension, it also declared from the outset of the Brooke–Mayhew talks that the British claim to sovereignty in the Government of Ireland Act (1920) must also be on the table for negotiation.[14]

The effects of the change towards a more symmetrical conception of national sovereignty in transforming the basis of negotiation were profound, as revealed by the eventual success of the Joint Declaration (or Downing Street Declaration) signed in December 1993. In the meantime, as discussed below, the IRA was determined to underpin its challenge to British constitutionalism through massive explosive force, while more extreme strands of unionism demonstrated the continued currency of violent politics. In their reaction to the Irish government's use of Articles 2 and 3 as a *quid pro quo* for strengthening the Irish dimension, the DUP quoted the RUC's estimate that the rate of terrorist killings by loyalist had increased from 20 per cent to 46 per cent in the previous ten years and warned:

Such killings we unreservedly condemn as we have always done and would abhor any suggestion that these should be used to support a political argument. Yet our fear is that this substantial increase will continue in the atmosphere created by the belief that democratic politics cannot bring change. Nobody should be in any doubt that our sincere conviction is to work to avoid such a condition. It should be stated, however, that failure to remove the territorial claim will continue to act as a spur to IRA violence.[15]

VIOLENCE IN THE VACUUM

The republican movement was buoyed by the fact that yet another internal talks process had failed to produce an internal agreement for the government of

Northern Ireland, and the militants interpreted the secret contacts with Sinn Féin as a concession to the pressure of violence. The IRA campaign which punctuated the talks process and accelerated following its conclusion in the autumn of 1992 was intended to shift further the British government from its neutral arbiter position to that of an active persuader for an all-Ireland solution. As the Sinn Féin policy document *Towards a Lasting Peace in Ireland* stated in 1992:

> ... implicit in the public political posturing [of the British Government] is the suggestion that the responsibility for dismantling partition lies largely with Irish nationalists and their powers and ability to persuade an appropriate percentage of unionists that their best interests lie in a reunited Ireland. This is but a shallow attempt to displace responsibility for resolving a situation which was wholly manufactured by Westminster and whose disastrous consequences are almost wholly borne by the Irish people. No amount of public political posturing can change that.[16]

The implication of republican strategic thinking was that violence had revealed the limits of cooperative containment, had elicited a reaffirmation of British neutrality and, if escalated carefully, could eventually transform the British government's 'public political posturing' into a firm decision to disengage from its increasingly expensive commitment to Northern Ireland. This interpretation of republican strategic thinking is in direct contrast to that of M.L.R. Smith and Gary McGladdery, who have each argued that the IRA was hostage to its own tradition of physical-force means and could not target violence for specific strategic results.[17] Yet, evidence suggests that the republican leadership was well aware of its ability to affect British strategic thinking, in small but significant degrees, by combining military pressure with hints of political compromise. It was also aware of the limits of the military instrument and was seeking to develop a new departure that would produce a stronger weapon than Semtex: an alliance of the constitutional nationalist parties North and South. Subsequent events (discussed below) show clearly that the republican leadership was able to sell significant compromises of its doctrinaire positions to the majority of its followers, based on reciprocal exchanges within the wider nationalist bloc and with British governments.

From the middle of 1990, the IRA campaign involved two primary theatres of war, both aimed at increasing the financial and personal costs of Britain's commitment to Northern Ireland, in order to encourage British elites to become persuaders for an all-Ireland settlement. Attacks against security personnel continued but the primary emphasis was on massive explosions in commercial town centres across Northern Ireland and at RUC and army installations. In addition, from August 1990 the IRA threatened to kill anyone working for the security forces in an attempt to intimidate the large civilian workforce working on army and police barracks construction, and thereby drive up security costs. The worst incident in this category was the killing of 8 Protestant/unionist workmen at Teebane Cross on 17 January 1992. The UDA/UFF retaliated on 5

February by killing five Catholics/nationalists at Graham's bookie's shop on the Lower Ormeau Road in Belfast.

From the middle of 1990 the IRA caused massive explosions on commercial property in town centres, army installations and police stations across Northern Ireland. Along with a series of incendiary bombings, the town centre bombings continued into 1993, peaking in May when a series of bombs in Belfast, Portadown and Magherafelt caused an estimated total of £22 million in the space of just three days. The bombings continued through the summer, devastating town centres in Bangor (twice), Newry, Coleraine and Newtownards.

Figure 15 reveals the direct costs of the commercial bombings in Northern Ireland, as the combined costs of criminal damage and injury compensation alone more than doubled from £42 million to £102 million between the fiscal years 1990–1 and 1992–3. In addition, as Figure 16 shows, the proportion of security costs as a proportion of the overall subvention grew from 1987 to 1990. In December 1991 Brooke announced that public spending in certain areas would be frozen because of the costs of bomb damage. This was followed in December 1992 by a similar announcement of a diversion of funds from other public accounts and most tellingly in April 1993 by Mayhew's well-publicized gaffe in *Die Zeit*:

> A number of nationalist people have been encouraged by the terrorists to believe that the British government would never release Northern Ireland, we would very happily release Northern Ireland, to be perfectly frank with you, because we have no selfish interest, strategic interest.
>
> It's not quite right to say, I withdraw that, I don't want to say we would very happily do it. I don't want to say that. We would be no obstacle in the way. It costs us three billion a year net. Three billion for one-and-a-half million people – we have no strategic interest, we have no economic interest, in staying there.[18]

Mayhew's statement is particularly revealing when contrasted with the statement of one of his predecessors, Humphrey Atkins, in 1979:

> I think the whole House recognizes that to seek to defend the citizens of the UK against the kind of attack to which the people of Northern Ireland are subjected is a costly business. At the same time I do not believe that this House would begrudge the cost of seeking to defend our fellow citizens against this kind of evil.[19]

The commercial bombing campaign in Northern Ireland was mirrored by the IRA's campaigns in Great Britain and on the European continent. There were three primary targets. First, the targeting of British army personnel both in England and on the continent continued apace. Apart from the ten army bandsmen killed at Deal in September 1989 mentioned above, the IRA also mistakenly killed the wife of a army soldier in Dortmund, Germany, and in June killed two Australian tourists mistaken for off-duty soldiers in Roermond, the Netherlands. The IRA did manage to hit their intended targets in May when they killed one army sergeant at a recruiting office in Wembley, greater London, and again in June when they killed an army recruit on the platform of Litchfield train station, and the following day when they killed an army major in Germany.

The second target group were British elites associated with security policy or previous security roles in Northern Ireland. On 30 July 1989, just ten days after Brooke announced the breakdown of the procedural round of talks among constitutional parties, the IRA killed MP Ian Gow with a bomb attached to his car outside his London home. The assassination of Gow, a proponent of hardline security measures and one-time confidant of Thatcher, had echoes of the Neave killing (by the INLA); it was a direct attempt to impact the personal and political life of elite decision-makers. Gow's death was followed in August and September by unsuccessful attempts on the lives of Lord Armstrong, another Thatcher confidant and chief negotiator of the AIA; General Sir Anthony Farrar-Hockley, Commander of Land forces in Northern Ireland between 1970 and 1972; Air Chief Marshal Sir Peter Terry, former Governor of Gibraltar who had given the order to permit the SAS to operate there; and Foreign Office Minister William Waldegrave, who was speaking at a conference on terrorism. Other notable incidents in this category included a bomb attack at the Conservative Carlton Club in London on 26 June, which caused damage but no injuries. The most audacious attack in this group was the mortar bomb attack on 10 Downing Street on 7 February 1992 during a meeting of the war cabinet on the first day of the Gulf War. One of the three mortar bombs landed in the back garden of 10 Downing Street, causing no injuries but a significant propaganda coup for the IRA by displacing the first day of the Gulf War on the front pages of most of the UK's quality papers.

The third target group comprised commercial targets ranging from small incendiary devices planted in busy shopping areas, to bombs intended to disrupt the railway networks, to bombs at gasworks facilities in the north of England. The IRA's British campaign included two 'spectaculars' in the City of London (the financial district) on 10 April 1992 at the Baltic Exchange and a year later on 24 April 1993 at the NatWest Tower. These two bombs killed four persons in all and caused damage estimated at approximately £1 billion.[20] The amount of damage forced the government to pass the Reinsurance (Acts of Terrorism) Act in May 1993, in which the government assumed responsibility as the 'reinsurer of last resort' for potential targets of terrorism. Not since the War Damage Act (1941), when the government was forced to provide insurance following the refusal of the private sector to insure against bomb damage, has a British government intervened to such an extent in the private insurance market. The IRA then attempted to gain maximum impact from the bombings by sending a letter to fifty international financial companies with London offices which stated: '. . . no one should be misled into underestimating the seriousness of the IRA intention to mount future planned attacks in the political and financial heart of the British state'.[21]

Despite the tonnages of destruction, the IRA did not succeed in its strategic objective of forcing the British government to concede the republican interpretation of the principle of Irish self-determination (including the necessity of the British becoming persuaders for Irish unity). Martin Mansergh, Fianna Fáil's chief researcher, saw 'absolutely no evidence from our dealings with the British Government or indeed their dealings with anyone else that they were materially swayed by bombs in the City of London'.[22] Of course, the last thing a British negotiator would reveal to an Irish negotiator was evidence of being pressured by republican violence. On the other hand, I was informed (off the record) by a former Fianna Fáil minister that in his opinion, these bombs were 'the decisive turning point in the events leading to the Joint-Declaration'.[23]

The significance of the spectaculars and commercial bombings was both more balanced and complex than either of these accounts would indicate. For significant elements within the republican movement the political reaction to the escalation of the bombing campaign revealed the limits of militant tactics, but also confirmed its belief in the necessity of underlining its position by the implicit threat of violence, both to pressure the British government and, especially, to manage its base and prevent out-flanking. For the British and Irish governments, the persistence of the IRA's military capacity underlined the necessity of an inclusive rather than exclusive approach to conflict regulation. This view was also held by the leadership of RUC Special Branch whose intelligence indicated that the internal debate within the republican movement was leading to a determination to trade militancy for pan-nationalist constitutionalism, and also by the persistence of inter-agency rivalry, which hampered the security forces in their attempt to defeat terrorism.[24]

By early 1993, the decision facing the republican leaderships was not whether to call a ceasefire, but when and for what constitutional concessions. For the republican leadership there were four significant developments suggesting a hurting stalemate. First, the bluntness of the military instrument was revealed by events like 'Britain's Enniskillen': the deaths of two children (Johnathan Ball, aged 3 and Timothy Parry, aged 12) and fifty-six injuries by IRA bombs placed in a crowded shopping area in Warrington on 20 March 1993. The republican movement had survived Enniskillen, but in the context of their own 'peace initiative', where a central aim was to gain support from Dublin and Washington, this tragedy was damaging. President Clinton declared that 'the United States condemns in the strongest terms such violence and those who support and perpetuate it'.[25] Two days after Warrington, Adams applied for a visa to visit the US and was turned down because of his links with a terrorist organization.[26]

Secondly, as the limits to the 'Armalite' were increasingly apparent, the loss of Gerry Adams' parliamentary seat in the Westminster election of 1992 also revealed the limits of the 'ballot box' in the context of a hot war. Moreover, it was clear to the more forward-thinking elements of the republican leadership that it was precisely the use of violence that had limited Sinn Féin's growth as a political party North or South. According to the very author of the 'ballot box and Armalite' strategy, Danny Morrison, writing from prison in 1992, the republican movement faced an historic opportunity to break the historical cycle which invariably left republicans marginalized: 'Believe it or not, I think we can fight on forever and can't be defeated. But, of course, that isn't the same as winning or showing something for all the sacrifices.'[27] Furthermore,

> The IRA will never overthrow the government or drive out Crown Forces. The landscape of the struggle is a West European consumer society, with sectarian divisions, with vestiges of social democracy. And our starting position was the demand for civil rights and reform ... We should never ever allow the situation to decline to the extent that we face such a decision from the depths of an unpopular, unseemly, impossible-to-end armed struggle. Or, from the point of brave exhaustion another one of the glorious defeats with which our past is littered.[28]

Thirdly, the successes of the commercial bombing campaign and the spectaculars in Great Britain were offset by the strategically targeted escalation of violence by loyalist paramilitaries. Between October 1988 and August 1993 loyalists killed eighteen people with Sinn Féin connections.[29] Moreover, loyalist paramilitaries killed more people in 1992 than republicans for the first time in Northern Ireland's history. This escalation was exactly the loyalist paramilitary strategy, as stated by a member of the UVF: 'We are out to terrorise the [republican] terrorists. To get to the stage when old grannies up the Falls will call on the IRA to stop, because it is ordinary Catholics that are getting hit, not the Provos behind steel security doors.'[30] According to the late Billy Wright (known as 'King Rat') of the UVF: 'I genuinely believe that whenever the two communities started to hurt the same, it wasn't long before we started to talk about peace, negotiations and settlements ... It also brought home to the IRA that never again would there be a Teebane, never again would there be an Enniskillen without the nationalist people paying a very heavy price.'[31] Evidence suggests that loyalists were facilitated by elements within RUC Special Branch and British army intelligence whose use of informants and disinformation, as discussed above, suggested a purposeful attempt to level the killing field. This strategy was successful in terms of the counter-terrorism strategy but at the considerable price of undermining state legitimacy by subsequent disclosures of collusion.[32] These disclosures then became leverage points for Sinn Féin during the implementation phases following the Good Friday Agreement in 1998.

Fourthly, by March 1993 the secret negotiations between Sinn Féin and the British government had reached a point where the British had agreed to formal talks in exchange for a two- to three-week IRA ceasefire, during which time the British claimed they could persuade Sinn Féin that violence was counter-productive.[33] Though wary of being duped into a ceasefire such as the disaster of 1975, the republican leadership did suspect that the British government was looking for a way to include the republican movement in the process of achieving an accommodation. In that context, events like Warrington, and the intensification of the town centre bombings in May 1993, set this process back because they cast doubt on the IRA's intentions and, in turn, on Sinn Féin's ability to emerge as an *interlocuteur valable* by delivering an IRA ceasefire. As the British government message to Sinn Féin on 3 June stated: 'Before that process [publicly announced talks] could be completed renewed violence on a serious scale took place – with the inevitable consequence that the process itself had to be halted... The outcome will, as always, be affected by events on the ground. This is not a threat, merely a statement of reality.'[34] Thus although Sinn Féin emphasized repeatedly that the secret discussions had proceeded without assurances of a ceasefire, the British were making it clear that no substantive negotiations could occur while violence continued and, more importantly, that the Major government would not act as a persuader for a united Ireland. As a part of a conflict regulation strategy, this firmness was significant because by revealing its own 'bottom line' the British encouraged the republican leadership to believe that they were being stubborn, but sincere. Major successfully defended the unionist consent principle against any erosion by the militant or constitutional republicans.

LETTING THE POT BOIL: THE CULTIVATION OF A 'HURTING STALEMATE'

In November 1992 Mayhew announced that the failed three-stranded talks process would be shelved in favour of bi-lateral talks between the British government and each of the constitutional parties. The bi-lateral talks were a holding pattern while the real action was taking place in the secret talks with Sinn Féin and a renewed emphasis on the Anglo-Irish intergovernmental level. As such, this development can be compared to the shift from the inter-party to intergovernmental level, which led to the signing of the AIA. However, the crucial difference between this and previous conflict regulation strategies was that the British government was attempting, through covert negotiations with Sinn Féin, and aware of the Irish government's cultivation of the Hume–Adams initiative,[35] to include the republican movement into the constitutional talks process. The problem for the British Prime Minister was that the rebellion of nine 'Euro-rebels' made his government dependent upon the nine votes of the Ulster Unionists in the crucial vote on the Maastricht Treaty in July 1993. The price for unionists was a pledge to establish a Select Committee for Northern Ireland (at Westminster), which unionists hoped would secure the union and provide more accountable direct rule.

The result of this confused strategy was, predictably, an intensification of violence and threats of violence as constitutionalist norms were breached. Loyalist paramilitaries interpreted the Hume–Adams dialogue as the establishment of a 'pan-nationalist front.' Unionist alarm was raised further in July 1993 when UUP leader Jim Molyneaux and MP John Taylor claimed that the Northern Ireland Office (NIO) had presented the IRA with peace proposals at the end of 1992. The UDA had already widened its list of targets to include the SDLP, and had carried out a series of attacks against the homes of SDLP members from January to March, 1993. In July, following Irish Tánaiste (Deputy Prime Minister, who was also Foreign Minister) Dick Spring's advocacy of a form of joint authority, Molyneaux responded that such a proposal would lead loyalists to take 'the paramilitary road'.[36] On 8 September, one day after the UFF killed a hairdresser on the Falls Road, John Taylor stated: '[i]n a perverse way the increasing fear amongst Catholics might be helpful because they were beginning to appreciate the fear in the Protestant community'.[37] Tory party Chairman Sir Norman Tebbitt further underlined the efficacy of violence when he stated: 'I suspect that the only thing that will take Articles 2 and 3 out of the Irish Constitution is when the bombs begin to blow in Dublin in the way that they have been in Belfast and in London.'[38] In December, future UUP leader David Trimble accused Irish Taoiseach Albert Reynolds of 'surrender by stages' to the IRA.[39]

While attempts at creating a level killing field may have contributed to the development of a hurting stalemate, in the short term it created a crisis as republican and loyalist paramilitaries escalated their violence. Like the 1975 ceasefire, unionist and loyalist anxiety was increased by the fact that the process of inclusion was covert and imbalanced towards republicans. This killing frenzy peaked in late October and early November 1993 when the IRA killed nine Protestants/unionists civilians (plus, accidentally, their own bomber, Thomas Begley) on the Shankill Road with a bomb meant for the leadership of the UDA/UFF.[40] Gerry Adams demonstrated solidarity with the IRA by carrying Begley's coffin, sewing consternation among US and British officials. The UFF responded swiftly by killing seven Catholics/nationalists a week later at a pub in Greysteel, Co. Londonderry, followed by six more Catholics/nationalists in the following two weeks.

The response to this crisis demonstrated that the contest for the control of force remained central to the pre-negotiating process. The British government had received a draft from the Irish government in June 1993 that was a synthesis of the (unpublished) Hume–Adams proposals and the Irish government's own proposals, developed largely by Martin Mansergh and Albert Reynolds. The fallout from the Shankill bombing clearly concentrated the minds of the Irish and British negotiators and a draft joint declaration was agreed in Brussels four days after the Shankill bombing. However, the British thought the Irish proposals did not protect sufficiently the separate right of self-determination for the unionist community. In addition, following the damaging revelations of the government's secret contacts with Sinn Féin in early December, the British government attempted to cover its unionist/loyalist flank by putting forward a new proposal which limited the provision of self-determination to Northern Ireland. In response, according to Brendan O'Brien, Albert Reynolds apparently told the British: 'that unless they accepted the concept of self-determination on an all-Ireland basis they were all wasting their time. The IRA campaign and the bloody conflict would continue. Reynolds left the British in no doubt that he would walk away from the process if needs be.'[41] This implicit threat was successful as the British withdrew their counter-proposal and negotiated the final declaration based on the original proposals agreed in Brussels incorporating the essential elements of the Hume–Adams agreement on self-determination.

From the British side the implicit threat of increasing loyalist violence was also used, if not orchestrated, to warn Dublin against seeking too much of a nationalist agenda. In late November, just days before the crucial 3 December summit, the seizure of a shipment of arms from Poland allegedly destined for loyalist paramilitaries was highlighted in the British media, amidst warnings that loyalists may have been acting on Tebbitt's advice to bomb Dublin. Evidence suggests that the arms shipment was in fact a hoax organized by army intelligence, meant to highlight the threat of a loyalist escalation.[42]

DEVELOPING *INTERLOCUTEURS VALABLES*

Having cultivated and recognized the 'hurting stalemate', it remained necessary to cultivate political alignments within nationalist and unionist blocs to move towards inclusive negotiations. The key to this process was the mutual recognition by the British and Irish governments of the need to modify sovereignty claims, which created the basis for a progressive set of reciprocal exchanges that reaffirmed the parameters of a settlement established with the AIA. More specifically, the bi-national, intergovernmental conflict regulation strategy shaped the strategic and tactical choices of the parties and movements in Northern Ireland, creating more stable negotiating blocs with the two governments as the *interlocuteurs valables,* leaders capable of taking their followers into a settlement. But this was not simply an elite-led, top-down process of 'lowing the horses slowly' into a British–Irish paddock. The conflict regulation process also required elites to recognize the legitimacy of the motivations of republican and loyalist paramilitaries, as well as cultivating 'sufficient consensus' between constitutional unionist and nationalist parties, grounded in the respective polities. Thus, there was a clear relationship between the development of an inclusive process (bringing paramilitaries into constitutional negotiations) and the opening of sovereignty to negotiation in a more symmetrical, bargainable exchange relationship than existed hitherto.

While significant political obstacles limited the strategic choices of the Major government, there were two primary reasons for the decisive shift in conflict strategy leading to the Downing Street Declaration (Joint Declaration) of December 1993. First, the alternative 'twin-track' strategy based on reaching agreement among moderates, while defeating terrorists, had failed for the fifth time since 1973 and the third time during the Conservative government's tenure since 1979. The shift in approach is revealed, for example, in Major's memoirs where his analysis of the situation in the early 1990s reveals a subtle departure from the focus on constitutional politics *in* Northern Ireland: 'We were beginning to see the fruits of our long term policy of addressing legitimate Nationalist grievances, building support for the democratic process across the political spectrum inside *and outside Northern Ireland*, and squeezing out terrorism by every means, *persuasive as well as military.*'[43]

Secondly, and perhaps more importantly, the Irish government was cultivating the republican leadership into the constitutional fold by acknowledging and encouraging the Hume–Adams dialogue which centred on a process of national self-determination acknowledging the principle of majority consent for any changes to the status of Northern Ireland. This process entailed an important shift by Fianna Fáil-led governments towards accepting the parameters of the Anglo-Irish Agreement. Despite Fianna Fáil's opposition to the AIA,[44] once in office, successive Fianna Fáil Taoiseach, Charles Haughey, (1987–92) and Albert Reynolds (1992–4), used the IGC, and, according to Martin Mansergh, Fianna Fáil's most influential advisor on Northern Ireland: 'The Irish Government (1991–4) were determined not to subscribe to anything, which would be clearly at variance with its international obligations, *principally the Anglo-Irish Agreement.*'[45] In other words, the principle of majority consent within Northern Ireland for any change to the constitutional status of Northern Ireland (Article 1 of the AIA) had been elevated to a constitutional *grundnorm* or dominant principle in the Irish Republic, which Sinn Féin had to accept in order to participate in an alliance of nationalist parties North and South. But in exchange for relinquishing its ethno-centric claim to national self-determination (which denied unionists a separate right of self-determination), Sinn Féin was being offered an alignment of the constitutional nationalist parties (Fianna Fáil and the SDLP) which would insist on adjustments to the regulative aspects of sovereignty as declared in the New Ireland Forum, including a guaranteed process of national self-determination which would make a united Ireland possible; as well as a significant North–South 'Irish dimension', power-sharing and significant enhancements of political and civil rights for the Catholic/nationalist minority in Northern Ireland.

One particularly important facilitator of a ripe moment was the 1991 census result that showed the Catholic/nationalist population growing at a faster rate than many expected, from approximately 37 per cent of the population in 1971 to approximately 42 per cent in 1991.[46] This trend contributed to the arguments within the republican movement that demographics rather than demolitions could forward the goal of Irish unity. It also convinced some unionist leaders of the potential erosion of their demographic strength and the resultant risks associated with obstruction of the British–Irish process. As UUP negotiator Reg Empey (and future leader of the Ulster Unionist Party) explained to McKittrick and Mallie,

> If this all collapses, do we not prove that Northern Ireland is a failed political entity? How do you put together circumstances again when Unionism can negotiate from any strength? Instability works against Unionism. It drives people out. It sends our students away. It weakens our economy and therefore weakens the Union. However difficult it is with emotional issues such as prisoners, my argument was that we had to look at the bigger-picture issues in the long term.[47]

In this context, the potential for the 'pan-nationalist' alliance to deliver an IRA ceasefire put considerable pressure on the British government to respond in order not to be, in the words of a senior official in the Northern Ireland Office, 'left sucking the hind tit'.[48] But the core demand of the republican movement – that the British government commit itself to acting as a persuader for a united Ireland – was a step too far for the British government. Major's justification for the rejection of the republican demand clearly reveals his belief that shifting from a position of neutrality to one advocating a united Ireland faced both incumbent and regime-level obstacles because of the implications for the union in the context of debates over devolution and European integration.[49] By negotiating the removal of any 'persuader commitment, Major solidified a 'pan-unionist' alliance to counter the Irish 'pan-nationalist' alliance, thus establishing a more symmetrical set of *interlocuteurs valables* aligned hierarchically within each of the nation-state blocs. The value of this dualist alignment was emphasized by Irish Taoiseach Albert Reynolds who argued that the key to the success of the Joint Declaration (Downing Street Declaration, DSD) approach was that he would deliver the nationalist side if Major would deliver unionists.[50]

It is in strengthening the dualist British–Irish relationship that the external intervention of third parties like the US and EU had their most profound impact. The external intervention and facilitation from the Clinton White House gradually reduced the hierarchical, political and symbolic obstacles to a settlement. According to an Irish official interviewed by Mallie and McKittrick, the Irish government's 'psychology was to give republicans a bit and see if they would deliver. The British psychology was to box them in and then, when they were truly in the box, give a bit. *They were using a colonial psychology.* Clinton put the whole American weight behind the first model.[51]

A FRAMEWORK FOR SELF-DETERMINATION: BI-NATIONAL CONSENT

The Joint Declaration (Downing Street Declaration) signed in London on 15 December 1993 was a significant advance in British–Irish conflict regulation because it established agreement between the two governments on the primary regulative aspect of sovereignty: a process of self-determination requiring the consent of *both* a majority of people in Northern Ireland *and* a majority of people in the Irish Republic. Paragraphs 4 and 5 contained the heart of the exchange:

> *Paragraph 4:* ... The British Government agree that it is for the people of the island of Ireland alone, by agreement between the two parts respectively, to exercise their right of self-determination on the basis of consent, freely and concurrently given, North and South, to bring about a united Ireland, if that is their wish.

> *Paragraph 5:* [The Taoiseach] accepts, on behalf of the Irish Government, that the democratic right of self-determination by the people of Ireland as a whole must be achieved and exercised with and subject to the agreement and consent of a majority of the people of Northern Ireland and must, consistent with justice and equity, respect the democratic dignity and civil rights and religious liberties of both communities.

In addition, the Joint Declaration reiterated that the parameters of a settlement must be 'founded on consent and encompassing arrangements within Northern Ireland, for the whole island, and between these islands' (Paragraph 2).

The Joint Declaration was a decisive turning point because of its acknowledgement of the core causes of conflict and its bi-national ethos that addresses the historical state, governmental and societal levels of conflict, *in that order*. By agreeing in principle on a mechanism for self-determination, the Irish government's status was marginally increased *vis-a-vis* Britain based on the adjustment to the core regulative aspect of sovereignty. This form of self-determination went beyond a simple reaffirmation of Britain's neutrality regarding the constitutional status of Northern Ireland as established with the Anglo-Irish Agreement. By stating that the process of self-determination was for the Irish people alone, the citizens of the Irish Republic were being given a veto on unionists' preferences for self-determination (currently, *inter alia* further integration into the United Kingdom; independence; and majoritarian devolution).[52] Henceforth, *both* nationalist and unionist preferences for self-determination were required for any change in the status of Northern Ireland. For the first time since 1918 the rights to self-determination were subject to all-Ireland consent, exercised concurrently in both parts of Ireland. Equally, by stating that the British presence in Northern Ireland was a result of unionists' preferences rather than strategic or economic interests, the two governments were attempting to deny the republican claim that the onus was on the British government to persuade unionists to promote a united Ireland. Instead, the two governments reached agreement on the core aspect of regulative sovereignty first, to consolidate their intergovernmental relations and remove the sliding, precipitous thresholds of state contraction and expansion.

Politically, the Joint Declaration had two important short-term aims stemming from increasing intergovernmental symmetry. By opening the negotiations to representatives of the paramilitary groups (on the condition of verifiable commitments to end the use of violence (Paragraph 10), the two governments were attempting to consolidate the nationalist and unionist blocs and thereby limit the destabilizing effects of violence which impacted so negatively during the Sunningdale negotiations. Secondly, the primacy of the bi-national, intergovernmental axis was demonstrated as the two governments again responded to the failure of an internal, Northern Ireland-based approach (Brooke–Mayhew talks) with an international treaty. The Irish government affirmed conditionally its commitment to support changes in the Irish constitution 'as part of a balanced constitutional accommodation'... [to] reflect the principle of consent in Northern Ireland' (Paragraph 7). This process sent a clear signal to unionists of the British intention of deepening co-operation with the Irish government and a clear signal to republicans that they would not be able to bomb the British government into conceding on the principle of majoritarian consent for any change in the status of Northern Ireland.

The effects of the bi-national treaty in turn shaped the internal debates within republicanism and unionism over participation in negotiations. While the Sinn Féin leadership privately supported the Joint Declaration in its internal negotiations, the majority of the grassroots, especially in border areas and further south, believed it sold short by assuring a 'unionist veto' on unity and ancillary levels of reform.[53] One significant incumbent-level obstacle was vital in the delay in the IRA's decision to call a ceasefire: the British opposition Labour party's policy of promoting 'Irish unity by consent' established in 1981. Given the fragility of Major's Conservative government, which was deeply divided on further European integration, some IRA leaders felt it was worth seeing out the Major government with a costly 'commercial' bombing campaign, and then calling a future Labour government on its commitment to act as a persuader for Irish unity. Against this view, the surprising victory of the Conservatives in the British election of 1992, in the midst of recession, led to speculation that the British Labour party could never again win power.[54] IRA attacks continued while the internal debate was taking place, but the targeting and nature of the attacks (such as the firing of uncharged mortars at London's Heathrow airport on 9 March 1994) suggested that the IRA leadership was being steered towards accepting an unarmed strategy.[55]

In contrast to explanations that focus on the dearth of IRA strategic think-ing, the maintenance of an offensive capability was crucial in maintaining unity within the republican movement despite serious scepticism concerning British motivations, as revealed by one IRA member from south Armagh: 'The Brits are looking for a military solution, not a political solution...[as a result] the threat of violence is always necessary. We can't give up arms until there's a negotiated settlement. Nobody should give Britain a stick to beat us with.'[56] The mini-spectaculars and the commercial bombings in Northern Ireland helped the republican leadership sell the intentionally ambiguous 'Total Un-armed Strategy' / 'Tactical Use of Armed Struggle' (TUAS) to the grassroots as an honourable truce rather than a surrender. 'To sue for peace is a noble thing.' wrote Adams in 1995, 'The IRA's initiative was a brave one, and the 31 August [1994] commitment was made by a confident, united and unbroken army.'[57]

Adams' public confidence was offset by significant doubts within the IRA army council and the grassroots in border areas like Tyrone and south Armagh. While cognizant of the necessity for the IRA to bring its hardliners along, the continuation of the campaign, and particularly the timing of the mini-spectaculars, brought severe criticism from constitutional nationalist leaders in the SDLP,[58] the Fianna Fàil–Labour government, and the Fine Gael opposition, though a notable lack of criticism from either Hume or Reynolds. The contin-uation of the campaign was interpreted as a slap in the face for the Irish government, which had stuck its neck out by removing the broadcasting ban against republicans in January 1994, and supported Adams' successful bid for a visa to the USA. Fine Gael opposition leader John Bruton accused Reynolds of 'appeasing the terrorists' instead of seeking agreement among constitutional parties.[59] Nevertheless, the republican leadership was clearly emphasizing that its involvement in the new departure was conditional upon the maintenance of the right of Irish national self-determination. As Adams emphasized at Sinn Féin's 89th Ard Fheis in February 1994:

We have ... correctly recognised that a united Irish nationalist/republican voice in support of such an end (a lasting peace) and a process for its achievement, as being a potent political force, not just in Ireland itself but in Britain and internationally. The sub-theme of that, of course, is that Irish republicans, by ourselves, simply do not possess the political strength to bring about these aims. While that situation obtains, it must continue to influence the political and strategic thinking of Irish republicans. *However, we do possess the ability to create conditions which can move the situation towards these aims and we have the power to prevent another settlement on British government terms, which would subvert Irish national and democratic rights.*[60]

The delay required for internal consultations within the republican movement also tested the solidity of the constitutional nationalists' commitment to the new departure. According to Adams, there were three final pieces that completed the jigsaw. First, the consistent support for the inclusive process by the Clinton administration and the powerful Irish-American business lobby created a vital counter-balance against British hesitancy to move the process forward. In January 1994, despite strong British objections, Clinton authorized a 48-hour visa that allowed Adams to attend a conference sponsored by the National Committee on Foreign Affairs, a think-tank chaired by influential Irish-American businessman Bill Flynn.[61] Second, the republican leadership was reassured that the SDLP would only accept a settlement that could be interpreted as an 'interim step' towards Irish reunification. The consistent support of SDLP leader John Hume for a settlement that was inclusively negotiated, based on the principle of Irish national self-determination, was vital in this regard. Hume solidified the confidence of the republican leadership by consistently supporting Sinn Féin's demand for the British government to clarify the Joint Declaration and, just before the ceasefire, issued a statement with Adams which called for the British government to 'respond positively, both in terms of demilitarisation of the situation and in assisting the search for an agreed Ireland by encouraging the process of national reconciliation'.[61] Thirdly, Hume's influence in Dublin, along with public and private reassurances from Albert Reynolds, convinced the republican leadership that the Irish government would also pursue a stepping-stone approach to a settlement that had an all-Ireland dynamic.[63]

The symmetry of paramilitarism – levelling of killing fields – was also evident in the trend in loyalist violence. Up until their own ceasefire, declared on 13 October 1994, loyalist paramilitaries also underlined their position as the defenders of the unionists' own right to national self-determination. Apart from the continuation of lethal attacks against Catholic/nationalist civilians, from July 1993 loyalist paramilitaries committed sixteen separate attacks in the Irish Republic, including one car bomb,[64] four letter or parcel bombs,[65] eight incendiary devices and three small bombs. Following the attempted bombing of a Belfast to Dublin train, the UVF stated: 'This was a warning to the Dublin government that Northern Ireland is still British and we will not be coerced, forced *or persuaded* into a united Ireland.'[66]

In addition, loyalist paramilitary leaders made it clear that they would maintain a degree of independence from both the UUP and the DUP, for example, rejecting in May 1994 the plea from James Molyneaux to declare a unilateral ceasefire in exchange for a place at the negotiating table.[67] Also, by declaring after their ceasefire that they would not initiate a first strike, the loyalist leaders made it clear that they would not be the lackeys of unionist politicians in the case of an unfavourable negotiated settlement.[68] A pivotal development for the loyalist ceasefire was the personal assurance given by Albert Reynolds to the UVF's Gusty Spence that the IRA had not done a secret deal with the British or Irish government in exchange for their ceasefire.[69] Still, the loyalist ceasefire was explicitly conditional upon a continuation of cease-fires by the IRA and any other republican or nationalist group: 'The permanence of our ceasefire will be completely dependent upon the continued cessation of all nationalist/republican violence, the sole responsibility for a return to War lies with them.'[70]

The Ulster Unionist leadership's response to the Joint Declaration had been clearly determined by the implications for constitutive and regulative aspects of sovereignty. The consensus among party leaders was that unionist consent for any change in the constitutional status of Northern Ireland was protected by the declaration (the core regulative aspect). As for other regulative aspects, it was significant that while the declaration was a British–Irish document, the fact that UUP leaders had been briefed in advance meant that the bi-national intergovernmental process had been opened up to include parties in Northern Ireland.[71] But more threateningly, by 1993 the demonstrated strength of the intergovernmental relationship in standing up to unionist pressure against the Anglo-Irish Agreement and then responding to the failure of the Brooke–Mayhew talks with the Joint Declaration was a sobering reminder to unionists of the need for constructive engagement with the British government rather than obstruction.

In the short term, the parliamentary arithmetic meant that the UUP effectively held the balance of power in the House of Commons following Conservative backbench splits over the ratification of the Treaty on European Union (Maastricht). In parallel with the alignments of 1921, the integrative unionist position created a natural alliance with those trying to preserve empire, or in 1993 anti-European and anti-devolutionary UK unionism. After the IRA called its ceasefire on 31 August 1994, Ulster Unionists used their leverage to insist that Sinn Féin be barred from negotiations until the IRA began to decommission its weapons. In addition, the emotive, constitutive sovereignty question of negotiating with terrorists reinforced British Conservative strictures on questions of nationalism, presenting obstacles which made it difficult for the Conservative government to pursue fundamental constitutional and institutional change.[72]

In the longer term, the strengthened and more balanced intergovernmental relationship sustained momentum despite the significant internal and external obstacles. When the Fianna Fáil–Labour coalition fell in November 1994 and was replaced by a Fine Gael-led coalition,[73] which was less determined to maintain a strong nationalist bloc, Irish officials emphasize the importance of the continuity of contacts and thinking among senior British and Irish civil servants, which sustained the momentum of the process by publishing the Joint Framework Documents[74] in February 1995, and which became the basis of the negotiations leading to the Belfast Agreement.[75]

The Framework Documents represented an accumulation of areas of agreement between the two governments achieved in the Brooke–Mayhew talks, and the Joint Declaration. The two governments reiterated their commitment to Irish self-determination, qualified by the necessity of the consent of the majority in Northern Ireland for a united Ireland (paragraph 18). The British government outlined an internal power-sharing government for Northern Ireland based on a collective (three-person) executive, and committee system headed by members of an elected assembly, in proportion to their vote-share. The two governments proposed a North–South body with some executive powers, but left the allocation of powers to be decided by consent between North and South. The east–west dimension called for a strengthening of the Intergovernmental Council (IGC) to 'underwrite' an overall settlement and act as residual, and possibly, in some interpretations, as co-sovereigns.[76] The individual and collective rights of both communities were to be protected under a Charter or Covenant of Rights, which would transcend any change in the constitutional status of Northern Ireland. Lastly, to acknowledge and possibly rectify their competing constitutional claims to sovereignty, the two governments stated that they would modify or change their constitutional claims to sovereignty (the Government of Ireland Act (1920), as amended, and Articles 2 and 3 of the Irish constitution, respectively).

What was fundamentally new in the Framework Documents (FWD) was the explicit proposal (Pars. 20 and 21) to adjust constitutive sovereignty claims: the British declared their willingness to amend or replace the Government of Ireland Act (1920) while the Irish government committed itself to adjusting its constitution to reflect the principle of consent. This proposed exchange, represented by the dotted line in Figure 17, represents the first intergovernmental confrontation of the opposed constitutive sovereignty claims and therefore the first time that the status of the two opposing sovereigns was recognized by the British government as comparable, if not equivalent, to that of the Irish. Equally, this blueprint for a negotiated settlement reinforced the strength of the British–Irish incentive mechanism established with the AIA. Not coincidentally, John Major was awarded the 'golden rhubarb trophy' by the Plain Language Commission for his part in Paragraph 46 of the FWD, which proposed:

> Where either government considers that any institution, established as part of the overall accommodation, is not properly functioning within the Agreement or that a breach of the Agreement has otherwise occurred, the Conference [IGC] shall consider the matter on the basis of a shared commitment to arrive at a common position or, where that is not possible, to agree a procedure to resolve the difference between them.

Astute unionists, if not the Plain Language Commission, must have interpreted this paragraph as a stark reminder of the threat of creeping British–Irish co-sovereignty.

For nationalists the constitutional levelling demonstrated how the alliance with constitutional nationalists (Sinn Féin, the SDLP in Northern Ireland and particularly the Fianna Fáil party in the Irish Republic) could leverage a fundamental change in constitutive sovereignty.[77] In addition to the proposal for extensive North–South bodies with executive powers and the signalling of significant reforms of political and civil rights, the Framework Documents consolidated the nationalist bloc during a time of considerable unease between Sinn Féin and the Fine Gael-led government.

An important side-payment for unionists was the prospect of the revision of Articles 2 and 3 of the Irish constitution, thereby entrenching the separate right of self-determination for Northern Ireland. As emphasized in previous chapters, this recognition of Northern Ireland's separate right of self-determination had been central to the unionists' negotiating position during Sunningdale and indeed since at least the early 1880s. But the more powerful, negative incentive was the threat of a strengthened Intergovernmental Conference and creeping all-Ireland institutions if they stalled the process of agreement or its implementation. The fallout from the Framework Documents led to the resignation of the UUP leader James Molyneaux and his replacement by David Trimble, MP, who promised a harder line on paramilitary decommissioning and defence of the union against creeping North–South integration. Since the British government was dependent on the votes of the UUP in the House of Commons, the process of inclusive negotiations was stalled through 1995. The dualist, intergovernmental approach dictated that unionists had to be compensated for what was perceived as on balance a 'pro-nationalist' Framework Document. This compensation was delivered by Northern Ireland Secretary Sir Patrick Mayhew in his Washington III pronouncement that paramilitaries would have to give up weapons as an act of good faith before being allowed into negotiations.[78]

The response to the decommissioning impasse reveals the importance of the maintenance of the cooperative and symmetrical British–Irish intergovernmental relations, as well as the limited capacity of external facilitation. As the process began to unravel with warnings of the fragility of the ceasefire by Sinn Féin, an intervention was made by US President Clinton, whose Special Envoy George Mitchell was appointed by the British government to chair an International Body on Decommissioning. Since the statutory authority of the international 'body' was that of an advisory body to the British government, Major was able to 'cherry-pick' the report, implementing the recommendation for pre-negotiation elections to establish democratic mandates, but ignoring Mitchell's proposal for simultaneous movement of paramilitary weapons decommissioning and de-militarization and police reform, forms of linkage that would become central to the implementation of the British–Irish (Good Friday) Agreement of 1998 (see next chapter). Major's refusal to countenance such linkage led the IRA to end its ceasefire with a huge bomb at Canary Wharf in

London on 9 February 1996, followed by a series of commercial bomb attacks and warnings in Britain through the summer and autumn.

The collapse of the first 'peace process' demonstrates the potential and limitations of the bi-national intergovernmental process. While the solidification of the core regulative aspect of sovereignty, in the context of the more favourable geo-political and demographic conditions, had tempted Sinn Féin and the IRA into constitutional politics, unionists' concerns over the pace and extent of reforms, allied with their pivotal parliamentary position, created significant obstacles to progress. In addition, it is clear that the question of negotiating with representatives of paramilitary organizations presented substantial ideological obstacles to some members of the British government, civil service and military.[79] Major's pronouncement in the Commons that it would 'turn my stomach to negotiate with Gerry Adams' may have been disingenuous, as authorized secret discussions with Sinn Féin leaders had been ongoing for several years, but it certainly reflected a concern to placate members of his government and backbench Conservatives who were antagonistic to the inclusive approach.[80] In this sense, little had changed since the Liberal–Conservative coalition, led by Lloyd George, faced the dilemma of talking with 'murderers'. In other respects, as the next chapter shows, the inter-governmental relationship sustained momentum towards a stable peace.

Notes

1. Quoted in *The Independent*, 1 September 1994.
2. Quoted in *The Daily Telegraph*, 27 September 1994.
3. Quoted in *The Guardian*, 22 October 1994, emphasis added.
4. Quoted in the *Irish Times*, 16 November 1985.
5. Interview with Peter Brooke, Northern Ireland Secretary (1989–91), in the *Irish News*, 3 April 2000.
6. *The Independent*, 4 November 1989.
7. Brooke, Peter, 'Transcript of Speech to Conservative Association, 9 November 1990', in author's possession.
8. The British government contact, nicknamed the 'Mountain Climber' was Michael Oatley, an MI-6 agent who had negotiated a ceasefire with the Provisional IRA in 1974.
9. Other tracks had been developing simultaneously in Northern Ireland as a series of talks took place between the Sinn Féin leader Gerry Adams and the SDLP leader John Hume since 1988; between Adams and Protestant church leaders, as well as between the Sinn Féin leader and representatives of Fianna Fáil, the coalition-leading party of the Irish government. See Mallie, Eamonn and McKittrick, David, *The Fight for Peace: The Secret Story Behind the Irish Peace Process* (London: Heinemann, 1996) pp. 85–91, 134–7; O'Brien, *The Long War*, pp. 263–7.
10. Mallie, Eamonn and McKittrick, David, *The Fight for Peace*, p. 124.
11. Quoted in O'Brien, *The Long War*, p. 252.
12. Major, John, *John Major: The Autobiography* (London: HarperCollins, 1999) p. 438.
13. Interview with Patrick Mayhew, London, 23 May 1998.
14. Interview with Irish Official, London, March 1998; see also O'Brien *The Long War*, pp. 244–9.
15. Quoted in O'Brien, *The Long War*, p. 256.
16. Sinn Féin, *Towards a Lasting Peace in Ireland* (Belfast: Sinn Féin, 1992) pp.7–8.
17. Smith, Fighting for Ireland, pp. 169–94; McGladdery, *The Provisional IRA in England*, Chapter 7.

18. *Die Zeit*, April 1993. The quote is the Northern Ireland Office's own version of the transcript of Mayhew's interview with *Die Zeit*, as quoted in the *Irish Times*, 27 April 1993.
19. H.C. 6th Series, vol. 972, col. 603, 25 October 1979.
20. Bew and Gillespie, *Northern Ireland: A Chronology*, pp. 261, 298.
21. Quoted in *Belfast Telegraph*, 8 July 1993.
22. Mansergh, Martin, 'The Background to the Peace Process: Address to the International Committee of the Royal Irish Academy', 22 May 1995, p. 12.
23. Interview with author, Dublin, 7 August 1995.
24. Holland and Phoenix, *Phoenix*, pp. 195–225; Horgan, John and Taylor, Max, 'The Provisional IRA: Command and Functional Structure', *Terrorism and Political Violence*, 9, 3 (1997) pp. 1–32.
25. Quoted in Bew and Gillespie, *Northern Ireland: A Chronology*, p. 296.
26. Quoted in the *Irish Times*, 27 November 1995.
27. Quoted in *The Scotsman*, 23 September 1999.
28. Ibid.
29. McKittrick, *Endgame*, pp. 261–4.
30. Quoted in *The Guardian*, 19 October 1993.
31. Quoted in *The Guardian*, 30 December 1997.
32. The Stevens Report, published in an abbreviated version in May 2003, found evidence of collusion between army intelligence, Special Branch of the RUC and loyalist paramilitaries. Stevens reported wilful obstruction of his investigation by both agencies. He also noted that the RUC briefed the Conservative MP and QC, Douglas Hogg, as Under Secretary of State, Home Department, that 'some solicitors were unduly sympathetic to the cause of the IRA'. Stevens found that the minister was compromised when he related this intelligence to the Commons (on 17 January 1989). Stevens' investigations led to 144 arrests and 94 convictions as of May, 2003. *Report of the Stevens Inquiry* (HMSO: 2003); see also Tomlinson, 1998. 'Walking Backwards into the Sunset: British Policy and the Insecurity of Northern Ireland', in Miller, David (ed.), *Rethinking Northern Ireland: Culture, Ideology and Colonialism* (London: Longman, 1998).
33. Sinn Féin, 'Setting the Record Straight: Sinn Féin's Record of the Communications Between Sinn Féin and the British Government, October 1990–November 1993' (Belfast: Sinn Féin, 1994) pp. 25–8.
34. Quoted ibid, p. 35.
35. The meetings between Sinn Féin President Gerry Adams and SDLP leader John Hume were announced publicly from the end of March 1993, but had commenced sometime in 1988. The final agreement has never been published but has been summarized by Adams as including these seven points:
    1. The Irish people as a whole have the right to national self-determination.
    2. An internal settlement is not a solution.
    3. The exercise of self-determination is a matter for agreement *between* the people of Ireland.
    4. The consent and allegiance of unionists are essential ingredients if a lasting peace is to be established.
    5. The unionists cannot have a veto over British policy.
    6. The British government must join the persuaders.
    7. The London and Dublin governments have the major responsibility to secure political progress. Adams, *Free Ireland*, p. 215.
36. Quoted in *Fortnight*, September 1993, p. 31.
37. Quoted in *Fortnight*, October 1993, p. 33.
38. Quoted in the *Irish Times*, 21 July 1993.
39. Quoted in *Fortnight*, January 1994, p. 31.
40. A group of UDA/UFF leaders had been meeting in offices above the fish shop an hour before the bomb was prematurely detonated.
41. Quoted in O'Brien, *The Long War*, p. 293.

42. Tomlinson, Mike, 'Walking Backwards into the Sunset: British Policy and the Insecurity of Northern Ireland', in Miller, David (ed.), *Rethinking Northern Ireland*, p. 109. Journalist Ed Moloney subsequently reported: 'Thanks to military documents unearthed by BBC journalist John Ware and revelations by former FRU [Force Research Unit] members and ex-UDA personnel (including Johnny 'Mad Dog' Adair), we now know that FRU was working 'C' Company (of the UFF) like the accelerator pedal in a deadly armoured car.' *Ireland on Sunday,* 28 August 2000.

43. Major, *John Major,* pp. 432–3.

44. Fianna Fáil in opposition had publicly opposed the agreement, and on its return to power in 1987 tempted Ulster Unionists into negotiations in order to 'replace or transcend' the AIA. See Mansergh, ' The Background to the Peace Process', p. 14.

45. Mansergh, 'The Background to the Peace Process', p. 15, emphasis added.

46. 1991 Census: Religion and Gender by Geographic Area (Belfast: Northern Ireland Statistics and Research Agency, 1993).

47. Mallie and McKittrick, *End Game in Ireland* (London: Hodder and Stoughton, 2001) pp. 287–8.

48. Dennis Bradley 'Peace Process should be seen through', the *Irish Times,* 20 April 1999.

49. Major, *John Major,* pp. 440–55.

50. Interview with Irish official, London, March 1998; see also Kerr, *Imposing Power-Sharing*, p. 102.

51. Mallie and McKittrick, *Endgame in Ireland* (London: Hodder and Stoughton, 2001) p. 184.

52. See O'Leary and McGarry, *The Politics of Antagonism,* pp. 290–5.

53. Interview with IRA member, Crossmaglen, Armagh 18 December 1994. The reflexive consent principle was clearly at variance with Sinn Féin President Gerry Adams' previously stated conception. According to Adams, 'the consent, or assent, *of as many of our unionist fellow country men and country women as possible* should be obtained to the complex economic and legal aspects of a final all-Ireland settlement, and the time-scale of bringing this about'. Quoted in Adams, *Free Ireland*, p. 235, emphasis added.

54. Crewe, Ivor, 'Voting and the Electorate', in Dunleavy, Patrick, Gamble, Andrew, Holliday, Ian and Peele, Gillian, *Developments in British Politics 4* (Houndmills, Basingstoke: Macmillan, 1993) p. 92.

55. Following the Heathrow attack, eight more mortars were fired over the next three days, all of which contained explosives but were purposely de-activated: the point apparently was not to cross the rubicon of 'international terrorism', but to warn of the IRA's continued capacity to strike at vital economic targets in Britain. Ten days later in Northern Ireland, the south Armagh brigade of the IRA achieved a morale-boosting publicity coup by downing an army helicopter with a home-made mortar as it landed at the RUC/army base at Crossmaglen, Co. Armagh. On 12 July an RAF helicopter was forced to land after being hit by a mortar at an army base in Newtonhamilton, Co. Armagh.

56. Interview with IRA member, Crossmaglen, Armagh, 5 August 1995.

57. Adams, *Free Ireland,* p. 224.

58. Seamus Mallon, the local SDLP MP and deputy leader of the SDLP, complained: 'We're back into the syndrome where you have Sinn Féin and its spokesmen talking peace in the morning and carrying out these murderous attacks through the IRA in the evening', quoted in *The Guardian* 21 March 1994.

59. Quoted in *Fortnight*, May 1994, p. 29.

60. Adams, Gerry, 'Presidential Address: 89th Sinn Féin Ard Fheis (Belfast: Sinn Féin) p. 6, emphasis added.

61. Former congressman, Bruce Morrison, also led two delegations of leading Irish-American businessmen to Northern Ireland, one in September 1993, during which time the IRA observed an unannounced seven-day ceasefire, and again in August 1994, five days before the official ceasefire. These visits reassured the leadership that a peaceful republican movement would receive significant material and political support from Irish-America.

62. Quoted in Adams, *Free Ireland*, p. 221, emphasis added.
63. O'Brien, *The Long War*, pp. 321–2.
64. On 18 August 1993, a UVF car bomb exploded in Dublin, causing no injuries but IR£750,000 damage.
65. On 5 October 1993, a UVF letter bomb addressed to Irish Tanaiste Dick Spring was found in a Belfast sorting office.
66. Quoted in *The Guardian*, 13 September 1994, emphasis added.
67. *The Guardian*, 24 May 1994.
68. John White of the Ulster Democratic Party (UDP – aligned with UDA/UFF): ... [W]e recognize that the past 25 years have been futile. The Combined Loyalist Paramilitary Command is 100 per cent behind the peace process ... Paisley's attitude has done a disservice to the Unionist cause. People from abroad see him just as a loudmouth and a bigot. In our community people's anxieties are growing because of the fears of the politicians – but most of all people want peace (*The Observer* 26 February 1995).
69. O'Brien, *The Long War*, pp. 331–3.
70. Quoted in the *Belfast Telegraph*, 13 September 1994.
71. Cochrane, *Unionist Politics*, pp. 318–21.
72. O'Dowd, Liam, 'Constituting Division, Impeding Agreement: the Neglected Role of British Nationalism in Northern Ireland', in Anderson, James and Goodman, James (eds), *Dis/Agreeing Ireland: Contexts, Obstacles, Hopes* (London: Pluto, 1998).
73. The coalition government from 1994 was comprised of Fine Gael, Labour and Democratic Left, all parties with moral and political opposition to the Fianna Fáil strategy of inclusion of Sinn Féin in negotiations.
74. Two documents were published, one by the British government alone, *A Framework for Accountable Government in Northern Ireland*, and one jointly by the British and Irish governments, *A New Framework for Agreement: A Shared Understanding Between the British and Irish Governments to Assist Discussion and Negotiation involving the Northern Ireland Parties*.
75. Interview with Irish official, London, March 1998. See also, Cox, W. Harvey, 'From Hillsborough to Downing Street – and After', in Catterall and McDougall, *The Northern Ireland Question in British Politics*, p. 105.
76. O'Leary, Brendan, 'Afterword: What is Framed in the Framework Documents', *Ethnic and Racial Studies* 18, 4 (1995) p. 870.
77. While the Framework Documents were negotiated by a Fine Gael–Labour–Democratic Left coalition, Fianna Fáil laid the particular insistence on balanced constitutional change in the Brooke–Mayhew talks.
78. The complete statement required: 'A willingness in principle to disarm progressively; a common practical understanding of the modalities, that is to say, what decommissioning would actually entail; in order to test the practical arrangements and to demonstrate good faith, the actual decommissioning of some arms as a tangible confidence-building measure and to signal the start of a process.' Quoted in *The Independent*, 8 March 1995. The British government position was partly encouraged by the Irish government's ambivalence, for example when Irish Tánaiste Dick Spring stated on 1 June 1994 that the IRA would have to hand over some arms to verify any cessation of violence. *Fortnight* July/August, 1994, p. 31.
79. Anderson, James, 'Rethinking National Problems in a Transnational Context', in Miller, *Rethinking Northern Ireland*, pp. 139–40; Tomlinson, Mike, 'Walking Backwards into the Sunset: British Policy and the Insecurity of Northern Ireland', in ibid, pp. 113–17.
80. Mayhew claimed in an interview with the author (London, 23 May 1998) that he and Major were the only members of the cabinet who supported the inclusive talks process. Considering that Mayhew himself was extremely sceptical of the Joint Declaration strategy, it is clear that the ideological obstacles to negotiating with 'terrorists' presented a formidable obstacle to the cabinet. Irish Officials recognized the extent of the Conservative government's obstacles and made a strategic decision in January 1997

to brief (unofficially) the opposition spokesperson on Northern Ireland, Mo Mowlam, on the potential of an inclusive negotiating process to solidify Sinn Féin's engagement to constitutional politics (Interview with Irish Official, London, March 1998).

8

Triangulating the British–Irish (Good Friday) Agreements, 1997–2007

Seamus Mallon, the Deputy First Minister in the Northern Ireland Assembly, famously described the Belfast Agreement signed on Good Friday (10 April 1998) as 'Sunningdale for slow-learners', referring to the power-sharing agreement that lasted for only five months from December 1973 to May 1974.[1] Mallon was right to suggest that in its broadest outline, the Belfast Agreement was structured along the main parameters of the Sunningdale Agreement, including:

- Agreement between the British and Irish governments on a process of self-determination whereby the Irish government agreed that any change in the constitutional status of Northern Ireland as part of the United Kingdom requires the consent of the majority in Northern Ireland;
- A Northern Ireland power-sharing executive and 108-member representative assembly elected by proportional representation with powers devolved (excluding security and policing) from the Westminster parliament;
- An 'Irish dimension' creating cross-border institutions linking ministerial representatives from Northern Ireland and the Irish Republic.

In addition, an east-west council linking the devolved assemblies in Scotland, Wales and Northern Ireland with the parliaments in London and Dublin was incorporated into a new British–Irish Agreement.

However, the similarities in the basic outline of a settlement mask vital differences in approaches to conflict regulation that reflect evolving and pluralizing conceptions of both British and Irish nationalisms. A comparison of the following passages reveals a significant shift in approach to conflict regulation from Sunningdale to Belfast. Given our focus on violence and nation-state legitimacy, consider first Blair's attempt to reassure unionists that the IRA *should* have to begin to hand over weapons before taking up ministerial office in the new Northern Ireland Assembly:

> There can be no fudge between democracy and terror... We are not setting new preconditions or barriers. On the contrary we want as many people as possible to use the Agreement as their bridge across to an exclusively democratic path. We will encourage them to take this path. But it is surely reasonable that there should be confidence-building measures from these organisations after all the suffering they have inflicted on the people of

Northern Ireland. And we also have a responsibility to provide protection against abuse of *the democratic process*, and its benefits, by those not genuinely committed to it.[2]

Note the difference between the idea of a 'democratic process' and the more rigidly statist views of Labour Prime Minister Harold Wilson in May 1974:

We speak for the overwhelming majority of the House of Commons so recently elected, that we will not negotiate on constitutional or political matters in Northern Ireland with anyone who chooses to operate outside the *established* constitutional framework ... [3]

Both prime ministers insisted upon democratic means, but whereas Wilson assumed that the two governments and Northern Irish political leaders had agreed a static constitutional framework, Blair spoke of a 'process' which, while based exclusively on peaceful means, is explicitly open-ended with regard to the constitutional status of Northern Ireland, and the development of cross-border institutions between the Irish Republic and Northern Ireland. By extension, the recognition that the constitutional status of Northern Ireland was open to negotiation reflects the evolution of conflict regulation based on the necessity of consent and inclusion, rather than exclusion of proponents of violence. The recognition of the legitimacy of their separate ethno-national claims reflects the recognition that ethno-national as well as civic nationalist claims require constitutional protection and institutional means of implementation. This principle extends to consideration of national self-determination, including the possibility of territorial adjustment to existing states.[4] British–Irish relations and their regulation of the conflict in Northern Ireland suggests that such adjustments can be regulated where principal nations with opposing sovereignty claims can agree on border changes and on bi-national parameters for inter-state relations, governance and societal-level individual and collective rights protections.

In Northern Ireland, the reciprocal response by militants, republican and loyalist, has been, respectively, the acceptance of the principle of consent for the change to the constitutional status of Northern Ireland, in exchange for an acceptance by the present majority to accept a process that also requires the (simultaneous) consent of the majority in the Irish Republic. By addressing the self-determination issue left stranded in 1921, the inclusive approach recognized that proponents of violence differed primarily over means rather than ends, and therefore the representatives of the extremes of opinion on the national questions, the vanguards and defenders, were too strong 'nationally' to be marginalized.[5] This change is reflected in the answer to Sinn Féin's Martin McGuinness' rhetorical question, when asked why the IRA could not have left it long ago to the constitutional politicians to negotiate a settlement. McGuinness replied, 'Constitutional politics ... but *whose* constitution?'[6]

The answer for the foreseeable future is *both* British and Irish. In 1998 the British and Irish governments, the constitutional and 'semi-constitutional' parties, the peoples of Northern Ireland and the Irish Republic had endorsed a settlement based on power-sharing, sovereignty pooling and an agreed mechanism for self-determination, entrenched in *both* UK and Irish law. Citizenship laws were introduced that allow people living in Northern Ireland to be British, Irish *or both*. Upon taking their seats in the Northern Ireland Assembly, members must declare their status as 'nationalist', 'unionist' *or 'other'*. Individual and collective rights protections were enshrined in mirror-image in both British and Irish constitutions, in what McGarry and O'Leary have termed 'double protection' mechanisms that provide reciprocal cultural and political rights, taking into account the possibility of changes of juris-diction.[7] And when dissident republicans tried to wreck the historic deal by killing twenty-nine people in Omagh in August 1998, both governments introduced nearly identical anti-terrorism legislation.

If the British–Irish (Good Friday) Agreement was Sunningdale for slow-learners, it could equally be described as the Anglo-Irish Treaty 1921 for *really* slow learners, both paramilitaries and politicians, Irish and British. The parameters of the settlement reflect an understanding of the same causes of conflict that were left unresolved and coerced in 1921. This concluding chapter shows how the stabilization of conflict is directly related to the relative equalization of national status, as expressed in willingness and ability to adjust core aspects of sovereignty sufficient to create a British–Irish exchange relation-ship, founded on mutually agreed, if not necessarily symmetrical, conceptions of national status. This principle enabled the two governments to maximize consent for regulating the core causes of conflict at the state, governmental and societal levels.

But while the British–Irish Agreement (BIA) reflects a liberalization of opposing nationalisms, it does not represent a 'post-nationalist' solution. Instead, the evolution of conflict regulation from 1985 to 1998 reflects a bi-national trend addressing a remarkably stable set of national parameters: inter-state and intra-state territorial claims, institutionalized forms of culture, religion and governance which are dedicated towards opposing, but, I shall argue, not necessarily conflicting nation-state configurations. In the conclusion I discuss the implications for theories of conflict regulation in deeply divided societies with internal and external features.

ETHNICIZING 'LIBERAL INTERGOVERNMENTALISM'

In the previous two chapters I argued that a modified 'liberal intergovernmental' approach offered the best explanation of the failure of the British and Irish governments to offer sufficient side-payments to the ethno-national blocs in Northern Ireland during the negotiation and implementation of the Sunningdale Agreement (1973–4) and then following the Anglo-Irish Agreement (1985). The rigid, hierarchical conception of sovereignty over Northern Ireland meant that British governments approached the conflict primarily as a matter of internal rebellion, rather than as a conflict with the Irish Republic centred on opposing claims to sovereignty. As a result, successive British governments were not in a position to offer reciprocal exchange or modification of core claims to sovereignty sufficient to reflect the opposing claims to self-determination of nationalists and unionists in Northern Ireland. The ambivalent conception of the Northern question in the Irish Republic also contributed to the broken bi-partisanship separating Fianna Fáil from the Fine Gael–Labour coalition and contributed directly to the Provisional IRA's justification of violence against the British state. In sum, the absence of bi-partisan support for radical reconfigurations of national sovereignty in both Britain and Ireland stemmed ultimately from the hierarchical conception of British over Irish claims to sovereignty over Northern Ireland. In the absence of a mutualist relationship between the competing sovereigns, relations in Northern Ireland remained polarized as the extremes of nationalism and unionism perceived positional advantage through force and counter-force. Such positional advantage was reduced only when intergovernmental co-operation produced clarity on the parameters of self-determination, power-sharing and opportunity promotion through collective and individual rights protections.

Critics of the intergovernmental approach to conflict regulation in Northern Ireland tend to focus on the elitism and nationalism of British and Irish state-craft. They cast doubt on the stability of institutions that grant vetoes to ethnic and civic constituencies with opposing national aspirations. They warned, with some justification, that incessant contestation of sovereignty and challenges over the distribution of public goods would lead to rigid legalism and 'mega-constitutionalism'.[8]

These views echo the 'centripetalist' or 'civic integrationist' approach to conflict regulation. Inherently 'statist', these approaches tend to assume the givenness of the state and emphasize forms of governance that create or reinforce a shared sense of national identity. While they encourage the division of power among the executive, legislative and judicial branches of government to constrain populism, protect minorities and minimize the control of vested interests, they object to forms of power-sharing based on ethno-national divisions. Philip Roeder's comparative study of power-sharing systems found that formal consociational systems that guarantee ethno-national parties shares of power in parliamentary systems and through ethno-federal territorial autonomy arrangements are significantly more likely to lead to recurring violence than systems based on ethnic-blind power-dividing (such as non-ethnic federalism, separation of executive, legislative and judicial powers through presidentialism and functional (as opposed to ethno-national) devolution.[9] Dixon, Taylor and Horowitz object, in different ways, to the reification of ethno-nationalism inherent in power-sharing systems like that practised in Northern Ireland,[10] while Ruane and Todd doubt the stability of an agreement that rests on a balance of power inherent in a 'dualist' conception of the primacy of the British and Irish nation-states.[11]

These critics of ethno-national power-sharing and bi-national intergovern-mentalism rightly emphasize the polarizing potential of elite-led nationalist projects, and the problem of mega-constitutionalism, where negotiations move at the pace of the most intransigent, has been in evidence in Northern Ireland since

1998. Yet, while these approaches reveal significant obstacles to the transformation of conflict, they under-emphasize the bi-national division of Northern Ireland and the primacy of the British–Irish intergovernmental axis as the focus of contestation from the élite to the grassroots level. Instead they deny or denounce the centrality of nationalism as the focus of conflict. They also underestimate the transformative effects of a bi-national approach that considers the vertical links between society, government and the state. While they might have felt vindicated in their analysis by the political process since 1998, would they have predicted that Sinn Féin and the DUP, the poles of the nationalist–unionist spectrum, could agree to share power on the basis laid down in the Good Friday Agreement? By regulating self-determination and promoting multi-level governance based on ethno-national and civic national criteria, the British and Irish governments have, knowingly or otherwise, synthesized ethno-national power-sharing and civic national integration to encourage the pluralization rather than reification of opposing British and Irish nationalisms.

A BI-NATIONAL CONFLICT

The analysis of the historical relationship between Irish nationalism and the British state has, I hope, revealed the continued salience of conceptions of national status and territorial statehood. The national legacies are further revealed by contemporary evidence showing the primacy of opposing, if increasingly 'plural', nationalisms. British national identity is the primary political and cultural identity of the majority of Northern Ireland Protestants. Between 1978 and 1998, authoritative surveys consistently showed that the majority of Northern Ireland Protestants consider themselves to be 'British' (varying from 65 to 78 per cent between 1978 and 1998) with only 10 to 20 per cent declaring 'Ulster' identity and 11 to 16 per cent declaring 'Northern Irish' identity (see Figures 8 and 9).[12] While Todd, Cochrane, Miller and others correctly emphasize the complexity and conditionality of Protestant/unionist allegiance to British government, it is clear that British national identity remains the primary political allegiance of a clear majority of Northern Ireland Protestants.[13] Conversely, as Duffy and Evans have shown, a clear majority of Northern Irish Catholics define themselves as 'Irish' (63 per cent average between 1989 and 1998) compared with 25 per cent 'Northern Irish' and 14 per cent 'British'.[14]

These British and Irish identities correlate closely with aspirations for the constitutional status of Northern Ireland, with 87 per cent of Protestants supporting Northern Ireland's place within the United Kingdom and 59 per cent of Catholics supporting a united Ireland. Moreover, despite the extent of pluralism within Protestant and Catholic cultural communities, Hayes and McAllister have found support for latent British and Irish national identities based on 'a marked unwillingness – less than one per cent across all survey years [1989 to 1998] – of either the Protestant or Catholic population to cross traditionally established allegiances and claim either a nationalist or unionist identity'.[15] Thus even though there is a healthy pluralism of opinion on nation-state congruence, there remains a dominant dualism of Protestant British unionism versus Catholic Irish nationalism. As Peter Robinson, Deputy Leader of the DUP stated in Washington in April 2006, even if the Northern Ireland power-sharing assembly was restored, 'they [Sinn Féin] will still be our political opponents in relation to constitutional and many other matters'.[16]

Similarly, interviews conducted with leaders of political parties associated with extremes of the nationalist spectrum – (British) loyalist and (Irish) republican movements – confirm that both view their causes as based on opposing claims to national self-determination. For example, David Ervine, leader of the Progressive Unionist Party until his death in 2006, based his unionism on the fact that he was 'a citizen of the United Kingdom' and moreover, that this carried with it a subjective identification of Britishness.[17] Ervine also emphasized the primacy of the principle of majority consent to any change in the constitutional status of Northern Ireland as part of the United Kingdom, rather than the secondary question of weapons decommissioning (discussed below).[18] Conversely, interviews with senior republicans confirm their view of the centrality of the British claim to sovereignty over a part of Ireland as the central cause of conflict: 'Local Protestants and Catholics can work together. There are even Orange Lodges in the south (Irish Republic) and nobody troubles them . . . The big question is whether the British have the will to negotiate on the constitutional question and are they prepared to transfer sovereignty?'[19]

Evidence for the centrality and primacy of the opposing British and Irish nationalism explains why national governments with the will and public mandate to adjust aspects of sovereignty in what Brendan O'Leary identifies as confederal, federal and consociational dimensions[20] were able to structure parameters of a settlement accepted by clear majorities in Northern Ireland and the Irish Republic, representing concurrent expressions of national self-determination. The following section analyzes the events leading to the British–Irish Agreement, paying particular emphasis to the intergovernmental management of the process.

THE ELECTION OF *INTERLOCUTEURS VALABLES*

The incumbent and ideological obstacles blocking negotiations from 1995 to 1997 were removed or diminished with the election of the British Labour government in May 1997 with a majority of 177 and a more 'polycentric' approach to questions of nationalism in the United Kingdom and with regard to European integration.[21] Following the June 1997 general election in the Irish Republic, a Fianna Fáil–Progressive Democrat coalition was formed, re-creating the potential for the type of pan-nationalist alliance that led to the first IRA ceasefire in 1994. While the election of two governments with political and ideological propensity as *interlocuteurs valables* may appear as fortuitous, as contingency, the evidence suggests that these governments were elected in part because of their pragmatic position on re-negotiating national sovereignty (especially the British Labour government) and, in the Irish Republic because of Fianna Fáil's ability to negotiate a settlement in Northern Ireland.[22] Moreover, what the subsequent negotiations and settlement reveal is the reassertion of a dualist, bi-national hierarchy, which 'triangulated' an historic agreement and, to date, its halting but largely successful implementation.

A key development was the adjustment of Labour's policy towards a position of neutrality on the status of Northern Ireland, a change that re-balanced the bi-national intergovernmentalist alignments and which was vital in cultivating pro-agreement unionism (See Figure 17). While unionists no longer held the balance of power, the achievement of a negotiated settlement was dependent on a sufficiently large and cohesive unionist bloc to prevent the type of splintering that undermined Sunningdale. In this context, British Labour's policy from 1981 to 1994 of promoting 'Irish unity by consent' clearly disqualified the party as a patron of unionism. For example, in a reliable 1996 survey conducted by Evans and O'Leary, 0 per cent of declared unionists supported Irish reunification; and only 2 per cent of unionists supported British–Irish joint sovereignty,[23] both of which were central policy positions in Labour's pre-1994 manifestos. The British government's cultivation of a moderate unionist bloc was underlined with a leaked briefing to senior Irish-American congressmen and lobbyists in February 1998. Blair explained that Trimble:

> had come a good deal further than many Unionists wanted him to, for example, accepting North-South structures. People on the US side could help enormously by making clear that they understood the position of the Unionists. It was important to remember that Trimble was under constant attack from Paisley [DUP] and McCartney [UKUP], so that giving comfort to the Ulster Unionists was vital.[24]

The Fianna Fáil-led coalition, in turn, solidified the nationalist bloc by releasing republican prisoners (on licence) and maintained an open line of communication with the Sinn Féin leadership.

Thus, the negotiating alignments were decisively different from the arbitration attempt of 1973–4. From a British-led process handicapped by broken bi-partisanship, the relationship had evolved towards a more symmetrical British–Irish process with solid bi-partisanship in Britain and Ireland. Moreover, as argued in the last chapter, the logic of the mutual exposure of the core sovereignty claims dictated that the process of constitutional negotiating had to include the extremists because they were explicitly recognized as representatives of the opposing poles of national aspirations for self-determination. The vertical alignment of governmental and societal bi-nationalism was the decisive cause of stable conditions for subsequent negotiation and constitutional agreements.

British Prime Minister Tony Blair first steadied unionists with a speech in Belfast that inverted (intentionally or not) King George V's statement on the opening of Northern Ireland's parliament in 1921, declaring that in his opinion the union would last at least as long as the lifetime of the youngest person in the hall.[25] Blair then dropped the decommissioning pre-condition and invited parties associated with paramilitary groups into negotiations on the condition of renewed ceasefires and a commitment to the six Mitchell principles on non-violence. The IRA called a second ceasefire on 20 July 1997 and the main loyalist paramilitary groups reciprocated six weeks later. An Independent International Commission on Decommissioning was established in August and substantive all-party talks began in early October. The second largest unionist party, the DUP (Democratic Unionist Party), excluded themselves from the talks, along with the smaller UK Unionist Party. While this meant that unionist parties representing 43 per cent of the electorate were outside the process, this exclusion was voluntary rather than imposed like the exclusion of the DUP in 1973 from the Sunningdale talks. George Mitchell, the talks chairman, and political scientist Donald Horowitz believed that the self-exclusion of the DUP was an important factor in allowing a deal to be reached, as it gave the UUP more freedom to negotiate tactically. But stable ceasefires and inclusive talks also enhanced the chances of mutualist negotiation because the constitutional parties were freer to exchange concessions without being accused of selling out to threats of violence. Equally, the inclusion and recognition of the legitimacy of paramilitaries allowed them to make concessions on core demands with less fear of being seen to be defeated in the context of a hot war.

Despite the strengthening of external and internal parameters, little progress was made in the first three months of inclusive negotiations as dissident republicans attempted to destabilize the implementation process.[26] Thereafter, a clear pattern of British–Irish intergovernmentalism was responsible for progress towards the Belfast Agreement. Two further stages of British–Irish 'triangulation' can be discerned. First, in January 1998 the two governments published 'heads of agreement' of a proposed settlement. This paper was based on the familiar three strands, but was welcomed in particular by the UUP because it appeared to place the Northern Ireland power-sharing assembly on a plane above the North–South bodies linking Northern Ireland with the Irish Republic (the Irish dimension). After both Sinn Féin and the IRA rejected the draft, the Irish government moved to shore up the nationalist alliance by emphasizing the need for the North–South bodies to have executive authority and thereby 'pool sovereignty'.[27]

In early April, after several precarious months in which both loyalist and republican ceasefires were breached and their associated parties expelled temporarily from the talks, the two governments produced a draft agreement published in the name of the talks chairman, Senator George Mitchell.[28] The release of the 'Mitchell draft' on the Monday before Good Friday offers a particularly poignant example of British–Irish triangulation. UUP leader David Trimble subsequently claimed that his efforts to insert amendments into the crucial section on North–South bodies was blocked by an Irish official who claimed: 'You can't do that, this is a joint (British–Irish) text and it can't be changed.'[29] While the draft *was* subsequently changed to limit the scope of cross-border institutions, the gain for unionists was offset by the concession on the executive powers granted to these bodies and their anchoring in British and Irish legislation rather than subordinating them to the Northern Ireland Assembly. The anchoring of the cross-border bodies in bi-national legislation reflects the hierarchy of the British–Irish Intergovernmental Conference (discussed below), which shares the residual power to review and come to agreement on the effective functioning of any agreed institutions. Also, the continuity of the intergovernmental parameters set in the Framework Documents of 1995 was revealed by Irish Taoiseach Bertie Ahern's negotiating stance during Good Friday week when he insisted on a 'text that fulfils that very clear negotiating position outlined back in 1995 in the Framework Document. I will not be moving from that position and the Prime Minister understands that.'[30]

As one of its official names suggests, the British–Irish Agreement[31] signed on 10 April 1998 represents the pinnacle of bi-national intergovernmental conflict regulation. The agreement was ratified on 22 May 1998 in simultaneous referenda North and South by majorities of 71.12 per cent in Northern Ireland and 94.4 per cent in the Irish Republic, creating an all-Ireland majority of 85.4 per cent in support of the package. The outline of its structure, its ratification in referenda and its implementation all attest to the effectiveness of a bi-national, British–Irish hierarchy as a framework for maximizing consent for processes of self-determination for nationalists and unionists in both parts of Ireland.[32]

The first substantive section of the agreement establishes the core regulative aspect of sovereignty: an agreed process of self-determination, based on concurrent majorities North and South for any change in the constitutional status of Northern Ireland. This 'principle of consent' is then enshrined in changes to the constitutive claims to sovereignty in the British and Irish constitutions, with the reciprocal exchange of the rescinding of the British Government of Ireland Act (1920) for amendments to Articles 2 and 3 of the Irish constitution. In the Irish constitutionalist reading, these exchanges rescinded mutually both governments' opposing constitutive claims to sovereignty and agreed to base sovereignty on the current will of the majority of peoples in Northern Ireland and the Irish Republic.[33] The key passage in the new Article 3 of the Irish constitution states:

> It is the firm will of the Irish nation, in harmony and friendship, to unite all the people who share the territory of the island of Ireland, in all the diversity of their identities and traditions, recognising that a united Ireland shall be brought about only by peaceful means with the consent of a majority of the people, democratically expressed, in both jurisdictions in the island ... (British–Irish Agreement, Annex B: Irish Government Draft Legislation to Amend the Constitution).

By recognizing the existence of two jurisdictions on the island, this amendment represents the first Irish constitutional recognition of the legal status of Northern Ireland as a part of the United Kingdom. In addition, the Irish state commits itself to be bound by the British–Irish Agreement. In return, the Irish nation is granted a mechanism for re-unification through the commitment of the

British to allow Irish unification if majorities in Northern Ireland and the Irish Republic support such a change and a commitment to grant a poll on self-determination with a minimum interval between polls of seven years.[34] In addition, the Irish government is granted a share of executive power on an all-Ireland basis through the establishment of a North–South Ministerial Council (NSMC), modelled on the European Council of Ministers.[35] For the Irish government, the primacy of the all-island dimension was revealed by Irish Taoiseach Bertie Ahern when the North–South Ministerial Council and implementation bodies were set up, with a secretariat in Armagh, the 'ecclesiastic capital', in December 1999. Ahern stated he was more pleased about [the NSMC] than any other development since the start of the peace process. 'The formal ratification and the ceremonial parts are all very nice but today is what it has all been about. This is now the reality, that we are in there dealing with real issues on an all-island basis.'[36]

This bi-national hierarchy is reflected at the subsequent levels of government created by the agreement. The power-sharing government for Northern Ireland may be pioneering in the creativity of its 'cross-community' decision-making,[37i] but with no tax-raising or authority over policing and justice (until 2007), the Northern Ireland Assembly had less power than the devolved Scottish parliament. The same is true of the North–South Ministerial Council vis-à-vis the Irish government, leaving the two sovereigns with the (separate) retention of the majority of residual political and economic power, co-managed through the British–Irish Intergovernmental Conference. Even the naming of the expanded 'Strand Three' dimension linking the devolved institutions in Northern Ireland, Scotland, Wales, the Isle of Man and the Channel Islands with the British and Irish governments is instructive: unionists wanted to call it the 'Council of the British Isles' or 'Council of the Isles' but had to settle for the 'British–Irish Council' (BIC).

Yet, there is by no means perfect symmetry. The British claim to sovereignty over Northern Ireland trumps the Irish aspiration. This asymmetry is reflected in the legal commitments made by the two states in the agreement. The Irish state consents 'to be bound by the British–Irish Agreement' while the British state, bound only by parliamentary sovereignty, simply repeals one source of the claim to sovereignty over Ireland, the Govt. of Ireland Act 1920. Irish officials interpret the statement that 'this Act [approving the British–Irish Agreement] shall have effect notwithstanding any other previous enactment'[38] as meaning that the commitments in the BIA have priority over the Act of Union (1800). Yet, experience has shown that British governments have asserted British parliamentary sovereignty over the British–Irish treaty relationship. Thus, the core element of regulative sovereignty, the mechanism for self-determination, is subordinate to British parliamentary sovereignty. Clause 1 (2) of the legislation reads:

> But if the wish expressed by a majority in such a poll [for Irish re-unification] is that Northern Ireland should cease to be part of the United Kingdom and form part of a united Ireland, the Secretary of State shall lay before Parliament such proposals to give effect to that wish as may be agreed between Her

Majesty's Government in the United Kingdom and the Government of Ireland'[39]

Thus in theory a future British parliamentary majority could veto a united Ireland, though the liberal unionist commentators who interpreted these 'balanced constitutional changes' as Irish negotiating mistakes surely underestimate the symbolic and political meaning of these status-levelling changes, as revealed below in the implementation of the agreement.[40]

Neither is the identification of a bi-national hierarchy in the agreement a denial of the importance of the consociational features of government proposed for Northern Ireland, the thorough reform of political and civil rights in both jurisdictions, nor the integral design of the three-strands that makes them interdependent. What I am suggesting is that, given the historical origins of the conflict, the British–Irish intergovernmental relationship is causally prior to the 'solution' of ethno-national conflict between Catholics/nationalists and Protestants/unionists *in* Northern Ireland. That is why the agreement affirms the requirement of both states to recognize and protect the variety of identities and traditions, but ensure ... 'parity of esteem and of just and equal treatment for the identity, ethos, and aspirations of *both* communities'.[41] In other words, maximizing self-determination for both communities required a more symmetrical bi-national framework than existed hitherto in order to facilitate a mutualist exchange relationship. But within this bi-national hierarchy there is considerable flexibility on the devolution of power downwards, based on the same 'rolling devolution' incentive established with the Anglo-Irish Agreement. Thus in the absence of successful power-sharing, the British–Irish Intergovernmental Conference is given the residual power to 'deal with all-island and cross-border co-operation on non-devolved issues' (Article 5). The incentive mechanism established with the AIA is reaffirmed: if unionists want less Irish government involvement in Northern Ireland matters, they must share power in Northern Ireland and accept cross-border bodies. And if Irish nationalists (including republicans) want less British rule, they must recognize Northern Ireland as part of the United Kingdom, and gain the consent of unionists for the enhancement of links between North and South, or for eventual Irish unification.

The importance of the bi-national incentive mechanism is clearly revealed in the battle within unionism, which was almost evenly split over support for the agreement.[42] The central argument used by Ulster Unionist leader David Trimble was that the agreement strengthened the union with Great Britain while giving unionists a veto on the nature and scale of cross-border bodies. Trimble could support the agreement at his party's conference in October 1998 because the all-Ireland consensus on the process of national self-determination meant that: '[a]ll the parties, including the Irish nationalists and republicans, are signed up to the statement that the constitutional future of Northern Ireland is to be determined by the people of Northern Ireland, without any interference or coercion by anyone else. Of course, that makes the Union more secure.'[43] If we compare Trimble's position with that of Brian Faulkner, the Ulster Unionist Party leader who supported the Sunningdale Agreement in 1973–4, we can see that Trimble had the clear advantage of having secured the constitutional recognition of unionist self-determination by the political representatives of Irish nationalism. The recognition of the principle of consent extended to the scale of the devolved portion of the Irish dimension – the North–South Ministerial Council – and the implementation bodies, which were reduced considerably in comparison with both the Council of Ireland proposed in Sunningdale and the scale of cross-border institutions proposed in the Framework Documents.[44]

Figure 18 compares pro- and anti-agreement support within unionism and nationalism for the Sunningdale and British–Irish Agreements respectively. These election results, subsequent polling data[45] and internal decisions taken by the Ulster Unionist Party[46] show pro-agreement support holding up in comparison with the precipitous slide away from Sunningdale, while political violence has been reduced to pre-1969 levels. While the voting in the referendum and the assembly election revealed an almost even split within unionism, the largest anti-agreement party, the DUP, quickly declared its intention to recognize and participate in the new institutions, demonstrating a sceptical rather than outright oppositional approach to the agreement. Moreover, loyalist parties (PUP and UDP, the political allies of loyalist paramilitary groups UVF, UDA/UFF, respectively) supported the agreement, at least until July 2001 when the UDP/UDA/UFF announced an end to its support. Even then, the UDA made it clear that its ceasefire would remain intact as long as the Provisional IRA ceasefire held. More hopefully still, the small PUP with two seats in the Northern Ireland Assembly effectively held the balance of power within the unionist bloc. As a result, the anti-agreement bloc had no army, implicit or explicit, with which to threaten or liaise as they did in 1974 to bring down the Sunningdale Agreement.

Among nationalists, support for the agreement was nearly unanimous North and South. Yet the IRA leadership rejected the agreement as a valid expression of national self-determination:

> The leadership of Óglaigh na hÉireann have considered carefully the Good Friday document. It remains our position that a durable peace settlement demands the end of British rule in Ireland and the exercise of the right of the people of Ireland to national self-determination. Viewed against our Republican objectives or any democratic analysis, this document clearly falls short of presenting a solid basis for a lasting settlement. In our view, the two imminent referenda do not constitute the exercise of national self-determination and voters' attitudes to the referenda should be guided by their own view and the advice of their political leaders.[47]

Nevertheless, by *not* calling for a 'No' vote in the referendum, and most importantly by publicly supporting Sinn Féin's position during the imple-mentation phase, the IRA leadership tacitly accepted the agreement at least as an interim form of government. Those within the republican movement who rejected the agreement outright split from the IRA and Sinn Féin and some activists drifted into two separate organizations, the 'Continuity IRA' (formed after the first IRA ceasefire in 1994 and linked to an older republican split from 1986) and Óglaigh na hÉireann (which journalists translated as 'Real IRA'). The latter attempted to destroy the implementation process in August 1998 with a massive car bomb in the town of Omagh (Northern Ireland) that killed twenty-nine people and injured scores more.

What was significant about the fallout from the Omagh tragedy was the extent to which dissident republicans were 'triangulated' by the two governments, acting with the fresh mandate of the popular and parliamentary ratification of the Good Friday Agreement (GFA). The Irish government moved quickly to introduce draconian anti-terror legislation (which potentially allowed the police to prosecute alleged members of a proscribed organization based on the word of a police officer). The British government were reluctant to introduce such measures in their own jurisdiction, in large part because of their dubious legal grounding, but did so because of the need and opportunity to demonstrate the strength of the British–Irish relationship.[48] The two governments subsequently announced joint RUC–Garda training initiatives and moved in tandem against dissident loyalists and republicans in their respective jurisdictions. Moreover, with intergovernmental co-operation extending to the United States and beyond, the 'Real' IRA was dealt a series of setbacks, including the arrest of its leader, Mickey McKevitt, based on evidence compiled by an FBI informer, the arrest of key operatives in Croatia on arms-buying missions and a series of interceptions and arrests in the Irish Republic which suggested that the Real IRA's new cell structure was infiltrated by the Provisional IRA and/or Irish police informants.

Indeed, a similar pattern of bi-national triangulation can be seen in the tortuous process of implementation from the agreement (10 April 1998) to the establishment of the Northern Ireland Executive and North–South Ministerial Bodies in December 1999. In the autumn of 1998 after the parties failed to agree on the cross-border bodies and matching portfolios for the Northern Ireland Executive, the two governments injected momentum by publicly airing other aspects of the reform agenda (policing, prisoner releases, judicial reform, human rights legislation) in a way calculated to remind local leaders of the British–Irish determination to exchange regulative aspects of sovereignty by implementing the reform agenda.[49]

Yet, there were clear limits to the bi-national 'triangulation' process, revealed most poignantly in the successive failures in March and June 1999 and February 2000 to resolve the decommissioning issue. The UUP refused to form the power-sharing executive with Sinn Féin until the IRA had begun to dispose of its weapons, whereas Sinn Féin and the IRA refused to dispose of weapons because what they interpreted as an act of 'surrender' was outside the terms of the agreement and likely to cause a larger split within the republican movement.[50] Sinn Féin rejected the first proposal, negotiated by the two governments and the Northern Ireland parties at Hillsborough in March 1999, because it made decommissioning a pre-condition to the establishment of the executive and could thereby establish a precedent for unionists to renegotiate aspects of the agreement. Unionists then rejected a second attempted triangulation in late June that was based on a commitment by the IRA to decommission weapons after the executive and NSMC were established. The British and Irish Prime Ministers (Blair and Ahern) had failed very publicly to create a deal and they retreated, inviting the agreement's talks chairman, George Mitchell, to conduct a review of the implementation process from September 1999.

Despite these setbacks, the bi-national hierarchy established with the agreement sustained incentives for compromise over the crises of executive formation. First, the Mitchell review was clearly mandated by the two governments to preserve the sanctity of the agreement, meaning that neither Ulster Unionists nor Sinn Féin could renegotiate its terms. Secondly, before and during the review, the two governments made it clear that in the event of failure of the parties in Northern Ireland to form the power-sharing executive, the two governments would attempt to implement the reforms intergovernmentally.[51] Therefore, unionists' hopes of reducing the Irish government's input into Northern Ireland's affairs would be dashed, as would republicans' hopes of minimizing direct rule from Britain. The same type of negative incentive based on creeping British–Irish intergovernmentalism was clearly influential, along with the undoubted facilitation skills of George Mitchell, in reaching agreement on the formation of the executive in December 1999. UUP leader David Trimble accepted a formula, almost identical to that proposed by the two governments the previous June, in which decommissioning would occur as a product, rather than a precondition, of the implementation of the agreement.[52] But facing a serious out-flanking manoeuvre within his party, Trimble felt compelled to insert his own deadline into the sequencing deal, threatening to resign if decommissioning had not begun by 4 February 2000. The Provisional IRA rejected this and, despite private objections expressed by the Irish government, the British government suspended the institutions of the agreement on 11 February 2000.

By asserting the primacy of its sovereignty claim, the British government exposed the Irish government to potential constitutional challenge as the amendments to Articles 2 and 3 appeared to have been 'banked' by unionists and the intergovernmental review procedure of the British–Irish Agreement violated. By extension, the leadership of Sinn Féin was threatened as dissident republicans could point to the futility of an agreement that could be over-ridden by the Northern Ireland Secretary's reassertion of British sovereignty. The reassertion of force created a constitutional crisis as the agreed mechanism for joint British–Irish decision-making in review of the agreement was not invoked. In Brendan O'Leary's view, the repetitive assertions of British sovereignty severely undermined the constitutionality of the agreement. 'Everything in the Agreement – its institutions, its confidence-building measures, the promise that Irish unification will take place if there is majority consent for it in both parts of Ireland – is revisable by the current Westminster Parliament, and any future Parliament, irrespective of international law, or the solemn promises made by the UK negotiators in the run-up to, and in the making of, the Agreement.'[53]

How did the sanctity of the agreement survive unilateral assertions of sovereignty? By returning to cooperative bi-national intergovernmentalism, the two sovereigns restored the principle of mutualism while offering both side-payments and symmetrical incentives to the subordinate parties in Northern Ireland. The re-balancing of the process can be seen in the sustenance of equivalence between paramilitary weapons and the British state's weapons. More broadly, if we consider policing, security, military and judiciary as constitutive aspects of sovereignty, then the degree of adjustment to these aspects proposed in the British–Irish Agreement reveals a degree of levelling which would have been unthinkable in the absence of a reciprocal, bi-national framework. Thus, a British official was quoted as saying:

> He [Blair] is ready to offer a programme of rapid British military base closures, troop reductions and changes in security if Sinn Féin agrees to IRA decommissioning. But these will not go forward unless there is some movement from Sinn Féin. We are not in the business of giving out any more sweeties without knowing what is going to happen.[55]

Similarly, the Patten Commission's premise in proposing radical reforms of the predominantly Protestant Royal Ulster Constabulary was that constitutive sovereignty was challenged:

> Policing has been contentious, victim and participant in past tragedies, *precisely because the polity itself has been contentious*. The consent required right across the community in any liberal democracy for effective policing has been absent... Both in the past, when the police were subject to political control by the Unionist government at Stormont, and more recently in the period of direct rule from Westminster, they have been identified by one section of the population not primarily as upholders of the law but as defenders of the state, *and the nature of the state itself has remained the central issue of political argument*.[55]

The Irish government continually reinforced the equivalence between state and paramilitary weapons by insisting that Patten's proposals be upheld in full and implemented rapidly, and also supported Sinn Féin's demands for rapid demilitarization as a corollary of paramilitary decommissioning.[56]

The response to this impasse attests to the primacy of the bi-national inter-governmental relationship in managing relations between state and paramilitary force and all subsidiary aspects of the power-sharing process. First, in May 2001 the Irish government secured a commitment from the British not to suspend unilaterally the power-sharing institutions without the consent of the Irish government, though this did not extend to a repeal of the suspension legislation itself. Secondly, in the account of Irish Minister for Foreign Affairs Brian Cowen, 'in order to persuade republicans that there was something in it for them, the British–Irish talks had to be broadened to take account of "demilitarisation"' (reduced Army patrols, watchtowers dismantled) and police reform.'[57]

In response, the IRA made a very significant, though under-reported, concession in May 2000 during the crisis of executive formation. After emphasizing the authority and responsibility of the two governments, the IRA stated:

> The full implementation, on a progressive and irreversible basis by the two governments, especially the British government, of what they have agreed will provide a political context, in an enduring political process, with the potential to remove the causes of conflict, *and in which Irish republicans, and unionists can, as equals pursue our respective political objectives peacefully.* In that context the IRA leadership will initiate a process that will completely and verifiably put IRA arms beyond use ... [58]

A confidence-building gesture was offered in terms very similar to those offered by the IRA to the Free State government in 1923: the IRA would agree to allow three independent observers to inspect and re-inspect an unspecified number of arms dumps and report to the Independent International Commission on Decommissioning.

What is novel here is the public acknowledgement by the IRA of political status-equality between Irish republicans and unionists, and the recognition of separate political objectives. While not explicitly recognizing separate and equal constitutional rights to self-determination, nevertheless this was the furthest the IRA had gone in recognizing the principle of mutual consent as the basis of self-determination. Moreover, it was the re-establishment of equivalence between paramilitary and state weapons that allowed subsequent IRA recognition of unionists' separate political objectives. Whereas Trimble was seeking to establish equivalence between IRA decommissioning and the formation of the Northern Ireland power-sharing executive (and concomitant participation in North–South bodies), the IRA was insisting on linkage between its own acts of decommissioning and the British state's de-militarization and legislative commitments to fulfil the Patten report's suggested policing reforms.

These halting, seemingly reluctant increments towards disarmament and reconciliation were again not enough to help David Trimble halt the slide in unionist confidence in the agreement. The apparent concessions to republicans over judicial reform, prisoner releases and amnesties; the overt challenge to the symbols of the state, both from the Irish government and republicans: flags and symbols in public buildings; the continued stand-off at Drumcree; all eclipsed the abstract constitutional principle of consent.[59] Despite what many unionists interpreted as 'concessions' to Sinn Féin, the party continued to reject nominating members to the new Police Board (and district policing boards).

Like the Trinitarian conflict itself, the final straw for this phase of the process came in three: allegations of an IRA break-in at the high-security military intelligence complex at Castlereagh; allegations of IRA collusion with Columbian Marxist paramilitaries; and allegations of a Sinn Féin/IRA spy ring at Stormont, alleged to have access to Prime Ministerial minutes and inter-party negotiating briefings. The 'analytical' explanation – that these three targets of republican para-politics were gauged towards the areas which Sinn Féin claimed were implementation failures by the British government – cut little ice with unionists or the two governments. Out-flanking by the anti-agreement DUP was imminent. Peter Robinson declared that his party 'would not be signing up for a transition to a united Ireland, as the UUP has done...Nor would his party [DUP] accept those who are linked with active terrorism ruling over those they continue to terrorise'.[60] In survival mode, David Trimble resigned from the executive (and by extension the North–South Ministerial Council). To avoid the likely electoral meltdown of pro-agreement unionism, the British government suspended the agreement for the fifth time since its inception. On cue, the two governments played their now-familiar duet after a Prime Ministerial summit: they briefed key journalists, intimating that, as an alternative to power-sharing and what became known as paramilitary 'acts of completion', the Irish and British governments would act to co-regulate their respective sovereignties with regard to the wider British–Irish agenda.[61]

To understand why this set of exchanges has been progressive we need to place them in their broader historical and constitutional contexts. On the one hand, contemporary Irish governments have reluctantly learned to accept some pragmatic assertions of British parliamentary sovereignty. In exchange, the British government has grown to recognize the principled constitutionalism required to sustain the agreement. In the Joint Declaration of April 2003, the British government committed to rescinding the legislation introduced by the arch pragmatist – Peter Mandelson – declaring that: 'In the context of definitive acts of completion [by paramilitary groups] the British Government would be prepared to repeal the power in the Northern Ireland Act (2000) to suspend these institutions by order.'[62] The British government also committed itself to the full implementation of the Patten police reforms, including acceptance of 'the desirability of devolving policing and justice within the lifetime of the next Assembly, on a basis that is robust, and workable and broadly supported by the parties'.[63] For its part, the Fianna Fáil-led Irish government demonstrated its resolve against paramilitarism by ruling out any coalition with Sinn Féin as long as the IRA remained active. Since Sinn Féin has clear electoral ambitions in both parts of the island, the incentive for closure on paramilitarism was reinforced.

The Hillsborough round of 2003 was progressive for balancing the bi-national duopoly on legitimate force with the preservation of the federal and confederal principles agreed in 1998. The heart of the deal reached by the two governments in early March 2003, though rejected by the UUP and Sinn Féin, was based on the following exchanges:[64]

- The verifiable end to paramilitary activity by groups connected to parties in government, in exchange for a two-year timetable for demilitarization or 'normalization' by 2005;[65] and ancillary agreement on a judicial process for fugitives of justice (based on the recognition of offence in exchange for a conditional amnesty).
- Full(er) implementation of the Patten police reforms (especially the

transparency and accountability of the former Special Branch, and the restriction of the Northern Ireland Secretary's authority relative to the Police Board and Ombudsmen) in exchange for Sinn Féin participation in the Police Board and district policing partnerships.

- The creation by the two governments of an Independent Monitoring Commission, composed of two British (including one Northern Irish) one Irish and one American appointee with a three-fold mandate: to assess paramilitary activity; to assess the British government's commitment to 'security normalization'; and to assess the commitment of ministers or other elected officials to exclusively democratic means and to commitments made to the terms of the pledge of office.

The proposed agreement attempted to balance two opposing demands. First, the UUP demanded a sanction method to bar political parties associated with paramilitary organizations from office based on clear evidence of continued paramilitary activity on the part of groups with links to parties in the assembly. Secondly, the agreement addressed Sinn Féin's demand for assurance that the BIA would be implemented in full. The unilateral authority of the Northern Ireland Secretary to make determinations on breaches of the pledge of office would not be formally rescinded, but the creation of an Independent Monitoring Commission to report publicly to both governments on alleged breaches, including the authority to make recommendations for remedial action, set limits on the autonomy of the Northern Ireland Secretary and, in theory, provided an independent scrutiny of the two governments' implementation commitments. Most significantly, the bi-national, intergovernmental process was reaffirmed: after intensive negotiations failed to break the deadlock among pro-agreement parties and government officials, a bi-lateral agreement was sealed by substantive 'short-haul' diplomacy between Blair and Ahern. Reminiscent of the processes leading to the Downing Street Declaration, Good Friday Agreement, and all of the progressive stages of implementation, the two governments concluded agreement on a historic annex to the British–Irish Agreement. Like the previous treaties the two governments distilled elements of common ground among the Northern Ireland parties and established new parameters in an international treaty.

But are these treaties transformative or just desperate cobbling? Fudge or adobe? It would be tempting to argue, for example, that contingency played a large part in the breakthrough leading to the first act of decommissioning by the IRA in November 2001. In the post-September 11 world, and in the aftermath of alleged IRA collusion with Columbian *guerillas*, it could be argued that the IRA had little choice but to commit to constitutional methods and avoid being on the wrong side in the 'war on terrorism'. But as important as 11 September 2001 was in shaping contemporary conceptions of legitimate and illegitimate force, it is also clear that the decisive exchanges took place earlier, in the spring of 2000, in the aftermath of the first suspension, when the IRA agreed to allow inspections of their arms dumps in exchange for explicit linkage to demilitarization, police and justice reforms. It was also clear to the

Sinn Féin leadership from the beginning of the peace process that the IRA and its weapons would have to be removed from the political process in order to cultivate political support in both parts of the island and to remove unionist excuses for delay in accepting reform.[66]

The Irish government has also been guilty of playing politics with the BIA. The Citizenship Act, ratified by referendum in June 2004, was largely a response to significant increases of immigration to Ireland. A seemingly unintended effect of the act's limits on citizenship to children born on the island of Ireland to non-citizens was to violate a key clause of Article 1 of the British–Irish Agreement: '... the birthright of all the people of Northern Ireland to identify themselves and be accepted as Irish or British, or both, as they may so choose, and accordingly confirm their right to hold both British and Irish citizenship is accepted by both Governments and would not be affected by any future change in the status of Northern Ireland' (Article 1 (vi)). As recognized by O'Leary and others, this act was a precedent for the Oireachtas to establish its superiority over the stipulations of the BIA, in much the same way as the British government had done through the suspension legislation.[67]

More positively, given the degree to which the two governments have been able to promote exchanges, it is evident that the British–Irish relationship has been most successful when it is 'vertically integrated' with political parties and movements at the governmental and societal levels. For example, just as we emphasized the need for the sovereign governments to integrate the aspirations of both republicans and loyalists into the bi-national architecture of the Downing Street Declaration (1993), the Joint Declaration of 2003 recognizes and addresses the opposing interests and aspirations of clear majorities of both nationalists and unionists, as expressed in authoritative opinion polls. The British–Irish insistence on a verifiable end to paramilitarism addresses unionists' top priority in the post-agreement period,[68] while the linkage between paramilitary decommissioning and demilitarization plus police reform and prisoner releases addresses the top priorities of Sinn Féin supporters.[69] The SDLP was also rewarded, despite its marginalization from these exchanges. Its supporters' priorities in May 2000 were 'commitments to non-violence', 'Northern Ireland Assembly', 'Northern Ireland Executive', 'paramilitary decommissioning' and 'support for the victims of the "Troubles"'. Thus, the bridging of commitments to non-violence (including decommissioning), with obligations to preserve the devolved status of the power-sharing institutions, effectively bridges the unionist–nationalist political spectrum. Further evidence from the polling reported by Colin Irwin supports the transformation to pluralized nationalism, with cross-community support for integrated education, integrated housing and a bill of rights 'protecting the culture of each community'.[70] One poll published before the 2003 assembly elections showed only 28 per cent of Catholics supporting a united Ireland and 21 per cent of Protestants (down from 48 per cent in 1988) supporting integration in the United Kingdom as preferred options. A plurality (35 per cent) of all respondents preferred the restoration of the devolved government 'under the umbrella of the [GFA]'.[71] Futhermore, as Figure 19 demonstrates, Trimble was able to consistently secure bare majorities within his party's governing Ulster Unionist Council for major stages in the implementation process.

Additionally, there is evidence that the British–Irish commitment to full implementation has led to confidence-building at the level of political elites in Northern Ireland. Whereas in the negotiations of the BIA the Ulster Unionist Party refused to negotiate directly with Sinn Féin, by the spring of 2003 the leaders of the two parties, Trimble and Adams, met up to fifteen times in their attempt to agree a new sequence of confidence-building steps and, though they ultimately failed, were, according to Northern Ireland Secretary Paul Murphy, 'directly engaged with the issues', without the need for British ministerial arbitration.[72] Equally profound was the shift in relations between the DUP and Sinn Féin. Whereas the DUP refused to participate in the GFA talks because of Sinn Féin's presence, and then refused to sit with Sinn Féin representatives in the Northern Ireland Executive, by 2003 the party had worked with Sinn Féin in Stormont committees and accepted the reality of negotiations with Sinn Féin (though not face-to-face until 2007; see Conclusion) following the 2003 elections.[73] Despite the party commitment to wrecking the agreement from within, in a 2001 poll a clear majority of its supporters (59 per cent) supported the party's continued participation in the Northern Ireland Executive and 30 per cent of supporters said they would again vote 'yes' on a referendum for the GFA.[74]

Our penultimate test of intergovernmental relations suggests clear trans-formative potential, but also residual conflicts based on divergent British and Irish constitutionalism. Consider first the statement signed by P. O'Neill on 21 October 2003 affirming that Sinn Féin President Gerry Adams 'reflected accurately' the IRA's view when he stated that Sinn Féin's position 'is one of total and absolute commitment to exclusively democratic and peaceful means of resolving differences'... [and]... we oppose any use or threat of force for any political purpose'. As the more reflective commentators noticed, the IRA statement meant that any future violence committed by the IRA, if deemed by the new International Monitoring Committee to be political, would annihilate the credibility of Sinn Féin and put an end to its constitutional republican project. However cryptic the IRA's langauge, it meant that the main republican paramilitary group had accepted the bi-national consent mechanism for national self-determination, something they failed to do when Sinn Féin accepted the Good Friday Agreement in 1998. It is also clear that the IRA's decision to make its historic commitment was a by-product of the formal equivalence between paramilitary and military (and policing) implements made in the British–Irish (Hillsborough) Agreement establishing the International Monitoring Commission (2003).[75]

The profundity of these developments was not lost on David Trimble in the autumn of 2003. Nevertheless, he judged that the IRA's historic commitment and the safety net provided by the Independent Monitoring Commission was not enough to ensure his short-term political survival given the declining unionist confidence in the agreement. More worryingly, the British Prime Minister's clumsy attempt to be helpful to Trimble backfired spectacularly, revealing once again the dangers of pragmatic over principled constitutionalism. In response to Trimble's decision to halt the sequential process leading to a commitment to share power, Blair declared his intention to try to subvert the constitutionally entrenched confidentiality clause invoked by the IRA in putting arms beyond use. This lurch simultaneously undermined Trimble's position within unionism (by making him look like he had been a poor negotiator by failing to get transparency from the IRA) and damaged equally republican confidence in British constitutionalism by suggesting that the Independent International Commission of Decommissioning's (IIDC) mandate, based on British and Irish legislation, was also unilaterally alterable. Blair's temptation was quickly quashed by a threat from the IIDC head, General de Chastelain, to resign if the confidentiality clause was broken. The Irish government also warned against a unilateral breach and elections to the suspended Northern Ireland Assembly went ahead in November 2003. It is both unsurprising and reassuring that a general from the dominion of Canada was responsible for checking imperious constitutionalism.

ACTS OF COMPLETION

The results of those elections, in which Sinn Féin and the DUP eclipsed the SDLP and UUP as leaders of the nationalist and unionist blocs (respectively), the failure of subsequent talks and allegations of an IRA non-violent 'spectacular' raid of the Northern Bank in Belfast in December 2004 led some commentators in early 2005 to declare the Good Friday process over or at least fundamentally transformed away from the inclusive process. A careful analysis of these developments, however, suggests that the bi-national intergovernmental process has been successful in leading the 'maximalists' within each bloc towards the centre ground, including commitments to pluralist nationalist thinking and pragmatic power-sharing.

The negotiations in the second half of 2004 offer another example of the dangers of pragmatic over principled constitutionalism. Negotiations brokered by the two governments seemed to come within a 'photograph' of a deal that would trade the IRA as an active militant organization, for commitment by the DUP to share power at Stormont and in the NSMC. The talks broke down over the DUP demand for photographic evidence of decommissioning as a public act of IRA contrition for its terrorist campaign. Paisley's demand that the IRA wear 'sackcloth and ashes' probably indicates the DUP's private rejection of a deal that was very close to that which pro-agreement UUP leader David Trimble was on the brink of accepting in late 2003. The IRA refusal to allow the publication of photographs was a defence of the confidentiality clause that it had carefully negotiated in the GFA. Republicans continued to fear that significant alterations to the confidentiality principle would set a precedent for unionist re-negotiation of other aspects and also feared that publicized 'surrender' would invite more republican defections to dissident ranks.[76]

When the two governments published their blueprint for a way forward on 8 December, their proposals and subsequent statements appeared to endorse the DUP proposal for photographs, thus placing the burden of responsibility for the failure of talks onto the IRA and Sinn Féin.[77] It was only after this successive attempt to purge the confidentiality principle that the IRA leadership is alleged to have authorized the Northern Bank raid, in which £26 million pounds was stolen. The scale of the raid and subsequent allegations of criminality and money laundering have reinforced the view that the republican leadership never intended to accept the partitionist principles of the GFA. By extension, these developments appear to confirm the warnings of centripetalists like Horowitz and others who warn against inclusion of extremists.[78]

However, these pessimistic interpretations ignore the classification error committed by the British and Irish governments in the treatment of the means of violence. Treating complete IRA decommissioning as equivalent to DUP participation in power-sharing undermined the vertical integration of bi-nationalism identified above as central to the negotiation and implementation of the GFA. If the weapons issue had been maintained as the preserve of the IIDC, where it was treated as equivalent to both demilitarization and police reform, rather than subject to popular verification, it is likely that the IRA would have complied, even if the Rev. Ian Paisley had asked the IRA to wear 'sackcloth and ashes'. In the absence of the maintenance of the constitutional ideals, the republican leadership, or perhaps rivals or sceptics of the Sinn Féin peace strategy, apparently decided that the violations of the GFA can or should be countered by equivalent symbolic and political attacks against the British state – a 'non-violent' spectacular meant to warn the British and Irish governments not to take the IRA's cessation for granted.[79] Even if we treat these republican self-justifications cautiously (the allegations of the bank raid as a pension scheme for 'retiring' IRA leaders is just as plausible, though this does not rule out the political motive described above), the revival of the political process demonstrates again the potential for bi-national intergovernmentalism to transform violent politics into constitutional politics.

On 28 July 2005 the leadership of Óglaigh na hÉireann [IRA] announced that it 'formally ordered an end to the armed campaign'.[80] This announcement was followed in October by the supervized decommissioning of the remainder of the known arsenal. Unlike the flawed exchange proposed by the governments in December 2004, this process was conducted under the condition of confidentiality, returning to the letter of the IIDC mandate as specified under the terms of the GFA. The only modification to the GFA mandated process was the introduction of two clergymen who acted as independent witnesses, the Catholic Redemptorist priest Father Alex Reid and the ex-Methodist president Reverend Harold Good. This particular modification was not imposed by the government but negotiated with Sinn Féin and clearly echoed the proposals developed in the context of the ending of the Irish civil war (as described in Chapter 3). Most revealingly, this side-deal included British government commitments to publish its 'normalization' paper committing it to further de-militarization, further implementation of police reforms, the replacement of the single-judge 'Diplock courts' and, most symbolically, the disbandment of the Royal Irish Rangers.

While it is true that Sinn Féin and the IRA faced considerable domestic and international pressure over the alleged involvement of their members in the murder of Robert McCartney in a Belfast pub, allegations of IRA money laundering and continued criminal activity, the IRA had survived similar levels of criticism domestically and internationally in the past without budging. In the context of a return to the principle of equivalence between paramilitary and official implements of violence, and in the wider context of recognition of the constitutional sanctity of an agreement that can be interpreted as an expression of national self-determination, the IRA felt that it could honourably end its campaign of violence.[81] The IRA's Easter message in 2006 further consolidated its commitments to the political process as it 'repudiated criminality' and denounced those 'former members' who continued to be involved in criminality.

THE ST ANDREWS AGREEMENT

With others, Michael Kerr has questioned whether the more symmetrical British–Irish intergovernmental relationship has been successful in regulating the conflict in Northern Ireland.[82] Citing the British government's successive unilateral suspensions of the GFA, he has argued that the intergovernmental relationship remains hierarchical rather than symmetrical. Another liberal unionist academic, Paul Bew (now Baron Bew of Donegore), argued that the intergovernmental relationship was insufficiently strong to threaten unionists with joint authority. '[W]ho,' he asked in 2004, 'either in London or Dublin, is acting in a way that will reinforce that argument?'[83] Both of these views underestimated the continued salience of the British–Irish relationship and its ability to maintain symmetrical incentives for unionists and nationalists in Northern Ireland to accept the principles of the GFA. As this final section shows, by restoring a commitment to the sanctity of the GFA and to its bi-national principles the two governments were able to sustain symmetrical incentives to consolidate both Sinn Féin and DUP commitments to the political process. The deal reached between the British and Irish governments and the Northern Ireland political parties at St Andrews, Scotland on (Friday) 13 October 2006 defied both superstition and the numerous pundits who thought the peace or at least political process was over once the DUP and Sinn Féin emerged as the largest parties following the 2003 Northern Ireland Assembly elections. While this deal and its successful implementation did require an extraordinary amount of pragmatic deal-making, especially by Northern Ireland Secretary Peter Hain, its success was based on the maintenance of the core principles of bi-nationalism that underpinned the Good Friday Agreement. The following interpretation also differs from those that focus on the Northern Ireland-level deal between Sinn Féin and the DUP, as important as that was. Instead, the deal between the proximate antagonists was mainly a by-product of reinforced British–Irish intergovernmentalism.

First, the return to principles of confidentiality and state-paramilitary equivalence that led to the removal of the IRA from the political process in 2005 cascaded into a significant set of responses from the DUP, both symbolic and political. Peter Robinson, deputy leader of the DUP, reinforced the trajectory of his party's position when he told the Council on Foreign Relations in New York in April 2006 that if Sinn Féin and the IRA were able to demonstrate their commitment to the rule of law, that he could look forward to a time when 'the eternal values of liberty and democracy have prevailed and that the sons and daughters of the Planter and the Gael have found a way to share the land of their birth and live together in peace'.[84] Robinson was almost certainly referring to Northern Ireland (rather than the island of Ireland) as the territory in which power could be shared. Yet in April 2006 his party also ended its long-standing boycott of the British–Irish Inter-Parliamentary Body and attended its meeting in Killarney. While Robinson was accused of being too far in front of his leader, his party or the DUP electorate in positioning the party for a deal with Sinn Féin in 2004, evidence that Paisley was preparing the ground for a seismic shift came in October 2006 when he met Catholic Archbishop Sean Brady at Stormont. Beyond symbolism, the DUP also confirmed its agreement in principle to the St Andrews Agreement and participated constructively with Sinn Féin and the other parties in the New Programme for Government Committee from 17 October 2006 to agree priorities for the new power-sharing executive.

Secondly, the thaw in relations between unionism and nationalism cannot be explained without again considering the symmetrical incentives developed by the British and Irish governments. When they met in Armagh in April 2006 to announce a new schedule for the restoration of the power-sharing institutions, they presented the parties with a clear and familiar choice: share power in Northern Ireland and in the North–South bodies or watch passively as the two governments developed British–Irish 'partnership governance' over their heads. The two governments reinforced their threat by launching their 'Comprehensive Study on the All-Island Economy' in October 2006 and discussing publicly a single inward investment strategy, joint trade-promotion, a single energy market and enhanced links between the two health services on the island.[85] The Irish government outlined commitments to invest the equivalent of £400 million (sterling) in infrastructure projects in Northern Ireland as part of its six-year National Development Plan (2007–13).[86]

These familiar threats were reinforced in the months before and after the St Andrews Agreement with positive incentives – such as a generous financial package geared towards ending economic deprivation in nationalist and unionist working-class areas – and negative incentives meant to appeal to unionists and nationalists equally: the suspension of MLA salaries, and increased water and property taxes. Other incentives were geared more directly towards the DUP and Sinn Féin, particularly the new nomination procedures for First and Deputy Ministers, which created an electoral incentive that favoured each within the two blocs respectively. The DUP were enticed by the prospect of the two governments' insistence on final 'acts of completion', especially the requirement that Sinn Féin would have to recognize the reformed policing and judicial authorities before entering government, the forestalling of education reforms, favourable appointments to the Parades and Victims' Commissions, as well as the first three peerages ever given to DUP members.[87] Sinn Féin were offered devolution of policing and justice to the Northern Ireland Assembly, further de-militarization, the abolition of the Northern Ireland Act (2000) that gave the British government the power to suspend the GFA, the possibility of amnesty for persons wanted for terrorist offences, strengthened accountability procedures for police and security services (MI5). The abolition of the Assets Recovery Agency – which had been targeting suspected IRA 'kingpins' in border regions – was announced in January 2007 just before the Sinn Féin special Ard Fheis to debate recognition of the PSNI.[88] The US government also lifted the ban on Sinn Féin fundraising in the US in response to Sinn Féin's decision to approve the two governments' schedule for restoration and specifically its decision to hold a special Ard Fheis to endorse the PSNI. Here again, US facilitation was geared towards reinforcing the British–Irish triangulation process.

On 28 January 2007 at a special conference (Ard Fheis) in Dublin, Sinn Féin delegates voted to allow the Sinn Féin party executive (Ard Chomhairle) to recognize the policing and judicial authorities if and when they are devolved to a future power-sharing executive. While conditional, the British and Irish governments interpreted the vote as the final act of completion expected of the republican movement as a condition for participation in government.

Elections followed on 7 March 2007 to endorse the St Andrews Agreement. While ostensibly meant to renew mandates for power-sharing, these elections also offered the side-payments to the DUP and Sinn Féin to secure their ascendance over the UUP and SDLP respectively. The latter parties naturally preferred a referendum rather than elections. For Sinn Féin, an added bonus was to give it a running start for the Irish general election expected in the early summer of 2007. The DUP increased its status as the dominant unionist party and largest party in Northern Ireland, winning thirty-six seats with 30.09 per cent of votes, an increase of six seats and 4.38 per cent of votes compared to 2003. The UUP were the biggest electoral casualties, losing nine seats and 7.74 per cent of votes since 2003 (to eighteen seats and 14.94 per cent of votes). On the nationalist side, Sinn Féin won twenty-eight seats from 26.16 per cent of votes, increases of four seats and 2.64 per cent since 2003, while the SDLP lost two seats on a decline of 1.77 per cent of votes (to sixteen seats on 15.22 per cent of votes).

Despite their renewed mandate, the DUP remained internally divided over whether to follow the two governments' schedule for restoration of power-sharing. Here again, the two governments used the threat of British–Irish partnership government if the DUP refused, to concentrate the minds of the waverers and doubters. On Monday, 26 March 2007 the DUP leader, the Reverend Ian Paisley, and Sinn Féin President Gerry Adams held a joint press-conference in which they did not shake hands but did announce that their parties had agreed to share power on 8 May 2007. Adams' concession on the six-week delay was predicated on Paisley's pledge that no new conditions or party executive votes would be raised in the six-week interim and on the two governments' maintenance of the threat of partnership governance as an alternative to devolved power-sharing. These developments demonstrate clearly that the British and Irish governments were able to cultivate consent by maintaining the bi-national parameters of the GFA and the symmetrical incentive of greater British–Irish direct rule if the parties in Northern Ireland could not reach a compromise. To analyze the prospects for this latest 'historic' deal, we need to look more closely at the changes made to the GFA.

The St Andrews amendments to the Good Friday Agreement reflect mainly the interests and concerns of the DUP and Sinn Féin as the dominant parties in Northern Ireland. The DUP secured an amendment to create a statutory ministerial code to 'act in accordance with the provisions on ministerial accountability of the Code'.[89] The practical effect of this code will be to limit the autonomy of individual members of the executive who, under the GFA, had 'full executive authority in their respective areas of responsibility, within any broad programme agreed by the Executive Committee and endorsed by the Assembly as a whole'.[90] Under the new ministerial code, any three executive members will be able to refer any issues, including draft North–South Ministerial Council and British–Irish Council matters not supported unanimously in the executive to a cross-community vote. The DUP also secured an amendment to the nomination procedures for selecting the First and Deputy First Ministers. Whereas under the GFA these two positions were nominated from the largest parties and ratified jointly on a cross-community vote, the new procedure allows the two largest parties to nominate candidates individually for the First and Deputy First Minister positions, respectively, without the need for cross-community approval. This change serves two purposes. It spares the DUP blushes by removing the need for the party to support a Sinn Féin Deputy First Minister. More importantly, it provides for a more robust executive by partially removing incentives for any First Minister (FM) or Deputy First Minister (DFM) to resign in order to bring the power-sharing system down. Both David Trimble as FM and Seamus Mallon as DFM were able to assert leverage by threatening to resign with, in Trimble's case, the clear knowledge that a cross-community support did not exist for the resurrection of the executive. With a lower threshold for executive formation, the threat of resignation still exists but its power is limited by the provisions that allow the two largest parties to simply nominate replacement FM or DFMs.

The strengthened scrutiny and review powers over the executive increase the potential for executive grid-lock. Sinn Féin feared that the previously anti-agreement DUP would use these measures to undermine power-sharing and cross-border co-operation. Therefore, amendments were proposed to the pledge of office to 'require that Ministers would participate fully in the Executive and NSMC/BIC, and would observe the joint nature of the office of First Minister and Deputy First Minister'.[91] These new procedures remove the freedom of executive members to boycott or attend selectively meetings of the NSMC/BIC, as FM David Trimble did in 2002. Additional features included a strengthened human rights agenda,[92] a financial package for a newly restored executive, and new 'national security arrangements' that 'preserve and build upon the Patten reforms'.[93] Thus, all of the new arrangements are designed to enhance the core principles of bi-national governance and rights protections agreed in the GFA. The so-called 'extremist' parties have not been able to deviate substantially from the parameters established by the two governments as early as 1995. Instead, precisely because the British and Irish governments have jointly maintained these bi-national parameters, both the DUP and Sinn Féin have transformed their maximal, opposed ethno-national projects into 'plurinational' agreement.

CONCLUSION

The prospects for keeping the gun out of British–Irish politics are unprecedented as long as the temptations are avoided for unilateral assertions of sovereignty that could undermine the mutuality of the British–Irish relationship.[94] This will mean that future British governments will need to be mindful and nurturing of the new constitutional foundations for governance in Northern Ireland and, given the likely difficulties there, of maintaining official-level and inter-ministerial relations with counterparts in the Irish Republic.

Equally, Irish governments, nationalists and republicans would be well-advised to avoid the mistake of asking too much of unionism as they did during the Sunningdale period. The competition between Sinn Féin and the SDLP to achieve the mantle of the nationalist party with the most effective policy to achieve re-unification will likely exert pressure on both main parties in the Republic to promote unification, especially if Sinn Féin secures its left-nationalist niche within the Irish party system. Too much emphasis on expanding the remit of North–South bodies could undermine liberal unionism. By contrast, continued economic growth and the promotion of secularism through more substantive separation of church and state in the Republic are likely to reduce unionist fears of re-unification or evolution towards deeper federal and/or confederal relations. *If* demographic and political conditions tip eventually towards a nationalist majority in Northern Ireland, the result of this consensual process is likely to be more of a union than unity, and the confederal relationship with Britain a more historically and nationally acceptable one on both islands.

Conclusion: Implications for Theory and Practice of Ethno-National Conflict Regulation

The robe of the purple velvet, the sword, the sceptre, and a richly-gilt Bible were gifts to the Protector [Oliver Cromwell] from his Parliament. "What a comely glorious sight it is" said the Speaker, "to behold a Lord Protector in a purple robe, with a sceptre in his hand, a sword of justice girt about him, and his eyes fixed upon the Bible! Long may you prosperously enjoy them all, to your own comfort and the comfort of the people of these three nations [English, Scottish, Irish].[95]

J.R. Tanner

It's just amazing when you walk in there. The ambience of the place – you can almost see Oliver Cromwell and all the rest of them down the ages. You can see what sort of mentality has been in train...So all of that stuff is rumbling around there. I've met ministers like Sir Patrick Mayhew and it's like talking to someone who thinks that he's ten levels above you...At least with Tony Blair you're talking to someone on the same level. The question is whether he is part of that whole mindset – somehow I don't think he is. Gerry Adams and I get on well with him: one big advantage is that we're obviously from the same generation. I have to say that he's the first British Prime Minister in maybe several centuries who has seriously tried to deal with Ireland and in particular with Britain's role...That said, he's still the British Prime Minister and I'm an Irish republican. I know where he stands and he knows where I stand. He knows we want to see an end to British government rule in Ireland and the establishment of a 32-county Republic. [96]

Martin McGuinness

By accepting that state legitimacy was contested by opposing, but equally valid, assertions of national rights, the British and Irish governments were moved to regulate rather than avoid sovereignty disputes. In turn, parties and movements with opposing self-determination claims were persuaded to pluralize their own conceptions of nationalism and accept reciprocal forms of self-determination.[97] By contrast to this interpretation, approaches to ethno-national conflict that assume the legitimacy of the state cast too rigid a frame for understanding conflict regulation in divided societies.[98] In the British–Irish case, consociational government and cultural and civic rights protections were vital bargaining elements, and were specifically traded for modification of ethno-national claims to self-determination. While necessarily cluttering the polity with competing demands, these bargains were concomitant to pluralizing conceptions of nationalism and nation-state arrangements.[99] While Knox and Lusztig, for example, rightly point to the dangers of 'mega-constitutionalism', the sinews of the conflict analyzed over the *long duree* show that, given the contested sovereignty over significant territory, the statist, unitary alternatives were and are unacceptable to significant ethno-national minorities. In this concluding section I want to defend and explicate the bi-national thesis by answering some of the dominant alternative interpretations of conflict regulation/resolution in / over Northern Ireland.

The primacy of the bi-national, intergovernmental explanation contrasts with that of Donald Horowitz, who tries to explain the provenance (and inherent instability) of the miraculous, 'arctic rose' of hybrid consociational power-sharing government in Northern Ireland. Horowitz emphasizes three factors: Firstly, in agreement with O'Leary and Evans, the political and demographic erosion of the unionist bloc created incentives for unionists to negotiate a deal that would provide short and long-term security in terms of constitutional guarantees, political representation, and individual and collective rights protections.[100] Secondly, Horowitz emphasizes the fortuitous self-exclusion of the DUP from all negotiations and of Sinn Féin from matters to do with Strand 1, power-sharing in Northern Ireland. These self-exclusions simplified the structure of negotiations, removing potential out-flankers from the equation. Thirdly, Horowitz places a great deal of reliance on a residual force: 'lessons' and 'accretions' (or 'deposits') of history. For example, he emphasizes that the negotiators had a limited palette of power-sharing and rights protection institutions to choose from because of the reiteration of power-sharing attempts since 1973.

I have shown in the previous chapter where I agree with the importance of the first two factors – demographic equalization and self-exclusion of extreme parties simplified bloc alignments. Equally, as the study overall has emphasized, the 'deposits' or 'accretions' of history are indeed dominant structural factors in affecting mobilization, governance, negotiation and implementation. But where I differ is in terms of causal priority and in terms of the interactions between the different national dimensions of conflict. These have important implications for conflict in Northern Ireland and elsewhere.

The limited palette of power-sharing and rights protection models confronting the SDLP and UUP in Strand 1 negotiations were not just accretions of history but instead limited variations allowed for consideration by the British and Irish governments. Further, these deposits are not just deposits of 'history' but more specifically the aspects of the Government of Ireland Act (1920) and Anglo-Irish Treaty (1921) that had been coercively negotiated and negligently implemented since 1921.[101] In turn, these accretions represent much older, dominant political fault lines derived at least from the sixteenth and seventeenth century origins of the modern conflict.

Horowitz argued, for example, that Sinn Féin's self-exclusion from Strand 1 negotiations facilitated agreement between the SDLP and the UUP and, more importantly, that such a coalition of moderates should have formed the basis of any power-sharing system. Similar interpretations have been made by academics from the 'liberal-unionist' perspective such as Paul Bew, Michael Kerr and Richard English, all of whom have been critical of the British government for insensitivity to unionism and / or specifically abandoning David Trimble and the Ulster Unionist Party during the post-GFA implementation phase by offering too many concessions to nationalists and republicans in particular.[102] An alternative interpretation is that British and Irish governments felt it necessary to compensate the republican movement for its acceptance of a separate unionist right to self-determination. The IRA held out in the non-recognition of a Northern Ireland jurisdiction because it strengthened its negotiating position with the British government on core sovereignty issues such as prisoners, policing, de-militarisation-decommissioning, and parity of (national) esteem in all public bodies. Most importantly, Sinn Féin's position aligned with successive Irish government positions for the regulation of national self-determination itself, as modified in the Downing Street Declaration and developed through the Framework Documents and BIA.

The bi-national primacy of this approach is revealed by the UUP strategy to maintain majority consent in Northern Ireland *and* remove Articles 2 and 3 from the Irish constitution. They refused until the last week before the agreement to negotiate in earnest on North–South bodies. These selective self-exclusions reflected strategic considerations aligned according to the bi-national parameters of the conflict. The fact that the DUP, which had campaigned in the 1998 referendum against the ratification of the Good Friday Agreement, came to accept its key provisions by 2006 lends further weight to the transformative effects of the bi-national approach.

Consistent with his centripetal, majoritarian approach, Horowitz also argues that it was unnecessary to include the extremes into the Northern Ireland process. In his view, war-weariness and *rapprochement* between the SDLP and UUP leaderships since the Brook–Mayhew talks (1991–2) had created a sufficient nationalist–unionist majority on key issues. Once again, this view neglects the centrality of the agreement on a mechanism for self-determination for shaping subsidiary preferences and sustaining parameters for conflict regulation. The SDLP's insistence on the inclusion of Sinn Féin was recognition of the primacy of what we have called the core of regulative sovereignty: agreement on a mechanism of national self-determination, and input into the making of the overall constitutional settlement. Since, as Horowitz recognizes, Sinn Féin was being asked to drop its maximalist position on self-determination, it had to be compensated with guarantees that went beyond the protections offered in previous agreements, which the movement and its Irish republican cousin Fianna Fáil both rejected in 1973 and 1985. But more importantly, considering that Sinn Féin's maximalist demand was integral to the broader constitutional nationalist position, requiring reforms of constitutive sovereignty (Articles 2 and 3), it is not solely a side-payment to Sinn Féin but integral to the compensation of the Irish nation for participation in the decision to partition the territory. It is, to use the terms applied to the extension of English Common Law to Ireland in the late sixteenth century, a 'surrender and regrant'[103] to the two constituent territories recognized as the bearers of rights to national self-determination in the BIA.

So, overall, the 'balanced constitutional exchange' cascaded into sufficient consensus on a bi-national mechanism of self-determination. On one hand, a bare majority of unionists were persuaded that they had the maximum possible control over their national self-determination, within the jurisdiction they reluctantly accepted in 1921 and subsequently in 1925. On the other hand, a clear majority of nationalists in both parts of the island were persuaded that they had achieved a viable, consensual mechanism for re-unification that respected a separate right of self-determination for unionists but also allowed the South to veto any unilateral determination by a majority in Northern Ireland. Far from being a tactical choice in the design of institutions, the institutionalization of symmetry at the inter-state level imposed bi-national symmetry at the (Northern Ireland) governmental level. For this reason, the primacy of 'parity of esteem', emphasized by nationalists but accepted by forward-thinking unionists given their potential minority status, was also established as the basis of governance for Northern Ireland, as the basis for self-determination between the two jurisdictions on the island and as a set of reflexive rights protections for both 'traditions'. If the bi-national ethos is 'vertically integrated' with the hierarchical levels of government described above, then there is consistency between the requirement of bi-national cross-community consent for the sub-state, governmental level of sovereignty and cross-border, bi-national consent at the primary, constitutive level established in the Downing Street Declaration.

This is not to say that the consociational features are optimal. Experience has shown that the rigidity of the bi-national (cross-community) consent mechanism could be a liability if it impedes the growth of the 'other' category of political representation (such as the Alliance Party and the Women's Coalition). The price for DUP acceptance of power-sharing with Sinn Féin was the strengthening of the Northern Ireland Assembly's accountability mechanisms over the power-sharing executive and the North–South Ministerial Council. These mechanisms could increase the potential for legislative gridlock, though they are counter-balanced by more stringent commitments to fulfil ministerial responsibilities that should remove the temptation for unilateral resignations to force suspension. In the context of stable British–Irish oversight, such gridlock is unlikely to lead to a return to political violence, as happened after Sunningdale and in so many other comparable conflicts. But it does require that both governments continue to respect the constitutive basis of the wider agreement. As Ahern recognized in November 2003, 'everyone had to realise that the Agreement was a treaty in international law and that it had been endorsed in referendums in the Republic and the North'.[104] The British–Irish intergovernmental mechanism for encouraging power-sharing, federalism and confederalism continues to have the potential to encourage moderation of maximal demands from either republicans or anti-agreement unionists.

Contrary to Horowitz' claim that there is no necessity to include the extremists in power-sharing, the evidence suggests that maximalist positions of both Sinn Féin and the DUP have been softened by the 'double-protection' and 'double-opportunity' mechanisms. Instead of a coalition of moderates being out-flanked by republicans and anti-agreement unionists, the process of inclusion has brought these 'maximalists' into the centre ground.

Moreover, the decommissioning-demilitarization exchange (if broadened to include prisoners, police, and justice) reflected the linkage between contested sovereignty and inclusion (in negotiations and power-sharing institutions) of paramilitary groups with maximally opposed self-determination aspirations. And it was resolved precisely because of that relativization. The gradual exchanges of guns for government removed the primary source of unionist opposition to the agreement.

By contrast to explanations emphasizing centripetal power-sharing at the Northern Ireland level, the bi-national, intergovernmental approach better explains the transformative effects of agreement on a process of national self-determination, and the bi-national regulation of sub-national autonomy. The flexibility on the constitutional status, the careful pluralization of sovereignty combining federalist and confederalist features, and reciprocal adjustments of statist national claims by the British and Irish governments all define a process moving from coercive to consensual precisely because it reflects the persistence of opposing but equivalent nationalisms. Building institutional settlements on national fault lines may seem precarious, but the evidence suggests that in this case at least the bi-national framework is necessary, if not sufficient for diluting such cleavages.

A second focus of criticism of the British–Irish approach recognizes the abilities of the two governments to maintain broadly consociational and bi-national parameters, but doubts the sustainability or stability of the process because of the inattention to root causes. Academics like Rupert Taylor echo the 'emancipatory' approach of Ruane and Todd in arguing that the elite-led practice of consociationalism is regressive because it rewards party leaders who corral voters into ethnic blocs. Taylor argues that the British–Irish approach neglects the societal-level causes of conflict, entrenches divisions rather than transcending them, minimizes the prospects for social integration of Catholics and Protestants by perpetuating residential and school segregation and endogamous marriage patterns. Taylor's positive 'social transformation' approach is based on the social principles of human freedom and action through integration and participatory democracy. He cites (selectively) evidence to show that consociational governance is unnecessary and regressive because of the growing trend toward a non-nationalist ethic of civic responsibility and participatory democracy. But, as McGarry recognizes, Taylor's evidence for the rise in civic partnership and participatory democracy is limited: 95 per cent of Northern Ireland's students still attend segregated schools and residential segregation has increased during the Troubles.[105] The largest 'civic' associations, the Orange Order and the Gaelic Athletic Association, are predominantly ethnically segregated. Given the depth of cleavages, consociationalists therefore question whether integration and conflict *resolution* can or should be the primary approach to policy.

Societal-level integration is important to the quality of consensual authority – as is clearly evident in the agreements and intergovernmental ethos. But, as I have stressed, voluntarist integration is neither theoretically nor empirically restricted in the bi-national approach. Instead, bi-national intergovernmentalism in this case represents a synthesis of the social transformation and consociational approaches that is applicable to 'kin-state' disputes over territory, precisely because territorial disputes draw in two or more competing sovereign states.[106] Taylor explicitly contrasts consociationalism's ethno-nationalist premise with the social transformation approach's emphasis on human freedom and action; the static social system, characterized by elite political and institutionalism is contrasted with the dynamic (progressive) model of social action through integration and participation, consistent with the civic society approach discussed above. Taylor's exemplary case is South Africa, where the transition from racial apartheid to non-racial democracy is explained according to the development of integrationist devices at the state, government and societal levels. However, there is a key difference between South Africa and Northern Ireland: Apart from KwaZulu Natal and potential Afrikaaner secessionists, the South African state is already nationally 'determined' as there is super-majority support for the territorial and institutional sovereignty of the state. Further, there is no external state with a historical claim or contemporary aspiration for territorial re-integration. Northern Ireland, by contrast, is a contested part of a state, with a substantial internal minority aspiring to re-integrate with its national territory and a reciprocal aspiration for re-integration by a clear majority of the host state. Furthermore, it is also questionable whether South Africa's transition has been a product of civic integration and participation. Formal and informal power-sharing devices have substantial consociational components in terms of asymmetrical federalism, informal power-sharing; internal party practice of regulating ethnicity; language, schooling and recognition of some tribal authority.[107]

While we can accept that voluntarist integration is a good policy in principle and that the 'social transformation' model is consistent with a plurinational approach, in practice we need to consider the causal priority of the forces under-pinning conflict. As a host of scholars have recognized, the civic nationalist approaches ignore the centrality of the British–Irish contest over national self-determination.[108] We saw in Chapter 7 that the asymmetrical conceptions of self-determination limited the progress of both the Anglo-Irish Agreement and the Brooke–Mayhew talks of 1991–2. Opposing unionist and nationalist aspirations have been consistently determinative of the success or failure of all constitutional, governmental and societal level contests in modern and early-modern history. More positively, it is clear that bi-national consociation is progressive in terms of both ethno-national and civic national criteria. While accepting an ethno-national mechanism of self-determination, and a formal consociational form of government in Northern Ireland, the agreement also promotes civic national integration policies. A study by Hayes, McAllister and Dowds found that graduates of integrated schools express more plurinational attitudes and identities.[109] Taylor reports that integrated marriage patterns are increasing *despite* the consociational parameters that have existed since the Anglo-Irish Agreement (and before). O'Leary and Evans and Paul Mitchell have also documented potential, though little evidence, for STV PR to encourage the type of cross-ethnic vote-pooling sought by Donald Horowitz.[110] In sum, the bi-national approach allows for the accommodation and regulation of both ethnic and civic national identities and interests.

Like the dangers of confused governance, a synthesis of civic and ethnic national approaches needs to consider the range of ideational, institutional and structural dynamics as far as they affect elite and popular opinion. We need to be able to specify causal priority between and among variables interacting at the state, governmental and societal levels. I have emphasized the ideational processes of status-seeking, their historical significance and their relationship with institutional, political and structural sources of power. In so doing I hope to have contributed towards a more generalizable theory of action that explains a broader range of dynamics than that available in more purely historical and political and social science accounts of this and comparable conflicts.

The shift in British–Irish relations from 'sister kingdoms' to sister republics allows for a more symmetrical, flexible, but still ordered (systemic) set of status hierarchies, facilitating mutualist exchange relations. The grounding of the British–Irish Agreement in popular consent and the intergovernmental relations embedded in the European Union created much greater disincentives for unilateral assertions of sovereignty. As we saw in previous chapters, just as Thatcher was prevented from pursuing a primarily security-focused policy and as Reynolds was persuaded to accept British neutrality on the question of self-determination, the Blair government has had to temper its inclination towards pragmatic constitutionalism while the Ahern government has had to moderate its insistence on constitutional idealism.

Given the generational evolution of these intergovernmental relations it is safe to predict that British–Irish dualism will survive changes of government for the foreseeable future. On balance, economic factors are likely to enhance British–Irish relations. The political establishments in both countries share broadly neo-liberal economic philosophies, relative to continental European partners. Previous disagreements over the Common Agricultural Policy have reduced in salience as the proportion of the Irish economy in agriculture has declined from 20 per cent to 5 per cent over the past twenty years, moving towards the UK level of 1 per cent.[111] The current differential in corporate tax rates has caused tension in the short term as Northern Ireland business leaders' interests in harmonizing island-wide rates towards the Irish level of 12.5 per cent (compared to variable UK rates between 19 and 30 per cent, depending on company size and profitability) has been prevented by the UK Treasury, who fear knock-on demands from Scotland and Wales will upset current fiscal policies. Nevertheless, the shared neo-liberal economic approaches of the two countries are likely to lead towards convergence of British and Irish interests towards minimalist EU tax harmonization. On balance, continued economic prosperity is unlikely to determine the outcome of future exercises in national self-determination because economies of scale and regional growth clusters are likely to perform comparably in both UK and Ireland economies.

The most profound effects of economic prosperity are likely to be their re-enforcement of the type of plural nationalism that has been responsible for successful conflict regulation. Thus while economic development has not yet eroded religiosity in either Northern Ireland or the Irish Republic, it has contributed to a shift towards a more individuated, consumer approach to religious faith,[112] has profoundly decreased the institutional power of the Catholic Church in both parts of the island,[113] and increased ecumenical approaches to faith by all strands of Christianity, as symbolized by the meeting on 9 October 2006 between the Reverand Ian Paisley (moderator of the staunchly anti-Catholic Free Presbyterian Church in Northern Ireland) and Catholic Archbishop Sean Brady.

A final, hopeful indicator of pluralism and British–Irish reconciliation occurred on 24 February 2007 when the English anthem, God Save the Queen, rung around the citadel of Gaelic games, Croke Park in Dublin. Irish nationalists were compensated for this return of majesty by an Ireland win (43-13), but the civility of the contest on the pitch and in the arena was a testament to the maturation of British–Irish relations. This by no means drew a line under the past history of relations between the two nations, but it emphatically demonstrated the parity of esteem that has transcended historical antagonism.

COMPARATIVE IMPLICATIONS

For the comparative study of nationalism and conflict regulation, the British–Irish evidence lends support to neo-pluralist, or in Michael Keating's phrase, 'plurinational' normative thought and empirical analysis. Keating's evidence from his comparisons of nationalist mobilization in Spain, Belgium, the UK and Canada, like McGarry and O'Leary's comparative analysis of conflict regulation, shows the success of 'open' constitutional approaches that recognize and regulate opposing national sovereignty claims, recognize and protect competing ethnic and national identities, and pluralize sovereignty in terms of federal, confederal and consociational practices.[114] The comparative evidence suggests strongly that opposing territorial claims can be regulated. For theories of the state and state-craft like Ian Lustick, the implications of this study suggests that territorial contraction and expansion can be regulated intergovernmentally in ways that are more nuanced and systemic than through the more anarchic conceptions of 'wars of position' and 'wars of manoeuvre'. The analysis of British–Irish intergovernmental relations, as seen particularly from 1921 through to the late 1960s, suggests that there is some value in considering the independent political force of status conceptions for both elites and citizens. National issues over borders, sovereignty, rights protections, and law and order were central factors, along with economic dependence and strategic interests, in determining political coalitions and movements vying for state power.

Once mutual national status recognition was institutionalized, more positive intergovernmental relations developed, consistent with Keating's broader comparisons. He argues that there is neither logical reason nor empirical evidence for the feared slippery-slope between limited national self-determination and incessant contestation.

> On the contrary, one might argue that the tendency to respond with concessions of competences rather than bold forms of recognition is more destabilizing since it weakens the state while not satisfying the nationalities, leading to further concessions. Still less does recognizing plurinationalism entail condoning the excesses of nationalism in the Balkans and elsewhere; quite the contrary. It does, however, invite us to place the stateless nation on the same moral plane as the consolidated nation-state, rather than assuming that the latter represents some culturally neutral proxy for cosmopolitan enlightenment.[115]

The implications for conflict regulation, especially in bi-national, paired-antagonisms are clear: constitutional design that produces reward power through status recognition and through plural sovereignty can produce stable exchange relationships as the bedrock of intergovernmentalism, especially in developed democracies.[116] These relations are more likely to be functional and reciprocal if and only if they are grounded in 'sufficiently' agreed conceptions of national status recognition.

In this sense, the empirical evidence from the British–Irish case lends qualified support to Roeder's theory of 'power-dividing' over 'power-sharing' in that British–Irish intergovernmental relations that regulate internal and external self-determination have been more robust than the power-sharing dimension in Northern Ireland. The intergovernmental relationship has sustained parameters at the governmental and societal levels and sustained functional cooperation within the North–South Ministerial Council. But contrary to Roeder's general claims concerning the instability of consociational power-sharing, the British–Irish case suggests that where self-determination claims conflict and where significant residential segregation limits the potential for centripetal electoral devices, power-sharing at the sub-state level can complement the power-dividing policies of multi-level governance. Consensual governance can be cultivated by grounding authority in a constitutional bond, with substantive rather than merely procedural implementation at the state, governmental and societal levels.

Whether the prospects for plural national state-building are realistic outside of the developed, democratic and confederal European Union is unclear.[117]What is more clear is that reliance on coercive power is likely to increase subsequent costs of control by generating negative affect and contested conceptions of justice towards the super-ordinate power.

Notes to Chapter 8 and Conclusion

1.   For comparisons of Sunningdale and Good Friday Agreements, see Kerr, Michael, *Imposing Power-sharing*; Wolff, Stefan, 'Introduction: From Sunningdale to Belfast', in Neuheiser, Jorg and Wolff, Stefan (eds), *Peace at Last? The Impact of the Good Friday Agreement on Northern Ireland* (Oxford and New York: Berghahn, 2003).

2. British Prime Minister Tony Blair, Speech at Balmoral 14 May 1998, emphasis added.

3. Quoted in Dewar, Michael, *The British Army in Northern Ireland* (London: Arms and Armour, 1985) p. 101, emphasis added.

4. See Lustick, Ian, O'Leary, Brendan and Callaghy, Thomas (eds), *Right-Sizing the State: The Politics of Moving Borders* (Oxford: Oxford University Press, 2001).

5. For similar views see Guelke, Adrian, *Northern Ireland: the International Perspective* (Dublin: Gill and Macmillan, 1988), pp. 59–89; Carty, *Was Ireland Conquered?*, pp. 132–3.

6. Quoted in the *Irish Times,* 2 April 1998, emphasis added.

7. O'Leary, Brendan, 'Introduction: Reflections on a Cold Peace', Special Issue: 'A State of Truce: Northern Ireland after Twenty-Five Years of War', *Ethnic and Racial Studies*, 18, 4 (1995) pp. 706–8.

8. Lusztig, Michael and Knox, Colin, 'Good Things and Small Packages: Lessons from Canada for the Northern Irish Constitutional Settlement', *Nations and Nationalism* 5, 4 (1999): 543–63; O'Leary, Damian, 'Cultural Identity and Constitutional Reform: the Challenge of Northern Ireland', in Hanafin, Patrick and Williams, Melissa S. (eds), *Identity, Rights and Constitutional Transformation* (Aldershot: Ashgate, 1999) pp. 98–101.

9. Roeder's prescriptive conclusions suggest that conflict regulation works better where the units of a federal state cross-cut territorially concentrated ethnic minorities and where subdivisions of federal units are determined functionally rather than ethnically (such as water, health, education boards that cross-cut ethnic or national 'homelands'). See Roeder, Philip G., 'Power Dividing as an Alternative to Ethnic Power Sharing', in Roeder, Philip G. and Rothchild, Donald, *Sustainable Peace: Power and Democracy after Civil Wars* (Ithaca and London: Cornell University Press, 2005).

10. Dixon, Paul, 'Paths to Peace in Northern Ireland (I): Civil Society and Consociational Approaches', *Democratization* 4, 1 (1997), pp. 1–27; see also Horowitz, Donald, 'The Northern Ireland Agreement: Clear, Consociational, and Risky' and Taylor, Rupert, 'Northern Ireland: Consociation or Social Transformation?', both in McGarry, John (ed.), *Northern Ireland and the Divided World* (Oxford: Oxford University Press, 2001).

11. Ruane and Todd, *Dynamics of Conflict in Northern Ireland,* pp. 304–6.

12. Gallagher, Michael, 'How Many Nations Are There in Ireland?', *Ethnic and Racial Studies* 18, 4 (1995) Table 1; Hayes, Bernadette C. and McAllister, Ian, 'Ethnonationalism, public opinion and the Good Friday Agreement', in Ruane, Joseph and Todd, Jennifer, *After the Good Friday Agreement: Analysing Political Change in Northern Ireland* (Dublin: University College Dublin Press, 1999) Table 3.

13. Todd, Jennifer, 'Two Traditions in Unionist Political Culture', *Irish Political Studies* 2 (1987) pp. 1–26; Cochrane *Unionist Politics,* pp. 57–83; Miller, David, *Queen's Rebels: Ulster Loyalism in Historical Perspective* (Dublin: Gill and Macmillan, 1978).

14. Duffy, Mary and Evans, Geoffrey, 'Class, Community Polarisation and Conflict', in Dowds, L., Devine, P. and Breen, R., (eds), *Social Attitudes in Northern Ireland: The Sixth Report* (Belfast: Appletree, 1997).

15. Hayes and McAllister, 'Ethnonationalism', p. 38.

16. Peter Robinson, Deputy Leader of Democratic Unionist Party, speech to Council on Foreign Relations, New York, 6 April 2006.

17. Interview with David Ervine, leader of Progressive Unionist Party, Belfast, 4 June 2005; see also Cochrane, *Unionist Politics*, p. 57.

18. Interview with David Ervine, Belfast, 4 June 2005.

19. Interview with Sinn Féin Communications Director Jim Gibney, Belfast, 6 July 1996.

20. O'Leary, Brendan, 'Assessing the British–Irish Agreement', *New Left Review,* 233 (1999) pp. 66–96; see also his 'Comparative Political Science and the British–Irish Agreement', in McGarry (ed.), *Northern Ireland and the Divided World*, Ch. 3.

21. Robbins, K., 'Britain and Europe: Devolution and Foreign Policy', *International Affairs* 78, 1 (1998) pp. 105–117; see also Arthur, Paul, '"Quiet Diplomacy and

Personal Conversation". Track Two diplomacy and the search for a settlement in Northern Ireland', in Ruane and Todd (eds), *After the Good Friday Agreement*, p. 78.

22. The Conservative government's biggest liabilities were its loss of reputation for economic competence, the internal split over the pace and extent of European integration and the related and rigid opposition to Scottish and Welsh devolution. As for the Irish electorate's support for a change of government, an *Irish Times/MRBI* poll of May 1997 showed the prospective Fianna Fáil–Progressive Democrat alliance as likely to 'best handle the Northern Ireland problem' by a margin of 45 per cent to 30 per cent over the Fine Gael–Labour–Democratic Left coalition. See O'Duffy, Brendan, 'Swapping the Reins of the Emerald Tiger: The Irish General Election of 1997', *West European Politics*, 21, 2 (1998).

23. Reported in Evans and O'Leary 'Intransigence and Flexibility on the Way to Two Forums: the Northern Ireland Elections of 30 May 1996 and Public Opinion', *Representation*, 34, 3 & 4 (1997) pp. 208–18, Table 8.

24. Quoted in the *Irish Times*, 18 February 1998.

25. King George V had celebrated the nation-building potential of the union by stating: 'The eyes of the Empire are on Ireland today – that Empire in which so many nations and races have come together in spite of ancient feuds, and in which new nations [Northern Ireland] have come to birth within the lifetime of the youngest in this hall. See Chapter 2, pp. 40–41.

26. Dissident loyalists who rejected the talks process split from the mainstream Ulster Volunteer Force (UVF) and formed the Loyalist Volunteer Force which was responsible for the killing of five Catholic civilians between October and December 1997. A dissident republican group, the Irish National Liberation Army (INLA) assassinated Billy Wright, the leader of the LVF, in the Maze prison on 27 December 1997, which then sparked a further round of sectarian killing by the LVF, which killed seven Catholics and one Protestant in January 1998 alone.

27. Quoted in the *Irish Times*, 4 February 1998.

28. Mitchell, George, *Making Peace: The Inside Story of the Making of the Good Friday Agreement* (London: Knopf, 1999) pp. 150–60.

29. Quoted in Mallie, Eamonn, *The Long Good Friday*. Channel Four Documentary Film, 2 April, 1999.

30. Quoted in the *Irish Times*, 3 April 1998.

31. There are actually two agreements, one which resulted from the multi-party talks (referred to as the 'Multi-Party Agreement') and a second international treaty between the British and Irish governments ('Agreement Between the Government of the United Kingdom of Great Britain and Northern Ireland and the Government of Ireland').

32. For thorough descriptions and analysis of the structures of governance see Brendan O'Leary, 'The nature of the British–Irish agreement'; Ruane and Todd, 'The Belfast Agreement: Context, Content, Consequences' in their edited collection, *After the Good Friday Agreement*.

33. This is Brendan O'Leary's reading in 'Comparative Political Science and the British–Irish Agreement', in McGarry, *Northern Ireland and the Divided World*, p. 68.

34. The agreement on a seven-year interval exemplifies the intergovernmental bargaining as a compromise between the Irish government proposal for a five-year interval and the British proposal for a ten-year interval.

35. The British–Irish Agreement stipulated a minimum of twelve areas of North–South co-operation. After a further eight months of negotiation six implementation bodies were agreed: trade and business development; inland waterways; aquaculture and marine matters; special EU programmes; food safety and language (Irish and Ulster Scots). In addition, six further areas were outlined for co-operation based on existing bodies: agriculture; tourism; transport; education; environment and health.

36. Quoted in the *Irish Times*, 13 December 1999.

37. The agreement established a 108-member assembly, elected by proportional representation (Single Transferable Vote), and a 12-member Executive Committee selected from

the assembly using the d'Hondt procedure. The Executive is headed by a First Minister and Deputy First Minister with identical powers, elected by the assembly on a 'cross-community basis', requiring concurrent majorities of declared unionists and nationalists, or a weighted majority (sixty per cent) of all members, including forty per cent of each of the nationalist and unionist representatives. The same cross-community voting procedures are required for key decisions stipulated in advance, or for any decision following a petition of concern by thirty members of the assembly.

38. BIA, 'Constitutional Issues', Annex A: Draft Clauses/Schedules for Incorporation in British Legislation.

39. BIA, 'Constitutional Issues', Annex A: Draft Clauses/Schedules for Incorporation in British Legislation', Clause 1 (2) p. 3.

40. Hennessey, Thomas. *The Northern Ireland Peace Process: Ending the Troubles?* (Dublin: Gill and Macmillan, 2000) pp.140–5; Bew, Paul, 'Myths of Consociationalism: from Good Friday to Political Impasse', in Cox et al., *A Farewell to Arms*, p. 58.

41. BIA, 'Constitutional Issues', Article 1 (v)

42. Hayes and McAllister, 'Ethnonationalism'.

43. Quoted in the *Irish Times,* 26 October 1998.

44. Steven King, political advisor to David Trimble characterized the North–South Ministerial Council (NSMC) in the context of the agreement in his article 'The Executive, not the Cross Border bodies, is Where the Real Test Lies', *Sunday Tribune* (Dublin), 19 December 1999:

> The North–South Ministerial Council has none of the grandiosity of 1920 nor the shaky constitutional basis of 1973. Critically, unlike its two distant cousins, the NSMC is shorn of anything that might look like, or conceivably become, a parliament for the whole of Ireland. Furthermore, it operates in the context of an Irish Constitution which now embodies the principle of consent.

45. Seventy per cent of respondents in a *Belfast Telegraph* poll (9 February 1999) supported the agreement, only one per cent less than the referendum result. Seventy-three per cent of respondents to the *Ulster Marketing Surveys/Irish Times* poll (27 April 1999) supported the agreement.

46. The Ulster Unionist Party's governing body, the Ulster Unionist Council, supported the British–Irish Agreement by a margin of five to two, compared with a margin of approximately four to two for entry into negotiations based on the power-sharing White Paper of 1973. Immediately after the referendum result Trimble used his mandate to secure the nomination of pro-agreement candidates within his party (twenty-six of twenty-eight candidates eventually elected) and most boldly, moved against potential rivals, refusing to allow Jeffrey Donaldson, the most prominent anti-agreement member of the UUP, to stand for the assembly elections. Donaldson subsequently defected to the DUP.

47. Quoted in the *Irish Times,* 1 May 1998.

48. See, for example, 'A Frantic Race from Horror to Hope', *The Observer* 6 September 1998.

49. The Agreement states:

> All participants accordingly reaffirm their commitment to the total disarmament of all paramilitary organisations. They also confirm their intention to continue to work constructively and in good faith with the Independent Commission, and to use any influence they *may* have, to achieve the decommissioning of all paramilitary arms within two years following endorsement in referendums North and South of the agreement and in the context of the implementation of the overall settlement (*British–Irish Agreement,* 'Decommissioning, Par. 3). Sinn Féin negotiated strenuously for the inclusion of the word "may" in order to maintain the legal distinction between itself and the IRA.

50. The effects of the bi-national threat were revealed by Seamus Mallon, Deputy First Minister designate:

> Under circumstances where the agreement was not operated in its entirety then I

have no doubt the British and Irish governments would feel justified in making their decisions on an intergovernmental basis and implementing those decisions as they so decide. Unionism would have lost its input and lost it in a most substantial way. Quoted in the *Irish News,* 17 September 1999.

The threat of creeping intergovernmentalism was confirmed by Irish Taoiseach Bertie Ahern, who warned that if the Mitchell review failed: 'both governments would have to receive the report and try to engage with the pro-agreement parties to see how aspects of the agreement could continue to be implemented' (the *Irish Times,* 10 November 1999).

51. Thus the Assessment of the Independent International Commission on Decommissioning reaffirmed the causal ordering stipulated in the British–Irish Agreement:

While decommissioning is an essential element of the Agreement, our discussions over the past year and a half convince us that the context in which it can be achieved is the overall implementation of that Agreement. All participants have a collective responsibility in this regard (*Independent International Commission on Decommissioning,* 'Assessment' November, 1999).

52. O'Leary, 'Comparative Political Science and the British–Irish Agreement'.

53. Quoted in *The Sunday Times,* 18 April 1999.

54. Independent Commission on Policing for Northern Ireland, *A New Beginning: Policing in Northern Ireland 1999,* p. 2, emphasis added.

55. For example, Ahern in December 1999:

In areas like east Tyrone and South Armagh there have been no security problems since the summer of 1997, yet the level of security infrastructure in those areas is the same as it was in the mid 1970s. The situation is not similar and we have to reflect that (*Irish Times,* 10 December 1999).

56. Cowen quoted in McAskill, Ewan, 'My Spats with Mandelson, by Ireland's Bruiser', *The Guardian,* 4 July 2000.

57. IRA statement, 5 May 2000, as reported in the *Irish Times,* 6 May 2000.

58. Kerr, *Imposing Power-sharing,* pp. 104–7.

59. Quotation from BBC News Transcript, 16 January 2003.

60. According to the *Irish Times'* Frank Millar, 'The Taoiseach also stressed the role of the British–Irish Inter-Governmental Conference during any interim period as the key vehicle of bilateral co-operation between the two governments, to ensure the continuation of what one source called "the Weston Park agenda" on policing, justice and other reforms', the *Irish Times,* 10 October 2002. Similarly *Irish Independent* London Editor Bernard Purcell reported that 'The Irish and British governments are preparing for a form of joint administration if they are forced to suspend the power-sharing. It would involve an Anglo-Irish ministerial council with ministers and officials from Dublin and London taking over the work of the devolved administration at Stormont'. Quoted in the *Irish Independent,* 10 October 2002.

61. British–Irish *Joint Declaration,* 8 April 2003.

62. Ibid. Paragraph 20 and Annex 2 'Devolution of Policing and Justice'.

63. As reported by Frank Millar, 'Blair and Ahern confident of basis for North progress', the *Irish Times,* 6 March 2003. A familiar negotiating tactic was invoked here as the proposal to include a US role in the sanction-monitoring body responds to the Sinn Féin chief negotiator's call for a US role in securing full implementation of the agreement.

64. The draft British–Irish legislation establishing the International Monitoring Commission defined paramilitary activity broadly to include:

- Attacks on the security forces, murders, sectarian attacks, involvement in riots, and other criminal offences;
- Training, targeting, intelligence gathering, acquisition or development of arms or weapons and other preparations for terrorist campaigns;
- Punishment beatings and attacks and exiling

The list included in the British–Irish Agreement establishing the IMC included:

- demolition of towers and observation posts in Northern Ireland;

- withdrawal of troops from police stations in Northern Ireland;
- closure and dismantling of military bases and installations in Northern Ireland;
- troop deployments and withdrawals from Northern Ireland and levels of British Army helicoptor use;
- the repeal of counter-terrorist legislation particular to Northern Ireland.

Draft Agreement between The Government of the United Kingdom of Great Britain and Northern Ireland and the Government of Ireland establishing the Independent Monitoring Commission.

65. Interview with Gerry Adams, Sinn Féin President, Belfast, 6 June 2005.
66. Brendan O'Leary has emphasized the need for the British government to more explicitly recognize the status of Northern Ireland as a 'federacy, perhaps in the same manner as the United Kingdom's courts are instructed to make European law supreme over law(s) made by the Westminster Parliament, through full domestic incorporation and entrenchment of the relevant treaty'. Quoted in his 'The British–Irish Agreement' in McGarry (ed.), *Northern Ireland and the Divided World,* p. 68. However, given the precedent such incorporation would have for the wider UK devolution project, it seems unlikely that such thorough constitutional entrenchment could be achieved short of a formal federation of the United Kingdom.
67. Following the Hillsborough deal of May 2000, the top two priorities for DUP and UUP supporters were 'paramilitary decommissioning' and 'commitments to non-violence'. Reported in Table 12.12 in Colin Irwin, *The People's Peace Process in Northern Ireland* (London: Palgrave, 2002) p. 267.
68. Ibid. p. 267. The SDLP's priorities were 'commitments to non-violence', 'Northern Ireland Assembly', 'Northern Ireland Executive', 'paramilitary decommissioning' and 'support for the victims of the "Troubles".' Thus, the bridging of commitments to non-violence (including decommissioning) with obligations to preserve the devolved status of the power-sharing institutions effectively bridges the unionist–nationalist political spectrum.
69. Irwin, *The Peoples' Peace Process*, pp. 169–74.
70. The *Belfast Telegraph/Independent* poll, summarized in Thornton, Chris and McAdam, Noel, 'Devolution Under Agreement Top Choice', the *Belfast Telegraph,* 14 November 2003.
71. Quoted in Holland, Jack, 'No Meltdown of Moderate Parties', *Irish Echo Online,* 76, 45 (12–18 November 2003).
72. McCabe, Anton and Colgan, Paul T., 'Hay's Sinn Féin Comments Reflect Reality', *Sunday Business Post,* 12 January 2003.
73. *Belfast Telegraph/Independent* poll, as summarized in *Belfast Telegraph,* 24 May 2001. As reported by Irwin, *The Peoples' Peace Process,* Table 4.4, p. 95. The 30 per cent bloc of pro-agreement opinion among DUP supporters held up consistently in polls between 1998 and 1999. In a poll conducted in October 1999 before the Mitchell Review, 50 per cent of DUP supporters declared that they wanted the agreement to work. Ibid. Table 4.4, p. 95.
74. *Draft Agreement between the Government of the United Kingdom of Great Britain and Northern Ireland and the Government of Ireland establishing the Independent Monitoring Commission,* as reproduced in http://cain.ulst.ac.uk/events/peace/docs/biimc150903.pdf (accessed 6 April 2007).
75. O'Kelly, Barry, 'Republicans' Hostility to Leadership Growing', *Sunday Business Post,* 6 February 2005. Journalist Ed Moloney believed Sinn Féin leaders exaggerated internal opposition to increase their negotiating leverage. See his 'War and Peace' the *Irish Times,* 5 February 2005.
76. The IRA leadership denied that it had agreed to point five of the draft IICD statement which read: In addition, the IRA representative has told us that the IRA will have photographs of the weapons and materiel involved taken by the IICD, in the presence of the independent observers. These photographs will be shown by the IICD to the two Governments and the parties at the time of the final report on IRA decommissioning

and will be published at the time the Executive is established. Annex D of 'Proposals by the British and Irish Governments for a Comprehensive Agreement' (8 December, 2004).

77. Bew, Paul, 'Myths of Consociationalism: from Good Friday to Political Impasse', in Cox, Michael, Guelke, Adrian and Stephen, Fiona, *A Farewell to Arms? Beyond the Good Friday Agreement* (Manchester: Manchester University Press, 2006) pp. 65–6.

78. A 'senior British official' quoted in *The Guardian*, 13 March 2007, claimed that the Northern Bank raid was 'carefully planned by leadership figures. It was deliberate.' This view was shared by a different British official in an interview with the author, London, 23 May 2007. This official believed that while the IRA may have been attempting a 'non-violent spectacular', the reactions by unionists, the British and Irish governments and publics were both a public relations disaster and a negotiating setback as the price was raised for a deal with the DUP.

79. The rest of the IRA statement read: 'This will take effect from 4pm [1600 BST] this afternoon. All IRA units have been ordered to dump arms. All Volunteers have been instructed to assist the development of purely political and democratic programmes through exclusively peaceful means. Volunteers must not engage in any other activities whatsoever. The IRA leadership has also authorised our representative to engage with the IICD [Independent International Commission on Decommissioning] to complete the process to verifiably put its arms beyond use in a way which will further enhance public confidence and to conclude this as quickly as possible.

80. See O'Leary, Brendan, 'Constitutional Mission Accomplished', in Heiberg, Marianne, O'Leary, Brendan, and Tirman, John, *Terror, Insurgency and the State: Ending Protracted Conflicts* (Philadelphia, PA: University of Pennsylvania Press, 2007).

81. Kerr, *Imposing Power-Sharing*, p. 14.

82. Bew, 'Myths of Consociationalism', p. 67.

83. Peter Robinson, Deputy Leader of the Democratic Unionist Party, speech to Council on Foreign Relations, 5 April 2006, as reported in http://cain.ulst.ac.uk/issues/politics/docs/dup/pr050406.htm.

84. Interview with Barbara Jones, Irish official, Department of Foreign Affairs, Armagh, 2 June 2006; Colgan, Paul, 'Governments unite to put pressure on DUP, *Sunday Business Post*, 5 February 2006.

85. Cowen, Brian, 'Business Breakfast SDLP – Derry', Speech by the Minister for Finance, 28 February 2007.

86. Lord Justice Girvan found that Northern Ireland Secretary Peter Hain disregarded norms of merit in his appointment of DUP member Bertha McDougall as 'Victims' Commissioner' in November 2006.

87. McDonald, Henry, 'Downing Street Accused of Pandering to Sinn Féin', *The Observer* 14 January 2007.

88. *Agreement at St. Andrews*, Annex A, Para. 2.

89. Multi-party Agreement (Good Friday), Strand One: Democratic Institutions in Northern Ireland, Para. 20.

90. *Agreement at St. Andrews*, Para. 8.

91. These included a British commitment to publish an Anti-Poverty and Social exclusion strategy, establishment of a Victims' Commissioner for Northern Ireland, a forum on a Bill of Rights and additional powers for the N.I. Human Rights Commission, a Single Equality Bill, an Irish Language Act and support for Ulster Scots.

92. *Agreement at St. Andrews*, Annex E.

93. Mallon, Seamus, 'Filling Unionist Bowl at Too High a Price', *Irish Times*, 18 May 2000.

94. Tanner, J.R., *English Constitutional Conflicts of the 17th Century 1603–1689* (Cambridge: Cambridge University Press, 1966) p. 198.

95. Quoted in *The Independent*, 22 April 2002.

96. See O'Leary, Brendan, 'The Conservative Stewardship of Northern Ireland: Sound-bottomed Contradictions or Slow Learning?' *Political Studies*, XLV(1997) pp. 663–76.

97. For example, see English, Richard, 'The State and Northern Ireland', and Townshend, Charles, 'State and Public Security', in English, Richard and Townshend, Charles, *The State: Historical and Political Dimensions* (London: Routledge, 1999).

98. McGarry, John, 'Northern Ireland, Civic Nationalism, and the Good Friday Agreement', in John McGarry (ed.), *Northern Ireland and the Divided World.*

99. See O'Leary, Brendan, 'Assessing the British–Irish Agreement', *New Left Review,* 233 (1999) 66–96.

100. For example, the choice of the Proportional Representation (STV) system for the parliament of Northern Ireland is a minimalist form of electoral proportionality; the North–South Ministerial Council resurrects the principle of the Council of Ireland and the British–Irish Agreement regulates intergovernmental relations and modified 'regulative' sovereignty through 'balanced constitutional changes' and in the agreement on the mechanism for national self-determination.

101. Bew, 'Myths of Consociationalism', pp. 65–7; English, Richard, 'The Growth of New Unionism', in Coakley, John (ed.), *Changing Shades of Orange and Green: Redefining the Union and the Nation in Contemporary Ireland* (Dublin: University College Dublin Press, 2002) pp. 103–5; Kerr, *Imposing Power-Sharing,* 109–11, 190–1.

102. Recalling the Elizabethan land reform proposals to attempt to shift from suzerainty to sovereignty in the late sixteenth century.

103. Dowling, Brian and Purcell, Bernard, 'No Deals or Stealth on Peace Accord – Ahern', *Irish Independent,* 29 November 2003.

104. Poole, Michael A. and Doherty, Paul, *Ethnic Residential Segregation in Northern Ireland,* (Coleraine, N.I.: Centre for the Study of Conflict, University of Ulster, 1996). Based on the 1981 census, the report concludes that 58 per cent of the population of Northern Ireland live in areas where one of the two communities is at least two-thirds of the total, thus representing a 'dominant majority' in their terms.

105. Stefan Wolff compares British–Irish regulation of Northern Ireland with France–German regulation of Alsace and The Saarland; Austrian–Italian regulation of South Tyrol as well as Franco-Spanish Condominium of Andorra and Anglo-French Condominium in the New Hebrides. See his *Disputed Territories: The Transnational Dynamics of Ethnic Conflict Settlement* (Oxford and New York: Berghahn, 2003). See also Coppieters, Bruno et al., *Europeanization and Conflict Resolution: Case Studies from the European Periphery* (Gent: Academia Press, 2004), an analyses of the impact of Europeanization on conflicts such as Cyprus, Serbia and Montenegro, Moldova and Transnistria and Georgia and Abkhazia. Both of these works offer useful theoretical frameworks for understanding the 'multi-level' chess of these complex conflicts. Neither of them specify sufficiently the causal priority of bi-national intergovernmentalism vis-à-vis multi-lateral (European) and internal majority–minority (societal) levels of dispute.

106. See McGarry, John, 'Political Settlements in Northern Ireland and South Africa', *Political Studies,* 46, 5 (1998) pp. 853–70.

107. Whyte, *Interpreting Northern Ireland* (Oxford: Oxford University Press, 1990); O'Leary and McGarry, *Explaining Northern Ireland* and *The Politics of Antagonism* 3rd Edition; Arthur, *Special Relationships*; Guelke, *Northern Ireland: The International Perspective.*

108. Hayes, Bernadette, McAllister, Ian and Dowds, Lizanne, 'In Search of the Middle Ground: Integrated Education and Northern Ireland Politics', *Research Update* Ark Northern Ireland Social and Political Archive, 42, (2006). The authors do not use the term 'plurinational' but their conception of pro-state and anti-state attitudes is equivalent to Keating's conception of 'plurinationalism'. The study found that both Catholic and Protestant graduates of integrated schools were less likely to emphasize Irish or British national identities and less likely to express interests in promoting Irish or British sovereignty.

109. Evans, Geoffrey and O'Leary, Brendan, 'Northern Irish Voters and the British–Irish Agreement: Foundations of a Stable Consociational Settlement?' *Political Quarterly,* 71 (2000); Mitchell, Paul, 'Transcending an Ethnic Party System? The Impact of

Consociational Governance on Electoral Dynamics and the Party System', in Wilford, Rick, (ed.), *Aspects of the Belfast Agreement* (Oxford: Oxford University Press, 2001).

110. www.cia.gov/cia/publications/factbook/geos/ei.html#Econ (accessed 6 April 2007).

111. Garvin, Tom, *Preventing the Future: Why Was Ireland So Poor for So Long?* Dublin: Gill and Macmillan, 2004) pp. 268–70; cf. White, Timothy, J. 'Catholicism and Nationalism in Ireland: From Fusion in the 19th Century to Separation in the 21st Century', *Westminster Papers in Community and Culture*, 4, 1 (2007) pp 56–60.

112. Girvin, Brian, 'Church, State and the Irish Constitution: The Secularisation of Irish Politics?', *Parliamentary Affairs* 49, 4 (1996) pp. 599–615.

113. See also Lustick, et al (eds), *Right-sizing the State*.

114. Keating, *Plurinational Democracy*. Ted Gurr also found that the failure of federalism and devolution policies in divided societies was more often the result of the centre's inability to grant substantive devolution, rather than from the ethno-nations' growing demands for more autonomy. Gurr, Ted, *Minorities at Risk: A Global View of Ethnopolitical Conflict* (Washington, DC: Unites States Institute of Peace).

115. For comparative analyses of plural sovereignty and conflict regulation see Ghai, Yash (ed.), *Autonomy and Ethnicity: Negotiating Competing Claims in Multi-ethnic States* (Cambridge: Cambridge University Press, 2000); Keating, *Plurinational Democracy*: Alcock, Anthony 'Lessons from Europe', in McGarry (ed.), *Northern Ireland and the Divided World*; Lapidoth, Ruth, *Autonomy: Flexible Solutions to Ethnic Conflicts* (Washington, DC: USIP, 1996); Mann, Michael, 'A Political Theory of Nationalism and Its Excesses', in Periwal, Sukumar (ed.), *Notions of Nationalism* (Budapest: Central European University Press, 1995); Safran, William and Máiz, Ramón (eds), *Identity and Territorial Autonomy in Plural Societies* (London: Frank Cass, 2000); on Israel/Palestine see Klieman, Aharon, *Compromising Palestine: A Guide to Final Status Negotiations* (New York, NY: Columbia University Press, 1999).

116. The independent effects of European integration on conflict regulation is explored in my current project, a comparison of intergovernmental conflict regulation in/over Northern Ireland, Cyprus and Sri Lanka.

Appendix: Figures 1–19

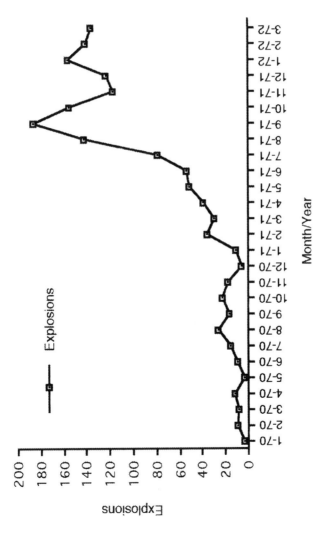

1. Monthly Explosions, January 1970 to March 1972

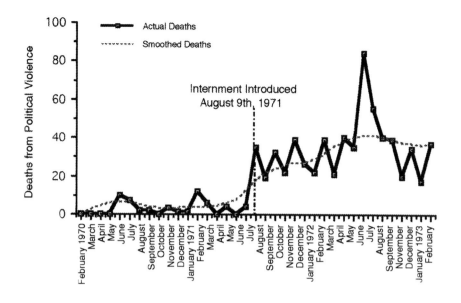

2. Monthly Deaths, February 1970 to March 1972

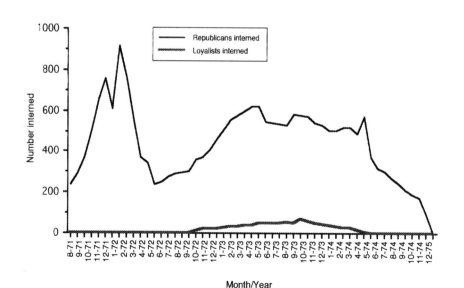

3. Monthly Internment of republicans and loyalists,
August 1971 to December 1975

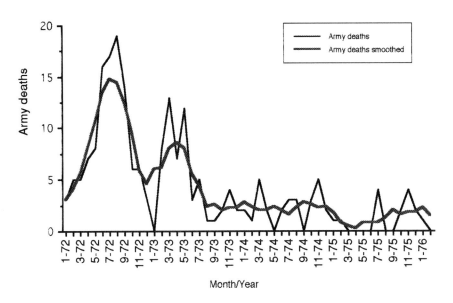

4. Monthly Army deaths, 1972–1976

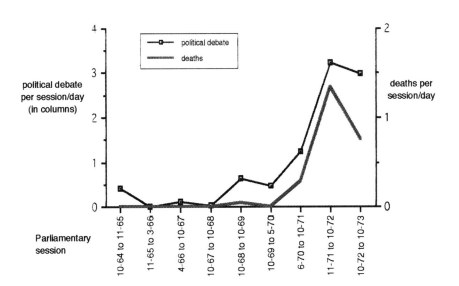

5. Deaths and political debate on Northern Ireland in the (UK) House of Commons, 1964–1973

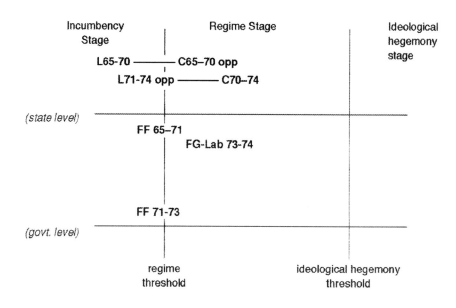

UK state-building (Ireland state-contracting)

Ireland state-expansion (UK state-contraction)

L = Labour (British)
C = Conservative (British)

FG = Fine Gael (Irish)
FF = Foamma Fáil (Irish)
Lab = Labour (Irish)
FG-Lab = Fine Gael-Labour coalition
opp = opposition party

6. Application of Lustick's classification of territorial state-building and
state-contraction to inter-governmental status conceptions in Ireland
and Britain, 1965–1974

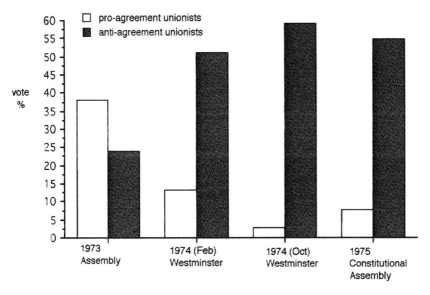

7. Pro- versus anti-agreement unionist vote (first preferences)
in Northern Ireland elections, 1973–1975

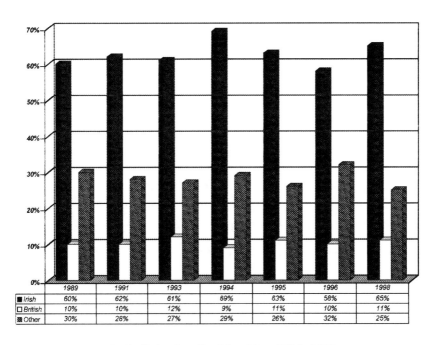

	1989	1991	1993	1994	1995	1996	1998
Irish	60%	62%	61%	69%	63%	58%	65%
British	10%	10%	12%	9%	11%	10%	11%
Other	30%	28%	27%	29%	26%	32%	25%

8. Catholic/nationalist identities, 1980–1998

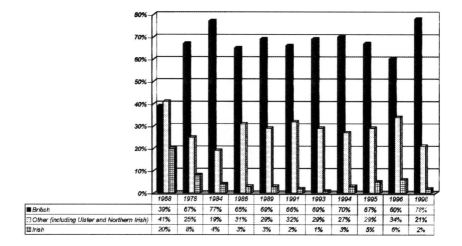

	1968	1978	1984	1986	1989	1991	1993	1994	1995	1996	1998
British	39%	67%	77%	65%	69%	66%	69%	70%	67%	60%	78%
Other (including Ulster and Northern Irish)	41%	25%	19%	31%	29%	32%	29%	27%	29%	34%	21%
Irish	20%	8%	4%	3%	3%	2%	1%	3%	5%	6%	2%

9. Protestant/unionist identities, 1968–1998

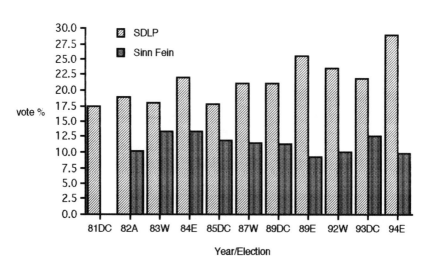

Note: DC=District Council; W=Westminster; E=European; A=Assembly.

10. The nationalist bloc vote in Northern Ireland, 1981–1994

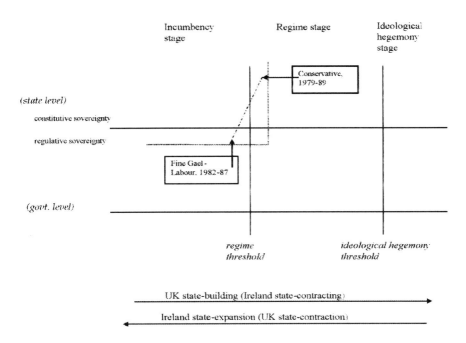

Note: Diagonal line (—·—·—·) represents inter-governmental institutions created by the Anglo-Irish Agreement (1985), including inter-governmental agreement on a mechanism for national self-determination for Northern Ireland. For an explanation of the terms used in this diagram see pp. 99–100

11. Application of Lustick's state-expansion/contraction classification to British-Irish inter-state relations established with the Anglo-Irish Agreement (1985)

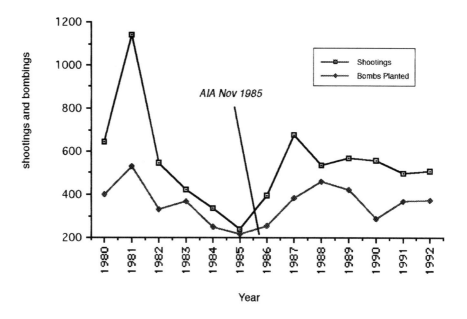

12. Explosions and shootings, 1980–1992

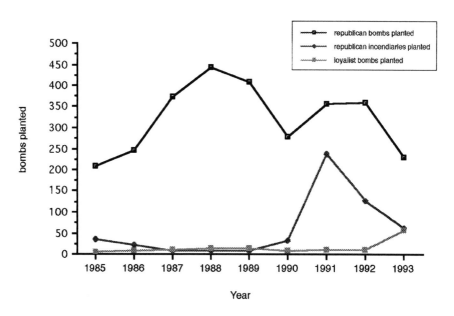

13. Republican and loyalist bombings in Northern Ireland, 1985–1993

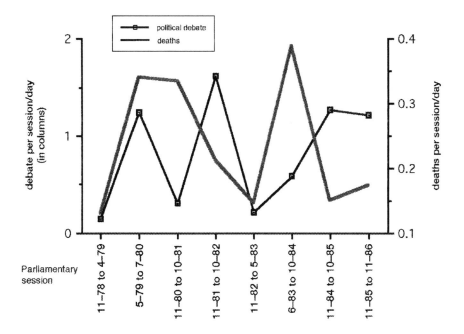

14. Deaths and debate on political/constitutional issues, 1978–1986

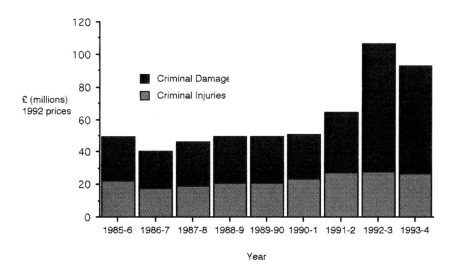

15. Criminal damage compensation expenditure, 1985–1994

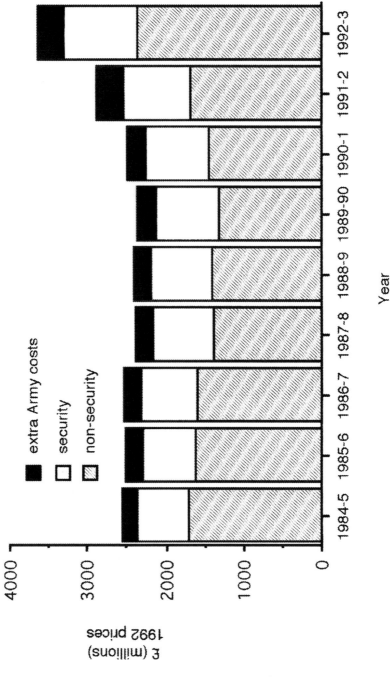

16. The UK subvention of Northern Ireland, 1984–1993

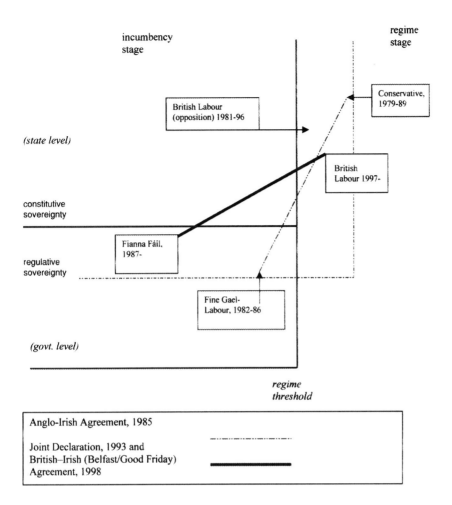

incumbency
stage

regime
stage

British Labour
(opposition) 1981-96

Conservative,
1979-89

(state level)

British
Labour 1997-

constitutive
sovereignty

Fianna Fáil,
1987-

regulative
sovereignty

Fine Gael-
Labour, 1982-86

(govt. level)

*regime
threshold*

Anglo-Irish Agreement, 1985

Joint Declaration, 1993 and
British–Irish (Belfast/Good Friday)
Agreement, 1998

Note: This figure represents the upper left section of the state-expansion, state-contraction model presented in Figure 1, as adapted from Lustick (1993). Arrows indicate shifts in party positions over time, where verticality represents hierarchical conceptions of the status of claims to 'constitutive' (above the state-level) and 'regulative' aspects of sovereignty. Thus, the vertical levelling of the positions of governments that negotiated the British–Irish Agreement (1998 ▬▬) represents increased symmetry, and in turn, a firmer foundation for mutualist intergovernmental exchange relations based on federal and confederal institutions. The horizontal movement represents mutual agreement on the consensus between governments on the necessity of consent for any either Irish state-expansion or British state-contraction.

17. British and Irish inter-state relations over Northern Ireland, 1982–2007

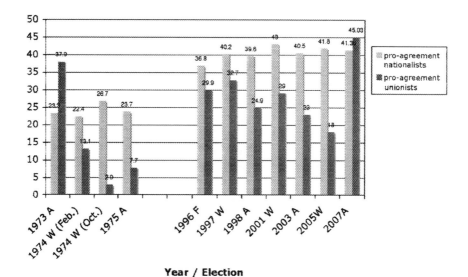

Year / Election

18. Comparison of pro-agreement nationalist and unionist parties, 1973–1975 and 1996–2007

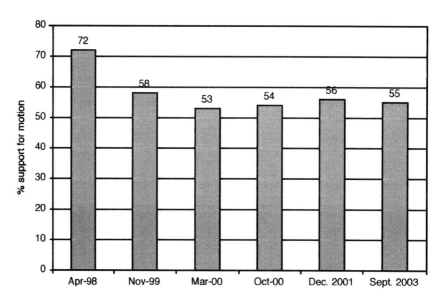

19. Pro-agreement votes (per cent) in the Ulster Unionist Council, 1998–2003

Bibliography

Official publications (British, Irish and International)
Union with Ireland Act (1800 c.67 39 and 40 Geo 3) (London: HMSO, 1800)
Act of Union (Ireland) (1800 c.38 40 Geo 3), (Dublin: HMSO, 1800)
Hansard Parliamentary Debates 1886–2001 (London: HMSO)
Report of the Census, 1911 (Dublin: Stationery Office, 1911)
A Return by Counties of all cases of shooting and bomb outrages, including firing
    at the person, into houses, etc, reported to the Police since the government
    dropped the Peace Preservation Act, HC, LXIX (1912–13), p. 725.
Government of Ireland Act (London: HMSO, 1920)
Official Correspondence relating to the Peace Negotiations. Part Two:
    Correspondence arising from the Conversations at London between
    President de Valera and the British Prime Minister, 13 August 1921
    (London: HMSO, 1921)
Hansard Parliamentary Debates (Northern Ireland House of Commons)
    1921–1972 (Belfast: HMSO)
Ireland (Confirmation of Agreement) Act (London: HMSO, 1925)
The Unity of Ireland: Partition Debated in Seanad Éireann, Official Reports,
    9 February 1939 (Dublin: The Stationery Office, 1939)
Dáil Debates, 1949–1998 (Dublin: Stationery Office)
Report of the Committee on the Constitution (Dublin: Stationery Office, 1967)
Disturbances in Northern Ireland: Report of the Commission Appointed by the
    Governor of Northern Ireland (Cameron Report) (Belfast: HMSO, 1969)
Report of the Advisory Committee on Police in Northern Ireland (Hunt
    Report) (Belfast: HMSO, 1969).
Report of the Inquiry into Allegations Against the Security Forces of Physical
    Brutality in Northern Ireland, Arising out of Events on 9th August 1971
    (Compton Report) (Belfast, HMSO, 1971)
Violence and Civil Disturbances in Northern Ireland in 1969 (Scarman
    Report) (London: HMSO, 1972)
Report of the Commission to Consider Legal Procedures to Deal with Terrorist
    Activities in Northern Ireland (Diplock Report) (London: HMSO, 1972)
Report of the Tribunal appointed to Enquire into the Events on Sunday 30th
    January 1972 which Led to Loss of Life in Connection with the Procession
    in Londonderry on that Day (Widgery Report) (London: HMSO, 1972)
The Future of Northern Ireland (London: HMSO, 1972)
Northern Ireland Constitutional Proposals (London, HMSO, 1973)
Report of a Committee to Consider, in the Context of Civil Liberties and

Human Rights, Measures to Deal with Terrorism in Northern Ireland (Gardiner Report) (London: HMSO, 1975)

Report of the Committee of Inquiry into Police Interrogation Procedures in Northern Ireland (Bennett Report) (London: HMSO, 1979)

Report of the New Ireland Forum (Dublin: Stationery Office, 1984)

Agreement between the Government of the United Kingdom of Great Britain and Northern Ireland and the Government of the Republic of Ireland (The Anglo-Irish Agreement) (London: HMSO, 1985)

Religious and Political Discrimination and Equality of Opportunity in Northern Ireland: Report on Fair Employment (Report of the Standing Advisory Commission on Human Rights) (London: HMSO, 1987)

Brooke, Peter, 'Transcript of Speech to Conservative Association', 9 November (1990)

Census of Northern Ireland, 1991: Religion and Gender by Geographic Area (Belfast: Northern Ireland Statistics and Research Agency, 1993)

Chief Constables' Reports, Royal Ulster Constabulary (Belfast: RUC, 1990–6)

Paths to a Political Settlement in Ireland: Realities, Principles and Requirements (Reports of the Forum for Peace and Reconciliation) (Dublin: Stationery Office, 1996)

Agreement between the Government of the United Kingdom of Great Britain and Northern Ireland and the Government of the Republic of Ireland (Anglo-Irish Agreement) (London: HMSO, 1985)

Joint Declaration on Peace (Downing Street Declaration) (London: Prime Minister's Office, 1993)

A Framework for Accountable Government in Northern Ireland (London, HMSO, 1995)

A New Framework for Agreement: A Shared Understanding between the British and Irish Governments to Assist Discussion and Negotiation Involving Northern Ireland Parties (London, HMSO, 1995)

Report of the International Body on Paramilitary Arms (The Mitchell Report) (London, HMSO, 1996)

The Ground Rules for All-Party Negotiations (London: NIO, 1996)

Agreement Reached in the Multi-party Negotiations (Good Friday / Belfast Agreement) (Belfast: HMSO, 1998)

Agreement Between the Government of the United Kingdom of Great Britain and Northern Ireland and the Government of Ireland (British-Irish Agreement) (Belfast: HMSO, 1998)

Agreements between British and Irish Governments in Respect of the North-South Ministerial Council, the British-Irish Council, and the British-Irish Intergovernmental Conference (BIIC) (London: NIO, 1999)

Joint statement by the Irish and British Governments at Stormont (The Way Forward) (London, NIO: 1999)

Assessment by the Independent International Commission on Decommissioning (Belfast: IICD, 1999)

A New Beginning: Policing in Northern Ireland (Belfast: Independent Commission on Policing for Northern Ireland, 1999)

Agreement between The Government of the United Kingdom and The Government of Ireland Establishing the Independent Monitoring Commission (London: NIO, 2003)

Final Report on the Report of the Inquiry into the Dublin and Monaghan Bombings, Irish Oireachtas's Joint Committee for Justice, Equality, Defence and Women's Rights, (the Barron Report), (Dublin: Stationery Office, 2003)

Report of the Stevens Inquiry (London: HMSO, 2003)

Proposals by the British and Irish Governments for a Comprehensive Agreement (Belfast: NIO, 2004)

Report of the Independent International Commission on Decommissioning (IICD) on the Decommissioning of IRA Weapons (Belfast: IICD, 2005)

Agreement at St Andrews, Joint Proposals, Issued by the British and Irish Governments, Aimed at Restoring the Devolved Assembly at Stormont, (Belfast: NIO, 2006)

Organisation for Economic Cooperation and Development (OECD), *Selection of OECD Social Indicators: How does your country compare?* 23 February 2007 (http://www.oecd.org/country/0,3021,en_33873108_33873500_1_1_1_1_1,00.html)

Business Breakfast SDLP – Derry, Speech by the Minister for Finance Brian Cowen, 28 February 2007

Public Records (British)

Intelligence Reports, 1914–16 CO 903/19 PRO Kew

Letter from Smuts to de Valera, 4 August 1921, DO 1119/1038 PRO, Kew

Diary of Negotiations, 27 May 1922, CAB 2111/257, PRO, Kew

Very Secret Memorandum of Interview between PM, Mr. Griffith and Mr. Michael Collins held in the Cabinet Room, 10 Downing St., 1 June 1922, CAB 211/257, PRO, Kew

Proceedings of Conference Between Representatives of the United Kingdom and Éire, 10–16 January 1938, CAB 27/164 I.N. Series, p. 24, PRO Kew

Cabinet Conclusions, 17 January 1938, CAB 27 I.N.C. (38), 198, PRO Kew

Memo from Maffey to Eden, 17 January 1940, DO 130/10, PRO Kew

The Effect of the War on Ireland's Destiny as a European Nation – Reflections by an Australian, 16 May 1940, PREM 4/53/2, PRO Kew

Memo from Maffey to Machtig, 3 June 1940, DO 130/10 f. 18,1. PRO Kew

Ernest Bevin to Churchill, 18 June 1940, PREM 4/53/2, PRO, Kew

Hand-written comment by Churchill to letter from Gough, 9 December 1941, PREM 4/53/4 PRO Kew

Letter from Churchill to Brooke, 12 June 1945, PREM 4 53/1 PRO Kew

Briefing Note on Lemass, Dec. (no specific date), 1965, PREM 13/982, PRO Kew

Notes of Downing St. meeting between Lemass and PM Harold Wilson, 26 July 1965, PREM 13/982, PRO Kew

Memo from Commonwealth Secretary (Arnold Smith) to PM Harold Wilson, 22 July 1965, PREM 13/983 (37/65), PRO Kew

O'Neill to Soskice, 4 April 1966, PREM 13/980, PRO Kew

Civil disturbances in Londonderry, October 1968, PREM 13/2841, PRO Kew
Contingency planning for maintenance of law and order, including military
    assistance and possible legislation to suspend constitution; part 3, 1969,
    PREM 13/2843, PRO Kew
Cabinet minutes, 1970, Cab 128/46, PRO Kew
Northern Ireland: Contingency Planning 22 July 1971, PREM 14/1010, PRO
    Kew
Situation in Northern Ireland, 27 July to 9 September 1971, CAB 164/879,
    PRO Kew
Draft letter, Heath to Lynch, 8 August 1971, 15/478/8, PRO Kew
PM Heath's summary of Cabinet meeting, 1 December 1971, CAB 130/522 p.
    13, PRO Kew

Public Records (Irish)
IRA activities, A12/1, NAI
Partition: Government Policy, 29 December 1969 – 23 April 1970,
    2000/6/101, NAI
Statement by the Taoiseach, Mr. J. Lynch, 13 August 1969, as reproduced in
    'Partition: Misc. Correspondence, Resolutions', 2000/6/150, NAI
Report to Taoiseach and Cabinet by Eamon Gallagher on trip to Derry, 29
    March 1970, 2000/6/150, NAI
Partition: Government Policy August 1968–August 1969, 2000/6/657, NAI
Religious tolerance in Ireland, January 1968–January 1969, 99/1/99, NAI
Memo from John Hume to George Colley, September (no date) 1971,
    2001/43/1393, NAI.

NEWSPAPERS AND PERIODICALS
British:
Daily Telegraph
Financial Times
Guardian
Independent
Independent on Sunday
Irish Post
London Review of Books
Observer
The Scotsman
The Times

Irish:
Ireland on Sunday
Irish Independent
Irish Times
Sunday Press
Sunday Tribune
The Pilot

The Nation

Northern Irish:
Belfast Telegraph
An Phoblacht/Republican News
Fortnight
Irish News

Other:
Die Zeit
The New York Times
The Scotsman

BOOKS AND ARTICLES

Adams, Gerry, 'Why I talked to John – By Gerry', *Fortnight* January 1988, pp. 6–7

Adams, Gerry, Presidential Address: 89th Sinn Féin Ard Fheis (Belfast: Sinn Féin, 1994)

Adams, Gerry, *Free Ireland: Towards a Lasting Peace* (Dingle: Brandon, 1995)

Adams, James, Robin Morgan and Anthony Bambridge, *Ambush: The War Between the SAS and the IRA* (London: Pan, 1988)

Adolphus, John, *The History of England: From the Accession of King George the Third to the Conclusion of the Peace in 1783*, Volume II (London: T. Cadell, Jun. and W. Davies, 1802)

Alcock, Anthony 'Lessons from Europe', in McGarry, John (ed.), *Northern Ireland and the Divided World* (Oxford: Oxford University Press, 2001)

Aldecoa, Francisco, 'Towards Plurinational Diplomacy in the Deeper and Wider European Union (1985–2005)' in Aldecoa, Francisco and Michael Keating (eds), *Paradiplomacy in Action: The Foreign Relations of Subnational Governments* (London: Frank Cass, 1999).

Amnesty International, *Northern Ireland: Human Rights Concerns* (London: Amnesty International, 1991)

Amnesty International, *Political Killings in Northern Ireland* (London: Amnesty International, 1994)

Anderson, Benedict, *Imagined Communities: Reflections on the Origins and Spread of Nationalism* (London: Verso, 1983)

Anderson, D., *14 May Days: the Inside Story of the Loyalist Strike of 1974* (Dublin: Gill and Macmillan, 1994)

Anderson, James, 'Rethinking National Problems in a Transnational Context', in Miller, D. (ed.), *Rethinking Northern Ireland: Culture, Ideology and Colonialism* (London: Longman, 1998)

Apter, David and Sawa, Nagayo, *Against the State: Politics and Social Protest in Japan* (Cambridge, MA: Harvard University Press, 1984)

Archer, Jeffrey, 'Constitutionalism and Violence: The Case of Ireland', *Journal of Commonwealth and Comparative Politics,* 22 (1984) pp. 111–27

Arendt, Hannah, *On Violence* (London: Allen Lane, 1970a)

Arendt, Hannah, *Thoughts on Politics and Revolution: A Commentary* (Orlando, FL: Harcourt, Brace, Jovanovich, 1970b)

Armstrong, Robert (Lord), 'Ethnicity, the English, Northern Ireland', in Keogh, Dermot and Haltzel, Michael H. (eds), *Northern Ireland and the Politics of Reconciliation* (Washington, DC and Cambridge: Woodrow Wilson Center Press and Cambridge University Press, 1994)

Arnold, Bruce, *Haughey: His Life and Unlucky Deeds* (London: HarperCollins, 1993)

Arthur, Paul, *Government and Politics of Northern Ireland* (London: Longman, 1984)

Arthur, Paul, 'Anglo-Irish Relations and the Northern Ireland Problem', *Irish Studies in International Affairs*, 2, 1 (1985) pp. 37–50

Arthur, Paul, 'Negotiating the Northern Ireland Problem: Track One or Track Two Diplomacy', *Government and Opposition*, 26, 2 (1991)

Arthur, Paul, 'Anglo-Irish Relations and Constitutional Policy', in Mitchell, P. and Wilford, R. (eds), *Politics in Northern Ireland* (Boulder, CO: Westview, 1998)

Arthur, Paul, '"Quiet diplomacy and personal conversation" Track Two diplomacy and the search for a settlement in Northern Ireland', in Ruane, J. and Todd, J. (eds), *After the Good Friday Agreement: Analysing Political Change in Northern Ireland* (Dublin: University College Dublin, 1999)

Arthur, Paul, *Special Relationships: Britain, Ireland and the Northern Ireland Problem* (Belfast: Blackstaff, 2000)

Aughey, Arthur, *Under Siege: Ulster Unionism and the Anglo-Irish Agreement* (London: Hurst, 1989)

Aya, Rod, 'Popular Intervention in Revolutionary Situations' in Bright, Charles and Harding, Susan (eds), *Statemaking and Social Movements: Essays in History and Theory* (Ann Arbor, MI: University of Michigan Press, 1984)

Bardon, Jonathon, *A History of Ulster* (Belfast: Blackstaff, 1992)

Barry, Brian, *Democracy and Power: Essays in Political Theory I* (Oxford: Oxford University Press, 1991)

Bartlett, Thomas, 'Indiscipline and Disaffection in the Armed Forces of the Crown in Ireland in the 1790s', in Corish, P.J. (ed.), *Radicals, Rebels and Establishments* (Belfast: Appletree, 1985)

Bartlett, Thomas, *The Fall and Rise of the Irish Nation: The Catholic Question, 1690–1830* (Dublin: Lilliput, 1992)

Bartlett, Thomas (ed.), *Life of Theobald Wolfe Tone: Memoirs, journals and political writings compiled and arranged by William T.W. Tone, 1826* (Dublin: Lilliput, 1998)

Barzilay, David, *The British Army in Ulster, 4 Vols* (Belfast: Century Services, 1973, 1975, 1978, 1981)

Beames, Michael, *Peasants and Power: The Whiteboy Movements and Their Control in Pre-Famine Ireland* (Sussex: Harvester, 1983)

Beames, Michael, 'The Ribbon Societies and Lower Class Nationalism in Pre-Famine Ireland', in Philpin, C.H.E (ed.), *Nationalism and Popular Protest in Ireland* (Cambridge: Cambridge University Press, 1987)

Bean, Kevin, 'The New Departure: Recent Developments in Irish Republican Ideology and Strategy' Occasional Papers in Irish Studies, No.6 (University of Liverpool: Institute of Irish Studies, 1994)

Beattie, Geoffrey, 'Divided They Stand', *The Independent on Sunday*, 11 September 1994.

Beck, Ulrich, *The Reinvention of Politics: Rethinking Modernity in the Global Social Order* (Cambridge: Polity, 1997)

Beckett, J.C., *The Making of Modern Ireland, 1603–1923* (London: Faber, 1966)

Bell, J. Bowyer, *The Secret Army: A History of the IRA 1915–1970* (London: Sphere, 1972)

Bell, J. Bowyer, *A Time of Terror: How Democratic Societies Respond to Revolutionary Violence* (New York: Basic Books, 1978)

Bell, J. Bowyer, *The Irish Troubles: A Generation of Violence 1967–1992* (Dublin: Gill and Macmillan, 1993)

Beloff, Max, 'Terrorism and the People', in *Ten Years of Terrorism: Collected Views* (London: Royal United Services Institute for Defence Studies, 1979)

Bennett, Ronan, 'The Party and the Army', *London Review of Books,* 18, 6 (1996) pp. 5–7

Beresford, David, *Ten Men Dead: The Story of the 1981 Irish Hunger Strike* (London: Grafton, 1987)

Beresford-Ellis, Peter, *Hell or Connaught: The Cromwellian Colonisation of Ireland, 1652–1660* (London: Hamish Hamilton, 1988)

Bew, Paul, *Land and the National Question in Ireland 1858–82* (Dublin: Gill and Macmillan, 1978)

Bew, Paul, *Conflict and Conciliation in Ireland, 1890–1910: Parnellites and Radical Agrarians* (Oxford: Clarendon, 1987)

Bew, Paul, *Ideology and the Irish Question: Ulster Unionism and Irish Nationalism, 1912–1916* (Oxford: Oxford University Press, 1994)

Bew, Paul, 'Myths of Consociationalism: from Good Friday to Political Impasse', in Cox, Michael, Guelke, Adrian and Stephen, Fiona (eds), *A Farewell to Arms? Beyond the Good Friday Agreement,* 2nd Edition (Manchester: Manchester University Press, 2006)

Bew, Paul, Gibbon, Peter and Patterson, Henry, *Northern Ireland 1921–1994: Political Forces and Social Classes* (London: Serif, 1995)

Bew, Paul, Gibbon, Peter, and Patterson, Henry, *The State in Northern Ireland, 1921–1972* (Manchester: Manchester University Press, 1979)

Bew, Paul and Gillespie, Gordon, *Northern Ireland: A Chronology of the Troubles 1968–1993* (Dublin: Gill and Macmillan, 1993)

Bew, Paul and Patterson, Henry, *The British State and the Ulster Crisis: From Wilson to Thatcher* (London: Verso, 1985)

Birrell, Derek, 'Relative Deprivation as a Factor in Conflict in Northern Ireland', *Sociological Review,* 20 (1972) pp. 317–43

Bishop, Patrick and Mallie, Eamonn, *The Provisional IRA* (London: Heinemann, 1987)

Blake, Robert, *The Unknown Prime Minister: The Life and Time of Andrew Bonar Law 1858–1923* (London: Eyre & Spottiswoode, 1955)

Boal, F. and Douglas, J., *Integration and Division: Geographical Perspectives on the Northern Ireland Problem* (London: Academic Press, 1982)

Bose, Sumantra, *Contested Lands: Israel-Palestine, Kashmir, Bosnia, Cyprus and Sri Lanka* (Cambridge, MA: Harvard University Press, 2007)

Boulton, D., *The UVF 1966–1973: An Anatomy of Loyalist Rebellion* (Dublin: Torc Books, 1973)

Bowcott, Owen, 'Heath was Urged to Share Ulster with Dublin', *The Guardian,* 1 January, 2002

Bowden, T., *The Breakdown of Public Security: The Case of Ireland, 1916–1921 and Palestine 1936–1939* (London: Sage, 1977)

Bowden, T., *Beyond the Limits of the Law: A Comparative Study of the Police in Crisis Politics* (Harmondsworth: Pelican, 1978)

Bowman, John, *De Valera and the Ulster Question 1917–1973* (Oxford: Oxford University Press, 1982)

Boyce, D.G., *Englishmen and Irish Troubles: British Public Opinion and the Making of Irish Policy, 1918–22* (Cambridge, MA: MIT Press, 1972)

Boyce, D.G., *Nationalism in Ireland* (London: Croom Helm, 1982)

Boyce, D.G., *The Irish Question and British Politics 1868–1986* (London: Macmillan, 1988)

Boyle, K., Hadden, T. and Hillyard, P., *Law and State – The Case of Northern Ireland* (London: Martin Robinson, 1984)

Bradley, D. 'Peace Process should be seen through' *Irish Times,* 20 April 1999

Breen, Richard, 'Who wants a United Ireland? Constitutional preferences among Catholics and Protestants', pp. 33–48 in Richard Breen, Paula Devine, and Lizanne Dowds (eds), *Social Attitudes in Northern Ireland: The Fifth Report* (Belfast: Appletree, 1996)

Breen, Suzanne, 'No Surrender', *Fortnight,* 331 (1994) pp. 16–17

Breen, Suzanne, 'Punch Drunk', *Fortnight*, 348 (1996) p. 7

Bright, Charles and Harding, Susan (eds), *Statemaking and Social Movements: Essays in History and Theory* (Ann Arbor, MI: University of Michigan Press, 1984)

Broeker, Galen, *Rural Disorder and Police Reform in Ireland, 1812–36* (London: Routledge & Kegan Paul, 1970)

Brooke, Peter (MP) 'The British Presence', Speech to Businessmen in London, 9 November 1990

Brubaker, Rogers, *Nationalism Reframed: Nationhood and the national question in the New Europe* (Cambridge: Cambridge University Press, 1996).

Bruce, Steve, *The Red Hand: Protestant Paramilitaries in Northern Ireland* (Oxford: Oxford University Press, 1992)

Bruce, Steve, 'Alienation Once Again', *Fortnight*, 317 (1993) pp. 18–19

Bruce, Steve, *The Edge of the Union: The Ulster Loyalist Political Vision* (Oxford: Oxford University Press, 1994)

Buckland, Patrick, *Ulster Unionism and the Origins of Northern Ireland* (Dublin: Gill and Macmillan, 1973)

Buckland, Patrick, *The Factory of Grievances: Devolved Government in Northern Ireland 1921–39* (Dublin: Gill and Macmillan, 1979)

Buckland, Patrick, *A History of Northern Ireland* (Dublin: Gill and Macmillan, 1981)

Budge, I. and O'Leary, C., *Belfast: Approach to Crisis – A Study of Belfast Politics 1613–1970* (Basingstoke: Macmillan, 1973)

Bull, Hedley, *The Anarchical Society: A Study of Order in World Politics* (London: Macmillan, 1977)

Bull, P.J., *Land, Politics and Nationalism: A Study of the Irish Land Question* (Dublin: Gill and Macmillan, 1996)

Burton, John, *Conflict: Human Needs Theory* (New York: St Martin's Press, 1990)

Callaghan, James, *Time and Chance* (London: Collins, 1987)

Campbell, David and Dillon, Michael (eds), *The Political Subject of Violence* (Manchester and New York: Manchester UP and St Martin's, 1993)

Canning, Paul, *British Policy Toward Ireland 1921–1941* (Oxford: Oxford University Press, 1985

Canovan, Margaret, *Nationhood and Political Theory* (Cheltenham: Edward Elgar, 1996)

Carroll, Terrance G., 'Disobedience and Violence in Northern Ireland', *Comparative Political Studies,* 14, 1 (1981) pp. 3–29

Carty, Anthony, *Was Ireland Conquered? International Law and the Irish Question* (London: Pluto, 1996)

Catterall, Peter and McDougall, Sean (eds), *The Northern Ireland Question in British Politics* (London: Macmillan, 1996)

Churchill, Randolph S., *Winston S. Churchill 1874–1965, Volume I, Youth, 1874–1900* (London: Heinemann, 1966)

Churchill, Winston, 'The Ulster Situation', in *The Complete Speeches of Winston Churchill 1897–1963, vol. 3, 1914–22* (London: Chelsea House, [1914] 1974)

Churchill, Winston, *The World Crisis 1911–1918,* Abridged and Revised Edition (London: Macmillan, [1931] 1942)

Clark, S., 'The Political Mobilization of Irish Farmers', *Canadian Review of Sociology and Anthropology*, XII, 4, 2, (1975) pp. 483–99

Clark, S., *Social Origins of the Irish Land War* (Princeton, NJ: Princeton University Press, 1979)

Clark, S. and Donnelly, J.S., *Irish Peasants: Violence & Political Unrest, 1780–1914* (Manchester: Manchester University Press, 1983)

Clarke, Liam, *Broadening the Battlefield: The H-Blocks and the Rise of Sinn Féin* (Dublin: Gill and Macmillan, 1987)

Clutterbuck, Richard, *Britain in Agony: The Growth of Political Violence* (London: Faber, 1978)

Cochrane, Feargal, *Unionist Politics and the Politics of Unionism since the Anglo-Irish Agreement* (Cork: Cork University Press, 1997)

Collins, Stephen, *The Haughey File: The Unprecedented Career and Last Years of the Boss* (Dublin: O'Brien, 1992)

Coakley, John (ed.), *The Territorial Management of Ethnic Conflict* 2nd Edition (London: Frank Cass, 2003)

Colgan, Paul, 'Governments Unite to Put Pressure on DUP, *Sunday Business Post,* 5 February 2006

Connolly, S.J., *Religion, Law and Power: The Making of Protestant Ireland 1660–1760* (Oxford: Clarendon, 1992)

Connor, Walker, 'Nationalism and Political Illegitimacy', *Canadian Review of Studies in Nationalism,* VIII, 2 (1984) pp. 201–28

Connor, Walker, *Ethnonationalism: The Quest for Understanding* (Princeton, NJ: Princeton University Press, 1993)

Coogan, Tim Pat, *The IRA* (Glasgow: Collins, 1987)

Coogan, Tim Pat, *The Man Who Made Ireland: The Life and Death of Michael Collins* (New York: Roberts Rinehart, 1992)

Coppieters, Bruno et al, *Europeanization and Conflict Resolution: Case Studies from the European Periphery* (Gent: Academia Press, 2004)

Corish, P.J. (ed.), *Radicals, Rebels and Establishments* (Belfast: Appletree, 1985)

Cox, Michael, 'Rethinking the International and Northern Ireland: A Defence', in Cox, Michael, Guelke, Adrian and Stephen, Fiona (eds), *A Farewell to Arms? Beyond the Good Friday Agreement,* 2nd Edition (Manchester: Manchester University Press, 2006)

Cox, Michael, Guelke, Adrian and Stephen, Fiona (eds), *A Farewell to Arms? Beyond the Good Friday Agreement,* 2nd Edition (Manchester: Manchester University Press, 2006)

Cox, W.H., 'Managing Northern Ireland Intergovernmentally', *Parliamentary Affairs,* 40, 1(1987) pp. 80–97

Cox, W.H. 1996. 'From Hillsborough to Downing Street – and After', in Catterall, P. and McDougall, S. (eds.), *The Northern Ireland Question in British Politics* (London: Macmillan).

Cronin, Sean, *Irish Nationalism: A History of its Roots and Ideology* (Dublin: Academy, 1980)

Crossman, Richard, *The Diaries of a Cabinet Minister, Vol. III: Secretary of State for Social Services, 1968–70* (London: Hamilton, 1977)

Crewe, Ivor, 'Voting and the Electorate', in Dunleavy, Patrick, Gamble, Andrew, Holliday, Ian and Peele, Gillian (eds), *Developments in British Politics* (London: Macmillan, 1993)

Cullen, L.M., *An Economic History of Ireland Since 1660,* 2nd Edition (London: Batsford, 1987)

Cunningham, Michael J., *British Government Policy in Northern Ireland, 1969–1989: Its Nature and Execution,* 2nd Edition (Manchester: Manchester University Press, 2001)

Curtis, L.P. Jr., *Coercion and Conciliation in Ireland 1880–1892: A Study in Conservative Unionism* (Princeton, NJ: Princeton University Press, 1963)

Curtis, L.P. Jr., 'Moral and Physical Force: The Language of Violence in Irish Nationalism', *Journal of British Studies,* xxvii, (1988)

Dangerfield, George, *The Strange Death of Liberal England, 1910–1914* (New York: Perigree, 1935)

Dangerfield, George, *The Damnable Question: One Hundred and Twenty Years of Anglo-Irish Conflict* (Boston: Little, Brown, 1976)

Danspeckgruber, Wolfgang, 'Conclusions', in Danspeckgruber, Wolfgang (ed.), *The Self-Determination of Peoples: Community, Nation and State in an Interdependent World* (London: Lynne Reinner, 2002)

Darby, John, *Conflict in Northern Ireland: The Development of a Polarized Community* (Dublin: Gill and Macmillan, 1976)

de Paor, Liam, *Unfinished Business: Ireland Today and Tomorrow* (London: Radius, 1990)

Deutsch, Karl W., *Nationalism and Social Communication: an Inquiry into the Foundation of Nationality,* 2nd Edition (Cambridge, MA: MIT Press, 1966)

Deutsch, R. and Magowan, V., *Northern Ireland: A Chronology 1968–73* (Belfast: Blackstaff Press, 1973)

Dewar, Michael, *The British Army in Northern Ireland* (London: Arms and Armour, 1985)

Dillon, Martin, *The Shankill Butchers: a Case Study of Mass Murder* (London: Hutchinson, 1989)

Dillon, Martin, *The Dirty War* (London: Hutchinson, 1990)

Dillon, Martin and Lehane, Denis, *Political Murder in Northern Ireland* (Harmondsworth: Penguin, 1973)

Dixon, Paul, 'Paths to Peace in Northern Ireland (I): Civil society and Consociational Approaches', *Democratization,* 4, 1 (1997a) pp. 1–27

Dixon, Paul, 'Paths to Peace in Northern Ireland (II): The Peace Processes 1973–74 and 1994–96', *Democratization,* 4, 2 (1997b) pp. 1–25

Doron, Gideon and Sened, Itai, *Political Bargaining: Theory, Practice & Process* (London: Sage, 2001)

Dowling, Brian and Purcell, Bernard, 'No Deals or Stealth on Peace Accord – Ahern', *Irish Independent,* 29 November 2003

Drudy, P.J. (ed.), *Ireland: Land, Politics and People* (Cambridge: Cambridge University Press, 1982)

Dudley, Ryan and Miller, Ross A., 'Group Rebellion in the 1980s', *Journal of Conflict Resolution,* 42, 1 (1998) pp. 77–96

Duffy, Mary and Evans, Geoffrey, 'Class, community polarisation and conflict', in L. Dowds, P. Devine and R. Breen (eds), *Social Attitudes in Northern Ireland: The Sixth Report* (Belfast: Appletree, 1997)

Elazar, Daniel J., *Federal Systems of the World: A Handbook of Federal, Confederal and Autonomy Arrangements,* 2nd Edition (London: Longman, 1994)

Elliott, John, 'Revolution and Continuity in Early Modern Europe', *Past and Present,* 42 (1969) pp. 35–56

Elliott, Marianne, *Partners in Revolution, the United Irishmen and France* (New Haven: Yale University Press, 1982)

Elliott, Marianne, *Wolfe Tone, Prophet of Irish Independence* (New Haven and London: Yale University Press, 1989)

Elliott, Sydney (ed.), *Northern Ireland Parliamentary Election Results, 1921–1972* (Chichester: Political Reference Publications, 1973)

Ellis, Steven, *Ireland in the Age of the Tudors 1447–1603: English Expansion and the End of Gaelic Rule* (London: Longman, 1998)

English, Richard, 'The state and Northern Ireland', in English, R. and Townshend, C. (eds), *The State: Historical and Political Dimensions* (London: Routledge, 1999)

English, Richard, 'The Growth of New Unionism', in Coakley, John (ed.), *Changing Shades of Orange and Green: Redefining the Union and the Nation in Contemporary Ireland* (Dublin: University College Dublin Press, 2002)

English, Richard, *The Armed Struggle: A History of the IRA* (London: Pan Macmillan, 2003)

Esman, Milton, *Ethnic Politics* (Ithaca, NY: Cornell, 1994)

Evans, Geoffrey and O'Leary, Brendan, 'Intransigence and Flexibility on the Way to Two Forums: the Northern Ireland Elections of 30 May 1996 and Public Opinion', *Representation*, 34, 3 & 4 (1997) pp. 208–18

Evans, Geoffrey and O'Leary, Brendan, 'Northern Irish Voters and the British–Irish Agreement: Foundations of a Stable Consociational Settlement?' *Political Quarterly*, 71 (2000)

Evans, P.B., Rueschmeyer, D. and Skocpol, T. (eds), *Bringing the State Back In* (Cambridge: Cambridge University Press, 1985)

Eveleigh, R., *Peace-Keeping in a Democratic Society: the Lessons of Northern Ireland* (London: Hurst, 1978)

Fanning, Ronan, *Independent Ireland* (Dublin: Helicon, 1983)

Fanning, Ronan, 'Small States, Large Neighbours: Ireland and the United Kingdom', *Irish Studies in International Affairs*, 9 (1998)

Farrell, Brian, 'MacNeill in Politics', in Martin, F.X. and Byrne, F.J. (eds), *The Scholar Revolutionary: Eoin MacNeill, 1867–1945, and the Making of the New Ireland* (Shannon: Irish University Press, 1973)

Farrell, Michael, *Northern Ireland: The Orange State* (London: Pluto Press, 1980)

Farrell, Michael, *Arming the Protestants: the Formation of the Ulster Special Constabulary and the Royal Ulster Constabulary, 1920–7* (London: Pluto, 1983)

Faulkner, Lady, *Brian Faulkner – Memoirs of a Statesman*, edited by John Houston (London: Weidenfeld and Nicolson, 1978)

Fearon, James D., 'Domestic Political Audiences and the Escalation of International Disputes' *American Political Science Review*, 88, 3 (1994) pp. 577–93

Finkel, Steven E., Muller, E.N. and Opp, K-D., 'Personal Influence, Collective Rationality, and Mass Political Action', *American Political Science Review*, 83 (1989) pp. 885–903

Fisk, Robert, *The Point of No Return: The Strike that Broke the British In Ulster* (London: Andre Deutsch, 1975)

Fisk, Robert, *In Time of War: Ireland, Ulster and the Price of Neutrality, 1939–45* (London: Andre Deutsch, 1983)

FitzGerald, Garret, *All in a Life: An Autobiography* (Dublin: Gill and Macmillan, 1991)

FitzGerald, Garret, 'Settlement a testimony to strong political leadership', *Irish Times,* 29 November 1999

Fitzpatrick, Brendan, *Seventeenth-Century Ireland: the War of Religions, New Gill History of Ireland, Volume 3* (Dublin: Gill and Macmillan, 1988)

Fitzpatrick, David, *Politics and Irish Life 1913–1921,* 2nd Edition (Cork: Cork University Press, 1998)

Fitzpatrick, David, 'Class, Family and Rural Unrest in Nineteenth-Century Ireland', in Drudy, P.J. (ed.), *Ireland: Land, Politics and People* (Cambridge: Cambridge University Press, 1982)

Fitzpatrick, David, *The Two Irelands, 1912–1939* (Oxford: Oxford University Press, 1998)

Flackes, D.W. and Elliott, S., *Northern Ireland: A Political Directory 1968–88* (Belfast: Blackstaff, 1989)

Foster, Roy, *Modern Ireland, 1600–1972* (Harmondsworth: Penguin, 1988)

Gallagher, Michael, *Political Parties in the Republic of Ireland* (Manchester: Manchester University Press, 1985)

Gallagher, Michael, 'How Many Nations are there in Ireland?', *Ethnic and Racial Studies*, 18, 4 (1995) pp. 714–39

Garvin, J.L., *The Life of Joseph Chamberlain, 3 Vols* (London: Macmillan, 1932–1934)

Garvin, Tom, *The Evolution of Irish Nationalist Politics* (Dublin: Gill and Macmillan, 1981)

Garvin, Tom, *Nationalist Revolutionaries in Ireland 1858–1928* (Oxford: Clarendon, 1987a)

Garvin, Tom, 'Defenders, Ribbonmen and Others: Underground Political Networks in Pre-famine Ireland', in Philpin, C.H.E (ed.), *Nationalism and Popular Protest in Ireland* (Cambridge: Cambridge University Press, 1987b)

Garvin, Tom, 'Unenthusiastic Democrats: the Emergence of Irish Democracy', in Hill, Ronald J. and Marsh, Michael (eds), *Modern Irish Democracy: Essays in Honour of Basil Chubb* (Dublin: Irish Academic Press, 1993)

Garvin, Tom, *1922: The Birth of Irish Democracy* (Dublin: Gill and Macmillan, 1996)

Garvin, Tom, *Preventing the Future: Why Was Ireland so Poor for So Long?* (Dublin: Gill and Macmillan, 2004)

Gearty, Conor, *Terror* (London: Faber and Faber, 1991)

Gellner, Ernest, *Nations and Nationalism* (Oxford: Blackwell, 1983)

Geertz, Clifford, 'The Integrative Revolution: Primordial Sentiments and Civil Politics in the New States', in *Old Societies and New: The Quest for Modernity in Asia and Africa* (New York: The Free Press, 1963) pp. 1–26.

Geldard, Ian and Craig, Keith, *IRA, INLA: Foreign Support and International Connections* (London: Institute for the Study of Terrorism, 1988)

Ghai, Yash (ed.), *Autonomy and Ethnicity: Negotiating Competing Claims in Multi-ethnic States* (Cambridge: Cambridge University Press, 2000)

Gilbert, Paul, *Terrorism, Security & Nationality: An Introductory Study in Applied Political Philosophy* (London: Routledge, 1994)

Gillespie, Paul, 'From Anglo-Irish to British–Irish Relations', in Cox, Michael, Guelke, Adrian and Stephen, Fiona (eds), *A Farewell to Arms? Beyond the Good Friday Agreement,* 2nd Edition (Manchester: Manchester University Press, 2006)

Gilmour, Ian, *Riot, Risings and Revolution: Governance and Violence in Eighteenth-Century England* (London: Hutchinson, 1993)

Girvin, Brian, 'Constitutional Nationalism in Northern Ireland', in Barton, B. and Roche, P.J. (eds), *The Northern Ireland Question: Perspectives and Policies* (Aldershot: Avebury, 1994) pp. 5–52

Girvin, Brian, 'Church, State and the Irish Constitution: The Secularisation of Irish Politics?', *Parliamentary Affairs* 49, 4 (1996) pp. 599–615

Githens-Mazer, Jonathan, *Myths and Memories of the Easter Rising: Cultural and Political Nationalism in Ireland* (Dublin: Irish Academic Press, 2006)

Goldstone, Jack, Gurr, Tedd, and Moshiri, Farrokh (eds), *Revolutions of the Late Twentieth Century* (Boulder, CO: Westview Press, 1991)

Graham, Thomas, 'A Union of Power?' The United Irish Organization: 1795–1798', in Dickson, D. Keogh, D. and Whelan, K., *The United Irishmen: Republicanism, Radicalism and Rebellion* (Dublin: Lilliput, 1993)

Greer, Steven, 'Supergrasses and the Legal System in Britain and Northern Ireland', *The Law Quarterly Review,* April 1986, pp. 198–249

Greer, Steven, 'The Supergrass System in Northern Ireland', in Wilkinson, Paul and Stewart, A.M. (eds), *Contemporary Research on Terrorism,* (Aberdeen: Aberdeen University Press, 1987) pp. 510–35.

Greer, Steven, *Supergrasses: A Study in Anti-terrorist Law Enforcement in Northern Ireland* (Oxford: Clarendon, 1995)

Guelke, Adrian, 'Loyalist and Republican Perceptions of the Northern Ireland Conflict: The UDA and the Provisional IRA', in Merkl, Peter (ed.), *Political Violence and Terror: Motifs and Motivations* (Berkeley, CA: University of California Press, 1986)

Guelke, Adrian, *Northern Ireland: the International Perspective* (Dublin: Gill and Macmillan, 1988)

Guelke, Adrian, 'Back-to-front politics', *Fortnight,* 325 (1994) pp. 12–13

Guelke, Adrian, *The Age of Terrorism and the International Political System* (London: Tauris Academic Studies, 1995)

Guelke, Adrian, 'International Dimensions of the Belfast Agreement', in Wilford, Rick (ed.), *Aspects of the Belfast Agreement* (Oxford: Oxford University Press, 2001)

Gupta, D.K., Singh, H. and Sprague, T., 'Government Coercion of Dissidents: Deterrence or Provocation?' *Journal of Conflict Resolution,* 37, 2 (1993) pp. 301–39

Gurr, Ted R., *Why Men Rebel* (Princeton, NJ: Princeton University Press, 1970)

Gurr, Ted R., *Minorities at Risk: A Global View of Ethnopolitical Conflicts* (Washington DC: US Institute of Peace, 1993)

Gurr, Ted R., and Goldstone, Jack A., 'Comparisons and Policy Implications', in Goldstone, Jack A., Gurr, Ted R., and Moshiri, Farrokh (eds), *Revolutions of the Late Twentieth Century* (Boulder, CO: Westview, 1991)

Hadden, Tom and Boyle, Kevin, (eds), *The Anglo-Irish Agreement, Commentary, Text, and Official Review* (London: Sweet and Maxwell, 1989)

Hadfield, Brigid, 'The Northern Ireland Constitution', in Hadfield, Brigid (ed.), *Northern Ireland: Politics & the Constitution* (Buckingham: Open University Press, 1992)

Halévy, Daniel, *President Wilson* (London: John Lane, 1919)

Hamill, Desmond, *Pig in the Middle: The Army in Northern Ireland 1969–84* (London: Methuen, 1985)

Hancock, W.K., *Survey of British Commonwealth Affairs, Volume I: Problems of Nationality 1918–1936* (Oxford: OUP, 1937)

Hanf, Theodor, 'The Prospects of Accommodation in Communal Conflicts: A Comparative Study', in Giliomee, H. and Schlemmer, L. (eds), *Negotiating South Africa's Future* (Basingstoke: Macmillan, 1989)

Hart, Peter, *The I.R.A. and Its Enemies: Violence and Community in Cork, 1916–1923* (Oxford: Clarendon, 1997)

Hayek, Friedrich A. *The Constitution of Liberty* (Chicago: Regnery, 1960)

Hayes, Bernadette C. and McAllister, Ian, 'Ethnonationalism, Public Opinion and the Good Friday Agreement', in Ruane, Joseph and Todd, Jennifer (eds), *After the Good Friday Agreement: Analysing Political Change in Northern Ireland* (Dublin: University College Dublin Press, 1999)

Hayes, Bernadette, McAllister, Ian and Dowds, Lizanne, 'In Search of the Middle Ground: Integrated Education and Northern Ireland Politics', Research Update, Ark Northern Ireland Social and Political Archive, 42, (2006)

Hechter, Michael, *Internal Colonialism: The Celtic Fringe in British National Development, 1536–1966* (Berkeley: University of California Press, 1975)

Hechter, Michael, 'Explaining Nationalist Violence', *Nations and Nationalism*, 1, 2 (1995) pp. 53–68

Heiberg, Marianne, O'Leary, Brendan and Tirman, John (eds), *Terror, Insurgency and the State: Ending Protracted Conflicts* (Philadelphia, PA: University of Pennsylvania Press, 2007)

Hennessey, Peter, *Muddling Through: Power, Politics and the Quality of Government in Postwar Britain* (London, Indigo, 1996)

Hennessey, Thomas, *Dividing Ireland: World War I and Partition* (London: Routledge, 1998)

Hennessey, Thomas, *The Northern Ireland Peace Process: Ending the Troubles?* (Dublin: Gill and Macmillan, 2000)

Henry, R.M., *The Evolution of Sinn Féin* (Dublin: Talbot [1920] 1971)

Hepburn, A.C., 'The Ancient Order of Hibernians in Irish Politics, 1905–14', *Cithara* X, 2 (1971) pp. 5–18

Hepburn, A.C., *The Conflict of Nationality in Modern Ireland* (London: Arnold, 1980)

Hewitt, Christopher, 'Majorities and Minorities: A Comparative Survey of Ethnic Violence', *The Annals of the American Academy of Political and Social Science*, 433 (1977) pp. 150–60.

Hewitt, Christopher, 'Catholic Grievance, Catholic Nationalism and Violence in Northern Ireland During the Civil Rights Period: a Reconsideration',

British Journal of Sociology, 32, 3 (1981) pp. 362–80

Hewitt, Christopher, 'Explaining Violence in Northern Ireland', *British Journal of Sociology*, 38, 1 (1987) pp. 77–87

Hillyard, Paddy, *Suspect Community: People's Experience of the Prevention of Terrorism Acts in Britain* (London: Pluto Press in association with Liberty, 1993)

Hobson, B. 'Foundation and Growth of the Irish Volunteers, 1913–14', in Martin, F.X. (ed.), Irish Volunteers 1913–1915 Recollections and Documents (Dublin: Duffy, 1963)

Hogan, G. and Walker, C., *Political Violence and the Law in Ireland* (Manchester: Manchester University Press, 1989)

Holland, Jack, *The American Connection: U.S. Guns, Money, and Influence in Northern Ireland* (New York: Viking, 1987)

Holland, Jack, 'No Meltdown of Moderate Parties', *Irish Echo Online,* 76, 45, 12–18 November 2003

Holland, Jack and Phoenix, Susan, *Phoenix: Policing the Shadows* (London: Hodder and Stoughton, 1996)

Hopkinson, Michael, *Green Against Green: The Irish Civil War* (Dublin: Gill and Macmillan, 1988)

Hoppen, K.T., *Elections, Politics and Society in Ireland, 1832–1885* (Oxford: Clarendon, 1984)

Hoppen, K.T., *Ireland Since 1800: Conflict and Conformity* (Harlow: Longman, 1989)

Horgan, John, *Sean Lemass: The Enigmatic Patriot* (Dublin: Gill and Macmillan, 1997)

Horgan, John and Taylor, Max, 'The Provisional IRA: Command and Functional Structure', *Terrorism and Political Violence,* 9, 3 (1997) pp. 1–32

Horowitz, Donald, *Ethnic Groups in Conflict* (Berkeley, CA: University of California, 1985)

Horowitz, Donald, 'Making Moderation Pay: The Comparative Politics of Ethnic Conflict Management', in Montville, Joseph V. (ed.), *Conflict and Peacemaking in Multiethnic Societies* (Lexington, MA: Lexington, 1989)

Horowitz, Donald, 'The Northern Ireland Agreement: Clear, Consociational, and Risky', in McGarry, John (ed.), *Northern Ireland and the Divided World* (Oxford: Oxford University Press, 2001)

Hutchinson, John, *The Dynamics of Cultural Nationalism: the Gaelic Revival and the Creation of the Irish Nation State* (London: Allen & Unwin, 1987)

Huntchinson, John, *Nations as Zones of Conflict* (London: Sage, 2005)

Hroch, Miroslav, 'National Self-Determination from a Historical Perspective', in Periwal, Sukumar (ed.), *Notions of Nationalism* (Budapest: Central European University Press, 1995)

Irish Information Partnership, *Agenda Database* (London: IIP, 1986, 1990)

Irwin, Colin, *The People's Peace Process in Northern Ireland* (London: Palgrave, 2002)

Jackman, Robert W., *Power Without Force: The Political Capacity of Nation-States* (Ann Arbor, MI: University of Michigan Press, 1993)

Jackson, Alvin, *Home Rule: An Irish History* (London: Weidenfeld and Nicholson, 2003)

Jalland, Patricia, *The Liberals and Ireland: The Ulster Question and British Politics to 1914* (New York: St Martin's, 1980)

Jenkins, Brian, *The Era of Emancipation: British Government of Ireland, 1812–1830* (Kingston, Ont.: McGill-Queen's University Press, 1988)

Jones, Thomas, *Whitehall Diary, Vol. III, Ireland 1918–25* (London: Oxford University Press, 1971)

Kearney, Hugh, *The British Isles: A History of Four Nations* (Cambridge: Cambridge University Press, 1989)

Keating, Michael, *Plurinational Democracy: Stateless Nations in a Post-Sovereignty Era* (Oxford: Oxford University Press, 2001)

Keatinge, Patrick, 'An Odd Couple? Obstacles and Opportunities in Inter-State Political Co-operation between the Republic of Ireland and the United Kingdom', in Rea, Desmond (ed.), *Political Co-operation in Divided Societies* (Dublin: Gill & Macmillan, 1982)

Kee, Robert, *The Green Flag,* Three Volumes (London: Penguin, 1989)

Kelley, Kevin J., *The Longest War: Northern Ireland and the IRA* (London: Zed, 1988)

Kendle, J.E., 'The Round Table Movement and Home Rule All Round', *Historical Journal,* 11, 2 (1968)

Kendle, J.E., *Ireland and the Federal Solution: The Debate over the United Kingdom Constitution, 1870–1921* (Kingston and Montreal, Canada: McGill-Queen's University Press, 1989)

Kenny, A., *The Road to Hillsborough: The Shaping of the Anglo-Irish Agreement* (Oxford: Oxford University Press, 1986)

Keogh, Dermot, *Twentieth-Century Ireland: Nation and State, New Gill History of Ireland,* No. 6 (Dublin: Gill and Macmillan, 1994)

Kerr, Michael, *Imposing Power-Sharing: Conflict and Coexistence in Northern Ireland and Lebanon* (Dublin: Irish Academic Press, 2006)

Kidd, Colin, *Subverting Scotland's Past: Scottish Whig Historians and the Creation of an Anglo-British Identity, 1689–c. 1830* (Cambridge: Cambridge University Press, 1993)

Kidd, Colin, *British Identities before Nationalism: Ethnicity and Nationhood in the Atlantic World, 1600–1800* (Cambridge: Cambridge University Press, 1999) p. 156

Killen, John (ed.), *The Decade of the United Irishmen: Contemporary Accounts 1791–1801* (Belfast: Blackstaff, 1997)

King, Steven, 'Lemass Approach May Yet Bear Fruit in North', *Irish Times,* 25 November 1997

King, Steven, 'The Executive, Not the Cross Border Bodies, is Where the Real Test Lies', *Sunday Tribune* (Dublin), 19 December 1999

Kissane, Bill, 'The Not-So Amazing Case of Irish Democracy', *Irish Political Studies* Vol. 10 (1995) pp. 43–68

Kissane, Bill, *Explaining Irish Democracy* (Dublin: University College Dublin, 2002)

Kissane, Bill, *The Politics of the Irish Civil War* (Oxford: Oxford University Press, 2005)

Kitson, Frank, *Low Intensity Operations: Subversion, Insurgency, Peace-keeping* (London: Faber and Faber, 1971)

Kitson, Frank, *Bunch of Five* (London: Faber and Faber, 1977)

Klieman, Aharon, *Compromising Palestine: A Guide to Final Status Negotiations* (New York, NY: Columbia University Press, 1999)

Knox, Oliver, *Rebels and Informers: Stirrings of Irish Independence* (London: John Murray, 1997)

Korff, Douwe, *The Diplock Courts in Northern Ireland: A Fair Trial?* (Utrecht: Netherlands Institute of Human Rights, 1984)

Kovalcheck, Kassian, 'Catholic Grievances in Northern Ireland: Appraisal and Judgment' *British Journal of Sociology,* 38, 1 (1987) pp. 77–87

Kratochwil, Emil, 'Of Systems, Boundaries and Territoriality: An Enquiry into the Formation of the State System', *World Politics,* 39, 1 (1986) pp. 27–52

Laffan, Michael, 'The Unification of Sinn Féin, 1917', *Irish Historical Studies,* XIV (1971) pp. 353–79

Laffan, Michael, *The Partition of Ireland 1911–25* (Dublin Historical Association: Dundalk, 1983)

Lapidoth, Ruth, *Autonomy: Flexible Solutions to Ethnic Conflicts* (Washington, DC: United States Institute of Peace, 1997)

Laski, Harold J., 'The Sovereignty of the State,' in *Studies in the Problem of Sovereignty* (New Haven, Conn: Yale University Press, 1924)

Lawler, Edward J., 'Power Processes in Bargain', *Sociological Quarterly* No. 33 (1982) pp. 17–34

Lawler, Edward J. and Yoon, Jeongkoo, 'Power and the Emergence of Commitment Behavior in Negotiated Exchange', *Sociological Theory,* 11 (1993) pp. 268–90

Lawler, Edward J. and Yoon, Jeongkoo, 'Commitment in Exchange Relations: Test of a Theory of Relational Cohesion, *American Sociological Review,* 61 (1996) pp. 89–108

Leahy, Pat, 'Majority Want a Nation Once Again', *Sunday Business Post,* 2 April 2006

Lecky, W.E.H., *A History of Ireland in the Eighteenth Century, Vol. III* (London, [1892] 1909)

Lee, J.J., *Ireland 1912–1985: Politics and Society* (Cambridge: Cambridge University Press, 1989)

Lichbach, Mark I., 'The Effects of Repression: Deterrence or Escalation', *Journal of Conflict Resolution,* 31, 2 (1987) pp. 266–97

Lijphart, Arend, *Democracy in Plural Societies* (New Haven, CT: Yale University Press, 1977)

Linz, Juan, *The Breakdown of Democratic Regimes: Crisis, Breakdown and Reequilibration* (Baltimore and London: Johns Hopkins University Press, 1978)

Longford, L. and O'Neill, T.P., *Eamon de Valera* (Dublin: Gill and Macmillan, 1970)

Lustick, Ian, 'Stability in Deeply Divided Societies: Consociationalism versus Control' *World Politics,* 31, 3(1979) 325–344

Lustick, Ian, *State-building Failure in British Ireland & French Algeria* (Berkeley, CA: Institute of International Studies, 1985)

Lustick, Ian, 'Becoming Problematic: Breakdown of a Hegemonic Conception of Ireland in Nineteenth-Century Britain', *Politics and Society,* 18, 1 (1990) pp. 39–73

Lustick, Ian, *Unsettled States, Disputed Lands: Britain and Ireland, France and Algeria, Israel and the West Bank-Gaza* (Ithaca: Cornell University Press, 1993)

Lustick, Ian, O'Leary, Brendan and Callaghy, Thomas (eds), *Right-Sizing the State: The Politics of Moving Borders* (Oxford: Oxford University Press, 2001)

Lusztig, Michael and Knox, Colin, 'Good Things and Small Packages: Lessons from Canada for the Northern Irish Constitutional Settlement', *Nations and Nationalism* 5, 4 (1999) pp. 543–63

Lyne, Thomas, 'Ireland, Northern Ireland and 1992: The Barriers to Technocratic Anti-Partitionism', *Public Administration,* Vol. 68 (1990) pp. 417–33

Lyons, F.S.L., *Ireland Since the Famine* (London: Fontana, 1973)

Macardle, Dorothy, *The Irish Republic* (Dublin: Irish Press, 1937, 1957)

MacDermot, Frank, *Tone and his Times* (Dublin: Anvil, 1980)

MacDonagh, O., *States of Mind: Two Centuries of Anglo-Irish Conflict, 1780–1980* (London: Allen & Unwin, 1983)

MacDonagh, O., *The Hereditary Bondsman: Daniel O'Connell, 1775–1829* (London: Weidenfeld and Nicolson, 1988)

MacDonagh, O., *The Emancipist: Daniel O'Connell, 1830–47* (London: Weidenfeld and Nicolson, 1989)

MacDonald, Michael, *Children of Wrath: Political Violence in Northern Ireland* (Cambridge: Polity, 1986)

MacFarlane, Leslie, 'Human Rights and the Fight Against Terrorism in Northern Ireland', *Terrorism and Political Violence,* 4, 1 (1992) pp. 89–99

MacMillan, Gretchen, *State, Society and Authority in Ireland: The Foundations of the Modern Irish State* (Dublin: Gill and MacMillan, 1993)

MacNeill, Eoin, 'The North Began', *An Claidheamh Soluis,* 1 November (Dublin, 1913)

MacStiofáin, Sean, *Memoirs of a Revolutionary* (Edinburgh: Gordon Cremonesi, 1975)

Maitland, F.W. 'Translator's Introduction', in Gierke, Otto, *Political Theories of the Middle Age* (Cambridge: Cambridge University Press, 1900)

Major, John, *John Major: The Autobiography* (London: Harper Collins, 1999)

Mallie, Eamonn and McKittrick, David, *The Fight for Peace: The Secret Story Behind the Irish Peace Process* (London: Heinemann, 1996)

Mallon, Seamus, 'Filling Unionist Bowl at Too High a Price', *The Irish Times,* 18 May 2000

Mann, Michael, *The Sources of Social Power: Volume II, The Rise of Classes and Nation-States 1760–1914* (Cambridge: Cambridge University Press, 1993)

Mann, Michael, 'A Political Theory of Nationalism and Its Excesses', in Periwal, Sukumar (ed.), *Notions of Nationalism* (Budapest: Central European University Press, 1995)

Mansergh, Martin, 'The Background to the Peace Process: Address to the International Committee of the Royal Irish Academy', (Dublin, Royal Irish Academy, 1995)

Mansergh, Nicholas, *The Irish Question 1840–1921,* 3rd Edition (London: Allen and Unwin, 1975)

Mansergh, Nicholas, *The Unresolved Question: the Anglo-Irish Settlement and its Undoing, 1912–72* (New Haven: Yale University Press, 1991)

Martin, Joanne, and Murray, Alan, 'Catalysts for Collective Violence: The Importance of a Psychological Approach', in Folger, Robert (ed.), *The Sense of Injustice: Social Psychological Perspectives* (New York: Plenum Press, 1984)

Maudling, Reginald, *Memoirs* (London: Sidgewick and Jackson, 1978)

Maume, Patrick, 'Young Ireland, Arthur Griffith, and Republican Ideology: the Question of Continuity', *Éire-Ireland*, XXXIV, 2 (1999a) pp. 155–74

Maume, Patrick, *The Long Gestation: Irish Nationalist Life, 1891–1918* (Dublin: Gill & Macmillan, 1999b)

McAllister, Ian, *The Northern Ireland Social Democratic and Labour Party: Political Opposition in a Divided Society* (Basingstoke: Macmillan, 1977)

McAskill, Ewan, 'My Spats with Mandelson, by Ireland's Bruiser', *The Guardian,* 4 July 2000

McCabe, Anton and Colgan, Paul T., 'Hay's Sinn Féin Comments Reflect Reality', *Sunday Business Post,* 12 January 2003

McCrudden, Christopher, 'Northern Ireland and the British Constitution', in Jowell, Jeffrey and Oliver, Dawn (eds), *The Changing Constitution*, Third Edition (Oxford: Clarendon, 1994)

McDonald, Henry, 'Downing Street Accused of Pandering to Sinn Féin', *The Observer,* 14 January 2007

McDowell, R.B., *Public Opinion and Government Policy in Ireland, 1801–1846* (London: Routledge and Kegan Paul, 1952)

McGarry, John, 'Political Settlements in Northern Ireland and South Africa', *Political Studies,* XLVI (1998) pp. 853–70

McGarry, John (ed.), *Northern Ireland and the Comparative World* (Oxford: Oxford University Press, 2001)

McGarry, John, 'Northern Ireland, Civic Nationalism, and the Good Friday Agreement', in John McGarry (ed.), *Northern Ireland and the Divided World* (Oxford: Oxford University Press, 2001)

McGarry, John and O'Leary, Brendan (eds), *The Future of Northern Ireland* (Oxford: Oxford University Press, 1990)

McGarry, John and O'Leary, Brendan (eds), *The Politics of Ethnic Conflict Regulation* (London: Routledge, 1993)

McGarry, John and O'Leary, Brendan, *Explaining Northern Ireland: Broken Images* (Oxford: Basil Blackwell, 1995)

McGarry, John and O'Leary, Brendan, *The Northern Ireland Conflict:*

Consociational Engagements (Oxford: Oxford University Press, 2004)

McGartland, Martin, *Fifty Dead Men Walking* (London: Blake, 1997)

McGladdery, Gary, *The Provisional IRA in England: The Bombing Campaign 1973–1997* (Dublin: Irish Academic Press, 2006)

McGuinness, Martin, 'Statement by Sinn Féin Ard Chomhairle member, Martin McGuinness', 2 December 1993 (Belfast: Sinn Féin)

McGuire, Maria, *To Take Arms* (London: Macmillan, 1973)

McIntyre, Anthony, 'Modern Irish Republicanism: the Product of British State Strategies', *Irish Political Studies*, 10 (1995) pp. 19–43

McKittrick, David, *Dispatches from Belfast* (Belfast: Blackstaff, 1987)

McKittrick, David, *Endgame: the Search for Peace in Northern Ireland* (Belfast: Blackstaff, 1994)

McKittrick, David, Kelters, Seamus, Feeney, Brian and Thornton, Chris, *Lost Lives: The Stories of the Men, Women and Children who Died as a Result of the Northern Ireland Troubles* (Edinburgh: Mainstream, 1999)

McCrone, David, *The Sociology of Nationalism: Tomorrow's Ancestors* (London: Routledge, 1998)

Migdal, Joel, *State in Society: Studying How States and Societies Transform and Constitute one Another* (Cambridge: Cambridge University Press, 2001)

Miller, David W., *Queen's Rebels: Ulster Loyalism in Historical Perspective* (Dublin: Gill and Macmillan, 1978)

Miller, David (ed.), *Rethinking Northern Ireland: Culture, Ideology and Colonialism* (London and New York: Longman, 1999)

Mills, C. Wright, *The Power Elite* (New York: Oxford University Press, 1956)

Mitchell, Arthur, *Revolutionary Government in Ireland: Dáil Éireann, 1919–22* (Dublin: Gill and Macmillan, 1995)

Mitchell, George, *Making Peace: The Inside Story of the Making of the Good Friday Agreement* (London: Knopf, 1999)

Mitchell, Paul, 'Party Competition in an Ethnic Dual Party System', *Ethnic and Racial Studies,* 18, 4 (1995) pp. 773–96

Mitchell, Paul, 'Transcending an Ethnic Party System? The Impact of Consociational Governance on Electoral Dynamics and the Party System', in Wilford, Rick (ed.), *Aspects of the Belfast Agreement* (Oxford: Oxford University Press, 2001)

Molm, Linda D., *Coercive Power in Social Exchange* (Cambridge: Cambridge University Press, 1997)

Moloney, Ed, *A Secret History of the IRA* (London: Penguin, 2003)

Moloney, Ed, 'War and Peace', *The Irish Times,* 5 February 2005

Montville, Joseph V., 'The Arrow and the Olive Branch: A Case for Track Two Diplomacy', in McDonal, J.W. Jr. and Bendahmane, D.B. (eds), *Conflict Resolution: Track Two Diplomacy* (Washington, DC: Foreign Service Institute, US Department of State, 1987)

Montville, Joseph V. (ed.), *Conflict and Peacemaking in Multiethnic Societies* (Lexington, Mass.: Lexington, 1989)

Moody, T.W., Martin, F.X. and Byrne, F.J., *A New History of Ireland, Vol. IX,*

Maps, Genealogies, Lists (Oxford: Clarendon, 1984)

Moody, T.W., *Davitt and Irish Revolution 1846–8* (Oxford: Clarendon, 1981)

Moravcsik, Andrew, *The Choice for Europe: Social Purpose & State power from Messina to Maastricht* (Ithaca, NY: Cornell University Press, 1998)

Morrill, John, 'The Fashioning of Britain', in Ellis, Steven G. and Barber, Sarah (eds), *Conquest and Union. Fashioning a British State, 1485–1725* (London: Longman, 1995)

Morris, Christopher W., *An Essay on the Modern State* (Cambridge: Cambridge University Press, 1998)

Mullin, Chris, *Error of Judgement: The Birmingham Bombings* (Belfast: Poolbeg, 1987) Munger, Frank, 'The Legitimacy of Opposition: The Change of Government in Ireland in 1932', *Contemporary Political Sociology Series*, 06, 006, 1 (London: Sage, 1975)

Murphy, John A., 'The Achievement of Eamon de Valera', in O'Carroll, J.P and Murphy, John A. (eds) *The Life and Times of Eamon de Valera* (Dingle: Brandon, 1983)

Murray, Fr R., 'Political Violence in Northern Ireland 1969–77', in Boal, F.W. and Douglas, J. (eds), *Integration and Division: Geographical Perspectives on the Northern Ireland Problem* (London: Academic, 1982)

Murray, Fr R., *The SAS in Ireland* (Dublin: Mercier, 1990)

Neeson, E., *The Civil War, 1922–1923* (Dublin: Poolbeg, 1969)

Nelson, Sarah, *Ulster's Uncertain Defenders: Protestant Political, Paramilitary and Community Groups and the Northern Ireland Conflict* (Belfast: Appletree, 1984)

Newman, Saul and Piroth, Scott, 'Terror and Tolerance: The Use of Ballots, Bombs and Bullets by Ethno-regional Movements in Advanced Industrial Democracies', *Nationalism and Ethnic Politics*, 2, 3 (1996) pp. 381–414

Newsinger, John, *British Counterinsurgency: From Palestine to Northern Ireland* (Basingstoke: Macmillan, 2002)

Nordlinger, Eric, *Conflict Regulation in Divided Societies* (Cambridge, MA: Harvard University Centre for International Affairs, 1972)

Nordlinger, Eric, *On the Autonomy of the Democratic State* (Cambridge, MA: Harvard University Press, 1981)

O'Brien, Brendan, *The Long War: The IRA and Sinn Féin: From Armed Struggle to Peace Talks*, 2nd Edition (Dublin: O'Brien, 1995)

O'Brien, Conor Cruise, *States of Ireland* (London: Granada, 1974)

O'Brien, Conor Cruise, *Herod: Reflections on Political Violence* (London: Hutchinson, 1978)

O'Callaghan, Margaret, *British High Politics and Nationalist Ireland: Criminality, Land and the Law under Forster and Balfour* (Cork: Cork University Press, 1994)

O'Clery, Conor, *Phrases Make History Here: Political Quotations in Ireland 1867–1987* (Dublin: O'Brien, 1987)

O'Clery, Conor, *The Greening of the Whitehouse* (Dublin: Gill and Macmillan, 1997)

O'Clery, Conor, 'Why Sunningdale Failed', *Irish Times*, Special Section: The Path to Peace, 24 February 1999, p. 2

O'Connell, Daniel, *A Memoir of Ireland: Native and Saxon* (New York, London: Kennikat Press, [1843] 1970)

O'Connor, Fionnuala, *In Search of a State: Catholics in Northern Ireland* (Belfast: Blackstaff, 1993)

O'Day, Alan and Stevenson, John, *Irish Historical Documents since 1800* (Dublin: Gill and Macmillan, 1992)

O'Doherty, Malachi, 'Durkin's Push for Irish Unity', *Fortnight,* Issue 407 (October), 2002

O'Doherty, Malachi, *The Trouble with Guns: Republican Strategy and the Provisional IRA* (Belfast: Blackstaff, 1996)

O'Dowd, Liam, 'Constituting Division, Impeding Agreement: The Neglected Role of British Nationalism in Northern Ireland', in Anderson, James and Goodman, James (eds), *Dis/Agreeing Ireland: Contexts, Obstacles, Hopes* (London: Pluto, 1998)

O'Duffy, Brendan, 'Containment or Regulation? The British Approach to Conflict Regulation in Northern Ireland', in McGarry, J. and O'Leary, B. (eds), *The Politics of Ethnic Conflict Regulation* (London: Routledge, 1993)

O'Duffy, Brendan, 'Violence in Northern Ireland 1969–1994: Sectarian or Ethno-National?' *Ethnic and Racial Studies,* 18, 4 (1995) pp. 740–72

O'Duffy, Brendan, 'The Price of Containment: The Effect of Violence on Parliamentary Debate on Northern Ireland, 1964 to 1993', in Catterall, P, and MacDougal, S. (eds), *Northern Ireland in British Politics* (London: Macmillan, 1996)

O'Duffy, Brendan, 'Swapping the Reins of the Emerald Tiger: The Irish General Election of 1997', *West European Politics,* 21, 2 (1998) pp. 178–86

O'Duffy, Brendan, 'British and Irish Conflict Regulation from Sunningdale to Belfast. Part I: Tracing the Status of Contesting Sovereigns, 1968–1974', *Nations and Nationalism*, 5, 4 (1999) pp. 523–42

O'Duffy, Brendan, 'British and Irish Conflict Regulation from Sunningdale to Belfast. Part II: Playing for a Draw 1985–1999', *Nations and Nationalism,* 6, 3 (2000) pp. 384–99

O'Duffy, Brendan and Githens-Mazer, Jonathan, 'Status and Statehood: Exchange Theory and British–Irish Relations, 1921–41', *Commonwealth and Comparative Politics*, 40, 2 (2002) pp. 120–45

O'Ferrall, Fergus, *Catholic Emancipation: Daniel O'Connell and the Birth of Irish Democracy* (Dublin: Gill and Macmillan, 1985)

Offe, Claus, 'Democratic Welfare State in an Integrating Europe', in Greven, M.T. and Pauly, L.W. (eds), *Democracy Beyond the State? The European Dilemma and the Emerging Global Order* (Oxford: Rowman and Littlefield, 2000)

O'Halloran, Clare, *Partition and the Limits of Irish Nationalism: An Ideology Under Stress* (Dublin: Gill and Macmillan, 1987)

O'Hearn, Dennis, 'Catholic Grievances, Catholic Nationalism: A Comment', *British Journal of Sociology,* 34, 3 (1983) pp. 439–45

O'Kelly, Barry, 'Republicans' hostility to leadership growing', *Sunday Business Post*, 6 February 2005

O'Leary, Brendan, 'Introduction: Reflections on a Cold Peace', in the Special Issue: 'A State of Truce: Northern Ireland After Twenty-Five Years of War', *Ethnic and Racial Studies,* 18, 4 (1995a) pp. 695–714

O'Leary, Brendan, 'Afterword: What is Framed in the Framework Documents?', in the Special Issue: 'A State of Truce: Northern Ireland After Twenty-Five Years of War', *Ethnic and Racial Studies,* 18, 4 (1995b) pp. 862–72

O'Leary, Brendan, 'The Conservative Stewardship of Northern Ireland, 1979–97: Sound-bottomed Contradictions or Slow Learning?' *Political Studies*, 45, 4 (1997) pp. 663–76

O'Leary, Brendan, 'Assessing the British–Irish Agreement', *New Left Review*, 233 (1999) pp. 66–96

O'Leary, Brendan, 'Comparative Political Science and the British–Irish Agreement', in McGarry (ed.), *Northern Ireland and the Divided World* (Oxford: Oxford University Press, 2001)

O'Leary, Brendan, 'The IRA: Looking Back; Mission Accomplished?', in Heiberg, M., O'Leary, B., and Tirman, J. (eds), *Terror, Insurgency, and the State: Ending Protracted Conflicts* (Philadelphia, PA: University of Pennsylvania Press, 2007)

O'Leary, Brendan and McGarry, John, *The Politics of Antagonism: Understanding Northern Ireland,* 2nd Edition (London: Athlone, 1996)

O'Leary, Brendan and McGarry, John, *The Politics of Antagonism: Understanding Northern Ireland,* 3rd Edition (London: Routledge, 2007)

O'Leary, C., Elliott, S. and Wilford, R., *The Northern Ireland Assembly 1982–1986: a Constitutional Experiment* (London: Hurst, 1988)

O'Leary, Damian, 'Cultural Identity and Constitutional Reform: the Challenge of Northern Ireland', in Hanafin, Patrick and Williams, Melissa S. (eds), *Identity, Rights and Constitutional Transformation* (Aldershot: Ashgate, 1999)

O'Malley, Padraig, *The Uncivil Wars: Ireland Today* (Belfast: Blackstaff, 1983)

O'Malley, Padraig, *Biting at the Grave: The Irish Hunger Strikes and the Politics of Despair* (Belfast: Blackstaff, 1990)

Osborne, R.D., 'Voting Behaviour in Northern Ireland 1921–1977,' in Boal, F.W. and Douglas, J. (eds), *Integration and Division: Geographical Perspectives on the Northern Ireland Problem* (London: Academic Press, 1982)

Ó Siochrú, Micheál, *Confederate Ireland 1642–1649: A Constitutional and Political Analysis* (Dublin: Four Courts, 1999)

Ó Tuama Seán and Kinsella, Thomas (eds), *An Duanaire 1600–1900: Poems of the Dispossessed* (Portlaoise, Ireland and St Paul, MN: Dolman, 1981)

Pagden, A. and Canny, N., *Colonial Identity in the Atlantic World, 1500–1800* (Princeton: Princeton University Press, 1987)

Pakenham, Frank, *Peace by Ordeal* (London: Sidgwick & Jackson, 1972)

Pakenham, Thomas, *The Year of Liberty: The Bloody Story of the Great Irish*

Rebellion of 1798 (London: Panther Books, 1972)

Pape, Robert A., *Dying to Win: The Strategic Logic of Suicide Terrorism* (New York: Random House, 2005)

Pappalardo, A., 'The Conditions for Consociational Democracy: A Logical and Empirical Critique', *European Journal of Political Research,* 9 (1981) pp. 365–90

Paseta, Senia, *Before the Revolution: Nationalism, Social Change and Ireland's Catholic Elite, 1879–1922* (Cork: Cork University Press, 1999)

Patterson, Gerald R., *Coercive Family Process* (Eugene, OR: Castalia, 1982)

Patterson, Henry, *The Politics of Illusion: A Political History of the IRA* (London: Serif, 1997)

Patterson, Henry, 'Sean Lemass and the Ulster Question 1959–65', *Journal of Contemporary History*, 34, 1 (1999)

Patterson, Henry, 'From Insulation to Appeasement: the Major and Blair Governments Reconsidered', in Wilford, Rick (ed.), *Aspects of the Belfast Agreement* (Oxford: Oxford University Press, 2001)

Phoenix, Eamon, *Northern Nationalism: Nationalist Politics, Partition and the Catholic Minority in Northern Ireland, 1890–1940* (Belfast: Ulster Historical Foundation, 1994)

Poggi, Gianfranco, *The Development of the Modern State* (London: Hutchinson, 1978)

Ponting, Clive, *Breach of Promise, Labour in Power 1964–1970* (London: Hamish Hamilton, 1989)

Poole, Michael A. and Doherty, Paul, *Ethnic Residential Segregation in Northern Ireland*, (Coleraine, N.I.: Centre for the Study of Conflict, University of Ulster, 1996)

Posen, Barry R., 'The Security Dilemma and Ethnic Conflict', in Brown, E. (ed.), *Ethnic Conflict and International Security* (Princeton, N.J: Princeton University Press, 1993)

Prager, Jeffrey, *Building Democracy in Ireland: Political Order and Cultural Integration in a Newly Independent Nation* (Cambridge: Cambridge University Press, 1986)

Purdie, Bob, *Politics in the Streets: the Origins of the Civil Rights Movement in Northern Ireland* (Belfast: Blackstaff, 1990)

Regan, John M., *The Irish Counter-Revolution 1921–1936: Treatyite Politics and Settlement in Independent Ireland* (Dublin: Gill and Macmillan, 1999)

Richter, Michael, *Medieval Ireland: The Enduring Tradition* (Dublin: Gill and Macmillan, 1988)

Robbins, K. 'Britain and Europe: Devolution and Foreign Policy', *International Affairs* 78, 1 (1998) pp. 105–17

Roeder, Philip G., 'Power Dividing as an Alternative to Ethnic Power Sharing', in Roeder, Philip G. and Rothchild, Donald, *Sustainable Peace: Power and Democracy after Civil Wars* (Ithaca and London: Cornell University Press, 2005)

Rose, Richard, *Governing Without Consensus: An Irish Perspective* (London: Faber and Faber, 1971)

Rowthorn, B. and Wayne, N., *Northern Ireland: The Political Economy of Conflict* (Oxford: Polity, 1988)

Roy, Olivier, *Globalised Islam: The Search for a New Ummah* (London: Hurst, 2004)

Ruane, Joseph and Todd, Jennifer, *The Dynamics of Conflict in Northern Ireland: Power, Conflict and Emancipation* (Cambridge: Cambridge University Press, 1996)

Ruane, Joseph and Todd, Jennifer (eds), *After the Good Friday Agreement: Analysing Political Change in Northern Ireland* (Dublin: University College Dublin Press, 1999a)

Ruane, Joseph and Todd, Jennifer, 'The Belfast Agreement: Context, Content, Consequences', in Ruane, Joseph and Todd, Jennifer (eds), *After the Good Friday Agreement: Analysing Political Change in Northern Ireland* (Dublin: University College Dublin Press, 1999b)

Rule, James, *Theories of Civil Violence* (Berkeley, CA: University of California Press, 1988)

Rumpf, E. and Hepburn, A.C., *Nationalism and Socialism in Twentieth-Century Ireland* (Liverpool: Liverpool University Press, 1977)

Ryan, Jeffrey J., 'The Impact of Democratization on Revolutionary Movements', *Comparative Politics* (1994) pp. 27–44

Ryan, Mark, *War and Peace in Ireland: Britain and Sinn Féin in the New World Order* (London: Pluto Press, 1994)

Safran, William and Máiz, Ramón (eds), *Identity and Territorial Autonomy in Plural Societies* (London: Frank Cass, 2000)

Sageman, Marc, *Understanding Terror Networks* (Philadelphia, PA: University of Pennsylvania Press, 2005)

Salmon, Trevor C., *Unneutral Ireland: An Ambivalent and Unique Security Policy* (Oxford: Clarendon, 1989)

Shannon, William, 'The Anglo-Irish Agreement', *Foreign Affairs*, 64, 4 (1986) pp. 835–50

Shils, Edward, 'On the Comparative Study of the New States', in Geertz, Clifford (ed.), *Old Societies and New States: The Quest for Modernity in Asia and Africa* (New York: The Free Press, 1963) pp. 1–26

Shinoda, Hideaki, *Re-examining Sovereignty: From Classical Theory to the Global Age* (London: Macmillan, 2000)

Sinn Féin, 'Towards a Lasting Peace in Ireland' (Belfast: Sinn Féin, 1992)

Sinn Féin, 'Setting the Record Straight: Sinn Féin's Record of the Communications Between Sinn Féin and the British Government, October 1990–November 1993' (Belfast: Sinn Féin, 1994)

Skocpol, Theda, *States and Social Revolutions* (New York: Cambridge University Press, 1979)

Smith, Anthony D., *The Ethnic Origins of Nations* (Oxford: Blackwell, 1986)

Smith, Anthony D., *Nationalism and Modernism: A Critical Survey of Recent Theories of Nations and Nationalism* (London: Routledge, 1998)

Smith, M.L.R., 'The Role of the Military Instrument in Irish Republican Strategic Thinking: an Evolutionary Analysis', Ph.D. thesis, University of

London, 1991

Smith, M.L.R., *Fighting for Ireland? The Military Strategy of the Republican Movement* (London: Routledge, 1995)

Smyth, Jim, *The Men of No Property: Irish Radicals and Popular Politics in the late Eighteenth Century* (London: Macmillan, 1992)

Sørensen, Georg, 'Sovereignty: Change and Continuity in a Fundamental Institution', *Political Studies*, XLVII (1999) pp. 590–604

Stalker, John, *Stalker* (London: Harrap, 1988)

Stewart, A.T.Q., *The Ulster Crisis* (London: Faber and Faber, 1967)

Stewart, A.T.Q., *The Narrow Ground: The Roots of Conflict in Ulster*, Revised Edition (London: Faber and Faber, 1989)

Street, C.J.C. ('I.O.'), *The Administration of Ireland, 1920* (London: Philip Allan, 1921)

Sutton, Malcolm, *An Index of Deaths from the Conflict in Ireland, 1969–1993* (Belfast: Beyond the Pale, 1994)

Tamir, Yael, *Liberal Nationalism* (Princeton, NJ: Princeton University Press, 1995)

Tanner, J.R., *English Constitutional Conflicts of the 17th Century 1603–1689* (Cambridge: Cambridge University Press, 1966)

Taylor, Rupert, 'Northern Ireland: Consociation or Social Transformation?' in McGarry, John (ed.), *Northern Ireland and the Divided World* (Oxford: Oxford University Press, 2001)

Thatcher, Margaret, *The Downing Street Years* (London: Harper Collins, 1993)

Thornton, Chris and McAdam, Noel, 'Devolution Under Agreement Top Choice', *The Belfast Telegraph*, 14 November 2003

Tilly, Charles (ed.), *The Formation of National States in Western Europe* (Princeton, NJ: Princeton University Press, 1975)

Tilly, Charles, *From Mobilization to Revolution* (Reading, MA: Addison-Wesley, 1978)

Tilly, Charles, *Coercion, Capital and European States*, AD 990–1990 (Oxford: Blackwell, 1990)

Tilly, Charles, *European Revolutions, 1492–1992* (Oxford: Blackwell, 1993)

Tilly, Charles, *Trust and Rule* (New York and Cambridge: Cambridge University Press, 2005)

Todd, Jennifer, 'Equality, Plurality and Democracy: Justifications of Proposed Constitutional Settlements of the Northern Ireland Conflict', in A State of Truce: Northern Ireland After Twenty-Five Years of War', Special Issue of *Ethnic and Racial Studies*, 18, 4 (1995) pp. 818–37

Todd, Jennifer, 'Two Traditions in Unionist Political Culture', *Irish Political Studies* 2 (1987) pp. 1–26

Tomlinson, Mike, 'Walking Backwards into the Sunset: British Policy and the Insecurity of Northern Ireland', in Miller, David (ed.), *Rethinking Northern Ireland: Culture, Ideology and Colonialism* (London and New York: Longman, 1998)

Townshend, Charles, *The British Campaign in Ireland 1919–21* (Oxford: Oxford University Press, 1975)

Townshend, Charles, 'Martial Law: Legal and Administrative Problems of Civil Emergency in Britain and the Empire, 1800–1940', *Historical Journal,* XXV (1982)

Townshend, Charles, *Political Violence in Ireland: Government and Resistance since 1848* (Oxford: Clarendon, 1983)

Townshend, Charles, *Britain's Civil Wars: Counterinsurgency in the Twentieth Century* (London: Faber, 1986)

Townshend, Charles (ed.), *Consensus in Ireland: Approaches and Recessions* (Oxford: Clarendon, 1988)

Townshend, Charles, 'State and Public Security', in English, R. and Townshend, C. (eds), *The State: Historical and Political Dimensions* (London: Routledge, 1999)

Urban, Mark, *Big Boys' Rules: The Secret Struggle Against the IRA* (London: Faber and Faber, 1992)

Valente, Joseph, 'The Manliness of Parnell', *Éire-Ireland*, 41:1&2, (2006) pp. 64–121

Valiulis, Maryann, *Almost a Rebellion* (London: Tower, 1985)

Vital, David, *The Making of British Foreign Policy* (London: Allen and Unwin, 1968)

Walker, B.M., *Parliamentary Election Results in Ireland, 1801–1922* (Dublin: Royal Irish Academy, 1978)

Wallace, M., *Northern Ireland: Fifty Years of Self-Government* (Newton Abbot: David and Charles, 1971)

Ward, Alan J., 'America and the Irish Problem, 1899–1921', *Irish Historical Studies,* XVI (1968)

Warner, Bruce, 'Extradition Law and Practice in the Crucible of Ulster, Ireland and Great Britain: A Metamorphosis?', *Conflict Quarterly*, 7 (1987) pp. 57–92

Watson, J. Steven, *The Reign of George III 1760–1815* (Oxford: Clarendon, 1960)

Weber, Max, *From Max Weber: Essays in Sociology*, translated, edited and with an introduction by Gerth, H.H. and Mills, C.W. (Oxford: Oxford University Press, 1946)

Whelan, Kevin, *The Tree of Liberty: Radicalism, Catholicism and the Construction of Irish Identity 1760–1830* (South Bend, IN: University of Notre Dame Press, 1996)

White, Barry, *John Hume: Statesman of the Troubles* (Belfast: Blackstaff, 1984)

White, Robert, 'From Peaceful Protest to Guerilla War: Micromobilization of the Provisional Irish Republican Army', *American Journal of Sociology,* 94, 6 (1989) pp. 1,277–1,302

White, Timothy J., 'Catholicism and Nationalism in Ireland: From Fusion in the 19th Century to Separation in the 21st Century', *Westminster Papers in Community and Culture*, 4, 1 (2007) pp. 56–60

Whitelaw, William, *The Whitelaw Memoirs* (London: Aurum Press, 1989)

Wilford, Rick (ed.), *Aspects of the Good Friday Agreement* (Oxford: Oxford University Press, 2001)

Wilkinson, Paul, *Terrorism and the Liberal State* (London: Macmillan, 1977)

Willer, D., Lovaglia, M.J. and Markovsky, B., 'Power and Influence: A Theoretical Bridge', in Willer, D. (ed.), *Network Exchange Theory* (Westport, CT: Praeger, 1999)

Whyte, John, *Interpreting Northern Ireland* (Oxford: Clarendon, 1990)

Wolff, Stefan, *Disputed Territories: The Transnational Dynamics of Ethnic Conflict Settlement* (Oxford: Berghahn, 2003)

Wolff, Stefan, 'Introduction: From Sunningdale to Belfast', in Neuheiser, Jorg and Wolff, Stefan (eds), *Peace at Last? The Impact of the Good Friday Agreement on Northern Ireland* (Oxford and New York: Berghahn, 2003)

Wright, Frank, *Northern Ireland: A Comparative Analysis* (Dublin: Gill and Macmillan, 1987)

Younger, Carlton, *Ireland's Civil War* (London: Frederick Muller, 1968)

Younger, Carlton, *A State of Disunion* (London: Fontana, 1972)

Zartman, I.W., 'Negotiations and Prenegotiations in Ethnic Conflict: The Beginning, The Middle, and the Ends', in Montville, J. (ed.), *Conflict and Peacemaking in Multi-ethnic Societies* (Lexington, MA: Lexington, 1990)

Zartman, I.W. (ed.), *Elusive Peace: Negotiating an End to Civil Wars* (Washington, DC: Brookings, 1995)

Zimmerman, Ekkart, *Political Violence, Crises, and Revolutions: Theories and Research* (Boston, MA: Schenkman, 1983)

Index

Fianna Fáil, Irish Republicanism and the Northern Ireland Troubles, 1968–2005

Catherine O'Donnell

Fianna Fáil: The Republican Party has been a party defined by its emphasis on partition and its ideological commitment to reunification. Through its use of anti-partitionist rhetoric it has been the most vociferous political party in the Republic of Ireland on Northern Ireland. Its emotive and divisive response to the outbreak of the Troubles in Northern Ireland seen most clearly in the Arms Crisis of 1970 which threatened to destroy the party and the stability of the State in the Republic. However, the party has been at the centre of the Northern Ireland peace process and the attempts at reconciliation between Unionists and Nationalists, and North and South. Yet there is no substantive study of Fianna Fáil's language, ideology and policy on Northern Ireland since the outbreak of the Troubles. How could 'The Republican Party' be such a central player in the political changes in Northern Ireland? Has Fianna Fáil changed its traditional republicanism and anti-partitionism? This fascinating and important new book provides an examination of Fianna Fáil's record on Northern Ireland since 1968. It outlines the party's response to the Troubles and its guiding principles in the search for the solution. O'Donnell argues that the relationship between Fianna Fáil and Sinn Féin is central to understanding Fianna Fáil's role in the peace process, which began with the Fianna Fáil-Sinn Féin talks in 1988. She investigates the implications of the peace process and the Good Friday Agreement for Fianna Fáil's ideology and policy on Northern Ireland and highlights the continued centrality of the relationship between Fianna Fáil and Sinn Féin to the peace process and politics in the Republic of Ireland. As Sinn Féin make further electoral gains in the Republic of Ireland, this book will be essential reading for anyone wishing to understand how Republicanism is a contested electoral resource within southern politics.

March 2007 288 pages
978 0 7165 3360 3 cloth   €60.00 / £45.00 / $70.00
978 0 7165 2859 3 paper   €27.50 / £19.95 / $30.00

The Provisional IRA in Ireland
The Bombing Campaign 1973–1997

Gary McGladdery

Foreword by Richard English

In this revealing and fascinating account, the impact of the Provisional IRA's bombing campaign in Britain on both British government policy towards Northern Ireland and the internal politics of the republican movement, are examined in detail. The book highlights the early thinking of the British government and draws on recently released public records from 1939, 1973 and 1974. It makes extensive use of television documentary footage to offer a broader analysis. The book also examines republican rationale behind the campaign, the reasoning behind the use of particular tactics and the thinking behind atrocities such as the Birmingham bombings.

Using a range of new evidence, the book highlights the bankruptcy of republican strategic thinking and challenges the notion that successive British governments appeased republicans because of the threat of bombs in London. The analysis of the campaign is placed within the wider context of the ongoing violence in Northern Ireland as well as the history of republican violence in England dating back to the nineteenth century.

2006   288 pages

978 0 7165 3373 3   cloth   €65.00 / £45.00 / $75.00

978 0 7165 3374 0   paper   €29.95 / £19.95 / $35.00

The Northern IRA and the Early Years of Partition 1920–1922

Robert Lynch

The years 1920–22 constituted a period of unprecedented conflict and political change in Ireland. It began with the onset of the most brutal phase of the War of Independence and culminated in the effective military defeat of the Republican IRA in the Civil War. Occurring alongside these dramatic changes in the south and west of Ireland was a far more fundamental conflict in the north-east, a period of brutal sectarian violence which marked the early years of partition and the establishment of Northern Ireland. Almost uniquely the IRA in the six counties were involved in every one of these conflicts and yet, it can be argued, was on the fringe of all of them. The period 1920-22 saw the evolution of the organisation from peripheral curiosity during the War of independence to an idealistic symbol for those wishing to resolve the fundamental divisions within the Sinn Féin movement, which developed in the first six months of 1922. The story of the Northern IRA's collapse in the autumn of that year demonstrated dramatically the true nature of the organisation and how it was their relationship to the various protagonists in these conflicts, rather than their unceasing but fruitless war against partition, that defined its contribution to the Irish revolution.

2006   264 pages
978 0 7165 3377 1   cloth   €65.00 / £50.00 $75.00
978 0 7165 3378 8   paper   €27.50 / £19.95 $32.00

The Evolution of the Troubles, 1970–72

Thomas Hennessey

This book explores the evolution of the Northern Ireland Troubles from an ethno-national conflict into an insurgency against the British state in Northern Ireland in the crucial years of 1970 to 1972. The book combines the decisions of 'high politics' with the experiences of those on the ground, for whom these decisions made the greatest impact. It tells the story of ordinary people caught up in extraordinary events covering the evolving Provisional IRA insurgency and the British Army's counter-insurgency. Key areas covered include: the Falls Road Curfew; Anglo-Irish relations; North–South relations on the island of Ireland; the fall of the Chichester-Clark Government; the premiership of Brian Faulkner; internment; Bloody Sunday; and the suspension of Stormont.

Dr Thomas Hennessey is Reader in History at Canterbury Christ Church University and a Fellow of the Royal Historical Society. He is the author of Northern Ireland: the Origin of the Troubles (2005); The Northern Ireland Peace Process: Ending the Troubles? (2000); Dividing Ireland: World War One and Partition (1998); and A History of Northern Ireland (1997).

October 2007   384 pages
978 0 7165 2884 5   cloth   €55.00 / £45.00 / $75.00
978 0 7165 2885 2   paper   €24.95 / £18.95 / $35.00

Crossing the Border
*New Relationships between Northern Ireland
and the Republic of Ireland*

John Coakley and Liam O'Dowd

This timely book provides the first sustained examination of cross-border relationships since the momentous sequence of events that began with the Good Friday agreement of 1998. It looks at changing patterns of North–South relations in three broad domains: politics and public administration, the economy, and civil society. Specific topics covered include the cross-border implementation bodies, the island economy, the voluntary sector, education, health, planning, public policy and the EU. The book draws on findings from a two-year research project embracing a large, multi-disciplinary team based in Dublin, Belfast, Dundalk and Armagh. The book also sets recent changes in perspective, outlining the evolution of cross-border relationships between partition in 1920 and the recent comprehensive settlement, and exploring the extent to which leaders North and South remained in denial about the evolving impact and implications of the border until the closing decades of the 20th century. The authors demonstrate how the search for a settlement in Northern Ireland has created a new dynamic in cross-border relationships, underlining the critical importance of these relationships in sustaining the peace process. In a trenchant assessment of future prospects, the book stresses the extent to which new North-South relationships have been dependent on external funding from the EU and the USA. It argues that the diminution of these funds potentially threatens the sustainability of successful cross-border programmes, putting the onus on the two governments to develop a more coherent and strategic approach to cross-border co-operation.

Crossing the Border is essential reading for anyone seeking to understand the island of Ireland in the twenty first century, for all those actively committed to consolidating peace in the island, and, in particular, for the wide range of policy makers and activists seeking to forge a new and mutually beneficial relationship between the two Irelands.

Contributors: John Coakley, Liam O'Dowd, Brian Ó Caoindealbháin, Robin Wilson, John Bradley, Kevin Howard, Etain Tannam, Cathal McCall, Andy Pollak, Patricia Clarke, Eoin Magennis and Ivo Damkat.

November 2007   272 pages
978 0 7165 2921 7   cloth   €60.00 / £45.00 / $75.00
978 0 7165 2922 4   paper   €24.95 / £19.95 / $32.50

Northern Ireland's '68
Civil Rights, Global Revolt and the Origins of the Troubles

Simon Prince
Foreword by Paul Bew

The Troubles may have developed into a sectarian conflict, but the violence was sparked by a small band of leftists who wanted Derry in October 1968 to be a repeat of Paris in May 1968. Like their French comrades, Northern Ireland's sixty-eighters had assumed that street fighting would lead to political struggle. The struggle that followed, however, was between communities rather than classes. In the divided society of Northern Ireland, the interaction of the global and the local that was the hallmark of 1968 had tragic consequences.

Drawing upon a wealth of new sources and scholarship, Simon Prince offers a fresh and compelling interpretation of the civil rights movement of 1968 and the origins of The Troubles. The authoritative and enthralling narrative weaves together accounts of high politics and grassroots protests, mass movements and individuals, and international trends and historic divisions. Prince shows how events in Northern Ireland and around the world were interlinked during 1968.

October 2007   272 pages illus
978 0 7165 2869 2   cloth   €65.00 / £45.00 / $75.00
978 0 7165 2870 8   paper   €24.95 / £19.95 / $30.00